PIMLICO

534

JOHN BUCHAN

Andrew Lownie was born in 1961 and educated at Fettes, Westminster and Magdalene College, Cambridge where he was President of the Union. Like Buchan he has been a law student, a journalist contributing to *The Times* and *Spectator*, a parliamentary candidate in Scotland and has worked in publishing. A Council Member of the John Buchan Society, he has written introductions to several Buchan novels and has edited collections of Buchan's poetry and short stories. He now lives in London.

Praise for *John Buchan*

'Brilliantly written and researched . . . Lownie draws on newly-released private papers to astutely pick his way through the public image and the passionately private man, painting a vivid and refreshingly readable literary portrait of one of the great unacknowledged and substantive figures in recent Scottish life.' *Catholic Life*

'He has been the subject of previous biographies, but Andrew Lownie's is a welcome addition . . . Mr Lownie has done him proud.' D. Cameron Watt, *Financial Times*

'Andrew Lownie's new life of him, though by no means hagiographic, should contribute to the Buchan revival.' John Grigg, *The Times*

'A well-written and helpful book. It is good on Buchan as war historian and rich in quotation and research as well as discoveries or rediscoveries to please or tease.' R.D. Kernohan, *Herald*

'Solid and readable . . . it goes deeper into Buchan's family life than Janet Adam felt able to.' John Gross, *Sunday Telegraph*

'Balanced and packed with information, much of which is new. Buchan fans should rush out and buy it.' Max Egremont, *Country Life*

JOHN BUCHAN

The Presbyterian Cavalier

ANDREW LOWNIE

PIMLICO

Published by Pimlico 2002

2 4 6 8 10 9 7 5 3 1

First published in Great Britain by Constable and Company 1995
Pimlico edition 2002

Pimlico
Random House, 20 Vauxhall Bridge Road,
London SW1V 2SA

Random House Australia (Pty) Limited
20 Alfred Street, Milsons Point, Sydney,
New South Wales 2061, Australia

Random House New Zealand Limited
18 Poland Road, Glenfield,
Auckland 10, New Zealand

Random House (Pty) Limited
Endulini, 5a Jubilee Road, Parktown 2193, South Africa

The Random House Group Limited Reg. No. 954009
www.randomhouse.co.uk

A CIP catalogue record for this book
is available from the British Library

ISBN 0–7126–9735–7

Papers used by Random House are natural,
recyclable products made from wood grown in sustainable forests;
the manufacturing processes conform to the environmental
regulations of the country of origin

Printed and bound in Great Britain by
Mackays of Chatham Ltd

To my father
who introduced me to the world of John Buchan

CONTENTS

CONTENTS

ILLUSTRATIONS

ILLUSTRATIONS

ACKNOWLEDGEMENTS

William Buchan, at the end of his memoir of his father, admitted that even he found his father an elusive character. 'For all his openness, courtesy, kindness, his geniality, his great knowledge which, at any time, he was ready to share, his charity and his questing, eager spirit . . . I believe that he held always a certain part of himself apart, inviolable and inviolate.' He concluded, 'by remembering him and re-telling his story I thought to come nearer to understanding a very complex and, I insist, mysterious man. Yet he eludes me still, as I believe he has eluded everybody.'[1] It is a feeling with which I have sympathy even after several years study of literally thousands of Buchan's letters to family and friends and hundreds of thousands of words written by him and about both him and his work. One can illuminate certain parts of his life and character but in the end Buchan is, more than most biographical subjects, someone of whom there can never be a definitive life. Indeed it is this sense of mystery, this inability to pin him down, this continual confounding of assumptions that for me is part of the attraction of this fascinating man.

My own interest in Buchan's life began while researching my last book, a literary guide to Edinburgh. Though I had read the Richard Hannay novels and knew the Scottish Borders, my knowledge of his life and work was limited. I subscribed to many of the popular preconceptions about him and his books – that they were old-fashioned, snobbish, anti-Semitic. The more I read about and by him the more I realised how false this picture was and how much more complex and ambivalent were his views. As I discovered more about him I was struck too by the fact that we had a similar background, interests and temperament. Like him I had been brought up and educated in Scotland before going south to university and I shared his interest in history, law, politics and literature.

A number of questions began to fascinate me. Why, given his ability and interest in politics, did he not rise more quickly in public life? Was he merely the anti-Semitic careerist of popular legend or a more complex and intro-spective man who turned his back on the 'glittering prizes'? How good a writer was he and was, in Cyril Connolly's memorable apothegm, the enemy of promise the pram in the front hall? Has history misjudged him, remembering him for a book he wrote in a matter of months rather than his historical fiction and biographies? As I talked to those who had known him, certain patterns emerged. Those who had never met him subscribed to the popular myths but all those who had known him well had nothing but praise. The present Lord Longford's memory of Buchan being the kindest man he had ever met was repeated by countless others. Many talked of him as being one of the most complete and serene people they had ever known, with a highly developed, almost mystical, sense of history and man's place in the world. The challenge in writing about Buchan has therefore been to bring out this inner life.

People repeatedly talked of his genius for friendship. It is an over-used cliché but has some validity in Buchan's case. When he died, the Editor of *The Times* said he had never before received so many spontaneous letters of genuine grief and respect from both politicians and the public, yet the contemporary image of Buchan is still the Karsh photograph, of a more forbidding figure with his thin face, tight lips, hook nose, and prominent forehead with its dramatic scar and inscrutable eyes.

His interests and activities were so wide and his energy so enormous that no-one can fully do justice to all he did. Writer, politician, soldier, publisher, journalist, imperial administrator, Buchan fitted more into his sixty five years than probably anyone else of his generation. His friend, Lord Lothian, has called him 'one of the most versatile men of his time'.[2] A Buchan biographer needs to have at least a nodding acquaintance with such varied topics as Scottish Church history, the nineteenth century Scottish education system, the Boer War and Reconstruction, propaganda during the First World War, the work of the publishing firm Nelson's and the news agency Reuters, domestic politics in the inter-war period, and competing philosophies of empire and interwar Canadian politics. That is before one even begins to analyse over a hundred books that range from several different genres of novel, short stories and children's stories to biographies, political studies, anthologies and a hand-book on the law of taxation.

It is not just Buchan's range that is a challenge to the biographer but also his productivity. Apart from his hundred or so books and hundreds of articles he still found time to write thousands of letters. For over fifty years he wrote to his mother almost every day and he wrote almost as often to his brothers and sister, wife, three sons and his daughter as well as to his many friends. A measure of the range of his contacts can be gauged by the fact that at his death there were several hundred letters of condolence.

Buchan and his books have increasingly generated numerous theses, books and articles. There have been studies of his political philosophy, his view of Empire, his brand of Scottish Nationalism, comparisons between him and Edgar Allen Poe and Richard Hannay and Flashman, articles on his villains, his heroines, his alleged anti-Semitism, his aesthetic consciousness and recreations of the journeys made by some of his characters.[3]

As with so much twentieth century biography, the problem has been too much material rather than too little. Yet for all that Buchan wrote, he rarely reveals much about himself. Surprisingly for a writer and an historian he did not keep a diary and threw away most of the letters he received. One therefore has to trace the correspondence either from his carbons or the letters that were kept by members of his family and are in the Buchan Collections at the National Library of Scotland and Queens University, Ontario or scattered in private and public collections around the world. By temperament and upbringing he was a reserved man who rarely confided his deepest thoughts to paper and again one has to gain insights into the private man from the letters and diaries of his friends and contemporaries. The picture which I hope will emerge is of a man more complex and much less dour than his public image. Pictures rarely show him smiling but in fact Buchan had a highly developed sense of humour and was a marvellous mimic, able to move in mid-sentence from his crisp English diction to Scottish Doric. He was devoted to his wife, even if he routinely forgot her birthday, and their early love letters are in turn passionate, affectionate, natural and moving.

Buchan has been described by the critic Gertrude Himmelfarb as 'The last Victorian', which is a reminder that almost forty per cent of his life, including his most formative years were spent when Victoria was on the throne. He was first published in the year that his great literary hero and influence, R.L. Stevenson, died and many of Buchan's attitudes are what we call Victorian – a sense of duty, a belief in hard work, honour and thrift, a faith in Britain and her empire. Though he shared some of the prejudices of his contemporaries, including a degree of anti-Semitism and racism, he was also in many ways far ahead of his time. He was one of the first statesmen to realise the importance of America in European affairs and of the power of film and propaganda. Far from being a narrow patriot, he showed himself in his books and life to have wide sympathies and a cosmopolitan outlook on life. His friends ranged from writers and academics such as Virginia Woolf, Rose Macaulay, Robert Graves, Elizabeth Bowen, Henry James, Arnold Bennett, Hugh

MacDiarmid, John Masefield and G.M. Trevelyan to politicians and statesmen as varied as the Red Clydesiders, Ramsay MacDonald, Stanley Baldwin, Arthur Balfour and Chaim Weizmann. Many of his books have a prophetic strain, anticipating twentieth century dictatorship, black power and child kidnapping and he was one of the first writers to put cars and planes at the centre of his books.

Professor David Daniell, who has done so much to raise Buchan's profile as a writer worthy of serious appreciation, is presently writing a literary study of Buchan and I have therefore deliberately concentrated more on Buchan's public life than on his work. It is now thirty years since Janet Adam Smith published her biography of Buchan. She knew the Buchan family and also the world within which they lived, but since her pioneering portrait was published much new historical and literary research has emerged, allowing a more detailed and less impressionistic picture to be presented.

I would like to thank Janet Adam Smith, Lady Adeane, Rupert Allason MP, the late Lord Amery of Lustleigh, Margaret Anderson, Myrtle Anderson-Smith of the University of Aberdeen Library, Ann Armstrong, James Armstrong of Lambeth Palace Library, Loila Armstrong, Theo Aronson, Lady Helen Asquith, Hon David Astor, Sir Alfred Beit, Sir William Benyon, Sir Isaiah Berlin, Doris Blowers, Anne Brown of Hutchesons' School, Lord Boyd-Carpenter, Elizabeth Boardman the Brasenose College Archivist, Michael Bott of the University of Reading, Toby Buchan, Ursula Buchan, Kathleen Cameron of the University of Saskatchewan Library, Alastair Campbell of Airds, Dame Frances Campbell-Preston, John Carswell, Sandy Campbell, Mr Justice Cazalet, Richard Childs and Alison McCann of West Sussex Record Office, the late Somerset de Chair, Kenneth de Courcy, Roy Court, Lady de Bellaigue, Richard de Peyer of Dorset County Museum, Lord Deedes, The Marchioness of Dufferin and Ava, Alexander Dunbar of Pitgaveny, Sir Archibald Dunbar, The Earl of Dundonald, Dr David Dutton, Margaret Ecclestone at the Alpine Club Library, Janet Edgell of the Middle Temple Library, Lord Egremont, Norman Entract of the Kipling Society, John Entwisle of Reuters, Rt Hon Michael Foot, Sir Edward Ford, Professor Philip Gaskell, Sophia Gibb for her help with picture research, Jennifer Gill of the Durham Record Office, David Gilmour, Sir Alexander Glen, Sir James Graham, Bopet Grant, Keith Grieves, John Grigg, Lord Hailsham, Mrs E.A. Harris, Paul Harris, Sir Christopher Hartley, Professor Christopher Harvie, Alastair Hutton, Elizabeth Inglis of Sussex University Library, Lord Ironside, James Jones of St Andrew's Church Ottawa, Pamela King, Simon Lawrence my copy editor, James Lees-Milne, Lord Longford,

Andrew Lorimer, Mary Lutyens, Ian McIntyre, Reverend George Mackenzie, John MacLaren, Alastair Macpherson the Haileybury Archivist, Mary McRae, Robin Malcolm, Lady Mason, Willie Milne, Ronan Nelson, Max Nicholson, Tish Nugee, Lord Oxford and Asquith, James Park, Russell Paterson of the John Buchan Society, Christine Penney of Birmingham University Library, Hon John Pickersgill, Professor Nicholas Polunin, Mark Riddey and Dr Robin Darwall-Smith of Oxfordshire Archives, Faith Raven, Patrick Rayner BBC Scotland, Professor Donald Read, Charles Ritchie, Tim Robinson, Patrick Scrivener, Mark Seaman, David Seed, Rosemary Seymour, the late Earl of Selkirk, Lady and the late Lord Shackleton, Linda Shaughnessy of A.P. Watt, Dick Shaw of The Intelligence Corps Association, Christopher Sheppard of Leeds University Library, Lord Sherfield, Joysanne Sidimus, Dr David Stafford, Roger Strong of the Northern Ireland Public Record Office, Christopher Strang of St Columba' Church, Wilfred Thesiger, Iain Thornber, Ross Tolmie, Professor Donald Cameron Watt, Paul Webb, Lord Wigram, Sir Geoffrey Wilson, David Jackson Young, Jocelyn Withrop Young.

I am grateful to the Librarians and Archivists of the various collections I consulted especially George Henderson and his colleagues at Queen's University Archives in Kingston, Ontario and the staff of the National Library of Scotland. Permission to quote from the Papers in the Royal Archives at Windsor Castle has been graciously given by Her Majesty the Queen. The script was read by Dr Janet Adam Smith, William Buchan, Professor David Daniell, Andrew Davies, Reverend Robin Denniston, Reverend Jim Greig, Solange Lownie, Catherine Rachem, Dr Michael Redley and David Roberts and I am particularly grateful to them for their many valuable comments. In addition William Buchan kindly let me use the Buchan family photograph albums and my particular thanks go to him. It cannot be easy to watch someone almost fifty years younger writing the life of one's own father but despite that he patiently and with great charm answered numerous questions. Last, but by no means least, my thanks to Hugh Andrew and his colleagues at Canongate for all their help during the course of this revised paperback publication.

PROLOGUE

━━━━

February 22nd 1940

WESTMINSTER ABBEY, under the flickering light of the yellow wax candles, looked at its most splendid as it gradually filled up for the noon memorial service. On one side of the choir stalls were members of the House of Lords, including the former Prime Minister, Stanley Baldwin, now Lord Baldwin of Bewdley. On the other side were almost all the members of the Cabinet, led by the Prime Minister Neville Chamberlain, the Chancellor of the Exchequer Sir John Simon and the Foreign Secretary Lord Halifax. The Lord Chamberlain was there representing King George VI. Other guests in the Abbey included leading members of the diplomatic corps and aristocracy and famous names from the worlds of literature, journalism, academia and politics. Several hundred Canadian officers in khaki filled the aisles alongside scores of dark-suited individuals representing institutions as varied as the British Film Institute, the Boy Scout Association, the Alpine Club and the Institute of Philosophy.

The recent news headlines, five months after the outbreak of the Second World War, had been dominated by the German advance into Norway, a rash of IRA bombings, including one only that day which had injured thirteen people in Oxford Street, and the announcement of the engagement of the actor Robert Morley and the daughter of the actress Gladys Cooper. Ten days earlier, however, the lead story in all the papers and on all the broadcasts had been the announcement of the unexpected death of the figure now commemorated by this Memorial Service at Westminster Abbey. His death had made front page headlines around the world from South Africa and Australia to Canada and the United States and special tributes had been penned by such different journals as the *Fishing Gazette*, *Country Life*, *The Law Journal*, *The Baptist Times* and the *Ayrshire Post*.

Hundreds of personal tributes had poured in from, among others, King George VI and members of the British Royal Family, President F.D. Roosevelt, the Pope, Clement Attlee, the Italian Foreign Minister Count Ciano, General Smuts, the French statesman Eduard Daladier, His Imperial Highness Prince Chichibu of Japan and Douglas Fairbanks Jr. There had been some 1,500 messages of condolence, including messages from a hundred different branches of the Women's Institute and several Native American Indian tribes. The historian G.M. Trevelyan had summed up the general feeling a few days before this particular service when he wrote to the man's widow 'I don't think I remember any one who has died during my lifetime whose death ever had a more enviable outburst of sorrow and love and admiration, public and private.'[1]

Now the dead man was being remembered in London, the city where he had worked for almost forty years. At the same time memorial services were taking place across the country including St Giles Cathedral in Edinburgh and every parade ground within the boundaries of the Canadian training camp outside London. Here at Westminster Abbey the service was being led by the Archbishop of Canterbury, assisted by the Abbey clergy in their black and gold funeral copes. The 23rd psalm 'The Lord is my Shepherd' was followed by a reading from Revelations XXI and then Cecil Spring Rice's powerful anthem set to music by Gustav Holst 'I Vow to Thee My Country'. It was a far cry from the modest Scottish beginnings of the man whose life was being celebrated – the present Canadian Governor-General, Lord Tweedsmuir, better known the world over more simply as John Buchan.

[1]

A SCOTTISH YOUTH

THE Royal Burgh of Peebles is a prosperous county town of neat grey stone houses at the confluence of Eddleston Water and the river Tweed. The area, with its soft rounded hills, high-backed ridges and wide valleys, is ideal sheep country and has been famous for its textiles and woollens since the seventeenth century. During the nineteenth century the town began to expand, drawing people from Edinburgh, some twenty miles away, who were attracted by its fishing and attractive countryside. 'Peebles for Pleasure' became the proud boast of the railway posters touting for custom. During the nineteenth century it had also become the home of the Buchan family.

Though the Buchans originally came from Aberdeenshire, where they were kinsmen of Buchan of Auchmacoy, they had gradually worked their way south. John Buchan's grandfather, also called John, had been born in Kincardine, Perthshire in 1811 and had served a law apprenticeship in Stirling. He moved to Peebles in 1835 and for five years he worked as the chief clerk to the town clerk and then became the accountant to the City of Glasgow Bank when it opened a Peebles branch. When the Bank of Scotland succeeded the City of Glasgow Bank he moved across as sub-agent and then in 1867 was appointed agent of the newly-opened branch of the Commercial Bank. In 1881 the Commercial Bank took over the premises of the Union Bank at the west end of Peebles High Street. John's new home Bank House, 'the house with the red door', was henceforth always to be associated with the Buchan family.

John Buchan quickly prospered, set up his own law firm and in 1862 bought Stellknowe, a large house with about twenty acres in Midlothian, now called Leadburn House. In 1844 he had married Violet Henderson, the daughter of a blacksmith and small farmer in the nearby village of Whim, and it was to Stellknowe that their family of three sons (John, Thomas and Willie) and two daughters (Kate and Violet) would go for holidays. However, the crash of the City of Glasgow Bank in 1878 almost bankrupted the family. As a trustee of the bank he was liable for the debts, and though the case went to the House of Lords, John Buchan was forced to cover the losses. It broke his spirit and his health and forced the family, hitherto considered prosperous, to sell many of their assets. But by the time he died in 1883 the debt had been discharged.

His youngest son Willie, born in 1851, after completing his law studies at Edinburgh University took over the family law firm and, in 1880, was appointed to the important post of Town Clerk and Procurator Fiscal. He was to run the two in tandem until his death twenty-six years later, during which time he was responsible for building new gasworks, widening the Tweed Bridge and improving the town's water supply from Manor Water. As his obituary in the local newspaper noted: 'Business did not absorb his whole activities and there was much time for volunteering (military training), for angling, and much other open-air life, and, above all, for continued study in the humane subjects of which he was so fond.'[1]

Willie Buchan, thin, delicate with a neat beard and moustache, was to be a fixture in all the young Buchans' lives and it was he, a frequent traveller to the Continent, who was the first to nurture his nephew JB's interest in French literature. His job allowed him to indulge in his love of books and in particular folklore, antiquities, genealogies, heraldry and French language and literature. William Buchan, his great-nephew, has pithily described Willie's disparate interests as 'Gasworks and Maupassant, main-drainage and heraldry, railways and folk-lore.'[2]

The middle Buchan son, Thomas, seems to have been the black sheep of the family. Family legend relates he killed a man in a fight, but more probably he simply found Peebles too provincial a town for his high spirits. As a young man he ran away to sea and eventually settled in New South Wales. On the outbreak of the First World War he joined up, rising to squadron sergeant-major in an Australian mounted regiment. He stayed on in Australia, and turned from drink to religion but still remained unforgiven by his Peebles relations. When he died in 1940, the local minister wrote to say he was erecting a stone with the words 'A true son of the Church'. JB, mindful of Tom's past, suggested altering it to 'A true son of Scotland'.

John, the eldest son of John Buchan and JB's father, was born in 1847 and educated at Bonnington Park School in Peebles, where aged nineteen he helped found the local YMCA. It was intended that he should follow his father into the family law firm but he became caught up, while serving a law apprenticeship, in the religious revival of the 1860s and 1870s and decided instead to become a minister. After studying at the Free Church College in Edinburgh he was ordained at the age of twenty-six. This was some twenty-five years after 'The Disruption', the great split in the Church of Scotland when 474 Church of Scotland ministers had walked out of the General Assembly, over the right of local landowners to appoint ministers to parishes, to form their own Free Church. By 1875 there were 3,700 Free Church congregations in Scotland. To be a Free Church minister signified a man prepared to flout the establishment, a man dismissive of social hierarchy. The Reverend John Buchan was such a man.

John Buchan returned to be the temporary minister at Broughton, a small farming village twelve miles outside Peebles, for the winter of 1873–4 and there he met and fell in love with the sixteen year old daughter of a local sheep farmer, John Masterton. Helen Masterton was the second of five children, an attractive girl with long golden hair and bright blue eyes who had just returned to Broughton from a boarding-school, The Priory, in Peebles and cookery lessons in Edinburgh. Within months of meeting, John and Helen were engaged and on 2 December 1874 were married at Broughton Green. In the summer of 1874 the Reverend John Buchan had been given his first charge, the Knox Free Church in Perth. It was at the manse at 20 York Place in Perth that their first born, named after family tradition John, was born on 26 August 1875. Helen had only just celebrated her eighteenth birthday.

The Buchan family did not stay long in Perth. Soon after the birth they were off again, this time to the West Church at Pathhead, a small town between Dysart and Kirkcaldy on the north shores of the Firth of Forth where the Buchans were to stay twelve years. Here, four more children were born – Anna Masterton, named after her maternal grandmother, in 1877, William Henderson named after his Buchan uncle in 1880, James Walter in 1882 and Violet named after her Buchan aunt in 1888. The manse, a grey stone villa in Smeaton Road now demolished, had been built in the 1830s and had good views across the Forth to Edinburgh, the Pentlands and to the Lammermuir hills. It stood in a large garden, with a railway behind it and in front, across a muddy by-road, a linoleum factory, a coal-pit and a rope-walk, with a bleaching-works somewhere to the rear. Buchan's most vivid memory of the manse, he later claimed, was the overpowering smell from the factory.

It was a big house with a day-nursery as well as drawing-room, dining-room, a guest room and a study for the Reverend John Buchan. Though the Buchans were not rich, especially after the 1878 Glasgow City Bank failure had depleted the family fortune, they were able to afford two servants: Marget who worked in the kitchen and who was to remain with the family for many years and a nurse Ellen Robinson, known as Ellie Robbie. Kirkcaldy was an area rich in history and literary associations which were to feed the imaginations particularly of the two elder children. They would play on the seashore or around the nearby Ravenscraig Castle, immortalised in Sir Walter Scott's novels. During the holidays they explored the fishing hamlets of Wemyss and Buckhaven further up the coast and talked to the Dutch and Norwegian sailors who anchored there.

JB became the leader of a gang which would sometimes pick fights with the young men at the local factories or the sons of the local gentry. On one occasion his gang set forty tar-barrels alight and rolled them into a disused quarry. The opening scene of a future novel *Prester John* would be based on these childhood escapades. It was a happy, tolerant, if disciplined, childhood. Though he was later to admit: 'Our household was ruled by the old Calvinistic discipline . . . the regime made a solemn background to a child's life,' he also stressed it was one where 'a natural love of rhetoric, and the noble scriptural cadences had their own meaning for me, quite apart from their proper interpretation. The consequence was that I built up a Bible world of my own and placed it in the woods.'[3]

The Calvinism preached and lived by the Reverend John Buchan was not the frightening and narrow doctrine from which R.L. Stevenson sought to escape but that of a benevolent, if omnipotent, God who ruled by unalterable law and where good would always triumph over evil. As Janet Adam Smith has put it: 'the Devil appeared to John as he did to Burns – half-humorous, half-earthy, a Hallowe'en bogy, a scarecrow, a figure of fun . . .'[4] Even church could be turned into an adventure with Sunday School classes devoted to learning through games and far away places, such as Nyasaland brought alive by stories from visiting missionaries. It was for the Free Church Sabbath School that Buchan produced his first published work, a New Year's Hymn for 1887 which ran:

> To Thee, our God and Friend,
> We raise our hymn today,
> O, guard and guide us from above
> Along life's troubled way,

Though the Buchan children would attend church twice on Sundays the Sabbath was also a day for ham and eggs instead of porridge at breakfast and cakes and sugar biscuits for tea. They might not be allowed their toys but there were Bible games. They would march around the nursery table blowing on trumpets to make the walls of Jericho fall, and once set the nursery rug alight while pretending to be Shadrach, Meshach and Abednego in the fiery furnace. The manse was a focal point in the life of the community and the minister and his wife were important local figures. Parishioners would come for practical as well as spiritual advice and the Buchans were expected to set an example, adopt a strong pastoral role and live a life of sacrifice and duty. The result was an upbringing that set the family slightly apart from the community and nurtured many of the qualities later to be identified with Buchan's own fictional heroes and heroines.

At the age of five Buchan fell out of a carriage and the heavy wheel ran over him fracturing his skull. After emergency surgery he was forced to spend the next year in bed. It was a formative experience. The deep and very distinctive scar on his left brow was to remain all his life, giving him a slightly sinister and raffish appearance. After the accident he had to learn to walk again and catch up on a lost year. The time he spent in bed, where he was forbidden to learn to read, was to nurture his already developed imagination and make him rather more introspective than his younger siblings. It was also to harden him so that he changed from a delicate child into a tough and determined young boy. While he was ill he was the centre of his mother's attention and the strong bonds that united mother and son until her death some fifty years later were forged at this time. Helen Buchan was only eighteen years older than her eldest son, almost a child herself while Buchan was growing up.

Helen's husband, a kind but quiet soul, spent much of his time ministering to his parish and she was often lonely and homesick. Pathhead was only a hundred miles north of Peebles but the bleak, industrial town looking out to the North Sea was a far cry from the rolling Border countryside where she had grown up within a large and loving family. Separated from her relations this sensitive and emotional woman increasingly found comfort in the son she had almost lost. As he grew older and she suffered various family tragedies her dependency on him would grow.

The Reverend John Buchan was a more shadowy figure but was, his son later admitted, 'the best man I have ever known.' He had the ruddy complexion of a countryman and, as a young man, had grown huge bushy whiskers. JB thought it 'odd that he should have been by profession a theologian, for he was wholly lacking in philosophical interest or aptitude.'[5] A good classical scholar and keen naturalist, whose great passions in life, fishing and walking, he passed on to his sons, he also prided himself on being a poet, publishing in 1881 a collections of verse, *Tweedside Echoes and Moorland Musings* which celebrated the Tweed Valley and his family. Originally a Liberal, he became a

Unionist after the death of General Gordon and over the issue of Home Rule. In church politics too he always took a conservative view, partly out of 'a love of old ways and a fast-vanishing world', and partly because 'he whole-heart-edly disliked a glib modernism and the worship of fashion.'[6]

JB first went to a dame school, where he spent only a few months before he was expelled for upsetting a broth-pot on to the kitchen fire. From there he moved to a Board School at Pathhead, then the Burgh School of Kirkcaldy, walking three miles each way and finally he attended the High School at Kirkcaldy. Though a great reader he claims he was idle in class. 'School played but a small part in my life. It was an incident, an inconsiderable incident; a period of enforced repression which ended daily at four in the afternoon.'[7] The real education was at home where his father would sometimes play his penny whistle or sing songs. More often, however, he would read aloud: Bible stories, Border ballads, Norse mythology, fairy tales, Lewis Carroll, Mark Twain and perhaps the most important literary influence on Buchan's future writing, John Bunyan's allegorical *Pilgrim's Progress*, a book which was then regarded as second only to the Bible. Buchan later claimed he had completely memorized the book drawn by 'its plain narrative, its picture of life as a pilgrimage over hill and dale, where surprising adventures lurked by the wayside . . .'[8]

Another formative influence too was the two months the Buchan children spent each summer with their Masterton grandparents at Broughton. The Masterton farm, the Green, was a white-washed building on the Edinburgh-Carlisle road at the north end of Broughton Village. The children would travel down by train to Peebles where they would have tea with Willie Buchan and his two sisters Violet and Kate at Bank House before catching another train the dozen miles to Broughton. John Masterton was a mild-mannered man, an elder in Broughton Free Kirk who was often to be seen in baggy tweeds and an old panama hat driving about with pony and trap or chatting to his neighbours. His wife Anna was quite different. A strong personality, often outspoken or aloof, she ran her household with economical efficiency. Their three unmarried sons John, James and Ebenezer worked the farm. With Eben, only six years older than his nephew, Buchan formed a particularly close attachment.

Broughton Green was a large house full of delights for young children – a playroom called Jenny Berry, a garret known as Frizzel's End filled with bound copies of *Blackwood's* and *Punch*, and a garden with gooseberry and currant bushes. All around was the countryside where the Buchan children were free to roam, go on fishing expeditions, explore ruins, walk the hills and establish a sense of belonging. They would often go out with the local shep-herds and attend the sheep clippings and markets or spend a day with poachers on the Tweed or one of its tributaries. As a result the young Buchan came to respect the farmers and shepherds of the area and to pick up the soft idiomatic Border speech. He also developed a keen eye for the lie of country and a sense of the pervading spirit of place, all of which he would turn to good use when he later came to write.

It was at Broughton that the fertile imaginations of Buchan and his sister Anna were fed with the oral traditions recorded by James Hogg and Sir Walter Scott, the tales of the Covenanters and Bonnie Prince Charlie's army. The people, history and surroundings of Peebles would provide the material not only for his early novels and short stories but also for more mature later work such as *Witch Wood*. The home of John Murray of Broughton, secretary to Prince Charlie during the 1745 rebellion, which stood on the site of the present Broughton Place was to provide particular inspiration to the young Buchan. Murray's wife is a central figure in his novel *A Lost Lady of Old Years* and Murray himself is the subject of one of the essays in Buchan's collection *Some Eighteenth Century Byways*.

The Borders were always to be seen as 'a holy land', quite separate from the places Buchan lived for the rest of the year. There he could relax in a way not possible in his father's parish, there he was drawn into a large family environment, there he could establish roots not possible in the highly mobile life of a minister's family. It was in the Borders he later wrote, he could enjoy 'feelings of happiness and security, of enterprise and adventure, of sadness and nostalgia.' Broughton was to become increasingly important as a stable base after the family moved to Glasgow.[9]

2

THE GLASGOW YEARS

I N 1888 the Reverend John Buchan moved with his family to the John
Knox Church, otherwise called the Rose Street Church, a large Gothic,
black-sooted building about a quarter of a mile from the Clyde River. It
was the oldest Free Church in Glasgow and served the working-class area of
the Gorbals. At that stage the Gorbals did not have the reputation for crime
and violence it later acquired, but it was a depressed area with a declining
congregation since most of the local inhabitants either did not attend church
or were Catholics or Jews. Anna Buchan was to write of it later:

> It was known in the district as 'the scrapit kirk' because of its unpainted
> seats. Everything was as it had been at the beginning. No hymn had ever
> been sung in it, rarely, if ever, a paraphrase; a precentor in a box led the
> people in the Psalms of David. The congregation looked a mere handful in
> the large church, and I think my mother must have quailed in spirit at the
> wilderness of empty pews.[1]

The Reverend John Buchan was to remain there until his retirement some
twenty two years later in the course of which he turned it into an active and
attractive church. He replaced fittings and redecorated the inside. He introduced an organist and a choir to sing hymns as well as psalms and he encouraged social activities, Bible classes, prayer meetings and classes for young
communicants.

There is a possibility that he may have moved from Pathhead to Glasgow
on account of health problems owing to the strains of the work at Pathhead,
but it is more likely that he was looking for a new challenge and wanted to be
closer to good schools now that the children were growing up. Perhaps most

crucially his annual salary would more than double from £187 to £410. The church did not come with a manse but the Buchans found a house two miles away in a prosperous suburb, Crosshill, near the Queens Park. Queen Mary Avenue was a broad, quiet road of villas – some single, others semi-detached – inhabited by professionals who worked in Glasgow. Florence Villa, at No 34, was a plain, square, stone building, with a copper beech in front, and at the back a long narrow garden, bounded by an old brick wall. Buchan gives an evocative picture of the garden with its elms, birches and ashes, the privet hedge, lawn bordered by flower-beds and dilapidated green house in an essay 'Urban Greenery' in his book *Scholar Gipsies*.

The Buchan family now consisted of six children ranging from John the eldest at thirteen to Violet less than a year old. It was a household dominated by Helen Buchan, who ran it with the help of one maid. John Buchan's mother was highly domesticated and nothing gave her greater pleasure than to sort out a set of drawers, bottle some fruit, make jam or turn her hand to some cooking. The Reverend John Buchan was, on the other hand, outside his church activities a gentle dreamer. He took little part in the everyday life of the family and was in many ways as helpless as his children. His passion for the Gospels was only matched by his vagueness over money and frequently his wife would find he had walked home in the rain because he had given his tram money to a beggar.

Mrs Buchan's domestic skills were extended to the John Knox Church which she ran with the same no-nonsense approach as she did her own family. The Reverend John Buchan was happy to preach and to lead his congregation in prayer, less keen to visit the sick and elderly or run the social side of the church. These tasks Helen Buchan undertook with little complaint and considerable success. It was she who ran the Women's Meetings and the Girls' Bible Class, who organised the sewing-class, collected for the Sustentation Fund or Zenana Mission and commandeered family and friends to knit, bake or build for the annual sale of work. Her motto was 'Do what has to be done *at once*!' and her passion for hard work and her determined nature were to be passed on and most notably to her eldest son.

Increasingly, as the church became more active, it began to take over the lives of the children. On Sunday there were now services in the morning and afternoon, a young men's meeting, a mid-day prayer meeting, the Sabbath school, the Bible-class and sometimes a Mission meeting to close the day. Anna helped her mother visiting the congregation, conducting prayer meetings and with church soirees, while young John Buchan was persuaded into leading a Sunday School class for Gorbals boys. Once the topic for the day had been covered he would overcome their and his own boredom by regaling them with rather more secular tales of his own invention. It was these Gorbals boys whom he later celebrated in the Gorbals Die-Hards, those invaluable 'irregulars' at the centre of his trilogy of novels beginning with *Huntingtower*.

Though the Buchan children fulfilled their duties with good grace and were devoted to their parents, there were increasing signs of friction as they grew up. The children were high-spirited and intelligent and at an age when they were beginning to question many of their parents' central beliefs. Their parents' life was a busy one allowing them to spend less and less time with their older offspring. The Reverend John Buchan had little ambition and in his leisure moments was content to retire alone to arrange his flowers, play his penny whistle or read his Walter Scott. His wife was fully employed in running the church and taking care of the younger children. John and Anna, only two years apart and both sensitive and imaginative children, spent more and more of their time playing together or inventing stories. The Glasgow years were to cement the bond first formed in Fife. From both parents, however, John and Anna Buchan inherited certain qualities. From their mother they learnt practical good sense, from their father a sense of the moral dimension to their lives and from both a sense of purpose and responsibility.

In November 1888 Buchan started in Class VI of Hutchesons' Grammar School at a quarterly fee of 21 shillings. Hutchesons' had been founded in 1641 by two Glasgow merchants, George and Thomas Hutcheson. The school had a wide social catchment area ranging from the children of prosperous middle class professionals such as the Buchans and the Maxtons – James Maxton became a well-known Labour politician – to poor boys or more mature students on full bursaries. The school remains one of the best independent day schools in Glasgow. When John Buchan was there it was still situated at 211 Crown Street in the heart of the Gorbals and the only secondary school on the south side of the city. Part of its attraction was that it, and Hutchesons' Girls School which Anna attended before going to a private school in Edinburgh, was reasonably close to Queen Mary Avenue. Each day Buchan would walk the two miles from his home in Queen Mary Avenue, a walk which took him through some of the roughest parts of Glasgow, past pubs, tenement blocks and rows of houses, most of which had seen better times. Another attraction was its high academic standards. For example, Hutcheson pupils had fifty per cent more passes than the national average in 1889, the first year of the new National Leaving Certificate. At the end of his first term he won the eleventh of the twelve open scholarships thereby entitling him to free education, including books and stationery, for the next four years.

At Hutchesons', Buchan initially studied a curriculum that consisted of English, Grammatical Analysis, Composition, History, Geography,

Religious Knowledge, Higher Arithmetic, Algebra, Geometry, Drawing, Latin, French, Vocal Music, Drill and Fencing. Extra subjects for which additional fees were due were Pianoforte, Phonography, Violin, Chemistry, Swimming and Elocution. During his second year he switched to the Classical side, coming under the influence of an inspiring teacher, James Caddell. For the next two years he studied the History of English Language and Literature, Composition, Mathematics, History, Geography, Latin, Greek, Fencing and Rifle Drill. He also took an extra class in French though not to examination standard. Caddell, who had been Dux of the school in 1870, had originally trained to be a preacher. In 1882 he returned to his old school as a Classical Master, staying for thirty-eight years. On his retirement Buchan contributed an appreciation to *The Hutchesonian* in which he paid tribute to his 'old friend and preceptor' as 'the most enthusiastic of guides' and speaking for his Hutchesons' generation 'one of the shaping influences in our lives'. Another pupil was less tactful. He remembered him as 'a holy terror – fit to take on his weight in wild cats'.[2]

There were no organized games at the school and pupils were left to use their free time as they wished. During his time as a 'Hutchie bug' Buchan matured intellectually and made his first attempts at writing. He read widely from Gibbon and Scott to Dickens and Thackeray and by the time he left he knew much of Matthew Arnold's poetry by heart. It was while he was at school he wrote the first canto of a poem on Hell and to his schooldays probably belongs part of a novel *The Tale of a Midsummer Night: the Memoirs of Captain John Hepburn of His Majesty's Navy*.

Aged fifteen he had begun to keep a Commonplace Book in which he faithfully recorded extracts from his favourite writers such as Robert Browning, Shelley, Ruskin, Andrew Lang, Stevenson, Byron and Rider Haggard. There were passages in Greek and French and also some youthful attempts at verse.[3] In it he listed his twenty greatest books which included *Don Quixote, Robinson Crusoe, Tom Jones, Henry Esmond, Vanity Fair, Jane Eyre, Les Miserables, Anna Karenina, Lorna Doone, Far From the Madding Crowd*, Stevenson's *The Master of Ballantrae* and several Scott novels *Waverley, Redgauntlet, Old Mortality* and *The Bride of Lammermoor*. The Commonplace Book also carried notes for his works in progress – *My Lady Feigning's Daughter* which was to become *John Burnet of Barns*, and his plans to edit Sir Philip Sidney's *Arcadia* and compile a book of criticism entitled *Notes and Criticisms*.

In June 1891 Buchan took his Lower Grade Education Certificate in Mathematics, English and Latin and the following summer passed the same subjects at the Higher or Honours Grade. He also added a Lower Grade in Greek. Only one other boy in the school passed with Honours in Higher

English. Though he entered Class X, the highest class in the school, for the Session 1892–93 he stayed only a few weeks before going straight to Glasgow University to which he had just won a bursary. He had also managed to obtain another bursary worth £30 a year and one of the ten leaving bursaries awarded by Hutchesons. In time his brothers Willie and Walter and Alastair would follow him to the school.

When John Buchan went up to Glasgow University in the autumn of 1892 the university had only twenty years earlier moved from its cramped conditions in the old High Street to the towers and pinnacles of Gilbert Scott's new building at Gilmorehill overlooking Kelvingrove Park. He had chosen Glasgow in preference to Edinburgh, where his father and uncle had been educated, principally so that he could live at home. However it was a good choice intellectually, for Glasgow University even then had a world-wide reputation. Lord Kelvin was Professor of Natural Philosophy, Edward Caird was Professor of Moral Philosophy, John Veitch a neighbour in the Borders Professor of Logic, and A.C. Bradley held the Chair of English. Buchan was one of almost 2,000 students, most of them men (since women were only allowed to graduate in 1893), who crammed each day at 8 a.m. into the large lecture halls to take copious notes on their chosen subjects. Some classes were as large as 200. Each morning he would rise at 6 a.m. to walk the four miles to the university through the south side of Glasgow and across the Clyde, though occasionally if the weather was bad he would catch the London train at Eglinton Street Station. In his memoirs, he recalled 'the sight of humanity going to work and the signs of awakening industry. There was the bridge with the river starred with strange lights, the light shipping at the Broomielaw, and odours which even at their worst spoke of the sea'.[4]

He was taking the General MA course which consisted of seven compulsory subjects – Latin, Greek, Mathematics, Logic, Moral Philosophy, Natural Philosophy (which now corresponds to Physics) and English Literature. In his first year he took classes in Mathematics, Greek and 'Humanity' (Latin) in which, on the basis of a written examination, he was awarded Second prize for General Eminence. During the second year he concentrated on Senior Latin and Greek, coming Second in the latter, and finally in his last year attended classes in Moral Philosophy, Logic and Private Greek. A contemporary, Alec MacCallum Scott, later remembered how the Professor of Philosophy, Henry Jones, once when returning an essay to Buchan remarked aloud that he wished he himself had written it.[5]

This grounding in the Classics was to be an important influence on Buchan's future writing which was to be marked by its clear and economical prose style and use of Classical imagery. He later admitted it had also given him a sense of values, mellowing the Calvinism of his youth. He wrote in his memoirs '. . . if they exalted the dignity of human nature they insisted upon its frailties and the *aidos* with which the temporal must regard the eternal. I lost then any chance of being a rebel, for I became profoundly conscious of the dominion of unalterable law. Prometheus might be a fine fellow in his way, but Zeus was king of gods and men.'[6]

Buchan's Greek teacher was Gilbert Murray, then only twenty six, who had become Professor of Greek three years earlier. Murray later vividly remembered his first meeting with the precocious Buchan. The seventeen year old student had asked him which Latin translation of Democritus Francis Bacon had used in his essays. Murray was impressed, not least when he learnt the reason behind the question. Buchan had been commissioned to edit and write an introduction for a collection of Francis Bacon's essays and apothegms for a series published by the London publisher, Walter Scott. The book appeared in 1894 as volume 88 in the Scott Library with Buchan joining such eminent editorial contributors as Ernest Rhys, Havelock Ellis, Richard Garnett and W.B. Yeats. Quite how he came to edit such a prestigious title is unknown but most probably it was through the artist D.Y. Cameron, a friend of the Buchan family, who had illustrated a number of books in the series. In his 9,000 word introduction, Buchan showed himself to be familiar with the period and quoted extensively from Bacon's contemporaries. It is clear that he identified with Bacon as a man torn between his ambitions as a writer and as a man of public affairs.

Among Buchan's university classmates were three friends from Hutchesons': Charles Dick, Joseph Menzies and John Edgar, all of whom recognized his exceptional qualities. Another university friend, the future journalist and writer Alec MacCallum Scott, later described them as 'a small group of disciples who sat at his feet and who preached abroad that this schoolboy was destined to become one of the great Masters of English Literature.'[7] Dick, in particular, worshipped the undergraduate Buchan and the editor of the university magazine had to edit part of a review of one of Buchan's novels in which Dick had written extravagantly that the style was bettered only 'by Shakespeare and the better parts of the Bible.'[8] With Edgar and Dick, Buchan set up the Nameless Club whose Honorary Presidents were three heroes R.L. Stevenson, the essayist and aesthete Walter Pater and Prince Charles Edward. The rules of the club were that they meet once a year, membership was hereditary and each member 'condescends to nothing that is common or unclean.' Closed societies appealed to Buchan's love of romance and his strong sense of male friendship. The Nameless Club was to be the first of many such societies with which

Buchan became involved during his life and which he would scatter throughout his novels.

Other contemporary graduates included the future Labour Lord Chancellor Hugh Macmillan, a lifelong friend, who had come to Glasgow in 1896 to read for his LLB; Robert Horne, later Chancellor of the Exchequer, who took First Class Honours in Philosophy in Buchan's first year, and H.N. Brailsford who after taking a degree in Philosophy and Classics stayed on as Assistant to John Veitch. The Buchan circle included William Romaine Paterson, later a popular novelist under the pseudonym Benjamin Swift, John Roy Tannahill subsequently well-known for his translations of Verlaine, Archibald Charteris eventually Professor of Law at the University of Sydney and a future Church of England clergyman Donald Cameron. Alec MacCallum Scott later confided to his diary:

> I have watched with awestruck and somewhat curious admiration the steady march of Buchan from success to success since the days when we sat next each other in Professor Bradley's English Literature Class at Glasgow about 34 years ago . . . He was even then a kind of Admirable Crichton. He seemed to achieve success by a kind of royal right which none could challenge and which none could grudge. His merit was apparent to every one who was brought into contact with him and yet there was not a trace of ostentation or arrogance about him . . . He was calm, steadfast, assured of himself and with his mind quietly made up as to what he meant to do . . . and he was good company all the way. He was not priggish, or dull, or over serious, or too much concerned with himself or his career.[9]

Murray was an inspiring teacher who talked to his students rather than merely read his lectures like so many of his colleagues. Buchan, as one of his most able and ambitious students, was quickly taken under his wing and they found they had many interests in common, not least in politics and literature. It was Murray for example who first introduced his student to the work of Ibsen a powerful influence over the next few years. The young student would often visit Murray at home and soon became friendly with Murray's wife Mary, the daughter of the Earl of Carlisle, who it was said would demonstrate her egalitarian principles by taking tea with her maids by turns in the kitchen and the drawing-room. During Buchan's final year Henry Jones became Professor of Philosophy when Edward Caird succeeded Benjamin Jowett as Master of Balliol. Jones was to be another influence on the precocious student introducing Buchan to the work of Kant and Sidgwick and firing him with a passion for the subject. Under Jones the young Buchan's mind was carefully honed and the beginnings of a lifelong interest in philosophy, and particularly the teachings of Plato, generated.

Years later Buchan admitted 'I went to Glasgow and I left young . . .' and that he was 'utterly undistinguished'. His interests were primarily intellectual and his ambition then was to become a professor in a Scottish university. He tended to return home immediately after lectures to work late into the night over his books. He never spoke in a Union debate nor took part in student politics and Rectorial Elections. The sum of his contribution to university life was to read a couple of papers to college societies and write a few pieces for the *Glasgow University Magazine*. These included a story 'On Cademuir Hill', an obituary appreciation of R.L. Stevenson, a review of Walter Pater's *Greek Studies* and after he left the university two poems 'The Strong Man Armed' and 'To a Princess who was Forgotten' and a piece entitled 'A Gossip on Books and Plays'. Glasgow was for him only a stage in his education but it was important in his development as a writer both for inspiration and introspection. He later wrote 'there is much to be said for a University in a great city. It brings the student face to face with the other side of life . . . Also it teaches him detachment. He learns to live his own inner life regardless of his surroundings.'[10]

The university session lasted from October to April to allow many of the students to return and help their families on the farm. Buchan used the long summer breaks to spend time with his relations at Broughton and Peebles, to catch up on his academic work, to read and to write. He was also beginning to discover Scotland. In the summer of 1890 the Buchan family had gone to Arran, two years later they were in Rannoch though in 1893 they were back at Broughton. During that first summer vacation Buchan studied hard determined to win two university prizes; the Lorimer bursary in logic, philosophy and literature and the Blackstone prize for Latin and Greek but in both he proved to be unsuccessful. He also finished his edition of Francis Bacon and published his first article. 'Angling in Still Waters', which appeared in the *Gentleman's Magazine* in August 1893, is an evocative account of a day's fishing on the Tweed. If at times self-conscious and rather flowery it is an extraordinary piece of work for a boy still under eighteen. The subject was one that he knew and loved and already there are signs of his ability to convey the sights, smell and sounds of the countryside.

He was reading widely, not just the popular works of the time such as J.K. Jerome, Arthur Conan Doyle, R.L. Stevenson's *Kidnapped* and *The Master of Ballantrae* but also, under the patronage of his Uncle Willie, more erudite work such as Ibsen's *A Doll's House*. In June 1893 he told Charles Dick he was enjoying Swinburne's *Poems and Ballads*, Lockyer's *London Lyrics*, the

Shorter Poems of Robert Bridges, *Lorna Doone* for the seventh or eighth time, Saintsbury's *Essays on French Novelists*, Dumas' *The Black Tulip* and Guy de Maupassant's *Contes*. The Glasgow University Library register of the time shows him borrowing books by Pater, Socrates, Goethe, Matthew Arnold's Essays and on several occasions Walton's *Compleat Angler*.

The long summer holidays were also used to explore the Borders, often accompanied by Charles Dick. Sometimes they would take rods and fish the Leithen and Manor waters or the headwaters of Clyde, on other occasions they would make long journeys on foot or by bike north to Edinburgh and south once crossing the border into England at Coldstream. On one such bicycle expedition in June 1893 Buchan found a dead man by the roadside which frightened him enormously. He told Charles Dick 'I did not hold an inquest on the dead man; still less did I inform a policeman, since there wasn't one nearer than six miles, and that one was in bed. What I did was to bolt on as fast as a broken bicycle and a lame leg allowed me.'[11]

Tragedy struck the Buchan family in 1893. Violet, Buchan's younger sister, had been taken ill that spring and brought from Glasgow to Broughton in the hope the fresh country air might aid her recovery but sadly that was not the case. She died at the end of June aged five. Her death came as a great shock to the family, in particular her father and sixteen year old sister who had in effect become a surrogate mother. Buchan too was deeply affected by her death admitting to Charles Dick soon afterwards 'I had no idea a death in a family was such a painful thing.'[12] A happier event was the visit that October of his uncle Tom. Buchan regaled Dick with an account of his visit. 'My Uncle Tom – the sailor one – is home just now, full of curious and wonderful stories many of which I have jotted down. He told me among other things that he had lived for six months in Samoa and had often seen Robert Louis. He said that he is a sort of King there, but that he goes about with nothing on him except a blanket, worn toga-wise, and pinned at the shoulder with a Cairngorm brooch. Fancy! Sic a sicht for sair een! A decent honest Scotsman come to that.'[13]

In 1894 Helen Buchan gave birth to her sixth and last child, a boy who was christened Alastair Ebenezer after one of his Masterton uncles. Buchan called his youngest sibling, almost twenty years his junior, Peter and the name stuck for several years until Alastair became the Mhor, Gaelic for 'the great one'. Indeed each of the Buchan children had a nickname; JB was 'Johnnie' or 'Dodo', Anna was 'Nan' or 'Pudge', William 'Grey Rat' and Walter 'The Bird'.

During the spring holiday Buchan was busy writing a short story 'A Midsummer Night's Tale', which became 'Comedy in the Full Moon', and an article 'The Muse of the Angle' about the poetry associated with fishing, which became *Musa Piscatrix*. There were plans to follow his edition of Bacon's *Essays* with *The Compleat Angler* and Sir Philip Sidney's *Arcadia* for the same series. He was now also working hard for his Oxford entrance. At the end of 1894 he wrote to Charles Dick from Queen Mary Avenue 'Somehow or other I have been feeling rather dull, perhaps the influence of the weather and hard work. My life just now is a fine example of "Dying to Live".' The hard work paid off. Shortly afterwards he learnt that after several attempts, he had won the Lorimer Bursary for Philosophy and, from a field of 150 candidates, a Hulme Scholarship at Brasenose.

The following summer was a busy one. In August 1895 the Buchan family took a holiday at Kinghorn in Fife where at high tide the sea came to within six feet of their front door in St James' Place. There Buchan learnt to swim, played golf a good deal and went for long walks along the shore. Even so he was working some ten hours each day – studying five pages of Plato a day, preparing a paper he was presenting to the Philosophical, a Glasgow Student Union Society, and completing a collection of essays which he called *Scholar Gipsies*. Later in the month he went to stay with Gilbert Murray and his family at Sheringham in Norfolk. Earlier guests had included George Douglas Brown, later the author of *The House with the Green Shutters*, and H.N. Brailsford, to whom Murray had given a revolver when he vowed to go and fight for the Greeks. At Sheringham the party played golf, swam and read Thackeray's *Pendennis* aloud. It was in Norfolk too Buchan completed a volume of short stories which he called *Grey Weather*.

In October 1895 his first novel *Sir Quixote of the Moors*, which he dedicated to Gilbert Murray, was published. It is a charming tale set in the seventeenth century, with strong echoes of Stevenson, Scott and the French romance tradition. In it a French gentleman, the Sieur de Rohaine, recounts his adventures with various Covenanters as he rides from Galloway to Leith. Sending Murray a copy Buchan conceded 'Now that I have read it in print I don't feel at all satisfied with it. Some of it I like but in a good deal of it I think I have been quite unsuccessful. Of course you will understand that it is written in character, and that this accounts for the frequently exaggerated sentiment and style.'[14] The following week Buchan was still unsure of the book and confessed to Murray 'I can't quite make up my mind whether I like it or not.' He admitted:

One of the worst faults of the book, I think, is the tendency to mere sentence making. I think this is due partly to the excessive admiration which I have felt for four years for Stevenson, partly to the way the book was written. It was built up sentence by sentence at intervals during the last three weeks of the College session.[15]

It is certainly true that some of the construction is clumsy and the authorial voice intrusive but the book is an early demonstration of Buchan's ability to record the physical sensations undergone by his characters and to make a place a central feature in a story. Like most of Buchan's early books it is an historical romance set in an area of Scotland he knew well and, as in most of his books, honour and friendship play an important part in the story. He was also unhappy about the title, which the British publisher, T.F. Unwin, had changed from the original *Sir Quixote*, and by the American publisher Henry Holt giving the book a different ending, thereby completely undermining the sense of the story.

The young writer need not have worried. Though the book received little review coverage this was generally good. The reviewer in the *Glasgow University Magazine*, possibly H.N. Brailsford, wrote:

> He does not write a modern novel with a purpose, but yet his interest in conduct is so strong that he must puzzle us with the right and wrong of a situation which could only occur in a bygone century. He reproduces all the hesitation and conflict of a modern Angel Clare or Richard Feverel. He is too healthily modern to be satisfied with mere action, and he cannot save himself from scrutinising motive . . . It is this anachronism which lifts the romance far above such ingenious trifling as Mr Anthony Hope's *Prisoner of Zenda*.[16]

However, the review went on 'The book is neither novel of adventure nor novel of character, and this uncertainty of treatment is its gravest artistic defect.' The writer noted a crucial Buchan element. 'There is hurry and movement through it all', adding 'The style strikes us as too consciously archaic in the first chapter, but later it becomes thoroughly easy, graceful, and urbane.'[17] Increasingly critics have argued that this first novel written when Buchan was nineteen is very important. David Daniell, who devotes considerable space to it in his study of Buchan's writing, has called it 'a little masterpiece, astonishingly percipient for an adolescent Victorian'. And he has suggested that 'the understanding of complex contradictory powers inside religious experience, forced to a dilemma without solution, and linked with the awakening of passion and the multiple loss of innocence – these are the characteristics of a story by Henry James'.[18]

Buchan's studies at the University, and the growing confidence engendered by his writing, had made him more aware of the parochialism of his own family life. Much as he loved his parents he felt constricted by their limited horizons and ambitions which tended to centre around the John Knox Church. There was a tension in his life between the preachings of his father and the teachings of his university professors, between a world bordered by John Knox and the stimulation provided by Erasmus, Galileo and Hume. The end of the nineteenth century had seen a renaissance in the life of Glasgow, not just in the wealth generated by its heavy industry but in its appreciation of the Fine Arts. Lavery, Pirie and Crawhall were exhibiting at the Glasgow Art Club, rich merchants had discovered Sisley, Manet and Van Gogh before their colleagues in London, Charles Rennie Mackintosh was building the Glasgow School of Art but these developments had bypassed the young Buchan buried in his books in Queen Mary Avenue. Now, no longer a teenager, his mind stimulated by his studies this precocious young man felt he had outgrown the city of his youth. Like many before him his eyes turned south and like many his route out of Glasgow would be Oxford.

3

THE SPELL OF OXFORD

HE Oxford that Buchan was about to enter had hardly changed in a hundred years. The streets still resounded to the clatter of the hansom cab and a horse tram ran up the High Street from Magdalen Bridge to Carfax. It was the Oxford of C.B. Fry and Hilaire Belloc, of Max Beerbohm's *Zuleika Dobson* and Compton Mackenzie's *Sinister Street*. It was largely a male society with few female students and where dons either did not marry or their wives quietly lived away from collegiate life. There were few scientists or pupils from state schools. Most of the undergraduates had been to public school and regarded Oxford as an enjoyable interlude before entering one of the professions. This was the heart of the Establishment at the apogee of Empire, a world to which Buchan had long aspired and in which many of his future views would be shaped.

En route to Oxford he had paid a quick visit to London to meet the publisher John Lane, to whom D.Y. Cameron had given him an introduction. The two men discussed terms for two books – the fishing anthology *Musa Piscatrix* and the collection of essays *Scholar Gipsies*. The former was to be published in December and the latter in February with Macmillan doing the American edition. Buchan was particularly pleased that Charles Robinson, who had illustrated R.L. Stevenson's *Child's Garden of Verses*, would be doing the illustrations for *Scholar Gipsies*. He also saw David Meldrum at the Savage Club who had been charged by the editor Robertson Nicoll to elicit as much information as possible for a profile in the *Bookman*. The *Bookman* published the profile in its December issue. It drew attention to the influence of Walter Scott and R.L. Stevenson on Buchan's writing, noted his publishing history to date and his plans for the future and concluded that 'his record is an extraordinary and interesting one for a writer of twenty years of age.'[1]

1895

John Buchan arrived in Oxford on the afternoon of 11th October. Writing to Charles Dick that evening he noted 'My rooms are very queer, but interesting . . . The only expensive thing about them is that they are fully lit with three planes of electric light which is very nice for the eyes.'[2] He had first come to Oxford the previous winter when he had stayed at Exeter and sat his exam in Christ Church Hall. He remembered in his autobiography 'walking in the later afternoon in Merton Street and Holywell and looking at snowladen gables which had scarcely altered since the Middle Ages. In that hour Oxford claimed me, and her bonds have never been loosed.'[3]

He was assigned room 7 at the top of No 1 Stair of Old Quad. Others on the staircase included Prince Synd Ulice Meerza, the son of the Nawab of Bengal. Benjamin Boulter, who came up from Westminster on one of the other Junior Hulme Scholarships, arrived a week later and was given the room opposite, No 8. Over fifty years later Boulter remembered how his new neighbour 'a thick-set man with a large head scarred on the left brow, speaking Lowland Scots in tones now deep, now shrill', introduced himself.

'These pictures are going to be a problem; come and join the hanging committee.' Gainsborough's *Mrs Graham*, was as tall as the room, I believe. 'But first of all,' he said rather solemnly, 'he must be given his place of honour.' 'He' was a photograph of Gilbert Murray . . .[4]

Brasenose, a small college in the middle of Oxford with about 100 undergraduates, was famous for its sporting tradition rather than as a centre of academic excellence; a former member of the college was William Webb Ellis who had invented rugby football. For an ambitious Scot from Glasgow Balliol would have been an obvious choice, given the Snell Exhibitions and that the Master was one of Buchan's former teachers. Buchan later claimed he had chosen Brasenose because of its associations with that high-priest of aesthetic prose-style, Walter Pater, whom he had much admired. Pater had however died in July 1894 and it is more likely that he chose the college on the advice of Richard Lodge who had come from Brasenose in 1894 to the first Chair of History at Glasgow.

Brasenose by reputation drew its intake from the lesser landed gentry and the North of England. In fact of the thirty four undergraduates in Buchan's year six had been at Harrow, three came from Fettes or Loretto in Scotland and several from abroad including a twenty-five year old Yale graduate, John Foster Carr, with whom Buchan became particularly friendly. The Principal, Charles Heberden, had held the post since 1889 and with his introverted manner, falsetto voice and passion for music was an unusual choice for such a sporty college. His picture by Sir William Orpen shows a bird-like man with a hooked nose, and Buchan was to write of him in his memoirs that his 'slender figure with its scholar's stoop seemed at first out of place in the robust life of Brasenose. Slowly his gentle humanity came to be understood, and when he died in 1922 the College mourned for him as a close-knit family mourns for its father.'[5]

Three days after his arrival Buchan admitted to Gilbert Murray. 'I can't quite make up my mind whether I like it or not . . . My tutor Fox is perfectly delightful and I look forward with great pleasure to my work. The men appear to be a curious mixture of overgrown schoolboys and would-be men of the world . . . I like them but I think I should tire of them pretty soon.'[6] During his first week he penned his initial impressions in an article, 'Oxford and her Influence' for the *Glasgow Herald*. In it he noted there was none of the 'pinch-ing, the scraping for an education, the battling against want and ill-health, which make a Scots college such a noble nursery of the heroic. Again, there are not so many gentlemen with designs on the reformation of the world. Things are quieter, easier, more contented. It is like some comfortable, latter-day monastery.'[7]

By 22 October he was writing to Dick: 'I am getting on here steadily, begin-ning to like the place more and more, and working very hard. My plan of day is something like this . . . I work at Classics from nine to one, I work in the Bodleian from 3 to 4.30, I work at Classics from 5 to 7 and from 7.30 to 9. Then after that I do general work.'[8] Buchan's rigorous timetable, his decision not to eat in hall to save money and his refusal to join the Freshmen's Wine Club had made him unpopular in college. His fellow undergraduates, almost all of whom had been to English public schools, found it difficult to under-stand this serious, hard-working, openly ambitious, slightly older Scottish student who seemed continually to be counting his pennies and even in his first term was preparing for a number of the university prizes.

It was not all work however. He took up rowing, characteristically admit-ting to Dick: 'I don't think I shall get a place in the College boat, but I shall try.' He was canoeing and playing golf, especially with his tutor Herbert Fox, a natural sportsman who played off a handicap of 6. Fox had become a Classics Fellow at Brasenose in 1889 where he stayed for the next thirty-two years establishing himself as a leading expert on Thucydides and one of the College characters, instantly recognizable by the hole he cut into his shoes to allow an excrescence on one toe to extrude. In Fox, and his free-spirited wife, Buchan found kindred spirits similar to the Murrays and the three of them would hire bicycles from the future industrialist William Morris, at that time running a cycle shop in the High, for trips across the Berkshire countryside and into Gloucestershire. Buchan's other great travelling companion was another Brasenose Fellow, Francis Wylie. Wylie was only ten years older than Buchan and had been at Glasgow University before coming to Balliol. A Fellow of Brasenose since 1893, he later became secretary to the Rhodes Trustees.

In November Buchan was instrumental in setting up the Ibsen Society which met weekly to read and discuss the dramas of the Master. The membership was to be limited to eight and no person was to be eligible for admission who had 'any serious stain on his moral character such as being a Socialist, a Radical, a Manchester man, an earnest student.'[9] And at the beginning of December Buchan was elected, together with Foster-Carr as the only freshers to the college essay society, the Ingoldsby. The Ingoldsby, which was limited to eleven members, met every fortnight on a Sunday night between 8.15 and 11.00 p.m. in term during which they read papers or simply to each other. Subjects included Ibsen's *A Doll's House*, Beaumont and Fletcher's *Philaster* and George Meredith's *The Egoist*. In May 1896 Buchan opened a discussion on 'Principles in Arts' while in November the Society listened to a paper on Walter Pater. Buchan was to remain a keen member and eventually, like Foster Carr, to become its President. It was for the Ingoldsby that he gave a paper 'Our Debt to the North' which involved his discussing a current interest, Celtic and Norse poetry.[10]

Shortly after Buchan's coming up to Oxford John Lane had approached him to succeed Richard Le Galliene as a literary adviser, a job which largely involved reading and commenting on scripts submitted to the firm. It was an extraordinary compliment for a writer so early in his career and only just twenty years old and an indication of the regard in which the young Scot was held. Buchan eagerly accepted, welcoming the fees as a useful source of income to supplement his scholarships and equally importantly relishing the contact the job would bring with some of the leading writers of the day.

At the beginning of his second term he was elected President of the Crocodiles with Benjamin Boulter as Secretary. The Crocodiles, which met to read and discuss literature, had evolved from the fated Ibsen Society after Ibsen's plays had proved too demanding for Buchan's Brasenose contemporaries. The insignia of the revamped club was a tie of green, grey and white 'under the fatuous idea that this is the colour of a crocodiles back.'[11] Among the books the Crocodiles read were Kipling's *Life's Handicap*, R.L. Stevenson's *Island Night Entertainments*, Austin Dobson's *Old World Idylls* and Arthur Machen's *The Great God Pan*. Machen's influence was to be noticeable in Buchan's early writing, most notably *Scholar Gipsies*.

A constant theme of Buchan's own account of his time at Oxford was his poverty. He felt that he must support himself given his father's modest salary and that several of his siblings were still at school. Oxford was expensive and it was necessary to have a good private income or generous parents in order to enjoy it fully. This Buchan intended to do but as a result of his own efforts and not at the expense of his family. Working hard for prizes provided money both for himself and his family, but it also gave him a satisfaction that he was not wasting his time and money. He was showing he could combine the prudence of a Calvinist with the longings of a Romantic.

It is quite clear from a study of his battel accounts at Brasenose that he spent much less than his contemporaries. His bill for the first term came to just over £20 made up of £1. 18 shillings college dues, £4. 7 shillings establishment charges, £3. 13 shillings room rent £1. 19 shillings for the buttery, £5. 8 shillings for the kitchen (when most people paid at least double that) £3. 10 shillings gate money and small charges for coals, laundry, stores and lighting. As income from prizes, journalism and books began to come in he started spending more. By the summer he was spending £37 a term which rose to around £40 in his second year and then fell back to the £20 mark as he lived in lodgings and had fewer charges on the college account. His mother would have approved.[12]

From his first term he had been working hard for both the Stanhope history and Newdigate poetry prizes and was therefore disappointed to learn in the summer term that he had not won them. He now had a strict timetable where he rose at 6 a.m. and despatched all his academic work by lunchtime. Afternoons were to be spent with friends walking, cycling or canoeing and evenings kept for his reading for Lane or his own literary work. By June he was out on the river rowing most afternoons and actually coxed a boat in the pair races. The magic of an Oxford summer term was beginning to work on him. He wrote to Charles Dick 'Oxford is looking its best just now. All the trees are out, garden chairs are appearing in the quad and everyone is in flannels and straw hats.'[13]

Mrs Buchan continued to write to her son almost daily, reminding him to watch his morals and chiding him for not thanking her for the currant loaf she had sent or forgetting Willie's birthday; but there were signs that he was breaking away from his family in Glasgow. During the holidays he now preferred to go to Broughton or Peebles than to stay with his parents in Glasgow and when in June he learnt that he had been put forward as a deacon in the John Knox Church his reaction to Anna was immediate. 'I received your letter this morning, and was immediately thrown into a violent passion by hearing of some misguided person proposing me as a deacon. *I will not have it* . . . it is a mere farce supposing such a thing.'[14]

He was now beginning to contribute articles through his literary agent Alexander Watt to *Macmillan's Magazine*, *Chamber's Journal*, *The Academy* and in the United States *The Living Age*. This development of his writing career had given him financial independence and he took pleasure with the earnings in buying presents for his family, most notably a pendant for his mother and a bicycle for Anna. In January 1896 he, also began his association with Beardsley's *The Yellow Book*, a magazine which influenced both him and his sister Anna to the extent that she used to sit in a darkened room and burn sticks of incense. It was not an interest the Reverend John Buchan understood. On one such occasion when he fell over a footstool, she later remembered, he shouted to her in frustration: 'Why should we sit in darkness and a horrible stink. Get up, girl, and don't sit attitudinising there!' 'A Captain of Salvation', which appeared in January 1896, is about a man brought down by drink. He finds salvation working for the Salvation Army in London's East End until figures from his past come back to plague him. Among those appearing with him in the issue were some famous names: George Gissing, Kenneth Grahame, H.G. Wells and a fellow Oxford student Maurice Baring. Further Buchan stories 'A Journey of Little Profit' and 'At the Article of Death' appeared in April 1896 and January 1897.

In June Buchan paid a brief visit to John Lane, staying with him in his set in Albany. Arnold Bennett, whose novel *In the Shadow*, later published as *A Man from the North*, Buchan had just read and liked leaves an interesting portrait in his diary for 26 June 1896 after meeting Buchan at Lane's flat:

> A very young, fair man; charmingly shy: 'Varsity' in every tone and gesture. He talks quietly in a feminine exiguous voice, with the accent of Kensington tempered perhaps by a shadow of a shade of Scotch (or was that my imagination?). Already – he cannot be more than 23 – he is a favourite of publishers, who actually seek after him, and has published one book. He told me that his second novel, a long Scotch romance, was just finished, and that he had practically sold the serial rights ... A most modest, retiring man, yet obviously sane and shrewd. Well-disposed too, and anxious to be just; a man to compel respect; one who counts.[15]

The following month Buchan was back in London where he told Boulter 'I met all sorts of people from awful New Women, who drank whisky and soda and smoked cigars to John Murray, the publisher, who is a sort of incarnation of respectability. I never was in so many theatres and restaurants in my life.'[16]

At the end of the term the Foxes had asked Buchan and Boulter to join

them on a study trip to Kissingen in Germany. The idea was to combine a
study of Classics and German with fresh air and visits to the theatre. Buchan
declined partly because he was worried about the heat but mainly because he
had his own tight agenda of hard work and exercise in Scotland with which
nothing was to interfere. First he stayed with Uncle Willie at Bank House
where he devoted five hours a day to studying Horace's Odes, reading scripts
for Lane and fishing. Then he joined his family, first at Innerleithen and then
in August at the Free Church Manse at Gallatown, Kirkcaldy where his
father was filling in for an absent minister. John Edgar came to stay and the
two young men swam, played golf and went for long walks. He continued his
work for the Newdigate poem, the subject of which was Gibraltar, and the
Stanhope History Prize which had been set on Raleigh. He had also started
planning his new novel to be entitled *A Lost Lady of Old Years* – the title is
taken from Browning's 'Waring' – though he was still considering the title *A
Lady of the Cause*. Finally in September he went walking in Galloway where
he began to collect moorland tales for a volume of short stories which John
Lane had suggested. It was almost a rest to return to Oxford.

For his second year Buchan moved across the Quad to Staircase 6, Room
3, where he paid the slightly higher rent of £5. 6 shillings. It was also slightly
quieter with the History Fellow George Wakeling in Room 4. Buchan was to
stay here until he moved out of college in his fourth year. At the end of
September 1896 *Scholar Gipsies* had been published. It was dedicated to his
grandfather John Masterton and had etchings by D.Y. Cameron. Buchan
described it in the Preface as 'a few pictures of character and nature, pieces of
sentiment torn from their setting, a fragment of criticism, some moralisings of
little worth – the baggage of a vagrant in letters and life'. It was certainly a
mixed bag ranging from short stories and poems to essays on the joys of fishing
and one 'Ad Astra' on death, but all were linked by their setting in the Upper
Tweed Valley. The most interesting was the title piece. *Scholar Gipsies* demonstrates an impressive width of reading and maturity of mind for an undergraduate. In it Buchan puts some of his own feeling into discussing people torn
between urban and rural life, between the world of scholarship and success
and the meditative opportunities of nature. It was a theme he was to develop
in his later writing.

The book had a good reception with a column in *The Times* and two
columns in the *Academy*; it quickly went into a second edition. The *Nation*
praised his 'mature and cultivated style' and singled out his ability to portray
character while the *Bookman* wrote 'The sixteen short essays have very considerable merit and we foresee that in a few years their young writer may have
grown into something better than a refined and amiable sayer of pleasant

things. The tone is so modest, the sentiment so healthy that the worst symptoms of precocity are entirely absent.'[17] It was a view shared by the Oxford JCR:

> Mr Buchan is no mere fireside Arcadian. He evidently knows intimately the country he is writing about; he has himself felt the discomforts, as well as the idyllic delights, of openair life; and he is remarkably successful in reproducing the peculiar charm of the monotonous bleak uplands of the Borders, their freshness, their healthful silence. It is a book worth more than one reading, and this is praise which we are very chary of giving. The performance is admirable, but the promise is still greater, and we look for great things from a man who while so young has achieved so much.[18]

Buchan had now agreed to edit a series on Romantic Towns for John Lane with the book illustrator Edmund New as the Art Editor. The first in the series was to be Warwick and the Vale of Arden to be followed by the Fen Towns, the West of England Seaports, Carlisle and the English Border Towns and the Tweedside Towns.[19]

New Year was spent at Broughton Green where he worked on his Horace, Latin poetry and *A Lost Lady*, saw something of his uncles at Bamflat, 'slept deeply through a Xmas sermon delivered with an Aberdonian twang' and went for long walks. He wrote to Charles Dick on December 30th:

> On Monday I worked all forenoon, and had a really magnificent walk of about fifteen miles in the afternoon. I took the hills and walked straight to the foot of Caerdon, then through the hillpass and down the Holmes Water. A snow storm was drifting up against the setting sun, and I have rarely seen anything finer than the lurid crimson and yellow flaming behind the bald white domes of the hills. Yesterday I climbed Trahenna (2450 ft) . . . a very wet, unpleasant task, but made up for by the magnificent view. It began to hail and I was drenched to the skin. Today I shall try to get to Lindsaylands and see my friend Miss Cooper, but I may be lost in the mist . . . I have nearly finished another chapter of my *Lost Lady*. Here, not five hundred yards from the place which once was her home, I seem to write better. I have finished the song which I had to write for her and must show you it when I come back.[20]

John Edgar, another old school friend, had come up to Balliol on an Exhibition in the Hilary term after taking a First in History at Glasgow University. Through Edgar, Buchan widened his circle and began to spend more time in Balliol where his friends now included a group of intellectual Etonians, Wykehamists, Harrovians and Scots most of whom were reading either history or Classics and were active in the Union Society. They included Johnnie Jameson, Robert Ensor, Edmund Haynes, Cuthbert Medd and in Buchan's own year Richard Denman, Auberon Herbert, Arthur Steel (later Steel-Maitland) and Arnold Ward. The Balliol circle alone made up an intellectual and sporting elite. Ensor had been a scholar at Winchester, Haynes had come up on a Brackenbury History Scholarship from Eton, Arnold Ward, the son of Mrs Humphrey Ward and grand-nephew of Matthew Arnold, had been the Newcastle Scholar at Eton and also come up on a scholarship. Ensor, Medd, Steel, Edgar and Ward would all take Firsts and Medd and Steel become Fellows of All Souls. Denman would win the Stanhope, Ensor and Ward the Craven and Steel the Eldon Scholarship. Jameson would represent the University at boxing, swimming and water polo, Bron Herbert and Steel would row in the Oxford boat while Ward would captain the Balliol Cricket XI.

Through Jameson Buchan met two other Scotsmen who though slightly younger were to become close friends. Tommy, known then as Tom, Nelson had been at the Edinburgh Academy with Jameson and gone on to University College where he captained the Oxford Rugby XV. Stair, also called Sandy, Gillon had been at Haileybury before going to New College where he captained the college 1st XV. Other friends from New College included Harold Baker who had come up from Winchester on a scholarship in 1896, an Etonian, the Honourable Hugh Wyndham and another Scot, Alec Maitland.

At the beginning of February 1897 Buchan put his name down for the Middle Temple following in the family law tradition. The Bar was seen as a useful finishing school for an ambitious undergraduate and it offered the freedom to write. Like Sir Walter Scott, he had no illusions that he could entirely support himself on his writing and he may also have felt the particularly Scottish concern that writing was a useful hobby but it was not a proper job in itself.

His literary activities were increasingly impinging on his academic studies with consequent results. In May he received news of his performance in Mods. He wrote to Charles Dick 'I am very much aggravated about my Mods. It seems I got 6 alphas when 7 would have got me a first; and worse still, in the very subject in which I was supposed to be going to get an a+ – Roman poetry – I got a b–. So you see I had a very near shave.'[21] There was better news in June when he heard that on his second attempt he had won the Stanhope History Prize with an essay on Sir Walter Raleigh, to add to the college Bridgeman Essay Prize which he had just been awarded. The

Stanhope essay was published by Blackwell that July and reviewed by *The Oxford Magazine*: 'The essay of Mr J. Buchan on Sir Walter Raleigh seems to have thoroughly deserved the success which it obtained . . . the author is well up with his subject, and writes in a pleasing and sometimes very epigrammatic style. His estimate of the character of Raleigh is just, and his criticisms on his literary productions are incisive.'[22]

August 1897 was spent at Ayr and on a walking tour in Galloway with Taffy Boulter. Armed with a fishing-rod, a flask of cordial, a sketch-book, half a melon and the manuscript of a story Buchan was working on they walked from Dalry up the Ken and the Polharrow Burn to the Forest of Buchan. From there they went over the 2,500 foot Clints of Millfire, through the bog to the Back Hill of Buss and climbed the Wolf's Slock from where they were able to look down on Loch Enoch and beyond the lochs of the Dungeon – Neldricken, Arron, Valley, Macaterick and Trool. The two young men, Buchan with a blister 'the size of a crown', had covered 65 miles over rough ground in just over 24 hours.[23]

His 21st birthday on 26th August was a time for reflection, allowing him to look back on his successes and lay plans for the future. He carefully drew upon a piece of paper, under four columns – literary, academic, practical and probable income – a 'set of things to be done in the next four years'. The first year was to be devoted to arranging the publication of his novel *John Burnet of Barns*, write a book *Modern Criticism*, begin *The Lady of the Cause*, and prepare *Grey Weather*. He was also to take a greater interest in politics and stand for the Union Committee. Estimated income was to be £200 which characteristically would exactly match expenditure.

During his third year Buchan began to think of life after Oxford. Perhaps he was unconsciously modelling himself on Curzon, who after Oxford had travelled in India and the East. He wrote to Charles Dick 'My whole mind just now is filled with my future career. I want to take Greats in June, and travel in E. Asia Minor next year doing some historical work and writing letters to the *Chronicle* on the political aspect of the country.'[24] In January 1898 he was elected to a Senior Hulme scholarship at Brasenose. He boasted to Dick 'I am busy just now working at Political Philosophy and reading Machiavelli in the Italian. I am also writing a paper on Celtic and Norse poetry for the Ingoldsby.'[25]

Girls hardly figured in Buchan's life as an undergraduate. There were few in Oxford and even then he preferred to chase the glittering prizes. Every so often, however, there is an affectionate reference in his letters to a female. One such was Lillian Cohen who took the part of Juliet in an OUDS production of *Romeo and Juliet* in February though it seems her performance was not particularly memorable. *Isis* noted of her acting that it 'has few striking faults, but unfortunately has no very inspiring merits'.[26] Invariably it was male company he sought and relished, not least because with males he could drive himself physically as well as mentally. In the spring he and John Edgar went on a walking tour of the Highlands. Beginning at Bridge of Orchy they walked through the Black Mount to Kingshouse Inn on Rannoch moor and climbed the snow covered Buachille Etive. Then they walked down Glencoe to Ballachulish and Appin following the path of David Balfour and Alan Breck Stewart in R.L. Stevenson's *Kidnapped*. On the basis of the holiday Buchan wrote an article published that May in the *Academy* on 'The Country of Kidnapped'.

In March he jointly founded another society, the Horace Club. It met at various colleges when members 'supped on nuts and olives and fruits, drank what we made believe was Falernian, and read our poetical compositions'.[27] Its purpose was to read poetry under the aegis of an Arbiter, Arnold Ward being the first Arbiter in May 1898 and Buchan the second in June 1898. Ladies could be admitted as guests and there were twenty members including, apart from the founding members, Hilaire Belloc, Cuthbert Medd, Harold Baker, the Vice-President of Brasenose the Reverend Francis Bussell, the President of Magdalen T.H. Warren and a New College undergraduate Alfred Zimmern. Honorary members included Maurice Baring, Laurence Binyon, Sir Rennell Rodd, T. Humphry Ward and Basil Blackwell who as Keeper of the Records published a limited collection of 500 copies of the members' verses in 1901.[28] It was for the Horace Club that Buchan wrote 'Ballad of Grey Weather', 'The Gipsy's song to the Lady Cassilis', 'From the Pentlands looking North and South', 'The Last Song of Oisin' and 'The Soldier of Fortune'. Other contributions included Belloc's 'The South Country' and 'Sussex Drinking Song'.

Buchan's circle had now expanded to take in a number of younger under-graduates of whom the most prominent was another member of the Horace Club, Raymond Asquith, the son of the future Prime Minister Herbert Asquith. Asquith had been a scholar at Winchester and had come up to Balliol on a scholarship the previous autumn. Buchan was entranced by this charismatic and brilliant figure who within his first year seemed effortlessly to have won the Craven and been *proxime accessit* to the Hertford. He was drawn to Asquith by the quality of his mind, the range of his interests, his sophisti-cation and his sense of fun but part of the fascination was Asquith's irrever-ent attitude to Oxford and success which stood in sharp contrast to Buchan's own feelings. Buchan, who described him as an 'urbane and debonair scholar-gipsy', later wrote:

His scholarship was almost too ripe for his years, and he had already conquered so many worlds that he was little troubled with ordinary ambition. As the son of an eminent statesman he had seen much of distinguished people who to most of us were only awful names, so that he seemed all his time at Oxford to have one foot in the greater world.[29]

It was for a pastiche of the *Spectator* that the two jointly edited that Asquith wrote his Tennysonian elegy 'On a Viscount who died on the Morrow of a Bump Supper' satirising T.H. Warren the President of Magdalen.

At his third attempt Buchan finally won the Newdigate Prize for poetry, following in the footsteps of Matthew Arnold, John Ruskin and Oscar Wilde. Reviewing a copy published by Blackwell that May *Isis* praised Buchan's decision not to stick too closely to the chosen subject for the prize, the Pilgrim Fathers:

> So far is he from hampering himself by undue consciousness of his subject, that, without the title, it would be difficult to guess with what the poem dealt. The work is original in its form, which suggests everything by a process of question and answer. And greatest merit of all, it is not long . . . And he has managed to be poetical on a subject perhaps the most unfitted for poetry to a reflecting eye . . . If, however, we must speak of faults (and in criticising a young author, it can only do him good to mention his faults) it must be confessed that there is a sort of mysterical air about the writing which makes it difficult to understand. This difficulty is increased by the constant use of Biblical allusions . . . All through there is a flavour of Tennyson, particularly noticeable in the closing line 'till the brief dark that fadeth into day,' which sounds very like the 'Morte d'Arthur.' But with all these faults, Mr Buchan's work is both more readable than the average Newdigate, and – what is of more importance – seems to show greater promise of power.[30]

The *Oxford Magazine* were more cautious 'Mr Buchan is known to have done good work already; for a young man his output is remarkable, and no doubt he has a still larger quantity of unpublished matter. It is not easy to prophesy how far he may go.' It went on to praise his slightly different use of the heroic couplet 'which the success of his poem quite justifies. The dedicatory lyric "To the Adventurous spirit of the North", is a beautiful little piece of work.'[31] The *JCR* was rather more tongue in cheek 'His poem on the Pilgrim Fathers is invaluable to the student of history, though it is said that the author composed it after reading about the Canterbury pilgrims and Cowley fathers and combining his information.'[32]

The end of the summer term was celebrated at the New College Ball which he attended with Tommy Nelson, Johnnie Jameson, Stair Gillon and two sisters from Dumfriesshire Caroline and Olive Johnston Douglas. After breakfast in Stair's rooms they drove off for a picnic by the river and to dance reels barefoot on the grass. A few days later the men gathered at Jameson's home at Ardwall for some rough shooting, sailing and walking. They climbed Cairnsmore of Fleet twice, played billiards, lunched off pate de foie gras and Burgundy at the Dungeon of Buchan and rode horses on the Sands of Fleet. Buchan loved going to Ardwall. There was a freedom and style of living there with its packs of dogs and scores of visitors not to be found in the quiet tranquility of Bank House or 34 Queen Mary Avenue. Jameson's father, then Sheriff of Perth but ennobled as Lord Ardwall in 1904, was a larger than life character, a plain-speaking laird more reminiscent of the eighteenth than the late nineteenth century and it is easy to see the attraction he held for the young man.

From Ardwall Buchan returned to Glasgow from where he cycled to Broughton Green and back to his careful timetable of work. He would get up at 5.30 a.m. and work till noon with an interval for breakfast. The afternoons were spent swimming in the Tweed or hill-walking and then it was back to his books from 4.00 p.m. till 7.00 p.m. and generally from 9.00 p.m. till 10.00 p.m. The only interruption was when he was attacked while bandaging the leg of a Highland bull. As he explained to Dick:

> The beast went sort of crazy, kicked over the farm-servant, who fled incontinent, and began to plunge violently. Willie and I held on, and just then the rope broke. The beast came at Willie, who got clear and ran for the door. Meanwhile at the breaking I had fallen on my back in a narrow stall, and before I could get up the beast came at me. Luckily it was rather lame and I got off before it did me serious hurt, but it 'dinnled' my right arm, tore my coat and gave me a nasty knock in the forehead. So I have had headaches for several days . . . [33]

In June 1898, after a six month serialization in *Chambers' Journal*, *John Burnet of Barns* was published by John Lane. Buchan explained to Dick that it had 'been well reviewed by some papers, critically and sensibly by some others, and roundly abused by some of the baser sort (e.g. our dear friend Robertson Nicoll in the B.W.'[34] Buchan himself was not entirely pleased with it. He wrote to Gilbert Murray: 'I am so glad you find "JB" not strictly dull. To tell the truth I am rather ashamed of it; it is so very immature and boyish. I had no half serious interest in fiction when I wrote it and the result is a sort of hotch-potch.'[35]

Like *Sir Quixote of the Moors* the book is a first person romantic adventure set in the seventeenth century with Stevensonian undertones and a Covenanting background, but it is a much more ambitious novel. It is longer and though much of the setting is the Upper Tweed Valley, the action also moves across to the Low Countries. It is also more autobiographical. The central character, John Burnet, shares a background and interests similar to those of the young Buchan. Indeed many of Buchan's own experiences such as dealing with Border floods are incorporated into the book. Burnet lives at Barns, a large stone house still visible from the road between Peebles and Broughton, while the heroine Marjory Veitch comes from Dawyck further up the Tweed. Several recurrent Buchan themes emerge in the book as well as the motif of the Scholar Gipsy – the moderate placed among fanatics, the contemplative man forced to become a man of action, good triumphing over evil and the death plunge at the end. Nicol Plenderleith, Burnet's servant, too is the first of Buchan's independent, loyal and brave side-kicks of whom the most typical is Peter Pienaar. Originally Buchan had intended to dedicate the book to Lady Mary Murray but in the end it was dedicated to the memory of his dead sister Violet.

The JCR in a generally favourable review ('Mr Buchan's descriptions . . . can be seen and heard and smelt.') had two reservations. It thought the central character, John Burnet, 'at times too petty for a hero. He is inclined to be pedantic, even priggish' and that the villain Gilbert 'not definitely represented in our imagination as a living person.' One of the best reviews came from the *Labour Leader* who thought it 'a most remarkable work for so young a man' and remarkably free from 'Kailyarder nonsense.'[36] The reviews of this Buchan's second novel confirmed he was a writer to watch.

Buchan returned to Oxford for a fourth year in October 1898 and took up lodgings outside college with a black collie Dhonuill Dhu, John Edgar and Taffy Boulter at 41 High Street, almost opposite the Schools. Many of Buchan's friends now were people he had met through student politics, not just at the Union but also through the university's political clubs. He himself was a member of the Tory Canning Club but followed with interest the activities of the other political clubs. Three close friends Harold Baker, Cuthbert Medd and Geoffrey Gathorne-Hardy were respectively Presidents of the Russell Club, the Palmerston Club and the Social Science Club. This interest in politics was one, as Martin Green has written, 'which sailed away from party slogans, ordinary polemic, or ideological discipline; a politics which aspired (this was above all dear to Buchan) to a supra-party transcendence, by means of a national or imperial symbolism'. Buchan used to tell Tommy Nelson 'All sensible men have the same politics, but what these politics are no sensible men ever tells.'[37]

His principal political activity was in the Union Society which has been curiously ignored, given that it took up an increasing amount of his time as an undergraduate and that a large number of his university friends were made there, many of whom were to be helpful to him in later life. The Union Societies of both Oxford and Cambridge have always been overestimated outside the two universities and under-estimated within them. Each generation is never worthy of the one that came before it but there can be no denying that whatever their abilities many of those active in the Union have tended to go on to great things. Past Presidents making their mark in public life while Buchan was at Oxford included George Curzon, W. St John Brodrick, Alfred Milner, Herbert Asquith and George Goschen; one of its greatest former Presidents William Gladstone had died while Buchan was at Oxford. What the Oxford Union gave young men (women were not admitted until 1963) was an opportunity to discuss ideas, to develop their skills at public speaking and self-confidence and to introduce them to some of the leading personalities of the day.

Buchan had first spoken in the Union in his third term but surprisingly, given his interests and ambitions, he did not become actively involved until the end of his second year. This is interesting given the calibre of the Presidents during his first two years at Oxford. They included Lord Balcarres later as Lord Crawford a Cabinet Minister, F.E. Smith, the future Lord Birkenhead, the authors H.A. Morrah and Hilaire Belloc, a Brasenose man P.J. Macdonell later Chief Justice of Trinidad and Tobago, John Simon later a senior Cabinet Minister and F.W. Hirst later editor of the *Economist*.

In May 1897 he opposed Hilaire Belloc's motion 'That in the opinion of this House the progress of events in the East demonstrates the uselessness of the concert and the Incompetence of her Majesty's Government.' *Isis* noted 'Mr Buchan was good and to the point; with some slight improvement of manner he might rank high' while *The JCR* noted that he 'spoke clearly and fluently. We should like to hear him more often.'[38] The opportunity came the following month when he proposed, though unsuccessfully, the motion 'that in the opinion of the House the popular literature of to-day is a sign of national degradation.' *Isis* thought his 'speech was pleasant hearing, and at times very humorous; but speaking louder he would improve himself so far as style of speech goes.'[39]

In December 1897 he was on home ground when he proposed 'That this House condemns the Kailyard School of Novelists' in what *Isis* described as 'a very good and interesting speech . . . Mr Buchan made a very striking exposition of the nature of the real Scotland, the romance and the pity of its history, which he placed in strong contrast with the narrow, parochial view of Scottish character spread by these writers.' The Kailyard School were a group of Scottish writers, many of them Free Kirk Ministers such as S.R. Crockett and John Watson, who wrote sentimentally about the virtues of Scottish life. Buchan's opposition is interesting since he himself has been accused of belonging to the school and his sister Anna's books are certainly part of the Kailyard.[40]

In February 1898 he returned to his primary interest of foreign affairs when he spoke in a debate on the position of Britain within the powers in Europe, siding with Raymond Asquith against Cuthbert Medd and Harold Baker. 'Mr Buchan (BNC) has a way with him which makes the house listen with interest and cheer at the right places,' wrote *Isis*. 'His speaking is excellent, his points convincing and well-put . . . The hon member's speech was a great success.'[41] The JCR took the same view 'In opening the debate Mr J. Buchan (BNC) made an excellent speech. He traced the growing power of Russia from the time of the Crimean War, and with a delightful turn of phrase spoke of turning the mailed fist into a cat's paw. The lining of the cloud which threatened us was of depreciated silver. Mr Buchan does not like democracy to interfere in foreign politics, and indeed he seemed to support the motion from a Tory standpoint.'[42]

Buchan's route up the Union hierarchy was a clever one choosing the Library Committee, whose task consisted of choosing books for the Union's well-stocked library. Apart from his own interest in books he may have been encouraged by the fact that Walter Pater had for many years been the Senior Librarian, a post given to senior members of the University and which was now held by his tutor at Brasenose, Llewellyn Bebb. Buchan had first stood for the Union Committee at the end of his fourth term but missed it by four votes. Two terms later in June 1897 he stood again and this time was elected fourth with 95 votes. The following term he nudged up to third in the Committee hierarchy and finally in March 1898, was elected unopposed as Librarian, an office which he held for two terms.

On 5 May he successfully proposed with Raymond Asquith 'That this House has no confidence in the policy of Her Majesty's Government in the Far East'. *The Oxford Magazine* thought Asquith's speech 'the best of the evening, lively and brilliant except for an occasional tendency to sink too low and a monotonous tone of voice. He spoke as a Radical of Radicals, and his epigrams on Lord Salisbury and the Cabinet had all the bitterness of a fierce antagonist. His style was excellent; other members might take a lesson from it.'[43] On the other hand they thought Buchan 'spoke as a Conservative of Conservatives, forced into a reluctant disloyalty. Mr Buchan was not so good as last term on the same subject. His voice is lacking in power and compass, and on this occasion there was a certain hesitation and uncertainty at times about his utterance, which rather marred his close reasoning and pleasant style.'[44]

The following term in his position as Librarian he proposed the vote of thanks during the visit of the Archbishop of Canterbury but surprisingly, this leading light of the Caledonian Society, did not take part in the motion shortly after 'That this House sympathizes with the Scottish desire for a National Assembly', proposed by Stair Gillon and Johnnie Jameson and opposed by Cuthbert Medd. Finally in November he made his successful bid for the Presidency with 169 votes to 99 for Sydney Armitage-Smith of New College, later a distinguished civil servant and 67 for Henry Reilly of Corpus, later a High Court Judge in India. Raymond Asquith was elected unopposed as Librarian (where he was followed consecutively by Stair Gillon and Harold Baker), and Jameson beat Buchan's own nominee Robert Rait by 161 votes to 154 for the post of Secretary.

At the Presidential debate that month, speaking for the last time as Librarian, Buchan proposed with Asquith 'That this House does not believe in International Morality', which, despite good speeches from him and Asquith, was defeated 51 votes to 112. In their review *The JCR* wrote:

> Mr J. Buchan (BNC), Librarian, proceeded vigorously to dispute the advisability of international morality. We have it, however, on his own authority that the Librarian is an austere moralist in private matters. In international politics, Mr Buchan finds no scope for charity, – for self denial, – for turning the cheek to the smiter, and those virtues which in private life go to make up morality . . . Mr Buchan concluded with a good Scotch story, well told. We do not think we have ever heard the Librarian so good: we certainly have never known him so lively.[45]

It was an opinion shared by *Isis* who thought he 'spoke with more ease and fluency than we remember to have heard from him before. Mr Buchan was distinctly good.' The *Oxford Magazine* reported 'For a sincere, ardent and puritanical moralist Mr Buchan was surprisingly exhilarated and exhilarating,' but it was Raymond Asquith they felt who had given 'the best speech of the evening in matter as well as manner'.[46]

During his term of office, Hilary 1899, Buchan's debates covered a wide range of subjects – Home Rule, the Disestablishment of the Church of

Wales, the future of the Liberal Party, the position of France and 'That in the opinion of this House the Great Democratic Joke is almost played out' proposed by Cuthbert Medd and opposed by a Balliol undergraduate who had come up the previous term, Aubrey Herbert. An early indication of Buchan's interest in America can be seen in his choice of the second debate of the term 'That in the opinion of this House, any formal alliance with America would be both injudicious and impracticable.' Edmund Gosse came to speak on the subject of taste, and Buchan's mother and Anna also paid a visit during the term. Helen Buchan when told by her son that some of the young men she had met were probably Prime Ministers of the future just laughed and said 'Oh, poor things! They've a long way to go before they're fit to be Prime Ministers.'[47]

Buchan and Jameson made an effective partnership, their Scottish back-grounds the butt of numerous jokes. While never an inspirational speaker like F.E. Smith, Hilaire Belloc or his successor Raymond Asquith, Buchan always had something interesting to say and won plaudits for his skilful management of debates and the Society's administration. Even after he ceased being President, he took a keen interest in its activities opposing the motion 'The present Anti-ritualistic movement is unreasonable and dangerous' at the beginning of the Easter term 1899 and supporting Geoffrey Gathorne-Hardy against Raymond Asquith and Johnnie Jameson over Stair Gillon for President in the elections respectively for the Michaelmas 1899 and Hilary 1900 terms.

In June 1898 he had been the subject of the JCR Portrait Gallery in which reference was made to his sporting and literary interests and it was noted 'Is fond of climbing many things, Parnassus among others . . . Is an excellent Librarian of the Union. Has been known to catch fish.'[48] Now to mark the start of his term as President of the Union Buchan was chosen as *Isis* Idol. The tone of the profile is facetious and it was probably written with inside knowledge supplied by Boulter who illustrated the piece. It gives a useful picture of Buchan as presented to his contemporaries when he was at the height of his fame at Oxford and it is therefore worth repeating in full:

A bad accident happened to him while he was still very young, and his life was despaired of. His obituary was, indeed, actually in type when he recovered. It was a close shave for Scotland and the human race. Since that time the Buchan *dossier* in all the great newspaper offices has been growing steadily fatter.

His career may be said to have properly begun when it was
decided that, on account of ill-health, he should not go to a
public school . . . In 1895 our Idol descended upon Oxford and
began to carry all before him that he cared to trouble
himself with – one of the finest things about him is that he
has a very good idea of what is worth while and what is not.

It is no disrespect to Glasgow to say that he now became
really great; it is simply that he developed. Here his powers
ripened, his tastes matured, his knowledge of men and things
increased . . .

His powers of work are remarkable, and inspire awe in his
friends; he confesses to a deep-seated loathing for what is
called leisure. Yet there exists no keener lover of action in
the open than he, and no sounder authority upon all branches
of Scottish sport . . .

In politics he is a Tory-Democrat-Jacobite. Legitimacy is his
ruling passion . . . He collects etchings. He dislikes dancing, and
hates ladies. He has no high opinion of the literature of today, on the principle, doubtless, of 'we makes it'. He does not
like to hear about his own books; he refuses to be classed as
a literary man . . . We know of no one who has had more success,
or deserved it better. He is as popular with men as he is
with Fortune. We do hate eulogy; but we are helpless.[49]

He was by no means the first of his circle to be an *Isis* Idol. Tommy Nelson
had been profiled in November 1897, Bron Herbert in March 1898, Aubrey
Herbert in November 1898 and Sandy Gillon would follow in February
1899, Johnnie Jameson in May 1899 and Geoffrey Gathorne-Hardy in
October 1899.

One of Buchan's great abilities was the ease with which he was able to move
between different circles in Oxford while still maintaining his base in
Brasenose. There were intellectuals such as Harold Baker and Robert Rait
later to become Fellows of New College, wordly politicians and aristocrats as
well as many university sporting heroes. Indeed his future literary heroes
would share many of the same distinguishing features as his Oxford friends.
During that fourth year Auberon Herbert was Secretary of the Boat Club,
Tommy Nelson played rugby for Scotland as well as Oxford and Johnnie

Jameson was the inter-varsity middleweight boxing champion having been a varsity swimmer. At a college level John Edgar was rowing in the Balliol 1st VIII, Taffy Boulter in the Brasenose 1st VIII, Sandy Gillon captain of the New College 1st XV, Arnold Ward captain of the Balliol cricket XI and Raymond Asquith captain of the Balliol Football XI. Buchan, through the auspices of its president Tommy Nelson, had been elected to the premier sport- ing club Vincents.

Many of his activities and friendships also revolved around the Caledonian Club, which had been refounded in October 1898 with Nelson as President, Buchan as Secretary and Stair Gillon, Johnnie Jamieson and Duncan Warrand also active. Membership was confined to those who could claim Scots descent on both sides for at least three generations and members wore a dark green dinner-jacket with Thistle buttons and tartan facings. The Club met once a term to celebrate St Andrew's Day on 30 November, Burns Night on 25 January and hold a Ladies Concert in Oxford Town Hall in June.

Under the patronage of this wider circle Buchan's outings, previously con- fined to walking, canoeing and cycling, now became more sophisticated. Constantly they tested themselves against the elements, a mark of future Buchan characters. They would canoe as far as they could between winter's dawn and dusk, walk to London or Cambridge in twenty four hours, ride across country on a compass course regardless of gardens or flooded rivers, sleep out of doors almost as a reaction against the formality of Oxford acade- mic life. One day with Raymond Asquith he donned a wideawake hat, hired an open carriage and, with Baedeker in hand, drove to a neighbouring country inn where, pretending to be an American tourist, Asquith solemnly addressed an assembled crowd on the merits of abstinence before ordering beer all round.

At the centre of these exploits was Aubrey Herbert, who was five years younger than Buchan and had come up to Balliol from Eton in 1898. The second son of the Earl of Carnarvon, Herbert soon became a well known Oxford figure, becoming Vice-President of the Union and taking a First in History. It was, however, as a roof climber that he was best known. On one such occasion while reputedly singing Italian love songs he fell through the roof of a bank, whereupon he was held at gunpoint by the startled bank manager. Herbert's character and later career was to form the inspiration for one of Buchan's best-known literary characters Sandy Arbuthnot.

During this fourth year Buchan was asked to contribute a history of his own college in a series on Oxford colleges published by F.E. Robinson. It was an interesting choice and as the following views demonstrate one received with mixed feelings as Buchan extended the conventional bounds of the college history. He dedicated the book to his American friend in Brasenose John

Foster Carr. The Oxford Magazine in a rather pedantic review, which seemed directed at dismissing the college as much as the author of its history, took exception to its breezy style, Buchan's preference for writing about the social life of the college to its architectural detail and his emphasis on Walter Pater and an eccentric character Sir Tatton Sykes over some dull college worthies.[50] The JCR were rather more generous:

> We have nothing but praise for Mr Buchan's history of BNC. It has all the qualities one has been led to expect in a work from his pen. It is scholarly without being dull, and bright without being trivial: and above all, it is up-to-date . . . Altogether it is a notable contribution to the series and a most readable volume, even to one who is not a member of BNC.[51]

Isis was likewise impressed, writing:

> the book seems to us to fulfil the ideal of the publisher's prospectus more completely perhaps than any of the series yet issued. It is slighter and less voluminous than its predecessors, and its character is more popular than erudite. The result has assuredly justified the publisher's choice of a romanticist rather than a historian. For while the facts are based on such unimpeachable historic data as are supplied by Mr Madan in Mr Clark's 'Colleges of Oxford', they are related in a brilliant style, and lit up with pleasant humour . . . Every Brasenose man will add this volume to his library, and the general reader will find it as attractive as a romance.[52]

Buchan, always a devoted son of his college, was to return to a similar subject with his thirty page monograph 'Nine Brasenose Worthies' for the Oxford Historical Society, published by the Clarendon Press in 1909. The monograph looked at, among others, the former Prime Minister Henry Addington, H.H. Milman and Walter Pater. So prolific and varied was Buchan's output becoming that one of the student papers mischievously suggested that his list of intended books included 'A ten-volume history of the Jacobites, a short guide to the study of Philosophy, a history of Calvinism, five novels, – one of which deals with Oxford life, and a manual of sheep-farming.'[53]

In March 1899 Grey Weather, the collection of 'moorland tales of my own people' that John Lane had suggested a few years earlier was published. Again Buchan dedicated it to his dead sister, Violet. Most of the short stories centre round the daily life of the shepherds, drovers, poachers of the Upper Tweed

Valley and their constant battles against the elements. Many of them involve death and reveal man to be callous. In 'At the Article of Death' a dying shep-herd is forced to assess his life and finds no consolation in religion; in 'At the Rising of the Waters' a farmer discovers a drowned man and casts him back into the water as if returning a fish, and in 'The Black Fishers' two brothers abandon their dead father. The collection appeared in John Lane's Arcady Library with a goat-foot Pan on the cover. It sounded many Arcadian notes with references to Theocritus and comparisons made between the inhabitants of the Upper Tweed and Arcady. Like many authors of the period, such as Maurice Hewlett, Arthur Machen, E.M. Forster and most notably Kenneth Grahame whom he much admired, Buchan was influenced by this form of literary paganism. However his stories were rather more rooted in the pastoral than the other writers who used Pan as a symbol of revolt against convention and urban life.

During his final year he had been working hard for his finals in Greats, mindful of what had happened during Mods. He was on surer ground since he was no longer required to make close textual study of classical texts but could roam over philosophy and ancient history. Much of the philosophy work he had already covered at Glasgow and he was spending much more time during the vacations on academic work than he had before. The result was the long expected First.

In September *A Lost Lady*, serialized the previous winter in *Today*, was pub-lished by John Lane. The book was dedicated to his Caledonian Club friend Duncan Warrand. Sending a copy to Charles Dick Buchan wrote 'The only real merit the book has – apart from Lovat who after all is only a fragment – seems to me to lie in the atmosphere . . . the melancholy of those hopeless moor-land wars fought in the mists and rain.' He admitted 'I retain my interest in style and character, but the narrative – the proper fictional stuff – grows thin and wandering. Hence I have come to believe that to a person of my habits the short story is the real form, and indeed I consider my *Blackwood* stories my best work.'[54]

A Lost Lady is set during the 1745 Rebellion. The central character Francis Birkenshaw, an eighteen year old law apprentice from Border stock but now working near Pathhead in Fife, is sent inadvertently on a mission to Lord Lovat in the North of Scotland by the wife of Bonnie Prince Charlie's Secretary, Mrs Murray. After many adventures Birkenshaw meets the Prince and Lovat but is just too late to save Murray from capture and Lovat from the scaffold. The novel is a study of the romantic temperament and about conflicts of loyalty as Birkenshaw makes his spiritual and physical journey towards self-knowledge. Like many Buchan heroes he follows his instructions not for ideological reasons, here Jacobitism, but out of a desire to redeem his honour for a woman. It is a more ambitious and complex book than Buchan had previously attempted and perhaps as a result was less successful. The book too was a victim of Buchan's busy lifestyle, which prevented him from polishing it, and a long and spasmodic gestation. As a result it is stronger on description than narrative pace or plot. But there are some wonderful set pieces such as Birkenshaw's flight to Lovat and the Battle of Culloden. It received short but generally appreciative reviews in several literary magazines and did much to consolidate the reputation the twenty four year old undergraduate was beginning to establish.

In October 1899 Buchan, now a graduate, returned to Oxford to prepare for a Fellowship at All Souls. He took rooms with Stair Gillon at 105 High Street together with a man from New College, Humphrey Milford, who later, as Publisher of the Oxford University Press, would become his publisher. Like many others, Buchan had thought the All Souls Fellowship would be a foregone conclusion. Indeed such was his confidence that he was planning a new book '*Opportunism – an Essay in the Exposition of an Attitude* by John Buchan, Barrister-at-Law, Fellow of All Souls, Oxford'. The news when it came at the beginning of November was all the more shocking for being so unexpected. He wrote to his mother: 'The worst has happened. I have not got to All Souls.' Instead it had gone to Dougal Malcolm, whose father was already a Fellow. 'I am of course bitterly disappointed but I will recover . . . I am chiefly sorry that I did not get it for your sake and father's . . . I must cut my coat according to my cloth and take humbler lodgings in town than I intended.'[55] His tutor F.I. Wylie wrote as soon as he heard. 'I hear they have not taken you at All Souls. I am more sorry than I can say. We all feel it as a personal disappointment: and without knowing the man they took, we are convinced that they will be sorry one day that your distinctions are not part of the All Souls record.'[56]

Buchan tried to put a brave face on it but it clearly rankled. As he told Murray: 'I hate not to do the things I am expected to do.' Two days later he wrote to his father: 'All Souls, of course, have a perfect right to elect whom they please but if their aim is to get the best man I hope to make them in time very sorry for their action . . . I will not go again for All Souls for worlds.'[57] In fact he did have another try the next year, but again was unsuccessful. The feeling on both occasions was that Buchan had spent too much time on his literary activities and not done enough background reading. It would not be the first time he would be told he had spread himself too thinly. Buchan's failure to secure the final glittering prize was news even in political circles. Raymond Asquith wrote to his father Herbert on 12 November:

The only thing which people talk about much is the All Souls Election . . .
the history fellowship was awarded to a New Coll. man called Malcolm,
an Etonian, whose father was a fellow before him: he may have been up to
form, as he took a good first in Greats and his reputation for work was so
great that he was commonly known as the 'Louser'. But most people are
very indignant at John Buchan being passed over: he is certainly a much
more brilliant man than either of the others and would have found the
money more useful . . . The prestige of All Souls is being rapidly lowered
by this type of award.[58]

In other men the failure to be elected to All Souls, the icing on a glittering university career, might have affected them for life as it did Hilaire Belloc but
Buchan had other ambitions to satisfy. He spent the rest of the term studying
law in preparation for a stint in a solicitor's office in January.

In his autobiography Buchan admitted that Oxford had been a watershed
in his life, 'one of those boundary periods, the meaning of which is missed at
the time, but is plain in the retrospect.' He arrived as his tutor later wrote 'a
quiet and unassuming Scot' and left four years later having taken the glittering
prizes and with the world before him.[59] He had been introduced to a new
society, of which he had only hitherto read – the world of country weekends
and London dances, of political and literary salons. Now he was a constant
visitor treated as an equal and looked up to as a rising literary and political star.
He was the subject of profiles in the magazines and even had his own entry in
Who's Who where he listed his interests as 'golf, cycling, climbing, angling and
most field sports' and modestly gave his occupation as 'undergraduate' – certainly not the reason for which he had been included. Oxford had been intellectually stimulating, allowing a precocious boy to meet sophisticated and
intelligent contemporaries and expanding his mind under the direction of
some of the finest teachers in the country. It had also caused him to modify
some, but not all, of the Calvinism of his youth. 'Formerly I had regarded life
as a pilgrimage along a straight and steep path on which the pilgrim must keep
his eyes fixed,' he later wrote. He now accepted that 'I had some of my Gothic
corners smoothed away, but I still had a good many angles, and there remained
a large spice of the Shorter Catechist in my make-up.'[60]

Above all Oxford had brought out a latent sense of fun and had allowed
him to develop male friendships with a wide range of people. In his memoirs
he wrote: 'After the years of intellectual ferment in a Scottish university
Oxford was for me a stabilising influence, but still more was it a mellowing of
character through friendship.'[61] Many of these friends, such as Stair Gillon
and Johnnie Jameson, would remain with him all his life. Some would die

some fifteen years later in the First World War. Others would be re-created, together with their Oxford values, when he came to write his novels.

In August 1896 he had drawn up a list of 'Honours Gained and to be Gained' covering the decade from 1892. Almost all of them had been achieved – the edition of Bacon's essays, the Hulme Exhibition at Brasenose, the publication of *Musa Piscatrix*, *Scholar Gipsies*, *John Burnet of Barns*, *Sir Quixote*, the Bridgeman, Stanhope and Newdigate prizes, First Class Honours in his finals.[62] There were, however, some disappointments. He had also originally planned to take a First in English Literature, secure a Fellowship at Magdalen for 1899–1900, win the Chancellor's English and Latin Essay prizes for 1900–1901 and round it off by being offered the Professorship of English Literature at Edinburgh University. He also had sketched out two books for Macmillan – *Cloistered Studies* and *The Borderers*. Life however was to turn out quite differently. Buchan admitted in his memoirs that failing the All Souls Fellowship was probably a blessing in disguise. He was not temperamentally suited to academic life, even though he had considered staying at Oxford to teach philosophy.

> The supreme advantage of Oxford to me was that it enabled me to discover what talents I had and what I really wanted to do. Horizons had extended and revealed a surprising number of things which woke my curiosity. I wanted to explore the wider stages of life. Besides, I had become attached to the study of law . . . So I decided that my profession should be the Bar.[63]

4

LONDON INTERLUDE

As the new century opened Buchan found himself working in a law office with a Balliol contemporary Richard Denman, later a Liberal and Labour MP. He also spent some time in the offices of a Mr Rawle, then President of the Law Society, in Bedford Row. His work was varied and because the firm rarely took pupils he received special attention. He inspected documents, wrangled with other solicitors on the taxing of costs at Somerset House, monitored cases in court on behalf of clients and even dealt with divorce cases but, as he admitted to Charles Dick after one particularly harrowing case, 'I am afraid that I am rather too sentimental ever to do well in the divorce court.'[1] There were plans to devil for a specialist in commercial law, to spend two months in a bank and then be called to the Bar in January 1901. He was enjoying the law. 'Nothing has ever impressed me more with a sense of profound intellectual force than the decisions and pleadings of some of our great lawyers,' he told Charles Dick but he was also rather restless.[2]

The South African War had broken out the previous October; both Johnnie Jameson and Geoffrey Gathorne-Hardy had gone out to South Africa with the Imperial Yeomanry and Auberon Herbert as a *Times* correspondent. Buchan wrote to Dick: 'I have been leading a curious life lately, very busy and keen on my law, very gay, and at the same time tormented with proposals to go to the front, which unhappily fall in with my desires. These last I have now finally conquered, and I can now watch my friends go off without special bitterness.'[3]

Office hours were only 10 a.m. to 5 p.m. which gave him plenty of time to write, particularly articles for the *Spectator* and short stories for *Blackwood's*. He was also preparing a new edition of one of his favourite books, Izaak Walton's *The Compleat Angler*, for a Methuen series. However his planned books on

Disraeli and Calvinism were being pushed into the background. He kept a boat on the Blackwater in Essex and went off for sailing weekends. He shared a rod on a dry-fly stream in Hertfordshire with a fellow Borderer and writer Andrew Lang, whom he had first met at Oxford and to whom he had dedicated his fishing anthology *Musa Piscatrix*.[4] His social life also seemed to be flourishing. In January he had dined with Lady Arthur Russell in South Audley Stret before going in a party, which included the Home Secretary, to see *She Stoops to Conquer* at the Haymarket. 'Altogether, the whole evening had a sort of 18th century flavour which I found very pleasant,' he told Charles Dick. Part of the pleasure may also have come from knowing he was at the centre of events, privy for example to Cabinet information about the siege of Ladysmith.[5]

Much as he was enjoying life in London he still felt guilty about his exile from his family in Scotland and he was still in thrall to his mother and her distrust of London life. After seeing a performance of *Cyrano de Bergerac* at Wyndhams, he wrote to his father with a message for his mother. 'Tell her too that I am heartily sick of the theatre and only go when I am taken. It is the most tiresome way I know of spending an evening.'[6] But out of this active social life had come an invitation from the Duchess of Argyll to write the life of the eighth Duke. Buchan considered the request carefully then refused, worried about her motives in commissioning the book.

While still at Oxford, he had joined the Devonshire, a club which even then still had strong links with the Liberal Party. Now as a young man about town he entered into club life with vigour, joining the Cocoa Tree, a club with Jacobite associations – 'a place with a long and dubious history, of which the bronze cocoa-tree in the smoking-room, stuffed with ancient packs of cards, was a reminder.' He had also become a member of the Piccadilly and the Bachelors', then situated at the foot of Hamilton Place, from whose bay-windows he would watch 'the tide of fashion flowing between Hyde Park and Piccadilly.'[7] He was seeing many of his university friends, particularly Geoffrey Gathorne-Hardy, and occasionally the names of girls would appear in his letters, such as Lady Cecily Baillie-Hamilton and Lady Grizel Cochrane. In April 1900 he had stayed for ten days with Aubrey Herbert at Pixton on Dartmoor, where they had climbed hills, fished, slept out one night on the heather and rode with the Dartmoor Hunt and in August he had sailed among the Inner Hebrides. Then, in September, he rented Altarstone, a farm on the Tweed between Stobo and Broughton, for the family to gather before William, who had also won a Junior Hulme Scholarship from Glasgow, went up to read Classics at Brasenose.

On first moving to London Buchan had lived in what he called his 'East-

End dwelling' at 4 Brick Court in the Temple. This he shared with Richard
Denman in rooms that 'were small and new, reached by a staircase of lavatory
bricks, and with no prospects but chimney-pots.' In December 1900 he moved
to a large flat overlooking the Thames at 3 Temple Gardens, which he shared
with Harold Baker and Cuthbert Medd. The flat was superbly positioned and
Buchan would later fondly remember how at night in winter he could hear the
calling of wild birds in their flight upstream.[8]

He was also becoming very friendly with Lady Mary Murray, who in many
ways was becoming a surrogate mother, and he would often spend the
weekend with the Murrays who were now living at Farnham. In September,
he arranged for his publishers to send her a copy of his recently published novel
The Half-Hearted. 'It is my first attempt at a modern story and I am afraid it is
pretty much of a failure,' he wrote to her. 'Some of it I like, and I think the
general intention is good, but I am afraid that most of it is too ambitious.'[9]
Three months later he wrote to her again 'The Half-Hearted is a stupid book,
written during a period of violent prejudice at Oxford. I should not write it
now but indeed now I shall write nothing but a few short stories and my great
legal work on Lord Mansfield.'[10]

The Half-Hearted, which he dedicated to Raymond Asquith, Harold Baker
and Cuthbert Medd, is a very uneven book starting as a novel of manners and
developing into an adventure novel that questions the purpose of life. It very
much reflects Buchan's own state of mind after Oxford, torn between his own
Calvinist ambition and the affectations of his Oxford circle, and takes in the
contemporary pre-occupation about the Russian threat to India on the North
West Frontier. In it he was trying to reconcile the differing attitudes to life of
his Oxford circle with Asquith representing the 'careless and gay' and Buchan
himself 'the world's iron and salt'.

Lewis Haystoun, who is based on Asquith, is an existential hero, a young
Border laird who at Oxford 'got the best First of his year and the St Chad's
Fellowship . . . he was quite the ablest man that has been there for years.'
Haystoun is contrasted with the self-made, urban and vulgar Stocks who also
vies for the attentions of the independent and liberal heroine Alice Wishart.
Lewis, known at Eton as 'Vaulting Ambition' because 'he won the high jump
and was a cocky beggar in general' is directionless. He feels he is 'out of
harmony with his times.' When he fails to win the local parliamentary seat,
Gledsmuir, against Stocks and his platitudes Haystoun thinks he has let down
his friends and his class. His self-esteem further suffers when Stocks, not he,
rescues Alice from drowning and she becomes engaged to her rescuer. After
declaring his love for Alice Haystoun leaves for the North West Frontier, as an
unpaid member of the Intelligence Department, in order 'to make reparation'.

There he meets an heroic end saving India from impending invasion and in a memorable speech comes to full self-knowledge; 'The half-hearted had become the great-hearted.'

Melodramatic as it is, *The Half-Hearted* is important for a number of reasons, not least because this is Buchan's first contemporary adventure story and the first to be set on a wide canvas and in a part of the world he did not know. Many of the recurrent Buchan themes, recently explored in the short stories, are beginning to be fully developed – the sense of an international conspiracy, the drawing on real political events, the regenerative powers of nature, the romantic forced to prove himself as a man of action, the conflict between duty and self, between ambition and contentment. Marka is a prototype Buchan villain, a sophisticated man of no fixed nationality who has penetrated the Establishment. He is 'a capital sportsman, good bridge-player, head like a rock for liquor, and as generous as they make; but . . . a terribly cold-blooded devil'. Britain is being subverted, in this case by 'the whole gang of Jew speculators and vulgarians who would corrupt a great country.' In articulating his own and his friends' dilemma about their role in the world Buchan could be said to be speaking for many of his own generation brought up to rule the Empire but now aware of its roots being undermined.

He was enjoying his time in the law. He liked the sense of tradition, the fellowship, the intellectual discipline. At the end of 1900 he had become a pupil in the chambers of John Hamilton, as Viscount Sumner a future Lord of Appeal. When Hamilton took silk at the beginning of 1901 Buchan moved to the chambers of Sir Sydney Rowlatt, then acting as Counsel to the Inland Revenue and one of the juniors to the Attorney-General, Sir Robert Finlay. The move gave him his first opportunity to devil on a Parliamentary Bill. He claimed later:

> I had no ambition at the time except legal success, and politics I thought of only as a step to that goal. It seemed to me that the position of a judge was the most honourable, dignified and independent of any – ease without idleness, an absorbing intellectual pursuit in which daily one became more of a master.[11]

He also admitted that he:

> loved the appurtenances of it all – the Inns of Court with their stately dining-halls and their long histories, the ritual of the Bar and Bench, the habits of mind and the ways of speech of the profession, the sense that here was the hoar-ancient intimately linked to modern uses.[12]

In June 1901 he was called to the Bar, having failed at his first attempt six months earlier. His Inn of Court was Middle Temple and, interestingly, he joined the Northern Circuit rather than the more obvious circuits around London. As a result he was seeing more of his old Oxford friend F.E. Smith, with whom he would often stay in Liverpool. At Easter he went to Johnnie Jameson's home in Galloway, Ardwall, where he engaged in some pistol practice and in May he was at a weekend house party at Panshanger, Hertfordshire the home of Bron Herbert's uncle Lord Cowper. It was here he first met Arthur Balfour, then Conservative leader in the Commons and other important political and social contacts such as Lady Curzon and several of the Cecils.

Through an introduction from a former colleague in the Horace Club, Dr A.G. Butler of Oriel, Buchan also began his association with the *Spectator*. Then under the editorship of St Loe Strachey it had become the most respected political weekly of the day and its tone of independent Conservatism suited Buchan. Temperamentally, too, he was much happier sitting in the *Spectator* offices in Wellington Street than in a firm of solicitors in Bedford Row. His first piece, an article on Rabelais, appeared in May 1900 and within a few months he was writing for the magazine almost every month. His contributions ranged from biographical portraits to articles on the Coal Industry, Roman Catholicism and Canada. Increasingly too he was asked to deputize for Strachey, first during the holiday period in August 1900, then four months later when the editor was in Egypt and in January 1901 when Strachey was busy with Queen Victoria's funeral. Between May and August 1901 Buchan was more or less solely in charge of the paper. He left a picture of his time there in the centenary issue of the *Spectator*:

> You entered by a narrow door and ascended a kind of turret staircase. On each floor there was a single room, where you felt that anything might happen. On the first floor St Loe Strachey sat, surrounded by new books, writing articles on foolscap paper in his large illegible hand, breaking off to stride about the floor and think aloud for the benefit of the visitor, overflowing with gossip and quotations, so full of notions that it seemed as if no weekly journal could contain one half of them . . . In the room above, Meredith Townsend lurked and took snuff . . . On the next floor – there may have been others, but I never penetrated to them – Charles Graves had his dwelling and I my modest chair. It was our business to see to the base mechanical details of editing, to correct proofs, and, above all, to keep the great men below us straight.[13]

In June 1901 Buchan had written to Dick 'I think I have at last found my feet in London – that is, I can enjoy life and at the same time get through a great deal of work. Last year I was rather experimenting, gay and serious by turns, but now things have got relegated to their proper places.'[14] John Edgar, who had taken a First in History the previous year, was now a lecturer in history at the Khedivial College in Cairo and wrote often to Buchan. Many other friends also seemed to be leading exciting lives abroad such as Auberon Herbert, Johnnie Jameson and Arnold Ward. Travel had always been on Buchan's agenda for it appealed to his romantic nature and his desire to immerse himself in the problems of empire. The opportunity soon presented itself.

In March 1901 he had met his old Oxford friend Leo Amery, who had just returned from his post as *The Times* correspondent in South Africa and was working on a history of the Boer War for *The Times*. Buchan may well have expressed his desire to go abroad then, because a few months later when Lord Milner, the High Commissioner for South Africa, was in Britain to recruit staff for the task of reconstruction, Amery, unable to go himself, put Buchan's name forward. Milner already knew about Buchan from his writing in the *Spectator* and through mutual friends the Asquiths. So he summoned Buchan to the Colonial Office on 7 August and offered him an appointment as his Private Secretary on a two year contract of £1,200 a year. It was an attractive offer, not just because Buchan admired Milner and what he was attempting to do in South Africa, but also because the salary was far higher than anything he could expect to earn in the near future at the Bar and from writing.

It is easy to see the attraction that working for Milner held for Buchan. Though twenty years older he had himself been President of the Oxford Union and won several university prizes. On coming down, he had been elected a Fellow of New College, read for the Bar and stood unsuccessfully for Parliament. He combined a strong social conscience – he was a founder of Toynbee Hall – with a belief in Britain's imperial mission. In 1890 he had been appointed under-secretary of finance in Egypt and at the age of thirty-eight had been made chairman of the Board of the Inland Revenue. Since 1897 he had been High Commissioner for South Africa, where he was now engaged in recruiting able young men to help in the reconstruction of the two new colonies of the Transvaal and the Orange Free State.

Buchan's friends encouraged him to take the job. Sir Robert Findlay, the Attorney-General, told him it could only help him at the Bar and Strachey offered to hold open a job on *The Spectator* for his return. Only his mother was opposed. Buchan tried to persuade her of the benefits – the climate, the prestige, the fact he could save £600 a year from his salary – but he assured her:

> I am not going if it is to hurt you deeply. It would only be a temporary absence, I should probably be back once a year, and of course the post annihilates distance . . . Quite seriously, I think it is a great chance, an interposition of Providence, but *you* must be considered.[15]

Eventually she relented, Buchan cancelled his plans to shoot reindeer in Norway with the Gathorne-Hardys and spent his final few weeks with the family in the Borders. Two days before he left he held a farewell dinner with a group of friends, Cuthbert Medd, Richard Denman, Leo Amery, Harold Baker, Paul Phipps and two other Oxford contemporaries who were going out with him, Hugh 'Algy' Wyndham and Anthony Henley. His South African adventure was about to begin.

5

THE CRECHE

BUCHAN sailed on the Union Castle ship RMS *Briton* on 14 September 1901. His fellow passengers were a mixed bag ranging from government officials and entrepreneurs to relatives of those killed during the War who were going out to visit their graves. On board, he became friendly with a man called Watson from Kelso who was going out to run a fruit farm in the Cape and was rather taken by a Mrs Nelson who was going to join her soldier husband. 'She is one of the most beautiful creatures I have ever seen,' he wrote home.[1] *En route* the ship docked at Madeira where he climbed a mountain, at Teneriffe and Cape Verde before reaching Cape Town at the beginning of October. Here he collected the necessary passes at Government House and caught a train up country. He described the journey to Charles Dick:

> They gave me a carriage to myself, where I was fairly comfortable. The Boers were on the line about 100 miles from Cape Town, so we went very slowly. It was funny to see the watch-fires and the Kaffir scouts, to hear rifle shots, and to see the guard turning out from every blockhouse with fixed bayonets till the train passed. The upper part of C. Colony is a desert of immense stony hills with clumps of heath and prickly pears among the sand. I have never felt in my life such a Sabbatical stillness as sitting outside the train in the great desert, smoking my evening pipe, and watching the most intense sunsets over the blue hills.[2]

At the roadside stations in the Orange River Colony he was struck by the sight of the soldiers. '... people I knew in London as spick and span young men, but now mostly in rags, and – except for their white teeth and clean finger nails — with little to distinguish them from tramps.' One of the soldiers who joined him on the train was the future First World War general, Douglas Haig, who was going on leave and whom Buchan knew as a neighbour in the Borders.[3] Another night he dined with an Irish Hussar who had just got a VC 'for riding down the firing line, saving a wounded man, and then with two bullets in him riding till his horse was shot to warn his men about an ambush.' At Bloemfontein he stopped overnight, arriving in Johannesburg late on Saturday night where he dined with Milner and chatted for an hour before collapsing into bed. He had travelled 8,000 miles in three weeks.[4]

Johannesburg still had the atmosphere of a frontier town. Lionel Curtis, who had come out a few years earlier from New College to serve in the War and as Town Clerk, described it as a collection of 'tin-roofed shanties, with a few large new jerry buildings humped above them, a number of straggling dusty pines and gums, a bit of bare hillside in the distance, and a few attenuated mine chimneys.'[5] By the 8th October Buchan was established in his office and had met his colleagues, including a dramatic introduction the previous day to Lord Basil Blackwood who turned up with '7 lurcher dogs, 40 walking sticks and an Indian servant in a turban — a fine wild sight.'[6] Blackwood was the third son of the Marquis of Dufferin, in turn Governor-General of Canada and Viceroy of India, and had been at Balliol just before Buchan. He had come out to South Africa as a Deputy Judge Advocate during the War and then stayed on as Assistant Secretary for the Orange River Colony. Buchan leaves a picture of him in *Memory Hold the Door*:

> Slight in build, with a beautifully shaped head and soft, dark sleepy eyes, everything about him — voice, manner, frame — was fine and delicate. His air was full of quiet cheerfulness, with a suggestion of devilment in the background as if he were only playing at decorum . . . It was Basil who introduced the fantastic element that kept us from the usual ennui of a staff. His serene good temper was unshakeable, and I do not think he was ever bored in his life.[7]

A natural administrator like his father and, Buchan thought, with Raymond Asquith and T.E. Lawrence one of the three best letter writers he had ever met, Blackwood was an eccentric, more interested in pursuing a life of interest than material reward. Though trained as a lawyer his real passion was drawing. A friend of Hilaire Belloc, he had illustrated a number of his rhymes and he and Buchan planned to prepare a Child's History of South Africa.

Apart from Blackwood, Milner's staff comprised his Private Secretary

Osmond or 'Ozzy' Walrond, who had been with him since 1897, together with Hugh Wyndham, Gerard Craig Sellar a civil servant from the Colonial Office and Buchan. After Walrond had a nervous breakdown in the spring of 1903 he was replaced by Geoffrey Robinson who later as Geoffrey Dawson edited The Times. Major William Lambton of the Coldstream Guards acted as Military Secretary, with Lord Brooke and Lord Henry Seymour as his ADCs. Other colleagues included Patrick Duncan, a Balliol graduate recruited by Milner from the Inland Revenue, who was in charge of the Transvaal's finances (he later became Milner's Colonial Secretary and eventually Governor General of the Union); J.F. Perry who had been sent out by the Colonial Office the previous year to join the Secretariat, and had just been made Assistant Imperial Secretary with special responsibility for the native territories; Lionel Curtis, previously one of Milner's Private Secretaries, and now Secretary of a Commission drawing up a Municipal Constitution for Johannesburg and Lionel Hichens, whom Milner had brought from the Egyptian Ministry of Finance.

To these young men, many of them newly arrived from Britain, could be added older Administration officials with a great deal of experience of the country who would take up important posts with the creation of the two Colonies. They included Sir Arthur Lawley, the Lieutenant-General of the Transvaal, Sir Hamilton Goold Adams, the Lieutenant-Governor of the Orange River Colony, Sir Godfrey Lagden, Chief Commissioner for Native Affairs and Sir George Fiddes Colonial Secretary of the Transvaal. It is however the younger men, many of them in later life to exercise considerable influence on Imperial policy, who have become immortalized as Milner's Kindergarten. Almost all of them were Oxford graduates, many of them from New College, Balliol or All Souls. To Perry, Duncan and Wyndham might be added the names of a slightly later generation John Dove, Richard Feetham who succeeded Curtis as Town Clerk of Johannesburg and later became a Union High Court Judge, Philip Kerr, later Lord Lothian, who arrived in 1902 and worked on the Railway Committee, and Buchan's All Souls rival Dougal Malcolm who came as Private Secretary to Milner's successor Lord Selborne. Buchan, himself, did not stay long enough in South Africa nor form such a tight bond with the group in later life to be strictly speaking a member of the Kindergarten. He preferred to call himself a member of the Creche.[8]

Though he had been offered accommodation sharing with Lambton, Walrond, Henley, Brooke and Milner at the official residence Sunnyside, he preferred to share with Wyndham, Blackwood and Craig-Sellar a couple of miles outside Johannesburg. 'It is in a fir-wood, with a thirty mile view,' he told Charles Dick. 'We shall have an English housekeeper, English maids and an English valet, and some niggers to look after the horses. We are keeping a cow and hens, and I am standing out for a herd of blackfaced sheep.'[9] There he and his young friends attempted to re-create the sort of life they had enjoyed at Oxford, for example by dressing in black tie for dinner. The only difference was perhaps the quality of the food. Two weeks after his arrival he wrote to Stair, now studying law in Edinburgh. 'Life is very comfortable save that the meat (being trek ox and sheep which has died of its own accord) is pretty miserable.'[10]

Soon after his arrival Buchan admitted to Anna that though he was homesick the previous week had been 'the most stirring and varied of my life . . . It is a fine keen life, much in the saddle and at the same time crammed with the most serious intellectual interest . . . My work, of course, is confidential and so I shall never write about it to you . . .'[11] His initial job, acting as 'a sort of political Private Secretary', was 'to help draft despatches to Britain and prepare reports on subjects for His Excy.' The intention was to take much of the administrative burden off Milner to allow him to concentrate on policy. It meant in effect that Buchan was given considerable responsibility, even though he had little practical experience of the country or its problems.[12]

Those problems were numerous. The war had left the country physically and economically devastated, its inhabitants beaten but unbowed. Much needed to be done to restore the country's prosperity and to prepare it for more responsible government. The two most pressing concerns were to resettle the Boer farmers who had lost their farms during the war and to restore full production of the Rand goldfields, many of them suffering from labour shortage as well as physical damage. Milner's further plans for Reconstruction were complex and ambitious. Firstly he wanted to encourage large scale settlement of British farmers in the Transvaal and the Orange River Colony so that when Responsible Government was introduced the British would outnumber the Boers. A further element of this process was to introduce free elementary education and make English the principal language of school instruction, thereby reinforcing the anglicization process. He created an Inter-Colonial Council, which included Government representatives from each of the two new Colonies the Transvaal and the Orange River Colony, to liaise about future developments and nominated Legislative Councils as a preparation for self-rule in the two Colonies. Under Baden-Powell a joint constabulary was set up and attempts made to expand and unify the rail network. Much attention was also given to agricultural improvements with the encouragement of new farming methods, irrigation, veterinary research and locust control.

Part of the attraction of South Africa to Buchan was the distance it placed between him and his family. Though he remained the centre of their world, and his mother in particular took a fierce pride in his achievements he had grown apart from them and they were no longer the centre of his life. He was a dutiful son who loved and respected his family but he was also quickly bored when he saw them. He was determined to make his own independent way in the world and he was therefore not entirely happy to learn shortly after he arrived that his father had secured a temporary job in South Africa as a minister in Port Elizabeth. Buchan fought hard to dissuade them from coming. If it were a matter of his father's health he should go to Madeira or Egypt and Buchan would pay part of the cost. He warned them of the problems of living under martial law and that they would have 'the dreariest and most harassed months' of their life. His admonitions were to no avail and the Reverend John Buchan, his wife and Alastair, then aged seven, arrived in December 1901. The house in Glasgow had been let to members of an American sect of Bible Christians, whose activities the Buchans later discovered included performing miracle cures.

The visit was not entirely successful. Buchan's father had sunstroke, his mother was poisoned by a mosquito bite and Alastair fell ill from drinking too much tinned milk. There was some embarrassment too when the Reverend John Buchan made some unfortunate remarks about Milner's perceived views of the Boer and Ebenezer Masterton made enquiries about securing a job through his nephew's patronage in South Africa. The Buchan family returned suitably chastened with dozens of ostrich feathers, an African basket full of gifts and Alastair with a mongoose called Rikki and a tortoise which he installed in the back garden of Queen Mary Avenue.

Soon after his arrival Buchan was approached to act as legal adviser to the Johannesburg Town Council at a salary of £2,000 a year. Despite the larger salary he felt his loyalties were to Milner and he refused, preferring to concentrate on his principal task, dealing with the refugee camps. He knew something of the camps for he had written a leading article on them in the *Spectator* only a few months earlier. In it he had argued 'We have to remember that our charges, while they are the relatives of our enemies, are also the stock of our future citizens. We have to preserve good temper, patience and humanity, knowing that every misfortune will be only too readily interpreted as a crime.'[13] It was a brave statement to make at the time for feelings had run high against the Boers. It would prove rather harder to implement.

The refugee or, as they came to be called, concentration camps had been created during the Boer War to shelter the destitute and the wives of the Boer farmers who had joined a commando. Most of them had entered the camps voluntarily but conditions soon became desperate as a result of over-crowding and lack of medical care. The camps had passed from army to civilian control the previous June and Milner had made the resettlement of the 160,000 people in them a top priority. He was appalled by the standards of hygiene and consequent high mortality rate, 344 per thousand, as was Buchan who visited them with Milner in October. The young Scot admitted to Lady Mary Murray that 'The Refugee Camps have made my hair grey,' but added 'we have now revolutionised the whole system, and the death rate is down to something nearly normal now.'[14]

In a letter to Charles Dick Buchan was happy to take credit for the improvement in conditions. He claimed:

> that the change in organisation and the reduction of the mortality is chiefly my doing. I have visited most of the camps, sometimes risking a good deal, and it was terrible to find little children dying like flies. I have had to decide 'off my own bat' complicated questions of sanitation, hospital management, engineering and finance.[15]

Indeed by April 1902 the death rate had fallen to thirty two per thousand, lower than the death rate on the veld, but that was principally as a result of the work of Millicent Fawcett and the arrival of doctors and nurses from Britain and the Indian Medical Service rather than Milner's officials.

The year 1902 began badly when Buchan caught dysentery after drinking bad water while sleeping rough up country. 'They are a nasty conjunction,' he wrote to Walter, 'for you have to take opiates for the dysentery and they of course increase your fever.'[16] Though he quickly recovered the attack was to have repercussions on his health many years later.

One of the principal tasks of reconstruction was moving the Boers back to their devastated farms. Some £300,000 was provided for rebuilding and restocking the farms and plans made to introduce the latest scientific methods to maximize return on the land. From his experience in Egypt Milner was convinced that the introduction of improved irrigation and farming techniques would make farming more attractive and therefore encourage settlement, especially from Britain, Canada and Australia. Such settlement he hoped would help break down the racial and economic divisions that had contributed to the war originally. In January Milner offered to make Buchan head of Land Settlement with absolute powers and responsibility directly to the Home Government. Buchan again declined to leave Milner, so a special Land Settlement Department was set up in Milner's office with Buchan in charge. He was to hold the post until March 1903 when the Land Board was established with Dr Adam Jameson, a former Minister of Lands in Western

Australia, as Commissioner. Buchan's role was to facilitate the administrative process of resettlement but it also involved him visiting, often remote, farms on his trusty steed Alan Breck.

Under his supervision a number of measures passed into law, most notably the Transvaal 'Settlers' Ordinance of 1902 in which the former holdings were surveyed, valued and then publicly allotted after enquiry by a Central Board. This was followed by the Lands Disposal Act which he confessed to being pleased with and 'better than any other Colonial Land laws that I know.'[17] Following the successful passage of the Transvaal Ordinance he was asked to organize the Land Department in Pretoria. At first he commuted between Johannesburg and Pretoria as he explained to Anna 'making bricks without straw and trying to knock the maximum amount of work out of a pack of idiots.'[18] Then after June he was based permanently in Pretoria living in some style in the Residency and with a hundred officials reporting to him. His duties were numerous ranging from financial dispatches to the Secretary of State to drafting account forms and preparing ledger accounts. He was also involved in drafting land settlement plans for the Orange River Colony and in railway finance. 'My work is as multifarious as the Army and Navy Stores,' he wrote to Charles Dick in September. 'This week I have been sitting on a legal commission, drafting company prospectuses, organising relief camps, found, ing two new settlements and auditing the accounts of an Irregular Corps. It is a splendid training, but a little too much responsibility is thrown on my shoulders, and I shall be glad when I can turn over a lot of it to departments.'[19]

He was putting in long days rising at 5 a.m., riding till 7 a.m. and starting work at the office by 8 a.m. He would stay until 7 p.m., adjourn for an hour for dinner and return to his desk till 10 p.m. As he admitted it was 'A pretty heavy day, considering how full of worry and responsibility the work is.'[20] Despite the pressures of work he still found time to read. Apart from 'Virgil, Horace, Wordsworth, a good deal of history, and a little philosophy' he managed some Dickens, Boswell's *Tour of the Highlands*, *The Hound of the Baskervilles* which he found a 'stupid work' and the 'delightful' *Just So Stories*.[21]

On May 31 1902 the Peace Treaty of Vereeniging was finally signed. On 21 June Milner was sworn in as Governor of the Transvaal with Buchan at his side. There was a levee in Pretoria where Buchan wore his kilt and Milner was presented by Portuguese envoys with the Grand Cross of the Order of Jesus Christ. Of the 450,000 British troops who had taken part in the war 8,000 had died of wounds and a further 14,000 of disease. The war had cost the British taxpayer £200 million.

In August, Buchan trekked to the western frontiers of the Transvaal with a guide, a cook, two Cape-carts, a spring waggon and eight mules. The party travelled to Zeerust by Klerksdorp, Korannafontein and Lichtenburg returning to Pretoria by Rustenburg. It was a journey that took him past many rebuilt farms and gave him a good idea of how Reconstruction was working in practice. It also provided him with useful material that he would draw from in future books. Perhaps most importantly it instilled a love of the South African veldt that remained with him until his death.

He had originally come out for only two years but he was now thinking of staying on. He had written to Anna in April that Milner 'said that I had administrative talent of the highest order and that if I decided to take up this work finally I had a great career before me. He also said that if I stayed till he left he would be able to help me a lot. He was extremely kind and so I said that I would postpone my decision for another year. After that who knows?'[22] By November 1902 he had decided to stay on for just one more year. He told Anna mysteriously: 'After that unless one particular thing happens I will return to the Bar and the *Spectator* with an eye to Parliament as soon as possible.' A month later he wrote to say he had been offered a job as editor of the main Johannesburg paper with an annual salary of £3,000 rising to £4,000. 'I declined because though I might have stayed five years in the job and returned home with a modest fortune, yet I think if one does a thing purely to make money one is apt to make a mess of it.'[23]

News came at the end of November from Bron Herbert that Cubby Medd had been taken ill while travelling in Albania and Southern Italy with another Oxford contemporary Robert Brand. In July Medd had asked Buchan to find him a post at HQ working for Milner and he continued to make approaches until November. In fact Medd had already died on 24 November, one of his last thoughts in his delirious condition was to ask for 'JB'. Buchan was shocked and racked by guilt blaming himself for not persuading Medd to come out to South Africa sooner. He wrote to Anna on 21 December 'I think Cubby's death the saddest thing I have ever known,' continuing that he thought him 'one of the two or three ablest men I have ever known ... It seems such a stupid and senseless thing for a man so brilliant and courageous to die of a thing like fever in a place like London.'[24]

Over New Year 1902/1903 Buchan made the second of his longer treks, an account of which he later incorporated into *The African Colony*. This time he travelled north-east to the Wood Bush taking with him Brand, who had recently joined Milner's staff. They covered some 1100 miles in five days by train, waggon and horseback. Writing from Pietersburg Buchan told Anna:

I have been over to Wood Bush, an elevated plateau in the Zoutpansberg

mountains overlooking the low fever country. I have never been in such an
earthly paradise in my life. You mount up tiers of mountain ridge, barren
stony places, and then suddenly come on a country like Glenholm. Terrific
blue mountains rise to the South but the country is chiefly little wooded
knolls, with exquisite green valleys between. The whole place looks like a
colossal nobleman's park laid out by some famous landscape gardener.

Throughout his life Buchan would regard the Wood Bush as 'a kind of celes-
tial Scotland', a sacred and enchanted place.[25]

Just after Boxing Day 1902 the Colonial Secretary, Joseph Chamberlain,
accompanied by his wife arrived for discussions with Milner on
Reconstruction and its financing and how best to work towards a reconcilia-
tion between British and Boers in a common Empire citizenship. In Pretoria
he met a delegation led by Smuts and made a series of speeches. Buchan
thought him 'very good – the old professional among amateurs' and Mrs
Chamberlain 'perfectly charming and very pretty'.[26] But as he told Stair
Gillon, in a shrewd assessment, he also had his reservations:

He is as clever as paint, and sees a point a mile off. But he is too dapper and
business-like; he seems to lack vision and daemonic power. I cannot
imagine him leading men as Gladstone led them, or attracting men as Lord
Milner attracts them, or moulding the future as Rhodes attempted. He is a
business-like clever man from Birmingham, a man whom you want to
make General Manager of the British Empire, but whom you know will
remain for ever a General Manager and not a creator.[27]

While working in Pretoria Buchan often stayed with General Neville
Lyttelton, who had succeeded Kitchener as Army chief in South Africa.
Initially he pretended to be unimpressed by the Lyttelton daughters. This
former founder of the Brasenose Ibsen Society wrote half-jokingly to Anna
after one visit 'I find it hard to keep my conversation at the proper intellectual
level. Miss Lyttelton will talk about Dante and Ibsen and it is no good pretending ignorance and asking if they were horses.'[28] The following week he
admitted to his mother 'I have lost the art of talking to womenfolk and they
bore me to death.' South Africa had brutalized him. It was a man's world
where there was little time for women. It may also have been a defence mechanism. Though he would joke about it with contemporaries Buchan was now in
his late twenties and wanted to settle down. Many of his male friends were now
married and so too were a number of women he had been in love with such
as Lady Evelyn Giffard.[29] He wrote to his sister: 'I have had numerous letters

lately including one from Sandy Gillon in which he informs me that Tom Nelson has been captured by Miss Margaret Balfour. I think Tom might have done better than that long ill-made girl but he doubtless knows his own mind. Sandy is in despair about this spate of matrimony: he says that now he and I stand alone.'[30]

There had been plans for Sandy Gillon to come out in April to join him in an attempt on the unclimbed north-eastern buttress of the Mont aux Sources in the Drakensberg, but the trip had to be abandoned when Gillon failed his Bar finals. Instead, in March Buchan took time off to trek in Swaziland with Robert Brand.[31] Brand was to become one of Buchan's closest friends in South Africa. He claimed he preferred working with Buchan 'a thousand times' more than anyone else and respected Buchan's ability to stand up for his own views often against more senior colleagues. When Buchan left South Africa it was Brand who took on many of his responsibilities including cataloguing Milner's official library and answering questions concerned with the Board of Trade. During these final months in South Africa Buchan was handling many of the administrative problems, such as franchises, budgets and military commands, that had arisen as a result of the creation of the two new colonies, the Transvaal and the Orange River Colony, and in July he was appointed to the important position of Secretary of the Inter-Colonial Council.[32]

He was still giving thought to his future career. Strachey had written offering him a job on the *Spectator* for £300 a year with a rise to £1,000 when Meredith Townsend, the assistant editor, then aged 72, left. Having previously dismissed taking a job for the money, Buchan now seems to have changed his mind and given some thought to going into a financial house. As he explained to Anna: 'I have no money. I shall not make a fortune in journalism and though I might at the Bar I would be too old by the time it was made. I am sure Providence meant me to be a politician and to be a fair and honest politician one must be independent of office.'[33]

Writing to Charles Dick he laid out the three options open:

I can accept the '*Spectator's*' offer and go back to the Bar at the same time – with the intention of going into Parliament at the earliest opportunity. Or I may accept an administrative post, probably in Egypt. Something of the sort will probably be offered me, as I have made a sort of mild reputation out here. Or finally, I may do what Lord Milner urges me to do, and go into a great financial house for the purpose of making a fortune quickly, and then when I am independent go in for administrative work on a large scale. I have many plans which my wealth could enable me to realise. Not that I have any love of luxury – out here I have become a sort of Spartan – but you must have money if you are to do constructive political work.[34]

He seemed confused. One moment he wanted to return to Britain and settle down. The next he would write that 'people out here say I should have been a soldier, and I think I should have done well, for I am quite indefatigable and I can manage men and attach them to myself. A sedentary London life with clubs and parties and books – all that seemed once so attractive . . . I have become thoroughly undomesticated . . . marriage and settling down . . . seem poor ideas.'[35] From his first glimpses of South Africa from the train on his arrival he had fallen in love with the country. Now unsure of his future he even considered buying a farm between Pretoria and Johannesburg, until it was pointed out gleefully by his less romantic and more practical friends that it had no water supply.

The fact there were so many Scots was both pleasing and sad for it only accentuated his own loneliness and sense of isolation. His confidential clerks were Scots, as was the cook at his home. As he told his mother 'It is a pleasure to get proper scones and oatcakes and porridge again.' One consolation was that his old friend John Edgar had been appointed Professor of History at the South African College in Cape Town but otherwise he felt isolated from his friends and feared that for all the good work he might be doing he was wasting his time. In January he had signed off to Charles Dick 'Put up a petition for a wandering Scot the next time you tread Galloway or Tweeddale.'[36] He was homesick and aware that he was moving away from his old friends. To Dick, now a Church of Scotland minister, he wrote in May 'I have travelled a different road, but I suppose our ways will meet again when I have the pleasure of entertaining a certain eminent divine at that Highland shooting-box which is to come, and we cast a fly together again and have a long crack over a peat-fire.'[37] After a week's trekking to the Rhodesian border with Brand John Buchan finally left South Africa on 26 July.

Milner's attempt at Reconstruction had had mixed fortunes. Land Settlement, for example, was a failure for only 700 male settlers had moved to the Transvaal by the time Milner left in April 1905. Many of the reasons lay outside the control of the officials on the ground for much of the land was either unsuitable or too expensive. The British Government had not provided enough money to fund the scheme properly and some of it had been wasted. Buchan's own work drew a mixed response. Land had to be bought quickly at a time when land prices were temporarily inflated. Since rents were calculated as a proportion of the cost of the land they were high and therefore out of the reach of most settlers. On the other hand a special correspondent of The

Times who was writing a series on 'Land Settlement in the New Colonies' thought that Buchan had 'brought to bear upon his work, not only an intelligent interest in, and a practical knowledge of matters agricultural, but an aptitude for rapid decision and for taking responsibility.'[38]

There had been some successes, however, as Buchan pointed out in an article on Milner in the summer of 1905. Though the country was not united under the Union Jack strong foundations for Union had been laid and there were notable advances in several key areas. An Agricultural Department with branches dealing with botany, chemistry, entomology, veterinary and bacteriological science, irrigation and forestry had been founded and widely praised. The railway network had been expanded. 'Natal has been linked up with the great trunk line; the wheat districts of the Orange River Colony and the pasture-lands of the eastern Transvaal are being brought into touch with the Rand; and Johannesburg is to gain direct communication with both Kimberley and Rhodesia.[39] 'In a country denuded of supplies, with few roads, and only one or two trunk lines, and at a great distance from any port, over 70,000 people were restored to their homes, over 150,000 head of stock were issued, and over 40,000 acres were ploughed by departmental teams.'[40] The Education system had been reformed. 'At the end of 1898 there were 14,798 scholars on the rolls of government schools; to-day there are upwards of 29,700.' In the article Buchan dismissed claims 'that High Dutch, the people's tongue, was being stifled, High Dutch being as familiar to the average farmer as Icelandic.' As he pointed out the Boers want their children 'to learn English, the language to get rich by'.[41]

For Buchan South Africa had been an emotional maturing. 'I have had a wonderful two years here, and have grown very old in the process,' he told Charles Dick. 'So much responsibility quickly ages a young man. But I have also the memory of unforgettable shooting trips and wild expeditions to every part of the country.' He later admitted in his memoirs that he had 'had to be in some degree a jack-of-all-trades – transport-rider, seedsman, stockman, horsecoper, merchant, lawyer, not to speak of diplomatist.'[42] He had been a success not just because of his energy, intelligence and administrative ability but also because as a Scot he understood the Boers in a way impossible to many of his English colleagues. The Boers were like Border farmers – tough, proud and stubbornly independent. Time and time again in his letters he makes comparisons with Scotland whether it is the scenery, the people or 'fighting the Dutch Reformed Church over educational and revenue matters . . . exactly the case of 17th Century Scotland again.'[43]

His work for Milner appealed to his sense of order and justice, to his natural aptitude for administrative work and it had allowed him to combine a life of action and thought. It had been an intellectual challenge, but it had also been a physical one as he rode to remote farm communities and worked long hours. He had benefited from his close proximity to Milner and his able young officials and the wider experience of living away from the three centres that had shaped his life Glasgow, Oxford and London; the experience had also reinforced his distrust of the pettiness of domestic politics. The South African experience had also strengthened his views about the British Empire and its possibilities. 'The Empire, is not the possession of any one party; and any attempt to claim Imperialism as the perquisite of Liberal or Conservative deserves the gravest reprobation,' he wrote in the Quarterly Review. 'The Empire is part of the data of our politics; its wellbeing is, like the monarchy, an axiom of all sane political creeds.'[44]

He had no illusions about what would happen in South Africa. 'Nationalism is bound to come in South Africa, for it is the logical development; and our business is to see that it does not take a wholly antiBritish character.'[45] Contrary to subsequent opinion Buchan was never a diehard reactionary Tory fighting to preserve the Empire at all costs. By the time he left South Africa, for example, he no longer supported Milner's concept of imperial federation but felt the Dominions 'must be allowed full freedom to follow their own destinies.'[46] He was a Romantic Tory who regarded the Empire as above party politics, something that could and should evolve for the mutual benefit of all. As an historian he saw that the British could not economically or politically, let alone morally, sustain it without that sort of cooperation. As a politician he perhaps failed to realize just how quickly the pace of change was moving against the British.

South Africa had also been important in introducing him to the world of intelligence. The Boer War had demonstrated to the British the need to obtain good intelligence on the ground and, under David Henderson as Director of Military Intelligence, the seeds were sown for the creation of a formal intelligence organization. One of the most important agents was Edmund Ironside an artillery officer with a gift for languages. Ironside, five years younger than Buchan, had served in the Boer War before being seconded to do intelligence work in Hereroland and then SouthWest Africa. His exploits had included accompanying a German military expedition against the Hereros and being awarded a German military medal. Buchan would have been aware of Ironside, who had acted as interpreter for Milner in the discussions with Smuts, from both gossip and access to the official files. Some years later he was to draw on him when he created Richard Hannay, perhaps his most famous fictional character.

While in South Africa Buchan had continued to contribute to various magazines. There was a piece on Lord Mansfield in *The Atlantic Monthly*, a profile of Theodor Mommsen in the *Spectator* and 'Evening on the Veld' for *Blackwood's*. In 1902 Blackwood published a collection of five long 'short' stories which Buchan called *The Watcher by the Threshold* after one of the principal tales. The stories had first been published in *Blackwood's Magazine* between January 1899 and August 1901, with the exception of 'The Outgoing of the Tide' which appeared in *The Atlantic Monthly* in January 1902 but in fact had been written while at Oxford. All of them were set in Scotland and had been inspired by walking tours of Scotland during the university vacations. In the dedication to Stair Gillon, Buchan pointed out: 'It is of the back-world of Scotland that I write, the land behind the mist and over the seven bens, a place hard of access for the foot-passenger but easy for the maker of stories.'

All but the last, 'Fountainblue', have a supernatural element and many draw on the Calvinist doctrine of the 'divided self'. He had been fascinated by the supernatural from his childhood reading and had furthered his interest with a study of pre-Christian cults at Oxford. The stories are interesting in revealing both his possible state of mind at Oxford and as an early attempt at some classic Buchan themes. In all of them the central character is torn between the surface glitter of life, here represented by England, and more primeval longings found in the wilds, here represented by Scotland. In the first story, 'No-Man's Land' the narrator Graves, bearing many resemblances to Buchan himself, is a young academic specializing in ancient history and myths. While walking in Galloway he is captured by a tribe of Picts who have survived to the present day. Though he escapes, the experience traumatises him with tragic consequences.

'The Far Islands' introduces the Raden family, later to reappear in *John Macnab*, and is concerned with the question 'Can a particular form of hallucination run in a family for generations?' Colin Raden is an Oxford undergraduate who continually dreams of another world, the Far Islands, to which he is translated only at his death. He is reacting against the civilizing influence of an old Scots family intermarrying extensively with the great English houses and adopting English customs and education. The implicit warning of the story is that such a form of 'civilization' may be a debilitating one and that one should never abandon one's more primitive streak.

The third story, 'The Watcher by the Threshold', takes as its theme the survival of pagan rites in a supposedly Christian society and looks forward to Buchan's novel *Witch Wood*. The narrator is a barrister, and possible prototype for Buchan's character Edward Leithen, staying with the Clanroyden family, themselves to appear in several Buchan novels, in Perthshire. Ladlaw, a neighbour of the Clanroydens, is a 'commonplace man, with fair talents, a mediocre culture, honest instincts, and the beliefs and incredulities of his class . . . He had a kind of dull, bourgeois rationalism, which used to find reasons for all things in heaven and earth.' He is not the sort of man therefore who becomes possessed by a demon, a possession which requires drastic treatment by the local minister. 'The Outgoing of the Tide' is another exercise in diabolism and again has similarities with *Witch Wood*. 'Fountainblue', in which the Clanroydens reappear, was the second of the two novellas in the collection and as David Daniell has argued again about the 'hidden primitive influence exerted by the topography of Lowland or Western Scotland.'[47]

Two Buchan themes are developed – the power of place exerted over a long period of time and the hidden depths that lie within people and allow them to confound even their own expectations. The story also highlights a Buchan theme – the thin line of civilization – often assumed to have been introduced after the First World War. One of the principal characters, Maitland says: 'There is a very narrow line between the warm room and the savage out-of-doors,' and later he points out 'You call it miles of rampart; I call the division a line, a thread, a sheet of glass. But then, you see, you only know one side, and I only know the other.'

Buchan had a highly developed imagination and throughout his life remained susceptible to the mysterious forces in nature. In his memoirs he relates three occasions where he suddenly became inexplicably terrified while out in the wilds or felt himself being transported back in time to the same location. His Calvinist upbringing and his wide reading had made him aware of the hidden depths in people and how close to the surface the primitive existed even in the most sophisticated circles. The short stories in *The Watcher by the Threshold* were to be perhaps his most obvious exploration of this fascination.

At the beginning of 1902 he had written from Africa to Gilbert Murray:

I am writing a book! I could not help it . . . I am so much in love with this country and have so many things to say which I think might be said. It may be any time in the next two years and I can't find a title. I want to talk about the beauty and mystery of the landscape, the Union history, the Boer character, and the racial and economic questions ahead. A funny hotch-potch, but I think it will have a certain unity.[48]

The following month it had a title, *African Studies*, and he told Anna that with its study of the topography, sport, people and politics it would be similar to Alfred Lyall's *Asiatic Studies*. He added 'I think it might be an interesting memento of my sojourn here.' The book was published at the end of 1903 by

Blackwood under the title *The African Colony: Studies in the Reconstruction* and dedicated to Hugh Wyndham 'In Memory of Our African Housekeeping.'[49] Buchan in his own words was aiming it at '*l'homme moyen politique*' and divided the book into sections on South Africa's past history and its future, covering potential political problems such as Land Settlement, economic prosperity and Federation. The most vivid and interesting part of the book, however, are his accounts of five long trips to the High Veld, Wood Bush, Eastern Veld and along the Great North Road.

The book immediately generated interest. Lord Cromer wrote Buchan a ten page letter about it and Robert Brand, who was in a good position to judge its authenticity, told his mother that 'while somewhat imaginative' it was 'quite accurate in the main and very well-written.'[50] The general opinion was summed up by the *Oxford Magazine* which wrote 'as a handbook to the actual country it is delightful but as a handbook to the political conditions which exist in it must be received with caution, and as a guide to its previous history with positive distrust.'[51] It praised Buchan's powers of description, his ability to evoke mood and even his analysis of South Africa's problems but concluded '*The African Colony* is the work of an artist in words, not of an artist in administration, and for that reason it is disappointing.'[52] It seemed his primary legacy to South Africa was to rest with his writing rather than his work for Milner.

6

SETTLING·DOWN

ON his return from South Africa in October 1903 Buchan went
back to Rowlatt's chambers. He tended to work on Board of Trade
and revenue cases for the Attorney-General, Sir Robert Finlay, and
had begun to specialize in tax matters. When the Balfour Government fell at
the end of 1905 and Finlay lost his job Buchan went into private practice at 2
Harcourt Buildings where his South African experience and contacts proved
useful. He received several briefs from the Transvaal Chamber of Mines
which in one case required him to go out to Cape Town. The upshot of his
work at the Bar was another book *The Law Relating to the Taxation of Foreign
Income*, suggested by R.B. Haldane and dedicated to Finlay. Buchan explained
in the Preface:

> The writer's aim in this little work has been to collect the provisions of law
> specifically relating to the Taxation of Foreign Income, both for the benefit
> of the practising lawyer whose work leads him but rarely into the domain
> of revenue Law, and of the business man whose investments and interests
> lie partly abroad.[1]

Haldane, a future Lord Chancellor, described the book in the foreword as a
'scholarly and comprehensive treatise'. In it Buchan drew on over a thousand
cases to explain with great clarity a complicated part of the law. Though in
later life he was to play down his brief experience of the law it is evident from
this book that he could have become a quite formidable lawyer.

Buchan had met Haldane through the Asquiths and soon became a regular
guest at Haldane's home, Cloan, in Perthshire where he was made privy to
many high level discussions. The two men were drawn by a shared Scottish

Presbyterian background, a taste for English country-house life, a loyalty to Milner and an interest in walking, philosophy, religion, politics and literature as well as law. It was at Cloan in September 1906 that Buchan learnt at first hand of the discussions Haldane, then Secretary of State for War, had just had with the Kaiser and King Edward VII at Marienbad and at Cloan where he first met Lord Esher, chairman of a committee reporting on War Office organization, Sir John French and Sir Ian Hamilton formerly Kitchener's Chief of Staff during the Boer War.

After his two years away Buchan was back in his old bachelor rooms in Temple Gardens, with its dark walls and and carpets and deep leather chairs, where he was looked after by a gloomy manservant called Mole. This time he was sharing with Baker and 'an austere and charming Greek scholar', Austin Smyth, who divided his time between Cambridge, where he was a Fellow of Trinity, and the House of Commons where he was a Clerk. In 1908 he would become Librarian of the House of Commons.[2] Both Harold Baker and Raymond Asquith were practising at the Bar and Buchan would often go with them for long Sunday afternoon walks. His social life remained as active as ever. As he pointed out in his memoirs:

> London at the turn of the century had not yet lost her Georgian air. Her ruling society was aristocratic till Queen Victoria's death, and preserved the modes and rites of an aristocracy. Her great houses had not disappeared or become blocks of flats. In the summer she was a true city of pleasure, every window-box gay with flowers, her streets full of splendid equipages, the Park a showground for fine horses and handsome men and women. The ritual went far down, for frock-coats and top-hats were the common wear not only for the West End, but about the Law Courts and in the City.[3]

There were visits to Sweeting's Oyster Bar in Queen Victoria Street, Romano's or the Savoy Grill where he could indulge in his favourite devilled kidneys in mustard and after a dance he might go to Greenwich by hansom for a breakfast of whitebait at the Trafalgar Inn. And there were weekends at Panshanger, Polesden Lacey and Crabbet Park where he was able to converse with the leading statesmen and journalists of the day, men like Lord Lugard the High Commissioner of Northern Nigeria, Lord Selborne then about to succeed Milner as High Commissioner for South Africa and the future press magnate Lord Northcliffe with whom he spent a Sunday in Surrey 'rushing about a frost-bound country . . . in a magnificent motorcar.'[4]

A new acquaintance was Violet Markham, whom he met at a dinner shortly after his return from South Africa and who would become one of his closest friends. A grand-daughter of Sir Joseph Paxton, the architect of the Crystal Palace, she was almost the same age as Buchan and shared his interest in South African affairs. Coming from a rich Liberal coal-mining family with a social conscience she was able to devote herself to charitable works, local politics and championing the ambitions of her friends. She was to be a crucial supporter in Buchan's future career.[5] Buchan was also seeing many old friends from South Africa such as Gerard Craig-Sellar and the Lionel Phillipses and in December 1903, he had an enjoyable dinner with Robert Brand, Sir Percy Fitzpatrick a partner in the important South African firm of Ecksteins, and Hugh Wyndham who was about to return to South Africa to start a stud farm. He was mixing in some exalted circles and was clearly a popular man about town but even so he admitted to finding London 'a very muggy place'. It was dull and depressing after the excitement of Africa.

In mid-November 1903 he heard that Cromer wanted him in Egypt when a vacancy arose and that he should try and obtain a temporary job in the mean-time. 'I quite agree and am quite content to wait till the way opens up,' he wrote to Anna. 'I have always been a fatalist.'[6] Throughout the spring of 1904 he held out hope for a job but despite support from two senior officials in the Egyptian Service, Sir Eldon Gorst and Clinton Dawkins, there just were no vacancies.

The following May Strachey repeated his offer for Buchan to replace Meredith Townsend as assistant editor of the *Spectator*. Since his return from Africa Buchan had written several articles for the magazine and Townsend had become progressively more ill. Strachey's conditions, however, were tough. Buchan must give up the Bar and abandon all hope of working abroad. He was to be paid £750, not the £1,000 originally promised, and only £400 if Buchan decided to combine his journalism with law. He must also take 'an aggressive Free Trade attitude . . . to carry the war into the enemy's country and subject every artifice, literary and political, to bring Balfour and Joe into ridicule.' Strachey added 'I think I should if I were you refuse to throw in my lot with journalism instead of administration.'[7]

A number of other opportunities also presented themselves. In June after giving a lecture on the Future of South Africa Buchan was approached by the South Edinburgh Unionist Association to be their parliamentary candidate. It must have been tempting since already several contemporaries were begin-ning to go into politics and he had given careful thought to a political career while in South Africa. He realized, however, that without a private income – MPs were not paid until 1911 – that it was not an option and he had to refuse.

When in January 1906 Townsend resigned from the *Spectator* Strachey offered Buchan a tough choice. He could continue at the Bar and freelance on the Spectator at only £150 a year or take the job of assistant editor at £800. He would be required to leave the Bar, not write for any other papers and produce each week two leaders, some reviews and at least nine 'notes'. 'I shall quite understand if you think it would not be worth your while to give up the Bar where I suspect you have a very brilliant future,' wrote Strachey. 'Also you must consider the possibility of the political future.'[8] The offer was more attractive now that he had lost government work at the Bar and there was no chance of him going abroad. After much haggling Buchan finally accepted on the condition he could still do some legal work, was given six weeks holiday a year and his salary rose to £1000 on the death of Townsend. Buchan was a natural journalist able to write fluently and apparently knowledgeably across a wide range of subjects for though his articles tended to concentrate on foreign affairs, his book reviews covered such disparate topics as exploration, biography, history and poetry.[9]

On his return from Africa Buchan had continued to maintain an interest in Empire and was beginning to be regarded as an expert on the subject. He had contributed a chapter, 'The Law and the Constitution' to a book on imperial problems published by John Murray in 1905 as *The Empire and the Century* and he had joined a dining club, the Compatriots, whose members were keen Imperialists and Tariff Reformers. Founded in 1904 by Leo Amery and, after his return from South Africa, under the presidency of Milner, its members included journalists such as Leo Maxse, Saxon Mills and J.L. Garvin, academics such as William Hewins and Halford Mackinder and former members of the 'kindergarten' such as Gerard Craig-Sellar.

One member was Frederick Oliver who was to become a close friend of the Buchan family. Ten years older than Buchan, he had been educated at George Watson's and Edinburgh University before going on to Trinity College, Cambridge where he had became friendly with Austen Chamberlain. After a few years practising at the Bar Oliver was invited by a Trinity contemporary Ernest Debenham to join the family firm Debenham & Freebody. Though he liked to call himself a draper, Oliver quickly rose to run what became one of Britain's major retail businesses and make a fortune. His career allowed him to write and his biography of Alexander Hamilton, published in 1906, was to be an important influence in a generation's thinking on imperial policy.

In his memoirs Buchan was to write:

South Africa had completely unsettled me. I did not want to make money or a reputation at home; I wanted a particular kind of work which was denied me. I had lost my former catholicity of interests. I had no longer any impulse to write. I was distressed by British politics, for it seemed to me that both great parties were blind to the meaning of Empire . . . I began to have an ugly fear that the Empire might decay at the heart.[10]

While in South Africa he had been acutely aware of the changes in British society that had taken place with the death of Queen Victoria and the accession of Edward VII. He felt many traditional values were under threat with a greater emphasis on wealth and material possessions. It was these changes that he attempted to explore in a novel he started on his return. Set in Northumberland it was provisionally called *The Mountain*.[11] The central character Hugh Armstrong is a scholar gipsy. Not only has he won a Balliol scholarship but there is 'no shepherd in the Borders was his equal on the hills'. Against Armstrong are pitted two representative figures – Durward, a successful barrister and Tory Radical who is impatient with the old class structure and an old Tory who is worried that the new empire builders are motivated by greed rather than duty.

The novel was abandoned after a few chapters and instead Buchan completed a treatise about Empire which he called *A Lodge in the Wilderness* and which was published anonymously in November 1906. *A Lodge in the Wilderness* was an attempt at the country-house discussion novel, best exemplified in Lowes Dickinson's *A Modern Symposium* (1905), and a contribution to a political debate then current in Britain. A millionaire philanthropist, Francis Carey (based on Cecil Rhodes), gathers a group of high-minded and intelligent people to discuss the nature of imperialism. They include, among others, the former Conservative leader Lord Appin (a mixture of Lord Rosebery and Arthur Balfour), a Jewish financier Eric Lowenstein (Alfred Beit), Lord Launceston (Alfred Milner), a young journalist Lewis Astbury, a former Premier of Canada, Ebenezer Wakefield, Colonel Alastair Graham of the Intelligence department, Lady Warcliff (Lady Lyttelton), Mrs Deloraine who is 'considered the most beautiful woman in England' (Pamela Wyndham) and Marjory Haystoun. Lady Flora Brune was supposedly based on a current girl friend and the thirty year old Hugh Somerville, 'soft from civilised life', on himself.

The Bookman in its review of the novel felt the arguments 'to be traced as much to a novelist's love of character as to a philosopher's love of truth,' but the fact is that the characters are merely mouthpieces for the book's ideas. *A Lodge in the Wilderness* is of more interest to the biographer than the literary critic since it is hardly a novel in the conventional sense, merely a series of contrasting statements about the nature of empire which one character defines as 'not a creed or a principle, but an attitude of mind.'[12] The book comes to no firm conclusion about imperialism. Lord Appin accepts: 'There is room for

Carey's mysticism, and Wakefield's practical good sense, and Susan's Liberal principles, and Lady Amysfort's Torysim – room too for the hard scientific faith of young men like Astbury and Hugh; room even for Sir Edward's anar-chic individualism.'[13]

To a late twentieth century reader, its attitudes may appear patronizing but given the time Buchan was writing he shows himself to be far in advance of many of his contemporaries with his view of the empowerment of the indi-vidual and the empire as a liberalizing force for good. A number of Buchan themes are developed. Musuru, nine thousand feet above the Rift Valley with its thousands of books combines the civilized with the wild. Lord Appin's philosophy of Romanticism argues that 'Holiness was possible only as a result of the struggle of the soul with an alien world; happiness as the outcome of pain endured and difficulties surmounted.' It is a philosophy that imbues Buchan's fiction as well as his life.[14]

Buchan is sometimes accused of creating shallow, passive women. It cer-tainly cannot be said of this book, where the women are educated, liberated, shrewd in their comments and taken seriously by the men. Likewise there is little here to support the charge against Buchan of anti-Semitism. Lownstein is described as a 'modest, gentle soul' and 'one of the first financial geniuses alive.' 'If we must have magnates,' says one of the characters, 'I would rather Jews had the money. It doesn't degrade them, and they have the infallible good taste of the East at the back of their heads.'[15]

As a young man Buchan had spent many holidays walking and occasionally climbing in the Scottish hills, especially in Skye and in the Coolins. His first ascent of a rock face had been the 3757 feet Ben Alder, beside Loch Ericht in July 1892. Six years later he had made his first serious climb when he tackled Buachille Etive in Glencoe while on a walking tour with John Edgar. In January 1899 he had climbed Ben More, that August the Arran Hills and in September 1904 together with Walter and Stair Gillon, ascended Ben Nevis by various routes. In South Africa he had climbed the Drakensberg and Mont-aux-Sources in Basutoland and in Zermatt climbed the Untergabelhorn in deep snow and made several ascents of the Riffelhorn.[16]

Now on his return from South Africa and missing the outdoor life he seri-ously took up mountaineering, a hobby shared by several of his friends and most notably by Stair Gillon and Leo Amery. Mountaineering appealed to his need to push himself to his physical and mental limits. He enjoyed the chal-lenge of new summits and the combination of brawn and brain that was required. For the next few years he seized every opportunity to climb, usually

in Scotland but also 'on the granite slabs of the Chamonix *aiguilles*, or the sheer
fissured precipes of the Dolomites, or the gabbro of the Coolins.' He preferred
rock climbing to ice or snow work and tended to go with either his brother
Walter or Stair Gillon. Mountaineering brought him back to nature and his
own primitive instincts. He later wrote part of its attraction, was that one
'matches one's skill and endurance against something which has no care for
human life.'[17]

In an article for *Blackwood's* in May 1905 he wrote:

> There is an ecstasy in mountaineering as in all nobler sports, and the dullest
> soul, if indeed dullness can ever be predicated of the true climber, will find
> a strange sub-conscious self awaken on the rock-buttress or the last saddle
> of snow.[18]

In October 1904 he was successfully proposed by Stair Gillon for membership of the Scottish Mountaineering Club and later published several stories,
reviews and articles in its journal.[19] Two years later he was elected to the
Alpine Club partly on the strength of his writing on the subject, proposed by
a former President of the Club the author Douglas Freshfield and Arnold
Mumm, a partner in the publishing firm Edward Arnold. In an appreciation
written in *The Scottish Mountaineering Club Journal* after Buchan's death Gillon
gives a shrewd assessment of Buchan's expertise and enthusiasm:

> He never served an apprenticeship. He just went at it by the light of nature.
> When I knew him his methods were original, unconventional, individual-
> istic, but his movements were sure, decided, purposeful, and invariably he
> finished his climb. His assets were strong fingers and arms, rather short legs
> of enormous lifting power, an enviable poise, which reminded me of
> Raeburn's marvellous balance, and a body that had limpet qualities. One
> felt he couldn't slip off. He went uphill at any angle, whether hands aided
> feet or not, faster than any man that I, or indeed John Mackenzie, ever
> climbed with. His physical reserves were enormous. I never saw him tired.
> Mentally he had purpose indomitable, patience, courage, calm, self-control,
> and nerve.[20]

Speaking to the Scottish Mountaineering Club in December 1931 Buchan
confessed that though he had given climbing up after his marriage 'my love of
mountains remains, I think, the strongest passion of my life. Most men cherish
a devotion either to high mountains or to the sea. I love them both, but had I
to chose I would turn my eyes to the hills'. He was to use his mountaineering

knowledge in several novels most notably *Prester John*, *The Three Hostages*, *Mr Standfast* and the short story 'Space' while there are several essays on mountaineering feats in *The Last Secrets*.[21]

Though, as always, Buchan was leading a busy life it was rather empty. Most of his contemporaries were married and settled into proper careers. In contrast, now almost thirty, he was still living in rooms in the Temple and dabbling at a succession of jobs. All that was soon to change. He had kept in touch with the Lyttleton family and it was at a birthday party for Lucy Lyttelton in July 1905 that he probably first met Lucy's cousin Susan Grosvenor, then aged twenty three. Susan was a pretty girl with long fair hair and not unlike his mother at the same age and he was sufficiently taken to mention her in a letter to his mother a few days later.

Susan's father, Norman de L'Aigle Grosvenor, was the third son of Lord Robert Grosvenor and a grandson of Charlotte Arbuthnot Wellesley niece of the first Duke of Wellington. It was a family with a 'history'. Charlotte's mother, another Charlotte, had left her husband in 1808 for Lord Anglesey, now largely remembered for losing his leg at Waterloo; Anglesey in turn had already been cited as a co-respondent in the divorce of Charlotte's sister-in-law. Born in 1845, Norman Grosvenor had had a conventional aristocratic upbringing. After Eton he had joined the Grenadier Guards, where he spent five years, most of it at race meetings. At the age of twenty-five he took over the family seat of Chester in the House of Commons, representing it in the Liberal interest until he vacated it with some relief in 1873. In the summer of 1875, while in a house party at Penrith, Norman had met Caroline Stuart-Wortley, whose father had been Solicitor-General under Palmerston. They immediately fell in love but it was not until six years later that they were allowed to marry. Two daughters were born, Susan in 1882 and Margaret in 1886.

In spite of his background, Norman Grosvenor was not wealthy and he had to earn a living as an employee of the insurance company Sun Life, of which he eventually became Chairman. His real interests, however, were fishing, grouse shooting and music and he was happiest dressed in his oldest clothes, going fishing or studying harmony and counterpoint. As a Liberal agnostic he could not have been more different from his Conservative, social, church-going relations. His grandson, William, has written:

His relations thought him a dangerous radical, a leveller, a traitor to his class. In fact he was a gentle and liberal-minded man, intelligent, serious

and kind-hearted, through whose nature ran a consistent strain of melancholy and a vein of romantic idealism which made him especially susceptible to the ideas of William Morris and his school.[22]

Apart from Morris, Norman Grosvenor was friendly with Leslie Stephen,
the first editor of the *Dictionary of National Biography* and father of Virginia
Woolf. Other friends included the painter Edward Burne-Jones and Charles
Booth, with whom he helped research *Life and Labour of the People in London*.
Through Stephen and Booth Grosvenor met Frederick Myers, a co-founder
of the Society for Psychical Research, and became fascinated by the survival
of personality after death. In the 1870s he had founded the People's Concert
Society with Dr, later Sir, Walford Davies. Its purpose was to hold concerts
in the poorer areas of London. Admission was a penny and the quality of the
music depended on the generosity of the musicians who gave their services free.
The running costs came out of the pockets of the committee. Norman
Grosvenor was succeeded as organizer by Hubert Parry and the Society continued until just before the Second World War.

Susan Grosvenor had grown up at two addresses on the Grosvenor Estate.
It was however the home of her paternal grandparents Moor Park, a large
Palladian house in Hertfordshire with designs by Robert Adam and a park
laid out by Capability Brown, for which she was to have the fondest memories.[23] After the death of Norman Grosvenor from cancer in 1898 Caroline
took her two teenage daughters to Dresden to study German, music and painting where they lived cheaply in a pension opposite the King of Saxony's
Palace. Later Susan learnt Italian and art history in Florence, taking classes
with Raymond Asquith's future wife Katherine Horner. Though taught by a
governess chosen for her moral character rather than academic abilities in fact
the education Susan received was far superior to that of many of her background. She was a serious young girl more interested in reading than the social
and outdoor life to which most of her contemporaries devoted their time. She
also had a strong social conscience. She had paid weekly visits to Passmore
Edwards's settlement in Tavistock Square to help with dinners for crippled
children and when Buchan met her was spending several days a week working
in an office in Baker Street which was a clearing-house for charitable effort.

John and Susan's courtship was slow, complicated by the fact she was
already unofficially engaged to an officer in the Irish Guards, Viscount de
Vesci. In October, Buchan, signing himself John Buchan, sent her a copy of
The Watcher by the Threshold apologizing that 'the stories are rather crude' and
as if by way of explanation 'they were written at Oxford'.[24] She quickly
replied to 'Mr Buchan' thanking him for the book. 'I have just finished *devour-*

ing it and I must tell you how awfully good I think the stories. They are so well sustained and interesting . . . I hope we are going to see you again soon. If you would come in for tea or later any day you would always find us.'[25]

By December he was inviting her to join him at country weekend parties and calling her Miss Clara and in April 1906 sent her a copy of a book by Hilaire Belloc. He was now calling himself JB and it was to JB she wrote in April

I promised on my word of honour never to divulge who called you a 'ladies man' as the person who said it was so justly terrified at what he had done that he made me swear not to repeat it. I was very much amused indeed at your remarks about the Balliol set, especially the extreme 'hauteur' with which you speak of the woman hating accusation. To quote you 'The true members of the set never troubled themselves sufficiently about the subject to form any opinions.' I feel thoroughly put in my place along with the rest of my sex. I shall never err on the side of thinking we are important again.[26]

He in turn teased her about her 'Guardsmen'. For her birthday in April he sent her two French poetry books with his 'best wishes for many more happy years in this short, confused and unsatisfactory world,' and in July he sent her a copy of Pater's edition of Plato. JB and Clara were now corresponding on a regular basis, he from climbing trips in Chamonix, Skye, Auchterarder and Ardwall she from various country houses.[27] They would meet at dinner parties or at country house weekends where they could walk in the woods or boat on the lakes. Both were restless characters, he adjusting to a more sedentary life after South Africa and she as she later wrote of herself 'a frivolous young person with intellectual leanings'.[28]

Eighteen months after their first meeting Buchan proposed, following it immediately with a letter:

I used to think only of my ambitions, but now everything seems foolish and worthless without you . . . I have not very much to offer except chances. But I think I could make you happy, and one thing I can give you, the most complete devotion and loyalty. You are the only woman I have ever been in love with, and ever shall be in love with.[29]

At the same time he wrote to his mother explaining he had decided to leave the law and journalism with the aim of going into Parliament and that he had proposed to Susan. 'My dearest mother, I want you to be kind to me about this and not make it harder for me. I know you will. Burn this letter and keep what

I have told you private for the meantime.'[30] When Susan accepted his marriage proposal everyone was delighted and congratulations flooded in from old friends such as Stair Gillon, Lady Mary Murray and the Gathorne Hardys. Violet Markham, after meeting Susan, wrote to Buchan: 'What a charming person your fiancee is. I fell in love with her on the spot.'[31]

It was a good match. He was clearly someone with a promising future. More importantly he was kind and older. There was something didactic in the relationship with Buchan sometimes calling her 'My Dear Child'. Though Susan had studied on the continent and been brought up amid some of the great country houses, she was still quite immature and had had a lonely childhood. She missed her father and this intelligent and sensitive man in many ways took his place and opened up a new world of culture and political affairs hitherto denied to her.

Mrs Buchan immediately wrote to 'assure you of a very friendly welcome into our family which has always been a most happy one'. Her letter belied her real feelings. Helen Buchan was suspicious of this young girl who managed to represent two of her greatest prejudices – the Church of England and the Aristocracy. Her grandson William later wrote that she 'behaved with a stark ungraciousness which must have been as bewildering to her future daughter-in-law as it was painful to her son.'[32] Anna Buchan was friendlier:

> I have thought of you such a lot since John's note with his great news last Friday. John has been all the world to me since I can remember anything and I don't really think there ever was a kinder and more considerate brother. I used to wonder what I should do when John married but now that John has found the one woman in the world I find I don't grudge him or you in the least.[33]

The betrothal party was held at the Park Lane home of some friends from Johannesburg, the Ecksteins, and attended by among others Lord Milner. The food was almost all white and the menus were printed on silver bells.

Now he was to be married, Buchan was determined to have a higher income and he decided to leave the *Spectator*. He wrote to Robert Brand suggesting he replace him as assistant editor at the same salary of £800 a year with a view to his eventually becoming editor, an option that presumably had been open to Buchan.[34] At the same time he accepted an offer from his old Oxford friend Tommy Nelson to join the family's publishing firm Thomas Nelson as a partner on a two year trial. The job involved acting as chief literary adviser, vetting books submitted by agents and developing Nelson's publishing programme. For the first part of 1907 he was to be based in Edinburgh, staying first with Stair Gillon at 116 Hanover Street and then with the Alec Maitlands at 6 Heriot Row.[35]

Alec Maitland had joined the Scottish Bar at the same time as Stair Gillon and Johnnie Jameson. His wife, Rosalind, was the sister of Gerard Craig Sellar and had been courted a few years before her marriage by Neville Chamberlain. The Maitlands were to become close friends of the Buchans and their home in Heriot Row a refuge for the Buchan family for the next thirty years. It was a difficult separation and Buchan and Susan wrote to each other daily. For him she was 'My darling Susie', 'my own little angel', 'my own sweetest Susie' 'Susan Cat' and 'Little Mouffs'. To her he was always 'My darling John'.

In January Mrs Buchan and Anna came to London where they met Susan for the first time at Brown's Hotel. Then in May Susan went north to meet the Buchan family in Peebles armed with a set of prepared conversational topics: the poor for Mrs Buchan, flowers for the Reverend John Buchan and poetry for Walter. She visited the Masterton uncles at Bamflat, whose Scottish accents she scarcely understood, and Mrs Buchan's sister Agnes Robb at Broughton where she 'sat consuming scones in the little drawing room and listening to talk about the various ministers'.[36]

It was a different world but Susan adapted to it quickly. She wrote to her family:

John's father is such a joy. He has the most heavenly good-tempered way with him – and laughs and is laughed at by his family all the time. He plays the penny whistle delightfully ... There is something very keen and strenuous about the atmosphere here; to begin with one feels very fit – they all talk awfully well – so intelligently and keenly and the amount of poetry quoted is amazing. One feels very alive and invigorated.[37]

She dined with Buchan's friends – Lady Ardwall, Stair Gillon, Tommy Nelson, Johnnie Jameson, George Brown, the Alec Maitlands – at the North British Hotel and saw the Parkside works 'which are *fascinating*' before going on to stay with the Tommy Nelsons 'in a castellated building with the most awful middle-class furnishings imaginable'.[38]

Throughout the engagement period Buchan was working extremely hard and there were mounting tensions about the wedding, generally created by Mrs Buchan. In June it all became too much and he collapsed from nervous exhaustion. His brother William wrote from India, where he was now a member of the Indian Civil Service: 'I was very sorry indeed to hear of your slight breakdown. For Heaven's sake take care of yourself and get fit again. It

is so unlike you to go and get ill. Mother's distress at your engagement is swallowed up in anxiety about your health, which is a good thing.'[39]

Raymond Asquith was to be married about the same time and he and
Buchan had a joint bachelor dinner at the Savoy. Then on a sunny Monday
afternoon, the 15 July 1907, JB and Susan were married at St George's,
Hanover Square where, traditionally, Grosvenor brides held their weddings.
Susan arrived in the Grosvenor family coach lent by her cousin the Duke of
Westminster and, since her father was dead, was given away by her mother.
The organist, Walford Davies, played some of Norman Grosvenor's own
compositions as Susan walked up the aisle followed by eight bridesmaids,
including Anna, all dressed in pink and silver carrying baskets of sweet peas.
The service was conducted by Cosmo Lang, then Bishop of Stepney, but later
in the year appointed Archbishop of York, whom Buchan had known when
Lang was Vicar of St Mary's at Oxford. Though Lang was ten years older he
and Buchan shared a similar background, career and interests. Both were sons
of the Manse, had been educated at the Universities of Glasgow and Oxford,
had taken Firsts and been President of the Union, had practised at the Bar and
published romantic novels with a Scottish background. Hugh Wyndham,
Buchan's colleague from Oxford and South Africa, was best man and later
remembered how Mrs Buchan 'glowered' at Lang's High Anglican scarlet
cassock.

The only two points of tension were that the Reverend John Buchan had
not been allowed to take part in the service and a wedding photo was vetoed
because the wedding party wanted to leave quickly. There was a party afterwards at 30 Upper Grosvenor Street from where the happy couple left by train
to start their honeymoon at Tylney Hall, the Hampshire home of the Rand
millionaire Lionel Phillips. Buchan later remembered that the baths ran pink
scented water and he felt obliged to tip the butler what he felt was the exorbi-
tant sum of £25.

Susan had suggested they spend the rest of their honeymoon in Paris,
Zermatt, the Italian Lakes then Venice. In the end they chose Innsbruck,
Achensee, Cortina and Venice. It was rather an unusual honeymoon.
Though they went for long walks and rowed on the lake together John spent
part of it writing a novel, possibly *Prester John*. He also produced a book of
cartoons illustrating their holiday. Susan was not entirely well and Buchan
took the opportunity to explore the countryside on his own, as always pushing
himself to his physical and mental limits. 'He starts at 5.30 a.m.' she wrote to
her family 'and simply goes *miles* as hard as he can. I am delighted he should,
as it isn't enough for him to walk about with me.'[40]

They attempted to climb Monte Cristallo, the highest mountain in the

Dolomites, but were forced to turn back when Susan had vertigo. 'Mettez vos pieds dans le vide, madame' the guide would shout and Susan would shudder. From there they went to the Hotel L'Europe in Venice with its views over the Grand Canal. 'We really have found the Venice of the Italians and not of the tourists – and it is quite heartening,' Susan reported to her family.[41] They went for long walks, on gondola trips, one day hired a boat with an orange sail to cruise among the islands and even spent time at the Lido which was in the process of being transformed from a small fishing village to the resort that Thomas Mann pictured in *Death in Venice* just five years later. Susan later remembered it as 'a modest place with one or two hotels and little wooden booths where one could buy dried sea-horses and mushroomlike straw hats. We hired bathing dresses, massively striped, and bathed in the sparkling waters of the Adriatic.' From their 'heavenly honeymoon' they returned to start married life.[42]

Their first few weeks of married life were spent at Tommy Nelson's Gothic villa in Edinburgh while Buchan covered for Nelson who was on holiday. In the autumn of 1907 they moved into their first London home at 40 Hyde Park Square, a tall rather gaunt house, with a steep staircase. It was there in the conservatory that Susan made her first gardening experiments and at the house their first child Alice Caroline Helen was born on 5 June 1908. That evening Buchan dutifully spoke, with Winston Churchill, at the Oxford Union. The baby was named after her two grandmothers and given as godparents Gerard Craig-Sellar and a cousin of Susie, Alice Grosvenor. Three years later in November 1911 a son, named after his two grandfathers, John Norman Stuart was born. His god-parents were Stair Gillon and Lord Robert Cecil. By this time the family had moved to 13 Bryanston Street, near Marble Arch. The Buchan household was completed by Frances Earl, a rather domineering and irritable spinster whom the children called Old Nanny.

In 1912 the Buchans made their final London move, to 76 Portland Place, an Adam style house, famous for its drawing room ceiling by Angelica Kauffman. Susan later remembered how 'It had all the spaciousness and grace of an eighteenth-century house, with a courtyard at the back . . . The house had a charming hall paved with black and white squares of marble, and John's library (the room we used most), lined with bookshelves, was a pleasant room.' A graceful staircase with shallow steps wound its way up to the nursery floor.[43] The Buchans were sufficiently wealthy to employ three Scottish maids which allowed Susan to pursue her own interests. She was attending lectures at the LSE and, with Violet Markham, had helped start the Personal Service League, a charity studying the problems of poverty and unemployment.

The Buchans lived the conventional life of young newly-weds of their class.

There were dinner parties with friends from Oxford, South Africa and the *Spectator* though rarely from literary or publishing circles. These dinner parties might include such distinguished guests as R.B. Haldane, the Raymond Asquiths, F.E. Smith or Lord Milner. One evening Philip Snowden, then the Socialist MP for Blackburn, and his wife were invited to meet Robert Cecil and his wife, all six then being active in the Women's Suffrage Movement. Weekends were spent with friends such as the Lionel Phillipses at Tylney Hall or the F.S. Olivers at Checkendon near Reading and sometimes they would visit Lord Rayleigh (the scientist Robert Strutt) at Terling near Chelmsford. Two important new friends were Moritz Bonn and his wife. Bonn, two years older than Buchan, was a clever young Jewish economist who had come over from Frankfurt in 1903 to become one of the first teachers at the London School of Economics and had later spent some time in South Africa.

They saw much too of Susan's family, particularly the daughters of her uncle Neville Lyttelton. General Lyttelton had returned from South Africa in 1904 to become in turn Chief of the General Staff, Commander in Chief in Ireland and Governor of the Royal Hospital at Chelsea. It was through the Neville Lytteltons that the Buchans had also become friendly with the Liberal statesman, Lord Grey. Lucy Lyttelton had married Charles Masterman who had been elected a Liberal MP in 1906, while Hilda, who rose to be National President of the Young Women's Christian Association, had married in 1909 as his second wife a career soldier, Arthur Grenfell. Another daughter Hermione had married Lionel Hichens, a colleague of Buchan's in South Africa.[44]

One member of Susan's family whom they occasionally visited was her uncle Charles Stuart-Wortley who had married first Anthony Trollope's niece Beatrice and then Sir John Millais' daughter Carrie. Though an MP Charles Stuart-Wortley's main interest was music and his home in Cheyne Walk was frequented by Edward Elgar and W.S. Gilbert, amongst many other musicians. Sometimes too they would stay with Susan's aunt Margaret, a famous beauty in her time, and her husband Sir Reginald Talbot. Talbot had been attached to Sheridan's staff during the American Civil War and had later been military attache in Paris and he and Buchan would talk at length about military affairs and international politics.

Another favourite Stuart-Wortley relation was Susan's cousin Jack whom Buchan had first met in 1905 when Stuart-Wortley was on leave from Sudan where he was a Civil Commissioner. After Eton Stuart-Wortley had been apprenticed in the Merchant Navy where he had trained on the old four-masted clippers. During the Boer War he had enlisted as a trooper then joined the Criminal Intelligence Department before becoming at twenty two the youngest Captain in the British army.

Often too the Buchans would stay with Susan's aunt Mamie and her husband Ralph, the future Earl of Lovelace, either at Ockham, their Jacobean house near Woking or at Ashley Combe near Porlock. It was through the Lovelaces that Buchan first met the writers Henry James and Hugh Walpole, the former of whom had been offered a cottage on the estate. Mamie Stuart-Wortley had studied at the Slade with Sir Edward Poynter before marrying: her husband, a first class mathematician, was a slightly eccentric character whose favoured apparel was a Loden jacket, grey flannel trousers and string shoes, who spent his life either studying or playing the violin. He was also obsessed by his grandfather Byron and in 1905 had written a study of his marriage, *Astarte*, which Buchan had reviewed in the *Spectator*. In the autumn of 1909 Buchan and Henry James were asked to look at the archives and 'reach some conclusion on the merits of the quarrel between Byron and his wife.' In April 1910 they duly presented their report which vindicated Lovelace's grandmother. Life with the Lovelaces was never simple. Mamie kept a large and solemn cockatoo she called William of Ockham and two green parrots who used to roam under the tables during meals nipping at the ankles of guests. She was also opposed to smoking and Buchan, then a keen smoker, would have to retreat to his room, lie on his back and carefully blow his cigarette smoke up the chimney.

In spite of moving south Buchan kept up his ties with the Church of Scotland and regularly worshipped at St Columba's in Pont Street and in April 1912 he joined his old Oxford friend Arthur Steel-Maitland, now an MP, as an elder of the church. In the same year too he and Arthur Grenfell were involved in raising money to buy a portion of the Heights of Abraham to provide a public park marking Wolfe's famous victory. He continued to work at Nelsons, either at the London office in Paternoster Row or the Parkside works in Edinburgh. His job was to commission more contemporary and literary authors for the list and edit the Encyclopaedias, reputedly learning Spanish to do so. In particular he was responsible for launching the Nelson Sixpenny Classics, the shilling non-fiction series and the then revolutionary concept of the Sevenpenny Library which aimed to introduce good modern fiction to the public in an attractive and inexpensive format.

The Sevenpenny list ranged from Erskine Childers's *Riddle of the Sands* and Sherlock Holmes to Mark Twain's *Tom Sawyer* and *Huckleberry Finn* and George Douglas Brown's *The House with the Green Shutters*. Through the literary agent J.B. Pinker he bought novels by Henry James, George Gissing (who received a lower royalty because 'we cannot expect the same sale for him as for, say, Anthony Hope and Mrs Ward'), W.W. Jacobs, A.E.W. Mason, John Galsworthy and E. Phillips Oppenheim. Buchan made offers on Joseph Conrad's *Romance* and in turn Pinker sent him novels by among others Arnold Bennett. Two of the books he discovered for the two-shilling novel list were H.G. Wells' *Mr Polly* and a celebrated detective novel, *Trent's Last Case*, by an Oxford contemporary and friend E.C. Bentley. Many of the books on the non-fiction lists also reflected Buchan's own tastes and were written by acquaintances including Kenneth Grahame's *Golden Age*, Winston Churchill's *Malakand Field Force*, Hilaire Belloc's *Path to Rome*, Lord Rosebery's *Napoleon* and F.S. Oliver's *Life of Alexander Hamilton*.

Buchan worked well with Tommy Nelson, his brother Ian and their cousin George Brown, involving himself in the administrative and production side of the business as well as the editorial. It was Buchan who was responsible for briefing some of the Nelson sales force, who took the chair at the annual concert and judged the literary competition. He was also responsible for expanding the firm's operations abroad. He set up a series of Nelson's French, German and Spanish classics and there were plans for a Russian series when war broke out in 1914.

Another of his responsibilities was editing a weekly paper called the *Scottish Review*. Originally launched in July 1905 as the *Scottish Review and Christian Leader*, its intention was to be a cheaper and Scottish version of the popular English religious weeklies. Buchan became its editor in February 1907 and immediately replanned the paper, introduced new features and gave it a more tolerant outlook. There were 'more articles on literary and social subjects, a good class of serial fiction, and a plentiful supply of book reviews by first-rate writers.'[45] Contributors included old friends such as Hilaire Belloc, Robert Rait and Lord Haldane, who wrote on the 1907 Imperial Conference, as well as Neil Munro on 'The Scots in Sweden', Professor Robert Seton-Watson on European politics and Andrew Lang on 'Anagrams of Mary Queen of Scots'. The paper also printed some hitherto unpublished verses written by R.L. Stevenson at Edinburgh University. Buchan did much of the writing himself, producing each week a 1,200 word editorial which his co-editor W. Forbes Gray noted was completed in under an hour and without a correction.

He controlled the policy, and contributed several columns each week, including editorials, a survey of political happenings at home and abroad, numerous literary articles, and a London Letter. Buchan in short was responsible for most of the features which gave the *Scottish Review*, brief though its career was, a unique position among journals of its class.[46]

However Buchan's talents and ambitions for the paper were not appreciated by the existing readership for whom abroad began at the English Border. Though the paper did cover Scottish affairs there was for many readers an uneasy mixture of the ecclesiastical and the secular and too many leading articles on countries they had never heard of. As Gray put it 'his mind usually travelled on a higher plane than that of the subscribers to the paper.'[47] At the end of 1908 the *Scottish Review* was closed. Buchan wrote to Gray that day 'It has been a gallant and worthy little paper, of which none of us have any cause to be ashamed.' It had been an attempt to put Scotland at the centre of contemporary literary affairs and re-create the tradition of Francis Jeffrey's *Edinburgh Review*. Buchan had hoped to enlarge his reader's horizons beyond kirk and kailyard, to interest them in political events throughout the world and to introduce them to exciting contemporary writers such as Meredith and Flaubert. As such he had failed. *The Scottish Review* had been too intellectual for a penny paper and insufficiently parochial to satisfy Buchan's fellow Scots. The battle against the Kailyard had still not been won.[48]

7

WRITING AND POLITICS

BUCHAN had long considered a political career and had kept up his political interests, especially in Imperial questions. In 1909 he had been elected to the Political Economy Club, the following April lec, turing to it on 'A Project of Empire'. In the summer of 1910 he was a found, ing member of the Chatham Dining Club which was set up 'to bring together for the exchange of ideas men of various professions and political creeds who are anxious to overcome the obstacles in the way of the effective consolidation of the British Empire.'[1] Members, with their date of joining in brackets, included amongst others Sydney Armitage-Smith (1912), Basil Blackwood (1910), a future Director of Naval Intelligence Commander Barry Domville (1912), Maurice Hankey (1910), Philip Kerr (1912), Dougal Malcolm (1912), J. St Loe Strachey (1913), Clive Wigram (1912), Edward Wood, later Lord Halifax (1910). By the outbreak of the First World War Buchan was a leading member of the committee along with Robert Brand, Guy Dawnay, Cuthbert Headlam and the Honourable Jasper Ridley.

The Chatham Dining Club, possibly a prototype for Buchan's fictional 'The Thursday Club', helped shape Buchan's view of Empire and, during a period of widespread German spy scares, produce useful inside information for future books. Norman Angell, who had warned of the impending world conflict, spoke on 'The Great Illusion' in April 1911 and the Right Honourable Syed Ameer on 'Islam and the British Empire' the following year. In June 1911 Buchan spoke on 'Democracy and Representative Government' and other speakers to the Club included F.S. Oliver, Dougal Malcolm, Robert Brand and J. St Loe Strachey before the war and several individuals with strong Intelligence links such as Sir Basil Thomson, D.G. Hogarth and Aubrey Herbert immediately afterwards.

One of the early members of the Club was Edward Gleichen who was to become a close friend of the Buchan family, head the Intelligence Bureau at the Ministry of Information during the First World War and, as a senior intelligence officer be a crucial influence on Buchan's life and writing. Almost certainly Gleichen inspired elements of Buchan's future fictional heroes and provided him with the high level intelligence background and introductions that contributed to the authenticity of Buchan's later picture of the secret world. Born a count in 1863, Gleichen was the son of Admiral Prince Victor of Hohenlohe-Langenburg and the grandson, through his mother, of Admiral of the Fleet Sir George Seymour. At the age of eighteen he had joined the Grenadier Guards and within five years he had been seconded to the Intelligence Department of the War Office where he was to spend a large part of his future career. His facility for languages and disguise led to Gleichen's being used extensively on intelligence gathering missions in Morocco, the Sudan, Abyssinia and during the Boer War where he was wounded, twice mentioned in despatches and awarded the DSO.

In 1901 he was appointed Director of Intelligence in Egypt and two years later he became Military Attaché in Berlin where he remained until 1906 when he was posted to Washington. In 1907 he became Assistant Director of Military Operations at the War Office where he was responsible for the European Section, his colleagues including Edmund Kell the head of MI5. Gleichen maintained close links with the Royal Family, through his own relations and through his wife Sylvia, a Maid of Honour to both Queen Victoria and Queen Alexandra. He had also forged a career as a writer with a series of books about his exploits. It was perhaps inevitable given their shared interests that Buchan and Gleichen should become close friends.

The Chatham Dining Club also brought Buchan in to contact with a number of political figures and rekindled his political ambitions. Charles Masterman, now an Under-Secretary in the Home Department, and Leo Amery, who had unsuccessfully contested East Wolverhampton several times, were just two of his friends encouraging him to stand for Parliament. In February 1910 Susie had written to her husband, 'my own darling Gogg', saying she had just met Herbert Asquith:

Old Sickie whose face was flushed and eyes fixed — whether by having dined too well or by the fact that hordes of Liberals kept passing him, I don't know . . . Directly he saw us he said how much he had enjoyed his dinner here — then said 'What a brilliant fellow John is — he ought to be in the House . . . he is far too jolly a fellow not to be in it and we shall have such fun if he were there.[2]

Buchan had tried to find a seat for the 1910 General Elections but was unsuccessful. Finally in March 1911 he was adopted as the Prospective Unionist Candidate for Peebleshire and Selkirk, a large seat that stretched from the outskirts of Edinburgh almost to the English Border. He was an obvious choice for he had known the constituency since his youth and still maintained good local links. (In October 1909, for example, he had been elected to the Tweedale Shooting Club). He also had the advantage that both sides of his family were well-known in the area. The Mastertons were success-ful local farmers while his brother Walter had succeeded their uncle Willie as Town Clerk of Peebles in 1906 and was now Procurator Fiscal. The seat was held by a Liberal Donald Maclean – the father of the spy Donald Maclean – who had won it from the Unionists by 201 votes in December 1910. Maclean had already sat as the MP for Bath between 1906 and 1910 and was a popular and experienced politician. In an electorate of just over four thousand his majority was fairly comfortable and it was unlikely the seat would change hands. The Peebles News noted that Maclean was not too worried by his opponent in a seat they called 'a forlorn hope' for the Conservatives. At least, however, Buchan's political career was finally under way.

There was initially concern about which party Buchan would be repre-senting. After his adoption meeting the *Peebles News* wondered 'Is Mr Buchan a Liberal?':

> Mr John Buchan is rather advanced in his opinions to please some of the more rabid Tories. Part of his programme is stated to be: Abolition of the hereditary principle of the House of Lords, Free Trade, and a scheme of Small Holdings. How the Unionist Tariff Reformers will act with such a programme remains to be seen. Certain it is that some who attended the meeting are not at all keen on such an advanced programme.[3]

Most of Buchan's English friends and his Masterton relations were Liberals but though he shared Liberal views on Free Trade and the need for old-age, health and unemployment insurance, the Buchans were Conservative. It was an unusual position given that the Liberal Party were seen as the established Party in Scotland, but this may have been part of its attraction. Buchan's Conservative views were firmly engrained, particularly on the subject of Ulster, and he certainly had no illusions about the Liberal Party, of whom he later wrote:

> Its dogmas were so completely taken for granted that their presentation partook less of argument than of a tribal incantation. Mr Gladstone had

given it an aura of earnest morality, so that its platforms were also pulpits and its harangues had the weight of sermons. Its members seemed to assume that their opponents must be lacking either in morals or mind.[4]

A satirical portrait of a Liberal politician, supposedly based on the then Lord Advocate Alexander Ure, had appeared in his short story 'A Lucid Interval' published in *Blackwood's Magazine* in February 1910.

During the three and a half years that Buchan nursed the constituency he tried to spend as much time as possible there, taking the opportunity of stints at the Nelson offices in Edinburgh to make quick visits to the area. Most of the time he stayed with Walter and Anna, now living at Bank House, but during the summer of 1911 he rented, as he had the previous summer, Harehope, a large house in the Meldon Hills four miles from Peebles and in the summer of 1912 he took Broadmeadows Cottage, beside the river Yarrow. This allowed him to pay more attention to the Selkirk end of the constituency, which he toured in a car nicknamed 'Alfred the Elephant' borrowed from Susan's cousin Jack Stuart-Wortley.

Apart from a succession of speeches in drill halls and institutes across the constituency, he was called on to perform the various duties exacted of a prospective parliamentary candidate. He opened bazaars, addressed Burns Night suppers, attended social events and was present at various civic functions. Sometimes too he was able to combine his political campaigning with his writing career, such as when he spoke in December 1911 to the Peebles Parish Church Young Men's Guild on The Marquis of Montrose. Much of his focus was personal and local but occasionally he would bring in friends who were national figures such as Sir Robert Finlay, Robert Horne, Lord Robert Cecil and F.E. Smith who, speaking in support of Buchan at the Drill Hall in Peebles, noted that the young candidate had had the most distinguished Oxford record since Milner and prophesied he would quickly make the Cabinet. Johnnie Jameson, then the Conservative and Unionist candidate for East Edinburgh also came and spoke on his behalf.

William Buchan has described his father as 'too honest, too unprejudiced, too romantic and, in a sense, too innocent for the party-political game'. To an extent that is true; but he fought a vigorous campaign and knew how to exploit issues and turn them to his advantage. For example, there was a spirited correspondence in the local papers with Buchan challenging Maclean's claims that certain employers had used improper methods of coercion in obtaining signatures to the British Covenant on Ulster.[5]

As a result of his candidacy Buchan was seeing more of his parents. In 1910 his father had retired from Glasgow to Peebles exhausted from his time in the Gorbals and with the intention of writing two books, a study of Peebleshire Poets and a theological book *The Apostolic Evangel. Blackwood's* had already published a collection of essays in 1902 entitled *The First Things: Studies in the Embryology of Religion and Natural Theology*. Since the Reverend John Buchan's pension of £120 was not enough to support him and his family Buchan, William and Walter had each agreed to supplement it with a small contribution. The family concern about his health was quickly justified. Shortly afterwards while staying at the Grosvenor Hotel in London *en route* to Switzerland on holiday with Anna, Walter and Alastair the Reverend John Buchan had a heart attack and was forced to return to Peebles. Then in October 1911 Buchan's mother became seriously ill. She was already being treated for anaemia, now she had a fever and temperature of 106 and it was thought had only a short time to live. The strain of watching his wife suffer proved too much for the Reverend John Buchan who died suddenly on 19 November 1911, six days before the birth of his first grandson, who was immediately named after him.

The Reverend John Buchan had always been a rather shadowy figure in the Buchan household. He was overshadowed by his wife's strong personality and was content to leave the everyday running of the family to her. It was she who had had ambitions for her sons and kept the family together but his early death still came as a considerable shock. William wrote to his older brother after their father's death:

I am thankful that the end was so short and so easy, a fitting ending to such a gentle life. I am able now to recall him far more vividly. There is something wonderfully restful and soothing in all my recollections. It was a fine simple life and the meaning of it is a good possession of his children. One can feel no sorrow for father. He's got more pleasure out of life than most men and he left it easily.[6]

There were fears that Mrs Buchan might follow suit and William contemplated returning from India. The following July he did return, his first visit to Britain in three years, staying with Walter and Anna at Bank House and John and Susie at Broadmeadows Cottage. He had been in India since December 1903 first as an Assistant Magistrate and Collector in the remote districts of Barisal, Chapra and Gobindpur in Bengal, then in 1907 as Assistant Political Secretary to the Governor of Bengal. In January 1908 he had been appointed a Registrar of Land Banks and from that August was acting Director of Agriculture in Bengal. These Land Banks had been set up to help Hindu peasants who might fall into debt with moneylenders and William had taken a close interest in them. Thereafter he was known to the family as Bogley after the Collector of Bogley Wallah in *Vanity Fair*. While in India Willie had taken up polo and following in his brother's footsteps he had also begun to write, contributing an article to *Blackwood's* in April 1911 based on his trip to the approaches of Kangchenjunga the previous year.

Soon after his return William complained of back pains. In Scotland baths at the Peebles Hydro proved ineffective and X-rays revealed nothing. Rheumatism was suspected, but it was only when Willie caught pleurisy on his return from the Oban Gathering that the family and doctors realised just how serious his condition had become. In October, Sir Almroth Wright, who had treated Mrs Buchan the previous year, was summoned and diagnosed a pneumococcal infection which he thought might have been contracted while trekking in the Sikkim Himalayas. Willie was put into a Glasgow Nursing home where he would sit up in bed with a monocle in one eye and tease his youngest brother Alastair, then still a teenager, about his flirtation with the Fabian Society. It was in the nursing home that he died at 6 p.m. on 11 November 1912 aged thirty two.

Buchan had rushed to Glasgow as soon as he heard the news. Writing the next day from the Central Station Hotel to Susie he explained what had happened:

> He had been sinking ever since the morning and was scarcely conscious. Nan and Walter arrived at 4.30 and he recognised them by their voices. At the end he began to call on me in the same voice as he used to call me when we were boys. At 5.30 they decided to operate as a last chance and he died under the anaesthetic . . . O darling . . . what are we to do without the dear canny brave laddie![7]

Two days later a funeral service was conducted first at Bank House and then in Peebles Churchyard. The three surviving Buchan sons led by JB together with Helen's brother John, Stair Gillon and Johnnie Jameson acted as pallbearers. The *Times* in its obituary wrote 'In Mr Buchan the Indian Civil Service has lost an official of the highest and most public-spirited type', while in India the *Statesman* noted 'His work was thorough, his friendship was warm, and his sympathies wide. The loss of his personality will be felt not only in the circle of his intimate friends, but in every village in the Province where his visits were looked forward to by the people he tried to help.'[8]

Willie's death was a great shock to Buchan coming so soon after the death of their father and he immediately took three weeks' sick leave. Helen had now lost two of her six children while Buchan had lost the brother closest to him in age and interests. Something of his feeling is expressed in the poem 'Fratri Dilectissimo: WHB' which serves as the dedication of the first Montrose biography. Susan later wrote of Willie's death:

> Of all the sorrows and tragedies I have seen, this was one of the most poignant. We watched the worsening of his condition and the complete helplessness of the doctors in the face of his mysterious illness, and tried to gather fortitude from his stark courage. He was one of the finest looking young men I have ever seen, and his outstanding work in the Indian Civil Service was admired and recognized.[9]

It is difficult to speculate how Willie would have fared if he had lived longer but, given his abilities and his character, it is likely he would have reached the highest levels of the Indian Civil Service. His early death placed an additional burden of responsibility on the thirty-five year old eldest Buchan son. Just as the death of J.M. Barrie's favoured brother had increased the maternal pressure on him to succeed, so too one can speculate that Willie's death placed an extra, unconscious pressure on Buchan to prove himself. It is from this period that Buchan, hitherto an active and healthy young man, began to be troubled by the duodenal ulcer from which he would suffer all his life and which he would give to one of his characters, Blenkiron. It had been present since his South African days and its condition had been aggravated by the long hours, little sleep and irregular meals of nursing the constituency. Now hard work and family worries, especially about his mother, had led to an intensification of the illness and the frequent need to spend several days at a time in bed. He cut back on his smoking, was careful to avoid beef or fruit and began to take doses of castor oil. The man of action was having to come to terms with the fact he would henceforth have to take life rather more easily, that his dreams might have to be realized in prose rather than in reality.

The six years between Buchan's marriage and the outbreak of the First World War were to be relatively fallow for him as a novelist as he sought to support his growing family and began to develop his political career. In November 1908 *Blackwood* published a series of his essays under the title *Some Eighteenth Century Byways*. He dedicated the book to his mother, surprisingly enough, the first time he had done so. Some of the essays had previously appeared in *Blackwood's Magazine*, the *Atlantic Monthly*, the *Quarterly Review* and the *Spectator* between 1900 and October 1908: others were specifically written for the book. The eighteenth century was a period that had always fascinated Buchan and to which he would continue to return in his later historical novels. The subjects in the book however ranged over the centuries and

Buchan's wide interests. There were favourites such as Prince Charles Edward, Lady Louisa Stuart an ancestor of Susan and later the subject of a book by her, Lord Mansfield, John Bunyan and Arthur Balfour but also articles on Tolstoy and Rabelais.

Many of Buchan's writings during this period were introductions to the various Nelson series for which he was responsible. These included Edgar Allan Poe's *Tales of Mystery and Imagination* (1911) and selections from Ralph Waldo Emerson (1909) and Edmund Burke (1911, reprinted 1925). Buchan remained fascinated by Burke all his life and later included an essay on the philosopher in his *Homilies and Recreations* published in 1926. The fact that Burke was not a party political animal and was torn between a literary and political career appealed to Buchan. He wrote self-revealingly of Burke 'All his life he stood a little apart from his contemporaries, and his detachment gave him a curious distinction. He was never quite Whig and never quite Tory, but a kind of impersonal magazine of universal truths.'[10]

Between April and September 1910 the boys' magazine *The Captain* had published in monthly parts a Buchan serial *The Black General*, the story of an educated black man returning to Africa to lead an indigenous revolt. Buchan had started to write the book while he was in South Africa and it was dedicated to a colleague there, Lionel Phillips. The book was published in August that year by Nelson under the title *Prester John* and in America by Dodd Mead with the title *The Great Diamond Pipe*. This was to be Buchan's first real success as a novelist. Editions quickly appeared in Norwegian, Swedish, Hungarian, Czech, Finnish, Dutch, French (as *Le prêtre Jean* or later *Le collier du prêtre Jean*), Italian (*Il serpente sacro*) and Spanish (*La serpiente de rubies*).

Nineteen year old David Crawfurd is training for the ministry at Edinburgh University when his father dies and he is sent to make his fortune in Africa. As his schoolmaster colleague, Wardlaw, tells him *en route* 'You'll exploit the pockets of the black men and I'll see what I can do with their minds.' On the boat David comes across the same black man, the Reverend John Laputa, whom he vividly remembers seeing several years earlier tracing a circle around a fire on the Fife sea shore. When he arrives in the Transvaal David further discovers that Laputa has set himself up as the incarnate spirit of Prester John, the fifteenth century King of Abyssinia and successor to the Zulu leader Chaka who had figured in Buchan's 1905 story 'The Kings of Orion'. Laputa is, as one character puts it, 'a sort of black Napoleon'. *Prester John* recounts David's adventures in trying to thwart both the ambitions of Laputa to encourage a rising against the European settlers and the jewel smuggling of the Portuguese Jew Henriques.

Almost all the reviews, which were generally favourable, referred to the

influence of R.L. Stevenson, and especially *Treasure Island*, but there are
several other debts. The 'delectable Mountains' come from Bunyan's *Pilgrim's
Progress*, and many critics have noted similarities with Rider Haggard especially *King Solomon's Mines* (1886) and *She* (1887). Much of the book is autobiographical. Crawfurd's father is minister of Kirkcaple and the adjoining
parish Portincross (Kirkcaldy and Pathhead) and Crawfurd attends the
burgh school. One of the characters Mr Colles shares the name of a literary
agent with whom Buchan was then regularly dealing. Buchan also drew
heavily on his own South African experiences. Blaauwildebeestefontein is
similar to the area that had so fascinated him, the Wood Bush, Machudi's glen
is like Machubi's glen in *The African Colony* while the fictional Pietersdorp is
Pietersburg.

At the centre of the book is John Laputa who may have been inspired by
Pambani T. Mzimba a black priest sent in 1893 to attend the jubilee of the Free
Church of Scotland. Another model was probably the African leader
Bambata who had led a revolt in Natal in 1906. Buchan was also drawing on
Ethiopianism, a movement of the 1870s when black converts to Christianity
set up their own missions under black ministers which became more overtly
political when the Abyssinians defeated the Italians at Adawa in 1896.
Laputa's phrase 'Africa for the Africans' had been coined by a mission-
educated African, Joseph Booth, in 1897. Laputa, despite its African sound,
was in fact the name of the Flying Island in *Gulliver's Travels*.[11]

Buchan had clearly given thought to the problems implicit in educating
Africans beyond the capacity of the European colonies to assimilate them
within their present structures. In drawing on his own knowledge of African
history he was also making a prophetic statement about black nationalism.
Prester John, which anticipated the very similar Nyasaland Rising of the
Reverend John Chilembwe in 1915, was supposedly a favourite of black
nationalists such as Jomo Kenyatta. Laputa is a tragic and impressive figure
on the grand scale, and dominates the novel. Buchan was heavily influenced
by the Calvinist preoccupation with the 'divided self', most obviously seen in
Stevenson's *Dr Jekyll and Mr Hyde*. Like many of Buchan's villains Laputa has
mixed qualities; 'there is no villainy he would not do if necessary and yet . . .
there's fineness and nobility in him.' And like many of the subsequent stories
Prester John explores the idea of the lost leader, 'the powerful charismatic man
who is destroyed for dark and unacceptable reasons.'[12]

Within the conventional framework of a *Bildungsroman* lie other Buchan
themes; there is the spirit of kingship that can be passed through generations,
later explored in *The Path of the King*; there is the preoccupation with myth and
primitive superstition; and as always there are hurried journeys. The narrative

drive of the book is much more accomplished than in his earlier books and already a number of character prototypes are emerging. There is something of Sandy Arbuthnot in Captain Arcoll of the Intelligence Department and of Richard Hannay in Aitken.

Though the reviews at the time were good, recent critics have been more divided. Jefferson Hunter has called it 'a nearly perfect work' but has criticised it for 'the unpleasant assumption that a white man has every right to gain the ancient treasure of the blacks and then transform the veld into a fertile agricultural district.'[13] The most obvious manifestation of this is a passage at the end in which David concludes:

> I knew then the meaning of the white man's duty. He has to take all the risks, recking nothing of his life or his fortunes, and well content to find his reward in the fulfilment of his task. That is the difference between white and black, the gift of responsibility, the power of being in a little way a king, and so long as we know this and practise it, we will rule not in Africa alone but wherever there are dark men who live only for the day and their own bellies.[14]

That is Crawfurd's view but not necessarily that of Buchan who gives Laputa a speech in which he exhorts his followers to overthrow the white man for it is 'A bastard civilization which has sapped your manhood; a false religion which would rivet on you the chains of the slave.' Laputa has always argued that Negroes 'have something to teach the British in the way of civilization.'[15]

The book goes beyond being about the white man's burden and the noble savage. It contrasts progress and primitivism symbolized by the plateau and the plains. It is a struggle, as Janet Adam Smith has shrewdly noted, not between black and white; it is between civilisation, towards which Laputa could be leading his people, and savagery, to which he is pulling them back.'[16] Where Scotland in the past has symbolised wildness to England's staidness, here Scotland is portrayed as civilisation in contrast to Africa's savagery. 'Behind me was the black night, and the horrid secrets of darkness. Before me was my own country, for that loch and that bracken might have been on a Scotch moor.'[17]

Critics have sometimes accused Buchan of racism, reading into novels, such as Prester John, an assumption of the superiority of white over black and this is fair comment for similar sentiments appear in later novels such as Greenmantle and Mr Standfast. In terms of race Buchan was not ahead of his contemporaries. For example John Laputa is a noble savage who though favourably compared with the 'Portugoose Jew' Henriques is still 'a Kaffir. He can see the first stage of a thing, and maybe the second but no more. That is the native mind.' Buchan's views reflected a general candid attitude. 'They were,' as the critic Gertrude Himmelfarb has pointed out, 'descriptive not prescriptive; not an incitement to novel political action, but an attempt to express differences of culture and color in terms that had been unquestioned for generations.'[18] In *Prester John* Buchan was exploring the thin dividing line between civilization and savagery which had characterized his early short stories and would later mark his thrillers. His own sympathies seem to rest with both sides of the divide and indeed his short story 'The Grove of Ashtaroth' published in June 1910 during the serialization of *Prester John* movingly depicts the natural beauty of pagan ritual.[19]

Sir Walter Raleigh had always fascinated Buchan. Here was another scholar gypsy figure. Raleigh had been the subject of Buchan's Stanhope Essay at Oxford and he had written about him for the *Scottish Review* in 1907. In 1911 he revised his earlier work for a popular biography in a Nelson series aimed at boys. He had also continued to write short stories, mainly for *Blackwood's Magazine*. These were collected by Blackwood's and published in April 1912 as *The Moon Endureth*; the stories interspersed with poems. Buchan dedicated the book to his father, who had died only five months earlier. The *Athenaeum* in their review noted the collection demonstrated 'a marked leaning towards the mysterious and the bizarre'; and it also showed 'considerable imagination, and occasionally a touch of delicate satire.'[20]

In 'Space' Buchan combined his fascination with the philosophical teachings of Henri Bergson and H. Poincare with the practical difficulties of climbing the Chamonix Aiguilles to produce a haunting story about the nature of reality. In 'A Lucid Interval' a drug is administered to politicians which induces them to tell the truth with disastrous results. In 'The Company of the Marjolaine' four American emissaries arrive at an Italian inn with an interesting proposal while 'The Green Glen' and 'The Grove of Ashtaroth' are both about the power evoked by place. The collection introduced a number of Buchan characters, most notably the lawyer Edward Leithen who would figure in five more novels and another collection of short stories; Tommy Deloraine in 'A Lucid Interval' appears in *The Power House* while Virginia Dasent in 'The Green Glen' is no doubt related to the Barbara Dasent in *Courts of the Morning*.

In December 1912 Buchan was the subject of another *Bookman* Profile. It stressed his literary descent from R.L. Stevenson and his 'peculiar blend of what one might call the pastoral and the picaresque', but also argued that he was beginning to develop his own unique style:

He has breathed a new life into the moribund art of the novel; he has made the short story what a cameo might be when it is cut by the hand of a master, and he has even contrived to make the light essay and occasional article an entertaining and scholarly production.[21]

It concluded 'Mr John Buchan has now attained his literary majority; we still wait for the great work; the more ambitious flight of his matured imagination.'[22]

One historical character that had always intrigued Buchan was James Graham, Marquis of Montrose. He had already written an essay on him, reprinted in *Some Eighteenth-Century Byways*, and he was to return to Montrose's life for several subsequent lectures and books. It is not difficult to see the attraction of Montrose for Buchan for here was a Calvinist-Platonist hero, who combined a life of action and thought, the sort of scholar-gipsy that so appealed to Buchan's own temperament. A biography of Montrose was an opportunity to bring alive the history, characters and topography of seventeenth century Scotland, a period which Buchan had covered in some of his early novels and which would fascinate him throughout his life. Here too he could demonstrate his great capacity to write vividly about military strategy. The clash of Church and State was a strong theme and its particular consequences as a result of Montrose's activities ones which had deeply affected Scottish history. So it was not just Montrose as an individual that so fascinated him but also his place in Scotland's history.

The book was written during 1912 while in bed at Portland Place and published in September 1913. It was the first book he had published since his brother's death almost two years earlier and he took the opportunity to dedicate it to Willie with a poem that reveals much about their relationship and Buchan's feeling for history:

When we were little wandering boys,
And every hill was blue and high,
On ballad ways and martial joys
We fed our fancies, you and I.
With Bruce we crouched in bracken shade,
With Douglas charged the Paynim foes;
And oft in moorland noons I played
Colkitto to your grave Montrose.

The reviews were mixed. The *TLS* thought it 'a brilliant and sympathetic sketch of Montrose, full of information and distinguished both by its style and by its insight,' while G.M. Trevelyan wrote to Buchan 'There is not a dull page on it and it is perfectly fair . . .'[23] Commentators, however, were gener-ally agreed that Buchan had overpraised Montrose at the expense of Argyll and the Estates. D. Hay Fleming's review in Buchan's old favourite the *British Weekly* and the comments by W.L. Mathieson in the *Scottish Historical Review* anticipated many of the criticisms later to be directed at Buchan's non-fiction. 'Men of Mr Buchan's gifts and temperament should eschew historical writing and devote themselves to avowed fiction,' argued Fleming, while Mathieson noted 'an asperity of tone and an unguardedness of statement which suggests the brilliant litterateur rather than the cautious historian.' Buchan was upset by the critical reception to the book and it was to be many years before he returned again to writing a full-length biography.[24]

In the spring of 1910 he and Susan had travelled on the Orient Express through the Balkans to Constantinople where they joined Gerard Craig Sellar on his yacht the *Rannoch* for a month's cruise in the Aegean. They visited Mount Olympus and Troy, where they had a guard of Turkish soldiers, sailed among the islands of the Aegean, visited the Acropolis and the Parthenon, saw Salamis and Delphi and climbed Parnassus before returning via Venice. Buchan wrote from Corfu to Charles Dick: 'Constantinople is pure Arabian Nights. My experiences varied from lunching in state with the Sultan's brother and dining at Embassies to chaffering with Kurds for carpets in a sort of underground Bazaar. I don't know any place where one feels history more vividly.' The trip inspired the short story 'The Lemnian', written after seeing the battlefield at Thermopylae, and the short story 'Basilissa', which would develop into Buchan's 1926 novel *The Dancing Floor*.[25]

For the summers of 1911 and 1912 Buchan went with Tommy Nelson to fish the swiftly flowing waters of the Leardal in Norway, experiences he used in *The Three Hostages* and *The Island of Sheep*. Another summer holiday was spent at Rosensee in Bavaria with the Moritz Bonns, fishing, walking and boating. Buchan drew on the holiday for background in *Greenmantle*, *A Prince of the Captivity* and the *Huntingtower* trilogy. It was while climing the Alpspritz with a young forester on that Bavarian holiday that Buchan, always sensitive to atmosphere, had the premonition of a hostile spirit watching him which he later described in his memoirs:

Terror, had seized me also, but I did not know what I dreaded; it was like the epidemic of giggling which overcomes children who have no wish to laugh. We ran — we ran like demented bacchanals, tearing down the glades, leaping rocks, bursting through thickets, colliding with trees, sometimes colliding with each other, and all the time we never uttered a sound.[26]

He had taken up deer-stalking when he married, attracted by the opportunities it presented to spend time outdoors in wild countryside with countrymen and the thrill of the chase rather than the kill. Most holidays therefore were
spent in Scotland either with the Buchans and Mastertons in the Borders or
with friends. There were fishing or sailing holidays at Achnacloich, Tommy
Nelson's property on Loch Etive and visits to Johnnie Jameson's parents Lord
and Lady Ardwall near Gatehouse-of-Fleet which Buchan had known since
his days at Oxford. Johnnie's father had been appointed to the Scottish Court
of Session in 1904 and taken the title Lord Ardwall. Lord Ardwall was a
throw back to the eighteenth century. Susan later described him as 'a somewhat alarming host, with his stocky figure, cherry-coloured face, a shock of
white hair and flashing dark blue eyes. He roared his remarks to his family and
visitors in the voice of a bull.'[27]

Buchan was only too delighted to accede to a family request to write Lord
Ardwall's biography after his death in November 1911. The book was published in November 1913 by Blackwoods and is especially revealing of
Buchan's own feelings about Scotland, her traditions and her people. The first
part of the book is a conventional hagiography but it is enlivened with some
marvellous descriptions and epigrams and Buchan expertly conveys the
Falstaffian exuberance of his subject.

> He was not tolerant of folly; he was not very tolerant even of reasoned
> opposition; but there was never less bitterness in a human soul. He had
> always an honest difficulty in understanding the point of view of a Radical
> and was wont to attribute it charitably to some stomachic derangement.[28]

The best part of the book is Buchan's own personal recollections of Lord
Ardwall from the 1898 meeting at the Gridiron Club of 'a figure who might
have stepped out of a Raeburn picture' to their pursuit together of 'hares on
horseback with a greyhound over the briar-clad dykes and bogs of a Galloway
moor.' He understood Jameson well not just because they had been personally
acquainted but because they were both Scotsmen, lawyers and country gentlemen. As a result *Andrew Jameson, Lord Ardwall* was amongst the most perceptive of all his biographies.

During the first three months of 1914 Buchan was hard at work on a new
novel which marked a departure in subject matter. He had always been interested in American history and the early American settlers. As pioneers they
appealed to his sense of romance and adventure. *Salute to Adventurers* is about
a young Glasgow merchant in the tobacco trade in Virginia. At the centre of
the novel is mad Muckle John Gibb who, like Laputa, seeks to overthrow the

established state. Many of the recurrent Buchan themes and traits are there —
the secret grove associated with a girl, the ability to describe terrain and military tactics. For someone who had still not crossed the Atlantic Buchan evokes
the Jamestown manors and plantations with vividness and skill. The book
was published in July 1915 and dedicated to Susie's uncle by marriage Sir
Reginald Talbot, who had taken part in the American Civil War.

Throughout 1914 new clouds of war began to descend. At the end of June
the Archduke Franz Josef was assassinated and on 4 August Britain declared
war against Germany. A few days earlier Buchan had breakfast with Edward
Grey, the Foreign Secretary, at 28 Queen Anne Gate. As he reported to
George Brown he found '. . . there was such a change in him. All the lassitude has gone and there was a kind of sober competence about him which
impressed me deeply.'[29]

The summer of 1914 was a time of personal as well as public anxiety. Alice
needed a mastoid operation and Susan's family had financial difficulties which
required his intervention. In August in order to provide Alice, now aged six,
with some fresh air the family took lodgings at St Ronan's, a large house on
Stone Road, Broadstairs, close to the Arthur Grenfells, cousins of Susie, who
had been lent a house with steps down to a private beach on the North
Foreland. It was there Buchan completed the book with which his name is
indivisibly associated – *The Thirty-Nine Steps*.

8

TRIUMPH AND TRAGEDY

IN December 1913 Buchan's first attempt at a thriller, *The Power House*, had been serialized in *Blackwood's Magazine*. Its success – it was subsequently carried in the American magazine *The Living Age* in January and February 1914 – encouraged him to start another novel, the idea for which had been gestating for some time. In July 1914 he wrote to George Brown 'I am sending you the "shocker" which I spoke of.'[1] By the beginning of December, after another period confined to bed and a trip in September to Ardtornish, it was finished. Under the title *The Black Stone*, he sent it to George Blackwood with a note 'I have amused myself in bed writing a shocker of the style of *The Power House*, only more so. It has amused me to write, but whether it will amuse you to read is another matter.'[2]

Blackwood did find it amusing and thrilling. There was some discussion about the title which Buchan suggested changing to *The Kennels of War*. By 28th January the two had agreed on the title – *The Thirty-Nine Steps*. The book was serialized in *Blackwood's Magazine* in three parts between July and September under the pseudonymn 'H de V' and published by Blackwoods in October. No one knows why Buchan chose a pseudonym and why this particular name but a fellow member of the Ingoldsby at Brasenose had been a H. du Vallon. Buchan dedicated it to Tommy Nelson, describing the book as a 'romance where the incidents defy the probabilities and march just inside the borders of the possible.'[3]

Review coverage was limited. *The Athenaeum*, which reviewed it alongside D.H. Lawrence's *The Rainbow*, thought it had 'a literary flavour, and a distant echo of Stevenson's *New Arabian Nights*'. *The TLS* thought the book 'enthralling' and pointed out how part of Buchan's skill:

is to make the reader feel that he himself was the hero. It was we who showed all this courage and resource; it was we who read Scudder's cypher; we who whistled 'Annie Laurie' to the great Foreign Office personage . . . we are heartily grateful to Mr Buchan for giving the world so vivid and truthful a narrative of our adventures, escapes, and achievements.[4]

Cynthia Asquith after reading it noted in her diary 'It is well-written and quite fun, but too full of glaring improbabilities, not to say impossibilities, which do not always succeed in giving that 'willing suspension of disbelief'. The hero certainly has amazing luck.'[5] However her reaction was untypical. The novel struck a chord in a nation obsessed with German spy fever and, within three months of publication, The Thirty-Nine Steps had sold over 25,000 copies.

Richard Hannay, a thirty seven year old mining engineer, returns to London after thirty years in Rhodesia. One night in May 1914 near his flat off Portland Place he is stopped by an American who claims to have stumbled on a conspiracy 'to get Russia and Germany at loggerheads' and asks for Hannay's help. A plot has been uncovered to murder the Greek Premier, Karolides, possibly based on the then Greek premier Eleutherios Venizelos, while on an official visit to London on 15 June. The American, Franklin P. Scudder, is killed shortly afterwards but Hannay finds his notebook with a cryptic message about 'The Thirty-Nine Steps'. Hannay decides to flee to Scotland fearing he himself might be charged with the murder and with Scudder's murderers after him determined to take on Scudder's quest.

The novel is picaresque, consisting of a series of adventures, many of them drawn from Buchan's own experience. Hannay is chased across the Galloway moors by both the police and German spies. He meets an innkeeper with literary aspirations, speaks at a Liberal political meeting and encounters 'the Spectacled Roadman' and 'the Bald Archaeologist', before being captured by the Black Stone, the German spy-ring, when he takes refuge in a farmhouse which it transpires is their headquarters. He escapes using his knowledge gained as a mining engineer and heads for Artinswell on the Kennett, the home of the Permanent Secretary at the Foreign Office, Sir Walter Bullivant, godfather of the Liberal Candidate. There he learns that Scudder was known to Sir Walter and while he is there news reaches them that Karolides has been murdered.

He then goes to Bullivant's home in Queen Anne's Gate, in reality home to Lord Haldane, Sir Edward Grey, Harold Baker and the British Intelligence Service. Here he discovers that the First Sea Lord, Lord Alloa, has been replaced by a member of the Black Stone who in disguise attends a crucial meeting at which Britain's secret naval plans are discussed. However he betrays himself to Hannay by an involuntary flicker of recognition. Hannay works out that the thirty nine steps hold the key to capturing the gang and given the tides they must be a set of steps to the sea at the coastal town of Bradgate. The action moves to Bradgate and the refined tranquillity of Trafalgar Lodge owned by a Mr Appleton. The Black Stone is rounded up and three weeks later war is declared.[6]

The book was written and appeared against the backdrop of German spy scares. *The Thirty-Nine Steps* owed much, particularly in terms of its strong sense of atmosphere, to Erskine Childers' *The Riddle of the Sands* published in 1903 which Nelson had published in their Sevenpenny library series in 1910 and Buchan had certainly read. Reviewing a reissue of *The Riddle of the Sands* in *John O'London's Weekly* in 1926 Buchan described the book as 'the best story of adventure published in the last quarter of a century'. Buchan admired Childers and ten years later, paying tribute to him in *The King's Grace* thought that 'no revolution ever produced a nobler or purer spirit.'[7] Childers had been a Clerk in the House of Commons working alongside Buchan's flat-mate Austin Smythe when his book was published and it is possible that Buchan met Childers in this way. Another link was another Clerk in the Commons, Basil Williams, who had been Secretary of the Transvaal Education Department when Buchan was in South Africa. All three men were members of the same rambling club 'The Sunday Tramps' founded by Leslie Stephen in 1879. Other members included R.B. Haldane, Leonard Woolf, G.M. Trevelyan, Robert Bridges and John Simon. Buchan had joined in November 1908 and one of its most recent members was Stanley Baldwin.

The Thirty-Nine Steps is a more sophisticated thriller than those of Buchan's contemporaries such as William Le Queux and Phillips Oppenheim, though marred by some of the same reliance on coincidences and improbabilities. The quality of its writing, plot and characterization are for a start much higher. Its first person narrative gives the story pace and authenticity, helped by Buchan's ability to convey the cadences of Hannay's speech. Richard Hannay was to become the best known of Buchan's fictional characters. The present Lord Ironside has argued that Hannay 'was modelled, 100%' on his father Edmund Ironside and 'his secret service tours of duty in Pretoria and Hereroland in 1901 and in German South-West Africa in 1902–04.'[8] At the time, so the present Lord Ironside claims, Buchan was attached to Lord Methuen's staff as Head of Policy and Planning and the two men had met occasionally. Buchan was also able to draw from official secret records, to which he had access, to give authenticity to his story.

There are certainly similarities between Hannay and Ironside in that both spoke Cape Dutch or *taal* and both were adept at disguise. The identification of Ironside as the model for Hannay was confirmed by Buchan's son Johnnie shortly after his father's death and has since been commonly accepted by all writers about Buchan. However there are very real differences between the two men, not least that Ironside was a professional soldier while Hannay is a mining engineer drawn unwittingly into the drama. It is far more likely that, while Buchan no doubt drew on the exploits of Ironside, Hannay is a composite portrait which owes something to Edward Gleichen, Baden Powell and David Henderson. Henderson had been Director of Military Intelligence in South Africa during the Boer War and his book *Field Intelligence, its Principles and Practice* published in 1904, had had an introduction by General Sir Neville Lyttelton. Another possible influence is Archibald Wavell, the future Lord Wavell, a Russian speaker and a colleague of Gleichen's in the Intelligence Branch.[9]

One reason for the novel's enduring popularity is its strong narrative pace and Buchan's ability to capture the smells, sounds and sights of the wild Scottish moors which gives the story a power and an immediacy. However *The Thirty-Nine Steps* is a much richer book than one might assume, filled as it is with historical, literary and biblical allusions and with strong mythical undertones. Hannay has been called 'a twentieth-century Odysseus' and in his position as a man hunted by both the villains and the police has come to be recognized as an important symbolic figure in the history of the thriller.[10] Many Buchan themes are present, most notably the importance of disguise. Hannay passes himself off in turn as milkman, political candidate, road sweeper, tramp and shepherd while his enemies are equally adept at concealing their real identities. There is the theme of the 'hurried journey' as Hannay moves quickly from London to Scotland where he is pursued across the moors and back to London. Familiar territory such as Galloway and London are revealed to harbour frightening aspects. Above all *The Thirty-Nine Steps* is marked by Hannay's innocent enjoyment of the chase which he compares to 'schoolboy hare and hounds'.

Throughout the autumn of 1914 Buchan had continued to suffer from the ulcer that increasingly impinged on his daily life. At the end of October he was ordered by his doctor, Sir Bertrand Dawson, later Lord Dawson of Penn, to rest if he was to avoid an operation. His wife wrote to him: 'I must just say how I think the strength and beauty of your character is coming out now . . . You are facing it so cheerfully my own precious, darling. You are so everything to your Punchie Munch.'[11]

He, however, did not remain idle. He had tried to join the army but was rejected on grounds of his age and health. He immediately threw himself into a new kind of war work. He suggested that Nelson, partly as a public service and partly to provide work for the printing works, should produce a history of the war. At first there was concern among the Nelson partners about the format. Buchan wrote to George Brown:

> I do not think we shall get absolutely accurate details of most of the fighting till after the war, and therefore a history on the scale of the *Times* or the *Daily Mail* is impossible; but I am satisfied that three months after the fighting we shall know enough to write an accurate history on the scale which I propose – viz monthly parts.[12]

Arthur Conan Doyle was the first choice to edit the history but said he was too busy. At the beginning of September Buchan approached his Oxford friend, Hilaire Belloc, with a contract. Belloc was to write a 60,000 word text with maps by the third week of October for publication in the first week of November. Further volumes were to be delivered and published at three monthly intervals. Negotiation took some time with a shifting delivery date until in mid-October Belloc finally agreed to take on the task. At the last moment Belloc dropped out and Buchan was forced to take his place. One of Buchan's crowning, and largely unrecognized, achievements was the result.

The Nelson History of the War was to run to over a million words and occupy Buchan's attention for the next five years. Even with the research assistance he received it is a remarkable achievement, which becomes staggering when one realises what else he was involved in during the war. The *History* first appeared in February 1915 with a preface by Lord Rosebery. A further twenty three parts appeared at regular intervals throughout the war and the whole work was then revised for a shorter edition in 1922. The profits, including Buchan's own royalties, were donated to war charities or to the families of Nelson's men who had enlisted. In the *History* Buchan shows his customary skills as an historian and writer – his control of a vast amount of material, his ability to convey the excitement and ennui of war, a strong narrative pace, an analysis of military strategy – to produce a remarkably accurate account of the war on all its fronts.

It noticeably raised his profile and throughout the spring of 1915 he undertook a series of lectures to raise money for war charities with the result that *The Times* and *Daily News* decided to use him as a correspondent. He was one of five journalists to be attached to the British army, after pressure was put on the Government by Reuters and other news organizations. In May 1915 he was sent to write up the second Battle of Ypres and then in October 1915, the month *The Thirty-Nine Steps* was published, sent as an observer at the battle of Loos. Buchan was a natural journalist and the first hand experience of the Front proved useful for both his lectures and books. One admirer was Leo Amery who wrote to his wife:

> I read John Buchan's articles in *The Times* and thought them excellent. He is a born journalist in the very best sense of the word – he can sense a situation quickly and can with the minimum of effort make a vivid story of it . . . If John had seen all I've seen of this war he'd have made three most readable books of it.[13]

The articles in *The Times* brought Buchan into contact with the General Headquarters Staff, who offered him a job drafting communiques at Haig's HQ. Buchan had known Haig for many years as a Border neighbour, a former Brasenose man and an elder of St Columbas and was happy to join the GHQ staff. Throughout 1916 the War Office and Foreign Office also began to make more use of him and were particularly keen for him to continue with the *History of the War*. They saw it as useful for propaganda purposes though they were worried about its content, given the access he had to secret material. 'It would be very difficult for him to write his history without criticizing officers and actions on the Western Front,' wrote General Charteris to Lord Newton in July 1916. 'Such criticism should not, I think, come from anyone who has access to such papers as we propose to show Buchan.' It was suggested someone else might write the chapter on the Western Front, and Buchan even offered to give up the *History* but in the end he continued to write it alongside his more confidential activities at GHQ.[14]

One of the British Government's priorities was to persuade the Russians to contribute more to the Allied war effort and together with his Oxford contemporary, Humphrey Milford, Buchan became involved in preparing a series of pamphlets for translation into Russian with that aim in mind.[15] In February 1916 Buchan escorted a Russian press delegation, which included Vladimir Nabokov, the father of the novelist, to see the British fleet at Scapa Flow and in May, he organized a further trip to Scotland, this time of members of the Russian Duma. They went to Glasgow where they saw the University, a munitions works and the shipbuilders John Brown before again going on to Scapa Flow.[16] One of the consequences of his involvement with the Russians was his election at the end of March 1917 as a member of The Russia Company, membership of which was restricted to those with experience of Russian affairs. Among those elected the previous March had been a number of friends including Maurice Baring, Harold Baker, Lord Hugh Cecil and J. St Loe Strachey.

On 26 June 1916 Buchan arrived at GHQ France where he was reunited with Raymond Asquith then on the Intelligence Staff. The following week he was gazetted as a Second Lieutenant in the Intelligence Corps. The Intelligence Corps had been formed at the outbreak of war and among its early recruits had been a number of Buchan's friends, including Basil Blackwood. Anyone permanently employed on Intelligence work became part of the Intelligence Corps, but so too did personnel on support duties such as censorship, publicity and propaganda; it was under these auspices that Buchan joined the Corps, not because he was actually engaged in spying. He had a roving commission to handle press matters, particularly the organizations of visits to the Front by foreign journalists. He reported to General Charteris and was responsible for preparing communiques and weekly summaries of the action at the Front for transmission to British embassies throughout the world. One of his first tasks was to write an account of the initial phase of the Battle of the Somme, which he expanded from a volume of his *History of the War*. This was published in two volumes in November 1916 and the spring of 1917 as *The Battle of the Somme, First Phase* and *The Battle of the Somme, Second Phase* and was quickly translated into Dutch, Danish, Portuguese, Spanish and Swedish.[17]

Buchan's writing skills had also been utilized by Charles Masterman's War Propaganda Bureau. The purpose of the Bureau's books, many of which went into foreign editions, was to maintain civilian morale and encourage foreign support. Several of them were published by Nelson. This served the dual purpose of disguising their origin and keeping the Nelson plant in business. Buchan's contributions included *Britain's War By Land* (1915) published by OUP in a series of propaganda pamphlets aimed at foreign countries, a collection of his Times articles *The Achievement of France* (1915), *The Battle of Jutland* (1916) two books *The Battle of the Somme* and *The Battle of Picardy* the last of which had a preface by Lloyd George.[18]

The Somme books have been criticized as inaccurate and naive, not least by Peter Buitenhuis in his study of First World War propaganda:

> The account contains all the ringing cliches and exaggerations of the genre, and by representing that almost unmitigated hell in such glowing colours, Buchan falsifies the whole military situation on the Western Front. By his omissions and exaggerated claims he makes not only the common soldier but also the commanding generals look superb.[19]

However it does need to be remembered that the books were written with the express intention of raising morale and Buchan himself made no great claims for them as lasting works of history. The critical comments about the war scattered throughout his letters and the novels written at the time, reveal that he had no illusions about the folly of the War and its conduct.

He well knew the reality of the Somme. Stair Gillon had served as a captain in an infantry brigade there and Raymond Asquith had been killed during the second phase of the attack. In his account of the battle Buchan paid tribute to him in a phrase that has become part of the formula of Great War commemoration: 'debonair and brilliant and brave, he is now part of that immortal England which knows not age or weariness or defeat'.[20] In fact Buchan was keen to ensure that a proper record of the conflict was kept and suggested to Haig the idea of a Historical Department at GHQ. The plan was to have an officer attached to each Army headquarters with access to all the material being processed so that history could be recorded as it was happening. Before any decisions could be taken he was recalled home and nothing came of it.[21]

Buchan was a popular member of Haig's staff at GHQ. James Marshall-Cornwall, then an Intelligence Officer at GHQ and an outstanding linguist, remembered Buchan joining the officers' mess 'where his brilliant talk and dry Scottish humour made him a congenial companion'.[22] Another portrait of Buchan at the time comes from the writer Howard Spring, also attached to Haig's staff.

I remember John Buchan, a cavalier if ever there was one, always commanding our respect but never forgetting how to unbend. It is a mystery to me how he got through the days as he did. He was doing his work as an Intelligence Officer; he was writing his history of the war; and he was somehow fitting in novels as well.[23]

Spring tells the story of how Buchan insisted on giving his sergeant a Christmas present, at a time when it was unknown for an officer to give an 'other rank' a Christmas present, but this was typical of Buchan's warm personality. The sergeant had the sense to say flatteringly that he would like an autographed copy of Buchan's latest novel *Greenmantle*, 'a reply which suggests an aptitude for the Diplomatic Service rather than the Methodist ministry which I know he decorates, and I trust adorns.'[24]

By the autumn of 1916 Buchan was spending most of his time at the Front and his health was beginning to be affected by the long hours, irregular meals and poor conditions. In October he suffered an acute attack of indigestion in his billet and after hours of trying to attract the attention of a sentry was taken to a Casualty Clearing Station. He was suffering from what was thought to be appendicitis, but in fact was diagnosed as a duodenal ulcer and at the end of February 1917 he underwent a two hour 'short-circuiting' operation at Portland Place. It was a major operation which would have rendered most men bedridden for months. Instead Buchan spent a month convalescing at the Oliver's home, Checkendon, where Susan and the children had been evacu- ated and then started a new job.

In December 1916 Asquith had been replaced by Lloyd George and Milner was included in the small War Cabinet. He immediately brought his own 'Milner men' into key positions. Leo Amery was taken from the army to act as a political secretary to the War Cabinet, Arthur Steel-Maitland, the MP for East Birmingham and an Oxford Union colleague of Buchan, went as a Junior Minister to the Colonial Office and then to the Foreign Office with a responsibility for Intelligence. Philip Kerr, later Lord Lothian, became one of Lloyd George's Private Secretaries. Buchan was put forward to run a propa- ganda department.

Propaganda was not a new weapon in the Government's armoury. Shortly after war broke out Charles Masterman, now a Cabinet Minister, had been appointed to head a propaganda bureau based at Wellington House, Buckingham Gate. On 2 September 1914 he brought together twenty five leading British authors to discuss propaganda. They included J.M. Barrie, Arnold Bennett, Robert Bridges, G.K. Chesterton, Sir Arthur Conan Doyle, John Galsworthy, Thomas Hardy, Anthony Hope Hawkins, John Masefield, Gilbert Murray, Sir Henry Newbolt, G.M. Trevelyan and H.G. Wells. Rudyard Kipling and Sir Arthur Quiller Couch, though unable to attend, also offered their services. Surprisingly Buchan was not included. Since the beginning of the war there had also been several unofficial organiza- tions devoted to propaganda work. The Central Committee for National Patriotic Associations had been formed in August 1914 with Asquith as hon- orary president and the Earl of Rosebery and Arthur Balfour as vice-presi- dents. This central committee co-ordinated the activities of other groups such as 'The Fight for Right Movement', founded by Sir Francis Younghusband, whose members included Buchan, Thomas Hardy, Henry Newbolt and Gilbert Murray.[25]

At the beginning of 1917 Robert Donald, the editor of the Liberal *Daily Chronicle* and a friend of Lloyd George, was asked to prepare a report on pro- paganda. He argued that the propaganda effort needed to be less defensive and suggested three deputy directors be appointed, one of whom should be Buchan because of his work for Lord Newton, the present nominal head of propaganda. A few weeks later the Cabinet discussed the question of propa- ganda and the deputy director posts. Milner championed Buchan for the job of director but Lloyd George was 'inclined to think that Buchan was too purely a literary man, and had been told to get the help of a Manchester Professor called Ramsay Muir'. It was only an intervention by Curzon and then Amery seems to have helped Buchan secure the job.[26]

A Department of Information, with the responsibility for coordinating all foreign propaganda, was officially set up by the War Cabinet on 20 February, and announced the following day in *The Times*. Foreign propaganda had previously come under the wing of the War Propaganda Bureau, the Home Office's Neutral Press Committee and the News Department of the Foreign Office. Now at last there was some sort of rationalization of the propaganda effort with central financial control and one record office. A distinction was to be made between literary and news propaganda and more emphasis placed on propaganda abroad. Buchan was put in charge at an annual salary of £1,000 and on 25 February was gazetted an unpaid Lieutenant Colonel on the Special List.

The Department was divided into four sections: Charles Masterman at Wellington House was in charge of a Production Section responsible solely for books, pamphlets, photographs and the records by official war artists; the Press and Cinema Section under T.L. Gilmour, based in the Lord Chancellor's Office in the House of Lords, dealt with cables, wireless, press and cinema; the Intelligence branch at 82 Victoria Street under Lord Edward Gleichen replaced George Mair's Neutral Press Committee and ensured news was quickly disseminated from Government departments to the propagandists; finally the Administrative Division, under Hubert Montgomery, the Deputy Director, at the Foreign Office, dealt with finance and liaison with other Government Departments. Buchan was based in the Foreign Office but made a point of visiting the other branches as much as possible.[27]

He brought in as his personal assistant Stair Gillon, who had been wounded in Macedonia, together with a number of other Oxford contacts including the explorer Reginald Farrer, E.S.P. Haynes and the cricketer Pelham Warner. Other members of the department included Stephen Gaselee, the Librarian of Magdalene College, Cambridge, Hugh Walpole, who had been serving with the Red Cross in Russia, Ian Hay Beith, Sir Ernest Shackleton and the historians Arnold Toynbee, Robert Seton-Watson and L.B. Namier. The head of Reuters, Roderick Jones, whom Buchan had known in South Africa, was appointed to run the section on cable and wireless propaganda, F.S. Oliver went briefly to the British Dominions Section and Alexander Watt was made the Department's Literary Agent.[28]

Like Masterman, Buchan was scrupulous that propaganda should be an accurate account of events, which brought him into conflict with many who

ABOVE: John Buchan's birthplace, 20 York Place, Perth.
Reproduced by permission of Andrew Lownie.

ABOVE: The Masterton family farm, Broughton where J.B. spent most of his family holidays.
Reproduced by permission of Andrew Lownie.

ABOVE: John Buchan, J.B.'s Grandfather
Reproduced by permission of Lord Tweedsmuir.
BELOW LEFT: Uncle Willie who introduced J.B. to the French Classics.
Reproduced by permission of Lord Tweedsmuir.
BELOW RIGHT: The Reverend John Buchan, J.B's father.
Reproduced by permission of Strathclyde Regional Archives.

ABOVE: Masters and senior boys at Hutchinsons', 1891. James Cadell is seated second from right with J.B. standing behind him second from right.
Reproduced by permission of Hutchinsons' Grammar School.
BELOW LEFT: 34 Queen Mary Avenue, Glasgow, where J.B. lived as a child.
Reproduced by permission of Andrew Lownie.
BELOW RIGHT: The Rose Street Church, Glasgow where J.B.'s father was the Minister for over twenty years. *Reproduced by permission of Strathclyde Regional Archives.*

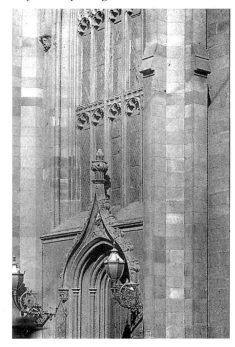

ABOVE: J.B.'s Oxford lodgings, 105 High Street (second house on left) during his final year in Oxford. *Reproduced by permission of the Oxford Photographic Archive.* BELOW LEFT: The Oxford Union Society Committee 1898. J.B., then Librarian, is seated left with his hands on Johnnie Jameson and E.C. Bentley, inventor of the clerihew, is seated extreme right. *Reproduced by permission of the Oxford Union Society.*

ABOVE LEFT: J.B. with Alan Breck in South Africa *c.*1902.
ABOVE RIGHT: J.B. on his bicycle in South Africa *c.*1902. *Both reproduced by permission of Lord Tweedsmuir.*
BELOW: Milners Young Men. Hugh Wyndham extreme left, Robert Brand standing third left, Philip Kerr sits on the floor centre with Geoffrey Robinson to his left. *Reproduced by permission of the South African Library.*

ABOVE LEFT: J.B. on honeymoon at the Venice Lido, August 1907. *Reproduced by permission of Lord Tweedsmuir.*
ABOVE RIGHT: J.B. and Susan skating. *Reproduced by permission of Lord Tweedsmuir.*
BELOW: J.B. with his first child Alice, in 1908. *Reproduced by permission of Lord Tweedsmuir.*

LEFT: J.B. with his parents, brothers, sister, wife and first child, 1908. *Reproduced by permission of Lord Tweedsmuir.*

BELOW: 76 Portland Place, the Buchans' home. *Reproduced by permission of the National Monuments Record.*

ABOVE: A weekend party at Terling, 1913. *Reproduced by permission of Hon. Guy Strutt.*
BELOW LEFT: J.B. with his two eldest children at Broadstairs in the summer of 1914 while writing *The Thirty-nine Steps. Reproduced by permission of Lord Tweedsmuir.*
BELOW RIGHT: St Cubys, the house rented by cousins of Suan Buchan at the top of the 'thirty-nine' steps. *Reproduced by permission of Andrew Lownie.*

felt there should be a more vociferous propaganda campaign. However a number of changes were made including a greater emphasis on newspapers and film. Indeed the Department expanded the use of film, for example of the Battles of the Somme and Arras, and made greater use of war artists, such as John Sargent, Wilson Steer, William Orpen, Muirhead Bone, Paul Nash and Christopher Nevinson, to bring the reality of the carnage home to the general public.[29] It is often assumed that Buchan personally championed sending war artists, such as Paul Nash, to the Front. In fact the opposite is the case. Buchan had visited Nash's exhibition at the Goupil Gallery in June 1917 and arranged to see Nash at the Foreign Office but he personally did not like Nash's work and it was only after testimonials from William Rothenstein and others that Buchan agreed to send him.[30]

One of Buchan's priorities was to keep American opinion informed about the course of the war. A British Information Bureau was set up in New York, lecturers such as Gilbert Murray were sent out and American journalists brought over from America on visits to the Front. His period at the Department of Information strengthened Buchan's belief in the importance of Anglo-American relations. One of his initiatives was to set up an informal Anglo-American Society in London with Gilbert Murray as President. At the same time a Press Bureau was set up in Paris and the work of the British Institute in Florence extended.[31]

Another of Buchan's responsibilities was briefing King George V on the progress of the war. In May 1917 he told his wife: 'I had a busy day yesterday, a good deal of it spent at Buckingham Palace. I have had many queer jobs in my life, but this is the queerest.' Buchan in later life liked to suggest that he had undertaken intelligence work. In his memoirs he wrote: 'I have some queer macabre recollections of those years – of meetings with odd people in odd places, of fantastic duties which a romancer would have rejected as beyond probability.' His son William remembers being told that his father would have meetings at the Cafe Royal under the pseudonym Captain Stewart.[32]

There is, however, no evidence that Buchan at this stage was directly involved in Intelligence work. As a report by Buchan to Sir Edward Carson of November 1917 stated: 'The Bureau has nothing to do with naval or military intelligence and is concerned with economic intelligence only so far as that affects politics. Its business is to collect information on the *political* situation and the trend of feeling and opinion in the different countries.'[33] However, the Intelligence branch did receive ordinary published intelligence reports, such Secret Service reports on political matters as the Foreign Office saw fit to provide and private communications. It is probably from such sources, rather than direct experience, that Buchan drew for the authenticity of his writing.

Meanwhile Susan was making her own contribution to the war effort. She was doing part-time administrative work for the V.A.D., twice a week went to an Infant Welfare Centre in Kentish Town and had helped set up a day-nursery in Gospel Oak Grove. She had now taken the family to Bidborough in Kent for the summer and Buchan was able to join them most weekends.

By the summer of 1917 Buchan was running into difficulties in the Department. At the beginning of June he was summoned to No. 10 and lec-tured by Lloyd George about being too much under the thumb of the Foreign Office. The following month Lord Burnham noted that Lloyd George thought Buchan 'was not the right man for the job, in which opinion we all agree'.[34] On the 7 August *The Times* joined in the criticism:

> We were in high hopes when Buchan was created 'Director of Information', a sufficiently comprehensive title. But Mr Buchan turns out to be virtually a subordinate of the Foreign Office where he works. His work, we are sure, is of the greatest national importance. The point is that he is merely that of an addition to the existing publicity departments, not that of a supreme co-ordinating centre.[35]

Buchan's principal difficulties were in obtaining information from the Service Departments and decisions from the Prime Minister. Leo Amery noted in his diary later that month: 'He can never get access to Lloyd George, who on the other hand continually sees that ruffian Donald of the *Chronicle*. He has no sufficient power to deal with questions like censorship, and the question is whether he should resign or confine himself strictly to foreign pro-paganda.'[36] Throughout 1917 Robert Donald had criticized both the Department and Buchan, partly motivated by his own desire for the job of running propaganda. There were suggestions of extravagance, of waste and inefficiencies, of too great an emphasis on film and too little on the expertise of journalists such as Robert Donald.[37] Donald was closely in touch with Lloyd George and persuaded him to set up an advisory propaganda committee, con-sisting of Northcliffe, or Beaverbrook while Northcliffe was in America, Lord Burnham the managing proprietor of the *Daily Telegraph*, himself and C.P. Scott of the *Manchester Guardian*, to keep an eye on Buchan.[37] Eventually, totally frustrated, Buchan appealed through Milner in September for someone to be appointed above him with a voice in Cabinet. Sir Edward Carson, who had been Attorney General and First Lord of the Admiralty before becom-ing a member of the War Cabinet without Portfolio earlier in the year, was brought in as the link man.

Official British Propaganda under Carson now had three branches.

Buchan was head of Foreign Propaganda with four divisions under him – Administration, Literary Production, Press & Cinema and Intelligence. Home Propaganda, previously the National War Aims Committee, was the responsibility of the Chief Whip Frederick Guest while military propaganda was left to M17 run by a colonel at the War Office. The change solved nothing. Buchan still found it difficult to obtain decisions from Lloyd George and was hurt to discover that the Prime Minister was supporting Donald's attempts to hold his own private inquiry into the Department. Meanwhile Carson, who had a poor relationship in any case with Lloyd George, was more concerned with problems in Ireland than the work of Buchan's Department.

In December Donald presented the report on the Department commissioned by Lloyd George two months earlier. In it he claimed propaganda was still dominated by the Foreign Office, there was a lack of unity and co-ordination, it was bureaucratic and more centralization was required. He said the Department had failed to use the foreign press sufficiently, the cables & wireless branch was amateurish, there were inadequate dealings with the British press, too much pamphlet material from Wellington House, no testing of the effectiveness of propaganda and too many people employed in the Department. He concluded: 'I am of the opinion that the Department's activities are altogether inadequate and in some cases misdirected. Much time has been lost and many opportunities missed, and the necessity for rapidity of actions is not yet fully appreciated.'[39]

They were harsh charges and not entirely fair. Both Buchan and Masterman suspected that Donald had capitalized on Lloyd George's distrust of officials and the inquiry was only part of a campaign to give journalists greater say in propaganda activity. They felt the investigations had been perfunctory and the criticisms lacked detailed evidence. Buchan was particularly upset that the inquiry report had been leaked to the *Daily Chronicle*.[40] He accepted that the Department was not perfect but pointed out how difficult it was to relay propaganda:

> Most men and all journalists consider themselves to be born propagandists, and readily point out where the Department fails. We welcome such criticism, when it is not merely ignorant gossip, for propaganda is not an occult science, but a matter on which every citizen has a right to judge, and on which his judgement is often valuable. Moreover, there is no finality to it, it may be improved but it can never be perfect.[41]

On the outbreak of the war Alastair had just completed three years of his four year general degree at Glasgow University. He decided not to matriculate for his final year and instead started work in June 1914 in a firm of local accountants. Shortly afterwards he enlisted as a private in the Cameron Highlanders and in the following spring, after a period at Aldershot and Bramshott was commissioned into the Royal Scots Fusiliers. At the end of 1915 he left for France with the 9th Battalion where he was wounded a few months later. He came back to spend the summer of 1916 training near Rosyth from where he was able to return to Peebles at weekends. Buchan was seeing as much of his youngest brother as his war work allowed and was proud of the only fighting member of the family. Alastair was nearly twenty years his junior, and Buchan treated him almost as a son. In June Buchan wrote to his brother reporting on a dinner with Winston Churchill, who between Cabinet posts had commanded the Royal Scots Fusiliers at the Front, and wishing Alastair a happy twentieth birthday:

> I dined with Winston the other night. He was asking a lot about you. He says he is very sorry to come back from the Front, but that there was no chance for him there, and he didn't want a Brigade. I wish I could make him see that his presence at home just now is ruinous to his reputation. He is a good fellow, and I don't want him to run amuck. At the moment he is one of the most discredited people in Britain.[42]

In October 1916, Alastair again returned to the Front where Buchan brought him a turkey, haggis and plum-pudding for New Year. Alastair was due to return on leave in March 1917 but the push on Arras, the nexus of the German railway system, meant all leave was cancelled. He wrote to his mother at the beginning of April

> We expect to move tomorrow and there may be a stoppage of letters for a few days, but don't worry, wee body . . . There may be things happening, but don't worry about me. I was just thinking last night what a good time I've had all round and what a lot of happiness. Even the sad parts aren't sad any longer, but in a queer way, a comfort . . .[43]

On the morning of 9 April, Easter Monday, Second Lieutenant Alastair Buchan of the 6th Battalion Royal Scots Fusiliers led his company into action. Almost immediately he was hit by shrapnel and had to be rushed to a Field hospital with a fellow officer Gervase Maude. That afternoon both men died from their wounds. Years afterwards Anna would write how the Nurse 'washed the battle-grime from their faces and smoothed their flaxen hair . . . and knowing that somewhere over the Channel hearts would break for these bright heads, before they were laid in the earth she kissed them for their mothers'.[44] In his letter of condolence Churchill wrote of Alastair: 'He was a most charming and gallant young officer – simple, conscientious and much loved by his comrades. I knew him well enough to understand how great his loss must be to those who knew him better, and to those who knew him best of all'.[45]

Susan received the news of Alastair's death in a telegram from Anna on 9 April. She immediately rushed by taxi to the Foreign Office where she was forced to wander through a maze of dark corridors as she waited for her husband to come out of a meeting. 'When I got into his room he sprang up smiling to greet me,' she recalled. 'All my carefully prepared words deserted me, and I held out the telegram to him simply saying "Alastair".'[46] The couple returned home to receive another shock. A telegram awaited them to say Tommy Nelson had also been killed in the same battle. On the morning of 9 April, as Alastair Buchan was leading his Scots Fusiliers over the parapets half a mile further north, Nelson was hit by a shell while standing in a trench near to the railway station at Arras. He died instantaneously.

Apart from being Buchan's business partner the handsome young Scot had for almost twenty years been one of Buchan's closest friends and represented all that was good and memorable from Oxford. It was on Buchan's suggestion that Nelson had recently transferred from the Lothian and Border Horse to become an Intelligence Officer in the Tank Corps and the two men had regularly met at the Front. Buchan later wrote of Nelson: 'His presence warmed and lit up so big a region of life that in thinking of him one is overwhelmed by the multitude of things which he made better by simply existing among them.'[47] Two days later Buchan had again to hear news of the death of a close friend. Robbie Macmillan, a Glasgow University contemporary of Walter Buchan and friend of Anna was killed in action. These deaths had a deep and lasting effect on Buchan. In the space of a few days he had lost a brother, his best friend and a possible brother-in-law. Already many of his Oxford contemporaries had been killed, most notably Raymond Asquith on the Somme in September 1916 and Bron Lucas who had been shot down over enemy lines in November 1916. Henceforth he would have to create his own heroes through his books.

In January 1918 Buchan started at the new Ministry of Information, based at Norfolk Street in the Strand but again he swiftly encountered problems. On 23 January he wrote to Northcliffe: 'the Department can only be worked under a chief who has authority with the War Cabinet, and by a director who has the confidence of that chief. The resignation on the same day of Carson from the War Cabinet, to devote himself to the Irish problem, provided the opportunity for a change. Beaverbrook, after some lobbying by the Chief Whip, Frederick Guest, and despite initial opposition from the King, was brought in at the beginning of February to take his place. Beaverbrook had been chosen, not just because he was a newspaperman of some energy who had already organized propaganda in Canada, but also because it was felt important that it was better to channel his activities against the German rather than the British Government.[48]

On 4 March 1918 the Ministry of Information was officially formed. It took over most of the functions of the Department of Information, except for enemy propaganda which was given to Northcliffe in Crewe House. Beaverbrook was made Minister of Information and Roderick Jones became the Chief Executive. Charles Masterman was made Director of Publications while Buchan became Director of Intelligence with Harold Baker and Hugh Macmillan his chief assistants. In time the Intelligence Department became known as the 'Power House'. 'Its business was to receive and digest all information necessary for the work of Propaganda and to inspire a suitable propaganda policy in the different countries. It translated the policy of the Government into terms of propaganda.'[49]

The Department received much confidential material from which it then prepared articles for foreign papers. Buchan's principal job was to interview diplomats and arrange for visits of British representatives to foreign countries but he also worked closely with senior military intelligence officers such as Lord Arthur Brown, Charles French, the liaison officer with MI6, and Walter Kirke. Buchan had first met Kirke when Kirke was head of Intelligence B at GHQ running networks in occupied France and Belgium. Another close colleague was Edgar Wells who at the beginning of May hosted a dinner for Buchan and various MO1, MO2 and MI8 officers with special responsibility for Russia. The likely subject of discussion six months after the Bolshevik Revolution was probably the question of aid to the White Russians.

Beaverbrook encountered many of the same problems that had so frustrated Buchan. The Service Departments and Foreign Office were reluctant to share their intelligence and Lloyd George would not give the support he wanted. Repeatedly he threatened to resign. Beaverbrook's ambitions for the Ministry, his nepotistic appointments and battles with other Whitehall departments soon became public knowledge and of some concern. The Ministry, and in particular Beaverbrook, came under attack from newspapers like the *Westminster Gazette*, and there was a full-scale debate in Parliament, led by the

Liberal MP Leifchild Jones who was worried by the possible conflict of interest of a newspaperman in government.

Among Buchan's innovations was the opening of a bureau in London for relatives to buy photos of the Front. These were used to bring home to the civilian population the conditions in the trenches and as an aid for relatives searching for missing soldiers. He also seemed to be involved in other war work. On 21 August he wrote to his mother that he had refused a job which ranked on the same level as that of ambassador. This was probably the post of British High Commissioner in Washington which only three days later Buchan himself was offering to Sir John Simon.[50] In the course of his activities Buchan was introduced to the American newspaper man Lowell Thomas who was in search of a dramatic story. After Thomas approached him in December 1917 Buchan arranged through the War Office for Thomas to go to Allenby's headquarters in the Middle East, where the guerilla exploits of T.E. Lawrence were already beginning to attract notice in official circles. It was Thomas who was to be largely responsible for bringing Lawrence's name to a wider public when he published *With Lawrence in Arabia* immediately after the war.

In October Beaverbrook took the opportunity of a glandular disorder to resign. He wrote to Buchan: 'perhaps on my retirement you will allow me the privilege of telling you, how much I have appreciated your work in the Intelligence Department. I have always felt how reliable you were in every particular and how much I was indebted to you . . .'[51] Though the war was clearly almost at an end morale was low. Beaverbrook had not been replaced and many of the Ministry's staff were ill with the influenza then sweeping the country. Two days after the Armistice Buchan was asked by the Cabinet to disband the Ministry by the end of the year, the first of the war ministries to be wound up. The general feeling was that propaganda, though a necessary evil in war, had no place in peacetime. Those departments that could not be closed were transferred elsewhere – propaganda to the Foreign Office and the profitable Art and Photography sections to the Imperial War Museum. Buchan had the difficult job of dismissing the staff. Anold Bennett noted in his diary on 15 November: 'Buchan the liquidator, came down to see me, and was very explanatory and apologetic. The behaviour of the Cabinet to me was of course scandalous. But they have treated many others similarly, so I was not surprised.' Buchan was equally relieved to be out as he told Charles Masterman the following month. 'I am not sorry to get quit of the business.'[52]

He was only too delighted at the same time to stand down as the candidate for Selkirk and Peebles and not contest the Khaki election of December allowing Donald Maclean to retain Peebles on the Coalition ticket. Buchan had always been sympathetic towards genuine conscientious objectors (one, Launcelot Wake, is at the centre of his novel *Mr Standfast*) and he now became involved with Gilbert Murray and Lord Parmoor in an appeal to free the 1,500 objectors still in prison.[53] In December he also offered his services to Murray, now involved in setting up the League of Nations:

> Now that my official work is nearly over and I am not implicated in party politics, I wish to say to you that I am at your service for any work in speaking or writing, that I can do on behalf of the League of Nations. I am every day more convinced that if we do not secure a workable scheme we shall not have won the war, and we shall have missed the greatest opportunity in all history. There is a great deal to fight against, hasty idealism as well as perverse stupidity, and I want to help. All the enthusiasm that I have always had for my own brand of Imperialism I feel now attaches to this creed, and any political work I do in the future will be done in its service.[54]

Robert Cecil persuaded him to become the Chairman of the Editorial Committee of the League of Nations Union, where he was responsible for publications ranging from the monthly 'The League' and 'The Covenant' to a series of pamphlets. His name was also put forward as a possible member of the British Delegation to the General Council of the Federation of League of Nations Societies to be held in Rome in the summer of 1920.[55] Just as after the Boer War Buchan's interest had been in Reconstruction so too after the Great War he wanted to channel his considerable energies into rebuilding a post-war world. Where before the War he had 'believed profoundly in the possibilities of the Empire as a guardian of world peace' he now transferred that hope to the League of Nations.

The First World War was an important break point in Buchan's life. Before it he had been a reasonably well known novelist whose initial promise at Oxford as a man of public affairs and writer had failed to materialize. He ended the war a household name whose books were read widely throughout society and who had run a major government department.[56] In March 1918 he had been elected to The Club, a prestigious and secret dining society founded by Sir Joshua Reynolds and Samuel Johnson in 1764. Its members had since included David Garrick, Charles James Fox, Adam Smith, Thomas Macaulay, James Boswell, Viscount Palmerston, Sir Walter Scott, George Canning, Sir Humphry Davy, William Gladstone, Edmund Burke, Alfred Tennyson and Matthew Arnold. Among the members were many of Buchan's friends such as Arthur Balfour, Edward Grey, Hugh Cecil, Lord Curzon, John Simon, the King's Private Secretary Lord Stamfordham and

Rudyard Kipling. Subsequent members would include Cosmo Lang as Archbishop of Canterbury, Henry Newbolt, Hugh Macmillan and H.A.L. Fisher. Winston Churchill and F.E. Smith on failing to secure membership had set up their own 'The Other Club'. It seemed that at last Buchan had reached the heart of the Establishment.[57]

In spite of the demands on his time during the War as a publisher, the author of the *History of the War*, a member of Haig's staff and responsible for his own government department, Buchan had still found time to write. The success of *The Thirty-Nine Steps* had encouraged him to reissue his first attempt at a shocker, a book written before *The Thirty-Nine Steps* and serial-ized in 1914 but never before published on its own. The book was called *The Power House*.

In the spring of 1913 the Buchan family had taken a cruise in the Azores. As Buchan told the writer Hugh Walpole: 'I shall amuse myself writing a real shocker – a tribute at the shrine of my master in fiction – E. Phillips Oppenheim – the greatest Jewish writer since Isaiah.' Buchan had always loved thrillers, particularly the work of Oppenheim, then the most successful writer of the day. Though *Prester John* had been reasonably successful Buchan realized that if he was to make any money from his writing he would have to be more commercial in his approach.[58] The cruise which took Buchan, Susie, Anna, Walter and Mrs Buchan to Madeira, Gibraltar, Lisbon, the Azores and Santiago, was not a complete success. Buchan suffered more gastric trouble, Susie had a cold, Anna was seasick and Helen, convinced she could write as well as her son, spent her time writing her memoirs in pencil in a small notebook. But the trip allowed Buchan the peace to write what would become *The Power House*. He was persuaded it should be reissued as a piece of light reading for the troops and it was published in May 1916 by Blackwoods. The book was dedicated to Sir Francis Lloyd, a General with whom Buchan had worked closely in war charity work, and was an instant success, selling 24,000 copies within its first six months.[59]

The book is narrated by Edward Leithen, a barrister and skilled fisherman with a seat in the Commons and a house, Borrowby, in the Cotswolds. Leithen, who had made his first appearance in print in 1910 in the short story 'Space', is generally accepted as the character most closely modelled on Buchan himself. One of Leithen's Oxford contemporaries Charles Pitt-Heron, an adventurer with similarities to Aubrey Herbert, has mysteriously disappeared. Pitt-Heron's wife tells Leithen that he was forced to flee and she has been told to make secret arrangements to join him. At the same time, in the course of his work at the Bar, Leithen comes across a retired East India mer-chant Julius Pavia and his evil-looking butler Tuke. Both Pavia and Pitt-

Heron have been buying a particular kind of bearer bond and both are con-
nected to a Mr Andrew Lumley 'a rich bachelor, a member of the Athenaeum
and Carlton Clubs, and a dweller in the Albany.'

Lumley is like Leithen (and Buchan) a collector of Wedgwood and agrees
to sell part of his collection, which he keeps at White Lodge, Pavia's home in
Blackheath, to the barrister. There Leithen sees a telegram written in French
and sent from Vienna by Pitt-Heron. Shortly afterwards Leithen is forced to
take shelter after a car crash with a mysterious gentleman who turns out to be
Andrew Lumley. The two discuss the rule of law, a central theme in the book.
Leithen enlists the help of Macgillivray, a former colleague at the Bar and now
working at Scotland Yard, but is constantly frustrated in his efforts to bring
Lumley's gang to book. Eventually in a confrontation in Albany Leithen
offers Lumley a deal whereby nothing is done about Pitt-Heron who is impli-
cated in the Power-House in return for Lumley's escape.

The novel was one of the first to develop a recurrent Buchan theme,
broached in his collection of short stories *The Watcher by the Threshold* – the
very real threat to civilisation which is often posed by the mole within. Lumley
tells Leithen: 'You think that a wall as solid as the earth separates civilization
from barbarism. I tell you the division is a thread, a sheet of glass. A touch
here, a push there, and you bring back the reign of Saturn.'[60] Buchan was
articulating a contemporary concern, that was to become a predominant motif
of the thriller over the next fifty years, that the old order was under threat, a
threat posed as much by individuals as by nations. The certainties of an
Imperial nation were being challenged and democratic government was
vulnerable to the machinations of able but unprincipled humans. Lumley
argues that there is weak government, that politicians have failed to give the
country a sense of direction. Into the power vacuum could easily step a person
or organization, which he calls the Power-House, which could work miracles.
Such a lost leader controlling an evil organization becomes a common theme
in Buchan's subsequent novels.

Andrew Lumley, supposedly based on the politician Arthur Balfour,
becomes an archetype Buchan villain. He is rich, sophisticated, accepted in
the highest circles – 'the most learned old fellow in Britain . . . he pulls the
strings more than anyone living'.[61] It is often assumed that the mark of a
Buchan novel is an exotic background but that is not always true. Here
London becomes a central and sinister character in the book as Leithen is
menaced in Piccadilly, trapped in a restaurant in Fitzrovia and attacked in
Green Park. 'Now I saw how thin is the protection of civilization. An accident and a bogus ambulance – a false charge and a bogus arrest – there were
a dozen ways of spiriting me out of this gay bustling world.'[62]

Buchan's next book *Greenmantle* is one of his best known novels and has been overall his most successful book, even outselling *The Thirty-Nine Steps*. It also remained one of his own favourites. Contracted in January 1916 for a £750 advance and written in London between February and June 1916, it was serialized in the magazine *Land and Water* that autumn and published in October 1916. Buchan dedicated the book to his mother-in-law Caroline Grosvenor. Its publication provided an opportunity for another *Bookman* profile which praised his versatility, again stressed the influence of R.L. Stevenson and singled out his articles for *The Times*. 'His war copy is free from highly coloured passages, and it is with calmness, dispassion, and in pellucid English that he records the happenings.' There was also a backhanded compliment. 'His literary career resembles the military and political career of Mr Winston Churchill in point of variety and effectiveness, and the future of Mr Buchan is just as hard to predict as that of Mr Churchill.'[63]

Greenmantle included many of the characters that had first appeared in *The Thirty-Nine Steps*, such as Richard Hannay and Sir Walter Bullivant, as well as introducing important new ones such as the Scottish aristocrat and adventurer Sandy Arbuthnot and the American, John Scantlebury Blenkiron. The book has resonances of *The Half-Hearted* and Buchan draws for his Constantinople on scenes from his 1910 visit to the area. However, the book is based on real events and a threat of which Buchan was well aware from his work in Intelligence and the compilation of the *History of the War* – the danger of a German-sponsored Muslim uprising which would threaten India.[64] The parallels between *Greenmantle* and the relevant chapter in the *History of the War* are fascinating. In the former the weak spot in the Turkish defence is the fort of Kara Gubek which in the latter Buchan argues was left undefended because the Germans believed the two mountain peaks on each side were inaccessible to artillery. Likewise Buchan in the story makes much of a traitor within Erzerum betraying the garrison to the Russians.

The book opens with Hannay convalescing after the Battle of Loos. A telegram arrives from Bullivant asking him to undertake a hazardous mission on which Bullivant's own son has just been killed. The Allies are worried that the Germans and Turks are attempting to encourage a mass uprising among the Muslims of North Africa, the Sahara, the Middle East and India. The only clue Hannay is given are the words *Kasredin, cancer vi*. In an attempt to foil the Jihad, Hannay enlists the help of Arbuthnot, 'a bloodbrother to every kind of Albanian bandit' and Blenkiron, a 'big fellow with a fat, sallow, clean-shaven face'. Each assumes a disguise; Arbuthnot goes East as a dancing dervish, Blenkiron pretends to be anti-Allies and Hannay goes through Germany as an embittered Boer determined to exact revenge on the British. The three plan to meet at a Constantinople tavern on 17 January 1916.

Arbuthnot, like many of Buchan's friends educated at Eton and New College, could be based on any number of people. There are traces of both Aubrey Herbert and T.E. Lawrence, who were involved in some of the real events on which the book was based, including the taking of Erzerum, but other possibilities include Captain Edward Noel, the grandson of the Earl of Gainsborough, who was a noted linguist with a penchant for travelling amongst remote peoples in disguise. Blenkiron was inspired by the American newspapermen with whom Buchan worked during the war. To Blenkiron he gave two of his own weaknesses – an ulcer and passion for playing patience.[65] Buchan's gift is to draw the reader into the story through a mixture of verbal dexterity and ability to invoke a giant conspiracy. Bullivant has an extensive intelligence system.

> I have reports from agents everywhere – pedlars in South Russia, Afghan horse-dealers, Turcoman merchants, pilgrims on the road to Mecca, Sheikhs in North Africa, sailors on the Black Sea coasters, sheep-skinned Mongols, Hindu fakirs, Greek traders in the Gulf as well as respectable consuls who use cyphers.[66]

Though he drew on his own inside knowledge for some of the detail it was meant to be a piece of escapism and there is the customary hyperbole. Peter is 'the bravest man I've ever met' and 'the finest shot I have ever seen in my life', Sandy 'a man of genius'. Bullivant calls Blenkiron 'the best man we ever had'.

The novels acted as a counterweight to Buchan's propaganda work. He did not have to regurgitate the official view of the war, though sometimes he did, but could advance another view, which need not be his own nor one that might appeal to his readership. He allows Hannay to reflect on the futility of war and the 'goodness' of some Germans, both after he is taken in by the woodcutter's wife and when he meets Gaudian, the German engineer building the Baghdad railway. He paints a sympathetic portrait of the Kaiser at a time when he was reviled by the Allies and only a year after Gallipoli pays tribute to the fighting skills of the Turk. The book has two villains: the effeminate Von Stumm, and the enticing devil queen Hilda von Einem with whom Sandy falls half in love. The name von Stumm was probably taken from a Balliol contemporary Ferdinand Carl von Stumm who eventually became Buchan's opposite number as Head of the Foreign Press and News Department at the Foreign Office in Berlin in 1918.[67]

Amongst those who read and enjoyed the book were Baden Powell and

members of the Russian Royal Family as they waited to learn their fate during
1917. Buchan wrote to his mother in October 1917: 'I saw a letter from the
Grand Duchess Olga saying that she and her sisters and Papa had been greatly
cheered and comforted in their exile by *Greenmantle*. It is an odd fate for me to
cheer the prison of the Tsar.'[68] Critical reaction was good. *The New York Times*
thought it a 'gorgeous yarn', the reviewer in the *Daily Express* described it as
'the best adventure story I have read for many a long day' while the *Daily
Telegraph* wrote:

> This is by no means an ordinary kind of story of war and adventure; it is
> one of the best things of its kind ever presented to readers. Ruse and risk,
> adventure and achievement, and mystery pervading all, with an easy, con-
> vincing, matter-of-fact style and abundance of incident and plausible cir-
> cumstance – these carry the narrative through to a fine conclusion.[69]

Sales were also good with 30,000 copies of the initial 35,000 print run sold
within the year and a further 50,000 copies sold of a cheaper edition in 1918.
In January 1918 Buchan sold the dramatization rights to Leon Lion with
whom he was to collaborate on a script but nothing came of it.

In 1962 Philip Toynbee, Gilbert Murray's grandson, chose the book for a
Punch series 'Good Bad Books'. Reflecting on what he argued was 'Buchan's
masterpiece', he concluded that '*Greenmantle* is richly inventive, and a book
which was once capable of creating in a boy's mind a whole world of living
myth.' He praised Buchan's 'narrative gift of the most enviable and congeni-
tal dexterity' and admitted that it was 'one of the books which have genuinely
enriched my imagination'.[70]

In 1980 Richard West also paid tribute to the book, writing in the *Spectator*:

> This masterpiece by the prince of thriller-writers reads better than ever now,
> and quite up to date . . . The plot, the humour and character drawing help
> to account for its lasting appeal, and so I think does its exaltation of old-
> fashioned virtues such as respect for the other man's point of view; courage;
> mercy; and chivalry to women.[71]

The third of Richard Hannay's adventures came with the publication in
May 1919 of *Mr Standfast*. Written between July 1917 and July 1918 during
London air-raids, a brief visit to Peebles in June 1918 and on visits to Susan
and the family in Kent it was dedicated to members of the South African
Brigade and serialized in *Popular Magazine* in January and February 1919.
Many of the characters in the previous books reappear – Richard Hannay

having commanded a brigade at Arras is now at the War Office working for 'Bullivant and his merry men', John Blenkiron has been cured of his stomach trouble as a result of the same short-circuiting operation Buchan had just undergone, Peter Pienaar has been invalided out of the RFC, Sir Walter Bullivant and Macgillivray remain as ever to play useful supporting roles as official members of the Security Services. And some new Buchan characters are introduced – Andrew Amos the shop steward and Border radical, Archie Roylance, Hannay's former subaltern in the Lennox Highlanders now training pilots for the RFC, Geordie Hamilton from Alastair Buchan's regiment the Scots Fusiliers and Mary Lamington who lives at Fosse Manor.

Hannay and his 'little confederacy' are asked to frustrate the activities of a group of German spies known as the Wild Birds. The book moves from London to Skye, from Switzerland to the South Tyrol, from a French chateau to the battlefields of the Western Front, all parts of the world Buchan knew well and which he evokes with great vividness. And, as in *Greenmantle*, real events such as the Second Battle of the Somme act as a backdrop to the story. The book's title comes from one of Bunyan's central characters in *The Pilgrim's Progress*. Pienaar, who is reading the book, shows himself to be 'Mr Standfast' and one of the themes of the book is the importance of fortitude, loyalty, moral and physical courage and friendship. *The Pilgrim's Progress* is used by Mary and Hannay as part of their code and references to the book are dotted throughout the text. Hannay and his colleagues show themselves to be on a pilgrimage and Hannay even at one stage compares himself to Christian.[72]

Mr Standfast was written while Buchan was at the Ministry of Information and one of its set pieces is the filming by a propaganda unit of a mock battle. He lets slip various espionage methods gleaned no doubt from his intelligence work; and the novel draws on his interest in military tactics and love of field sports. An underlying theme to the book is pacificism and the dangers of industrial unrest and even revolution on Clydeside. Blenkiron again pretends to be opposed to the war and several pacifists play supporting roles. Rather than indulge in the crude jingoism with which Buchan is often tarred, he in fact tried in the novel to present various views of the conflict. His own support for fairness in dealing with conscientious objectors after the war suggests that, despite his own commitment to Allied victory, his sympathies were rather wider than might be assumed.

One of the most interesting characters is a conscientious objector, Launcelot Wake, whose individualism is contrasted with Bullivant's merry men's support for the State. Janet Adam Smith argues that Wake is the first of Buchan's characters to be given the 'root-of-the-matter' treatment where an initially unattractive character is redeemed through a particular sympathy, ability or task. In this case it is Wake's skill as a mountaineer and his successful accomplishment of a mission towards the end of the book. Moxon Ivery, otherwise known as the Graf von Schwabing, is a typical Buchan villain, indeed turns out to be an old rival. He is 'the cleverest devil in the world', a master of disguise, a former Liberal candidate who 'has decorated the board of every institution formed for the amelioration of mankind'.[73]

Mr Standfast, written and set in the closing stages of the First World War, looks to the end of the war, questioning the justness of the conflict and what the future holds. The image Buchan presents is a pastoral one of 'a green English landscape with its far-flung scents of wood and meadow and garden'. It is to such an England, most particularly to the Cotswolds that in time will also become Buchan's home, that Hannay and his new bride return.[74] *The Times* noted that '*Mr Standfast* is redeemed from melodrama and crude sensationalism by the skill of the writer, his fine eye for scenery, his love of mountains and mountaineering, his admirable command of racy Scots talk, his artistic use of the element of the supernatural, to say nothing of his grasp of the military history of the war, and his personal knowledge of operations on the Western Front.'[75]

Reviewing the American edition the *New York Times*, while critical of Buchan's attempt to write American dialect and 'his desire to pile on the thrills', thought the book 'a good thriller. The author's style is vivid and while he falls too easily into the conventionalities of melodramatic fiction, he gives the impression of being superior to the clap-trap which he is describing.'[76] It is a much fuller and richer book than the previous two in the trilogy both in terms of characterization and its varied setting but shows signs of being written over a long period. Characters tend to appear and be dropped so that Amos disappears after the Scottish scenes and Peter Pienaar only properly appears when the book moves to Switzerland.[77]

Buchan had written poetry since he was a young man and his poems had appeared in several of his books, either as dedications or interspersed in collections of short stories; some now had begun to appear in anthologies. Many of them were written in Scots vernacular and drew their inspiration from people and places on the Tweed, others were inspired by history and classical literature. After his marriage, as his literary sympathies narrowed and demands on his time grew, he had written less poetry. His experiences on the Western Front and the loss of many of his closest friends had however restored his interest in both reading and writing poetry and the result was an eclogue *Ordeal By Marriage*, published in 1915, and *Poems, Scots and English*, a collection of twenty eight poems half of them in English and half in Scots, which was published in a limited edition of fifty copies in June 1917 and dedicated to Alastair.[78]

David Daniell has singled out the war poetry, 'the best of which can stand with Siegfried Sassoon', but contemporary critics preferred Buchan's earlier work. In its review the *TLS* wrote:

> Every one reading Mr Buchan's Scottish poems will be struck by the con-
> trast between those about the war and those of the older world. It is not
> merely that some of the poems are peaceful; it is more than that . . . They
> belong to any time or no time; they are contemporary with all Scottish verse
> of the school of Ramsay and Burns; they admit you to the pastoral eternity
> of that old world which lies at the back of the hills. The war poems, good
> as they are, have not this sort of magic quality . . .[79]

Another book apart from *Mr Standfast* that looked to the future of Britain after the war was *The Island of Sheep*, a symposium in the style of *A Lodge in the Wilderness*, which Buchan and his wife wrote, under the pseudonyms Cadmus and Harmonia, just after the end of the war. It was published by Hodder & Stoughton in August 1919 and by Houghton Mifflin the follow-ing year. The problems and opportunities of the post-war world interested Buchan greatly. He had taken part during the war in the discussions of the New Days Committee and was a great supporter of the League of Nations. Now the war was over he wished to develop those ideas on paper. *The Island of Sheep* is set in a shooting-lodge on a Scottish island where a series of repre-sentative figures – 'A progressive journalist', an 'American in England', 'A lady given to good works', 'A Liberal lawyer', 'A Labour Leader', an 'Imperialist', 'The Lady Guidwillie of Waucht – A Highland landowner' and a parish minister, John Macmillan, discuss among much else Socialism, Bolshevism, the nature of democracy, syndicalism, the League of Nations, Imperialism and America. It is a piece of fun where the characters have names like Merryweather Malone and Lord Linkumdoddie and Buchan almost seems to be sending himself up with one character described as 'the best man to hounds in Northamptonshire'. It is also an optimistic book with Buchan arguing that the innate commonsense of the ordinary British man can solve most problems. Some papers misunderstood it completely. Buchan's American publisher Ferris Greenslet, for example, took delight in telling Buchan of the review from one farming paper disappointed by its philosoph-ical speculation. The book quickly went out of print and is now a collector's item of interest in charting Buchan's immediate post-war concerns, but otherwise unmemorable.

9

COUNTRYMAN

BUCHAN ended the war an exhausted man and almost immediately retired to bed for several weeks. He was physically and mentally drained from his time at the Department of Information where he had worked fourteen-hour days. The war had shattered many of his ideals and he had lost many close friends. He felt too his war work should have been recognized by some form of honour. Though Beaverbrook tried to obtain a KCMG for him through Balfour, Buchan had received nothing except decorations from the Kings of Italy and the Belgians and an LLD from Glasgow University.

When pressed Balfour had written: 'Personally, I have the greatest possible regard for Col. Buchan, and hold his abilities in very high estimation . . . we only have a very small store and it would really not be fair to rob men who look forward to this Honour after many years under the Foreign Office in order to reward services, however meritorious, rendered to other Departments.'[1] Buchan had suggested a KBE 'which the Prime Minister can give off his own bat' but nothing was forthcoming. Partly there was unease in official circles about rewarding propaganda work, partly there were bureaucratic problems with regard to Buchan's status. In large part Buchan, the supposed opportunistic careerist, continued to be out-manoeuvred by his political and civil servant colleagues.[2]

The end of the war seemed the right moment to move out of London. His family were growing up and he felt they should be brought up in the country. Alice was now ten, John seven and there were two new additions to the family, both named after Buchan's dead brothers, William de l'Aigle born in January 1916 and Alastair Francis born in September 1918. The family had spent a large part of the war out of London either at Checkendon or in various houses in Kent. Buchan, after the demands of his war work, had a hankering for a quiet rural life where he could indulge in country pursuits and write in peace. The house, however, had still to be near to London as even with the success of the 'shockers' Buchan needed and wanted to keep his job with Nelsons.

As an undergraduate he had fallen in love with the countryside around Oxford, with its gently rolling hills and rich agricultural land. In January 1911 he and Susan had looked at houses a few miles outside Oxford and in September 1917 he and Susan had taken a four day holiday in the Cotswolds and decided that that was where they wished to settle after the war. Another factor was that Susan's sister Margaret, who had married an Australian, Jeremy Peyton Jones in 1916, now lived in the area. During the War Buchan had viewed properties, often accompanied by Hugh Macmillan and in October 1918 he had written enthusiastically to Susan about Weald Manor, near Bampton, but it proved too expensive. The house figures in his short story 'Full-Circle' published in *Blackwood's Magazine* and the *Atlantic Monthly* in January 1920.

In January 1919 the Buchans began their search in earnest. By May he was able to report to his mother that he had found exactly what he was looking for when a friend, the Treasurer of Christ Church, tipped him off that the college was buying the village of Elsfield four miles to the north east of Oxford and would sell him the manor-house and twenty acres around it. In November the deal was concluded for the then considerable sum of £40,000.[3] Elsfield Manor was a seventeenth century manor house built of Cotswold stone with some Victorian additions, but a dwelling had stood on the site since the Domesday Book. The house had associations with Dr Johnson, who had visited it in 1754 to have tea with its then owner, the Radcliffe Librarian, Francis Wise. Wise had laid out the garden with ornamental ponds, a gazebo and built a gardener's cottage in the style of a medieval chantry and little had changed by the time the Buchan family arrived almost two hundred years later. The grounds mixed the formal and the wild and one of Buchan's first actions was to plant a yew-hedge and copper-beech.

The house opened immediately on to the quiet village street and one entered into a white-panelled hall with a floor of stone flags. On the walls were two coloured plates of the second Lord Astor standing beside his horse Buchan, a print of some red-faced dons, a drawing by Basil Blackwood and some mounted deer antlers. At the far end a broad staircase led to the library and bedrooms. On the left was the morning room and straight ahead the drawing room, again panelled in white and with good views over the lawn to the Cherwell water-meadows and then over the Vales of Eynsham and Witney. Steep stairs led directly from the dining-room down to the kitchen. The basement also contained the scullery, the servants' hall, a store-room, cellars and larder. To the side was a stable-yard which had been a gun-park for the Parliamentary army during the siege of Oxford. Apart from stables and harness room the yard included a laundry, dairy, coach house which acted as a garage and brewhouse. The latter, however, supposedly out of consideration for Helen Buchan's feelings was never put into commission. The National Grid did not reach Elsfield until 1936 and therefore part of the area was also used to generate the household electricity.

The library, with its bookshelves stretching from floor to ceiling, was for Buchan perhaps the most important room in the house. Here, or sometimes in a study on the first floor, he wrote his books at a solid partners' desk which he shared with Susan, and here he 'transacted business, read aloud to his children, entertained his friends, smoked and pondered and made projects.'[4] Beside him was an inkstand and a converted Georgian knife-box in which he kept a stock of writing paper and nearby a table consecrated to his smoking things, which tended to include a pipe and sometimes strong Turkish cigarettes. On one side of the desk was a long oak table covered with books, magazines and pots of flowers from the greenhouse, and on the other a sofa and some armchairs. To the right of the desk was a shelf for press cuttings. Over the fireplace hung a picture of *Sir Walter Raleigh*, which had been painted by an Irishman who had taken part in the 1916 Uprising and was henceforth known as 'Papa's Sinn Feiner'.

The house required new bathrooms and electric light so the Buchans took the lease of Harberton House on Headington Hill for the winter of 1919/20, moving into Elsfield at the beginning of 1920. It was to be the Buchan family home for the next thirty four years, a place where at last Buchan could sink new roots and where he could write in peace. For Buchan the country had always been a place of refuge. In Glasgow there was Broughton, in South Africa the Wood Bush and, now that he had decided not to follow friends like Johnnie Jameson, who had been elected for West Edinburgh in the Khaki Election, into parliament, there was no need to be in London. He relished the opportunity to spend time with his wife and children and be free from the pressures of London social life. He kept an old charger named after his Transvaal pony Alan Breck and would ride in the early morning. At weekends he thought nothing of walking thirty miles over the surrounding countryside. Sometimes he would take friends such as Lord Edward Gleichen shooting on the four hundred acres he leased next to the Manor, but generally he preferred going out alone to shoot hares or woodcock. Eventually, after a few years he tired even of that and passed the land to a syndicate of farmers. He was far happier fishing alone, with Johnnie or Amos Webb, his chauffeur.[5] If before the war Buchan had hankered after a small estate in the Borders he was now reconciled to this small manor house with its pretty garden, splendid views and peaceful library. Here he could work undisturbed and entertain friends, many of whom lived nearby. There were the F.S. Olivers near Reading, the Gilbert Murrays on Boars Hill and old Glasgow friends such as W.P. Ker in Oxford itself.

Though Elsfield allowed Buchan to recover his energies after the war he did not let himself forget the tragedy which had just taken place. Buchan's son William was to write later:

> War and its tragedy was one aspect of a weighty past, always present, very often in elegiac terms, which, although we should have been shocked to find ourselves resentful of it, did keep continually before us standards which sometimes seemed impossibly high.[6]

Mementos of the war cluttered the house. To the left of the front door was a map showing the 'French chateau where Haig had had his headquarters, with black lines raying from it to various points of the compass indicating the chain of command to the divisions of his army, and the names and locations of villages and towns between'. In the library were coloured reproductions of portraits of the French Generals Foch, Joffre and Mangin alongside a signed copy of Sargent's portrait of Haig, 'a German bayonet, a gunmetal watch half-smashed by a bullet, a pair of Zeiss binoculars taken from a dead German officer'.[7] The First World War had a profound effect on Buchan and made him very much aware of 'how thin the crust was between a complex civilization and primeval anarchy.' He had seen the worst horrors of the Western Front and the experience was to shape much of his writing after the war.[8]

The months immediately after the war were devoted to one of the most personal and moving of his books, *These For Remembrance*. This was a memoir of six friends who had been killed during the war: Tommy Nelson, Bron Lucas, Cecil Rawling, Basil Blackwood, Jack Wortley and Raymond Asquith. It was privately printed at the Chiswick Press under the supervision of the Medici Society and dedicated to his children, 'for I want you to know something about my friends who fell in the Great War ... I hope it will never befall you which has befallen me – to look around and find a flat emptiness'. The number of copies printed is unknown but may only have been limited to a copy for each of the six families and Buchan's own copy. The title probably comes from Ophelia's lament in Hamlet '*That's for remembrance*' and the book begins with Gabriel Harvey's elegy after Agincourt:

> Ah, that Sir Humfry Gilbert should be dead:
> Ah, that Sir Philip Sidney should be dead:
> Ah, that Sir William Sackeuill should be dead:
> Ah, that Sir Richard Grenuile should be dead:
> Ah, that braue Walter Deuoreux should be dead
> Ah, that the Flowre of Knighthood should be dead,
> Which, maugre deadlyest Deathes, and stonyest Stones,
> That couer worthiest worth, shall neuer dy.

One of the book's greatest admirers was Buchan's old enemy Robertson Nicoll.

Though he never explicitly expressed this Buchan, like many of the First World War survivors, seems to have felt guilty that he had lived when so many of his contemporaries had died. It was this sense of guilt, as well as of history and duty, that drove him to compile several books on the conflagration in the years after the First World War. In his attempt to explain and understand the war he was not alone, for in the years immediately after 1918 a spate of books about the war's origins and its victims, accounts of the military and political strategies, memoirs from generals and politicians poured from the publishing presses. Buchan was however among the most prolific. There was a short book *The Battle-Honours of Scotland 1914–1918* for the Glasgow publisher George Outram in 1919 and at the instigation of Smuts *The History of the South African Forces in France* for Nelson in 1920.

Later in 1920 he published a memoir of the Grenfell twins *Francis and Riversdale Grenfell* with the profits going to the Invalid Children's Aid Association with which the twins had been associated. Francis and Riversdale Grenfell came from a well-known military family and were cousins of the better-known Billy and Julian Grenfell, who were also killed in the war. The twins had seven brothers of whom three had already died in the service of their country – one in the Matebele rising, one at the charge of the 21st Lancers at Omdurman and one in India. Of the surviving four brothers all served in World War One at the rank of Lieutenant Colonel or above. Buchan had met the brothers, cousins of Auberon Herbert, after their brother Arthur married Susan's cousin Hilda in 1909, but only became close to them immediately before the outbreak of the war. Always prone to hero-worship, Buchan had been drawn by their high spirits, their sporting prowess – both were excellent polo players – and their intellectual curiosity.

Rivy, as he was commonly known, had been killed in September 1914 just after Francis had received the VC during the retreat from Mons. Buchan had been Rivy's executor and in April 1915 had been one of seven guests with

Arthur Grenfell, Winston Churchill and Arthur Balfour for a farewell dinner for Francis at Claridges. The next month Francis, himself, was killed in a German gas attack. Buchan wrote the book principally for the Grenfell family and drew extensively on the twin's letters. It covers their Eton school-days, military service in India and South Africa and it begins like *These for Remembrance* with Gabriel Harvey's lament after Agincourt.

The process of exculpation went on through the 1920s with an account of the British Empire during the First World War, *Days to Remember* (1923), written with Henry Newbolt and aimed at secondary schools, *The History of the Royal Scots Fusiliers 1678–1918* (1925) – to which the Prince of Wales contributed a foreword paying tribute to Alastair Buchan – and numerous contributions to books on the War. These included *The Long Road to Victory*, the *John Buchan Annual* for 1920, which consisted of first person accounts of First World War battles including Buchan on the South Africans at Marrieres Wood, Maurice Baring on the Air Battles of the Somme and Francis Yeats Brown on the 17th Cavalry. There were biographical sketches of Raymond Asquith, Basil Blackwood and Auberon Herbert for the *Balliol College War Memorial Book* (1924) and, with another co-writer, a history of *The Fifteenth-Scottish-Division 1914–1919* (1926).

Buchan was also working on a revised version of his *History of the War*. Each of the twenty-four parts had to be revised now the conflict was over, a task that took much of his time until its completion in the summer of 1921. The new edition received a mixed response. Basil Liddell Hart, who had liked the original version, felt Buchan had written the new book too quickly and not taken into account all the new information now known. There was criticism too of his treatment of Lloyd George, most notably from the great man himself:

> When a brilliant novelist assumes the unaccustomed role of a historian it is inevitable that he should now and again forget that he is no longer writing fiction, but that he is engaged on a literary enterprise where narration is limited in its scope by the rigid bounds of fact ... The real explanation is that Mr Buchan found it so much less trouble to repeat War Office gossip than to read War Office documents.[9]

The History of the War is now recognized as one of Buchan's great achieve-ments, *The Edinburgh Review* going so far as to call it 'a book which will rank with Macaulay's *History of England*.' Perhaps the four-volume history, revised after the war, lacks the excitement and immediacy of the original but it is still a fine and evocative study of the conflict written only a few years after its end.[10]

It was a book that drew a large post bag. One correspondent admitted to having read all the volumes several times and wanted further volumes on Versailles and statistical information while another brought home something of its tragedy when he wrote after reading the first volume that he was the only survivor of his own twenty/first birthday party held a few years before the out/break of the war.

The prodigious output is even more extraordinary when one remembers that Buchan remained, even after his short circuit operation of 1917, an ill man. His duodenal ulcer continued to give him pain and in October 1921 he saw Sir Berkeley Moynihan at his clinic in Leeds 'to be thoroughly vetted – with some idea of a new operation'. He was forced to give up smoking and to follow a careful diet that largely consisted of steamed fish, milk and eggs with perhaps a small sherry or whisky.[11] He later had a spell at Freiburg im Breisgau in the Black Forest where he saw a Dr Marten, who specialized in discovering if there were psychological influences on physical ailments. Marten numbered many society figures amongst his patients including Lady Ottoline Morrell; Buchan's companions at the Kurhaus Hoven included among others Lady Salisbury, Lady Wemyss, Lady Plymouth, Lady Grey, Lady Cynthia Asquith, Lady Beatrice Ormsby/Gore and Hilda Grenfell. He wrote to Roderick Jones in November 1926 after a week's treatment at the hands of Dr Marten. 'He says that my trouble is purely mechanical, the result of my opera/tion, and that he can get it right, but he insists on my staying four weeks.'[12] Dr Marten was eventually forced to conclude: 'Never in my experience have I met anybody less frustrated or less crippled by inhibitions. He is free from neuroses. His trouble must be wholly of physical origin.' The experience however gave Buchan the beginning of his story 'The Loathly Opposite', which later appeared in a collection of short stories, *The Runagates Club*.[13]

Always disappointed at not having received an honour after the First World War, he had asked Beaverbrook to make approaches on his behalf to the Conservative leader, Andrew Bonar Law, for the 1921 New Year Honours List but nothing came of it. During the first part of 1922, perhaps sensing that Lloyd George's days were numbered and this might be his last chance, Buchan renewed his appeal enlisting the support of the Lord Chancellor F.E. Smith, now Lord Birkenhead, Sir Robert Horne, now Chancellor of the Exchequer and Lord Beaverbrook. He wrote to his old boss at the Ministry of Information asking if he would put him up for a KCB with the justification: 'I am now pretty well restored to health, and shall presently take up politics again, and I should greatly like to have some memento of my war service. I think we are agreed that my official and historical work combined give me a reasonable claim.'[14] Lloyd George seemed to be indifferent either way but there was opposition to the award elsewhere and Buchan was forced to renew his appeal to Beaverbrook again the following month adding: 'I am really anxious to bring off the thing, for my mother is getting pretty frail and I want to please her, that is for your private ear. It's no argument for anybody else.'[15] Beaverbrook wrote to Lloyd George's Private Secretary John Davies: 'I have spoken to the Prime Minister on occasions, and he appeared to agree that John Buchan would make an excellent subject for an Honour . . . I must say that Buchan worked very hard during the war, and I think he is deserving of an Honour.' Davies promised to raise it with the Prime Minister but again nothing happened.[16]

In May Buchan wrote to Beaverbrook: 'You told me to remind you about this time of the KCB business. I fancy the list is made up about the middle of May. I have jogged the memories of FE & Bertie Horne.' Beaverbrook asked Buchan to draft a letter he could send and suggested a KCMG. As well as his work at the Foreign Office, the Department of Information and the Ministry of Information, Buchan pointed out that:

> Apart from these special services he put his literary gifts wholly at the country's services, taking no payment for what he wrote. In addition to many pamphlets and articles he published the twenty-four volumes of his History of the War – a book which had throughout the world by far the largest circulation of any war publication, and which by its sanity, breadth of view and reasoned optimism, did much to balance and inform the public mood and had, notably in America, a far-reaching influence.[17]

Problems still remained. Both F.E. Smith and Robert Horne wrote on Buchan's behalf to Lloyd George but the Prime Minister pointed out that 'nobody outside the Civil Service & Fighting forces can get a KCB' while 'the old establishment of the British Empire is closed.' He recommended he, Horne, try on Buchan's behalf for 'a plain Knighthood, and the KBE later'.[18] Buchan was having none of it, pointing out that he had been a civil servant during the war and also linked with the Dominions thereby making the KCMG still a possibility. 'Failing either,' he wrote to Beaverbrook, 'could His Majesty, with whom I am on friendly terms, be induced to grant me a KCVO?' In the end Buchan's intransigence, combined with a lack of flexibility from the appropriate authorities, cost him his honour.[19]

The question needs to be asked why did Buchan press so hard for a honour and why was he denied it? He later claimed it was for the sake of his mother while his detractors have suggested it was pure vanity. It is certainly true such rewards mattered to him and characters such as Richard Hannay were to be festooned with the sort of honours that Buchan craved. He had a great respect for and belief in British institutions. An honour was literally such for him, and his Calvinist sense of justice made him feel that he was entitled to some sort of recompense for all he had done during the war. Many of his wartime col-leagues at the Ministry of Information had lobbied Beaverbrook and been rewarded. At the time Beaverbrook had ingenuously stated Buchan's problem: 'You are neglected because you do not care and consequently do not subject me to pressure. There is no influence which is operating against you: likewise there is no influence operating in your favour except mine.' In the end perhaps that was Buchan's greatest drawback. He was not a political operator. He would have to wait another decade to receive the honours he so coveted.[20]

The war also brought changes in Buchan's relations with Nelsons. In 1915 it had become a limited company and he was made a full Director but while he was working at the Ministry of Information his Nelson job had become sec-ondary. Buchan began working there again at the beginning of 1919, divid-ing his time between the Paternoster Row office in London and the Parkside works in Edinburgh when he would stay with the Maitlands in Heriot Row. Tommy Nelson had always been Buchan's mentor within the firm. Now he was dead and neither Buchan nor George Brown agreed with the direction in which Ian Nelson wanted to take the firm. The series of reprint copyright novels, the Sevenpennies, on which Buchan had worked so hard was not resumed and in 1921 George Brown resigned. Buchan himself found there were increasing personality conflicts with Ian Nelson.

These came to a head at the beginning of 1923 when Buchan was offered the job of Deputy-Chairman at Reuters. Nelson was worried that Buchan might not now devote sufficient time to the firm when they were down to two directors. There were also niggles about Buchan's takings from the firm and his expenses. Buchan felt aggrieved that they should be so pedantic when he had donated to the firm close to £10,000 worth of royalties on his books. The dispute rumbled on into the summer of 1923 when Buchan had to call in Hugh Macmillan to act for him to draw up a new contract with Nelson's. One element of the dispute was over money. When Buchan joined Nelson's at the beginning of 1907 he claimed it was on a Director's salary of £750 with a small share of the profits. In fact it was £1,000 p.a. with a guarantee that his income would not drop below £1,500 p.a. for the first two years.[21]

The firm had suffered during the war from labour and paper shortages and though it was now recovering was still not making a profit. Buchan, with four young children, now claimed he was earning less from Nelson's than he had some sixteen years before. Buchan represented to Ian Nelson that he devoted two-thirds of his working days in London and most of his weekends to the firm at the cost of more profitable activities like writing novels. He asked for a salary rise adding: 'I do not suggest any extravagant increase, for, as I told you, I am willing to sacrifice something to continue in a business to which I have a strong attachment.'[22]

Nelson was not easily moved, pointing out that Buchan's salary over the last few years had averaged £2,000 each year and that remuneration had been based on the partners/directors devoting all their energies to the business. He was upset that Buchan had taken on other directorships and activities, especially at a time when the number of directors had fallen from four to two, thereby increasing the pressure on each of them.[23] Eventually the two agreed that Buchan would remain at Nelson until October 1929 on a salary of £750 and he would be allowed to take on other work as long as it did not conflict or interfere with his responsibilities at the publishing business.

The dispute convinced Buchan that in future he would have to rely more and more on his writing for his income and that he needed to bring in fresh blood. Accordingly he asked the poet Henry Newbolt, with whom he had worked in the Ministry of Information, to act as an adviser to the firm. Together they compiled a series of books for the firm which included editions of nineteenth century poets such as William Morris, Robert Browning, Matthew Arnold and Dante Gabriel Rossetti which Newbolt edited and Buchan introduced. They also produced *A History of English Literature* with Buchan writing chapters on the Victorian period, 'The prose of reflection' and 'The end of the century' and contributions from among others the Shakespearian scholar John Dover Wilson. Between 1919 and 1921 Newbolt had been Chairman of a Ministry of Education Committee entitled English in National Education and he decided with Buchan to publish a series of books inspired by its conclusions. This became 'The Teaching of English' series and was followed shortly after by 'The Teaching of History' series. Buchan as General Editor of the latter produced eleven volumes between 1928 and 1930. Some of the writers were old friends such as Robert Rait, the Historiographer Royal for Scotland since 1919, others were the leading historians in their field such as George Coulton, J.D. Mackie and R.B. Mowat.

Though Buchan's principal publishers from 1916 became Hodder & Stoughton, he allowed Nelson's to do the cheap editions of his novels and wrote or contributed to thirteen books for them between 1920 and his resignation as a director. These included several books usually published in time for the Christmas market and aimed at young boys such as the John Buchan Annual series. In 1920 this was *The Long Road to Victory* and in the following year *Great Hours in Sport* with chapters, among others, on mountaineering by Geoffrey Winthrop Young, small-boat sailing by Hilaire Belloc, cricket by

Pelham Warner and fishing and 'sport and literature' by Buchan himself. *A Book of Escapes and Hurried Journeys*, published in September 1922, dealt with a dozen famous escapes or hurried journeys including King Charles II's dash after the battle of Worcester, Marie Antoinette's flight to Varennes, Bonnie Prince Charlie's escape after Culloden and Winston Churchill's adventures during the Boer War. In the preface Buchan, many of whose novels include a hurried journey and are in the romance tradition, gives his definition of a romance – 'that which affects the mind with a sense of wonder – the surprises of life, fights against odds, weak things confounding strong, beauty and courage flowering in unlikely places.' Four years after it was published the book became a school set book.[24] *The Last Secrets: The Final Mysteries of Exploration* stemmed from Buchan's lifelong interest in exploration and consisted of a series of chapters on the North and South Pole, the Mountains of the Moon, Mount McKinley and Mount Everest. Published in September 1923 it was dedicated to Cecil Rawling, with whom Buchan had planned to explore the northern side of Everest in 1913.

Part of the tension at Nelson's had arisen from Buchan's growing involvement with the news agency Reuters run by an old friend from South Africa, Sir Roderick Jones. Jones had been a Reuters correspondent in South Africa and came to Britain to head the South African section in London just after Buchan went out to work for Lord Milner. Jones returned to South Africa in 1905, still under thirty, where he made good use of his contacts with Botha and Smuts. In 1915 he became General Manager, helped by references from Lord Gladstone, Sir Matthew Nathan, Sir Starr Jameson and Sir Lionel Phillips. In 1916 the Foreign Office at the instigation of Milner took a stake in the recently reorganized company and Buchan became the nominee Foreign Office director. He resigned from the Reuter Board in June 1917 on becoming head of the Department of Information, which had financial dealings with Reuters and was succeeded by Dougal Malcolm. Jones however, despite much criticism, continued to act as the managing director of Reuter's and worked first for the Department of Information and then when the Ministry of Information was formed at the beginning of 1918 as the full-time, but unpaid, director of propaganda. He was rewarded by becoming one of the first knights of the new Order of the British Empire.

In 1919 Buchan rejoined Reuters' Board together with Dougal Malcolm now a Director of the British South Africa Company. Four years later when Jones was making plans to make a ten-month world tour of the Reuter's business he asked Buchan to become Deputy Chairman and take a more active role in the firm's activities. According to an agreement of 27 February 1923 Buchan was to be paid £1,500 in the first year, £2,000 in the second and £2,500 in the third year.[25] Impressed by his skill at assimilating and presenting complex information Jones, who had hoped Buchan would write the history of the company, left instructions that he should become Chairman should anything happen to him. As a result Buchan now spent more time at the Reuters building at 9 Carmelite Street off the Victoria Embankment where it had moved in November 1923 from 23–25 Old Jewry.

Buchan was a popular member of staff and Mrs Allan Harris, then a junior member of the news room, remembers how he was the only senior executive who would come down from the 5th floor to see them. 'He was always very courteous and interested in what we were doing.' He remained on the Board, continuing to hold one of the Reuters Trust seats when the Press Association took over in 1931, until he left for Canada in July 1935. However, he kept up his links and contributed a message to the first issue of *The Reuters Review* in January 1938 in which his own attitude to the firm is revealed. 'It is, and has always been, far more than a mere commercial organisation,' he wrote 'and every member of it can feel he is in the fullest sense a public servant.'[26]

Most summer holidays after the war were spent in Scotland either in the Borders or in the Highlands. There Buchan could regain his strength by rigorous outdoor exercise either fishing with Walter and Johnnie, or going for long walks during which he always carried a silver flask of whisky. From 1919 he took to leasing Gala Lodge a mid-Victorian stone villa at the southern end of Broughton village from his aunt, Agnes Robb. As his fame grew he was increasingly pestered by admirers and Gala Lodge had the advantage of allowing him to beat a hasty retreat on to the hills behind while the family kept the visitor talking at the door. Staying at Gala Lodge also allowed Buchan to see his mother, sister and brother without having to stay with them at Bank House. Though the family were still close Buchan's life was very different from that of his Peebles relatives, which revolved around the life of the town. It was only the past which really united them.

Anna by now – under the pseudonym O (for Olivia in Shakespeare's *Twelfth Night*) Douglas – had become almost as successful a novelist as her elder brother. Hodder counted her with her brother as one of their top five authors. Most of her novels were highly autobiographical, set in Peebles and were thinly disguised portraits of her immediate family. Her first novel *Olivia in India*, published in 1913, was based on a trip to India in November 1907 to see her brother William to whom the book is dedicated. It was followed in 1917 by *The Setons*, the story of a Scottish minister and his family, in 1920 by *Penny Plain* and then at roughly two year intervals *Ann and Her Mother, Pink Sugar, The Proper Place, Eliza for Common, The Day of Small Things, Priorsford, Taken by the Hand, Jane's Parlour* and *The House that is Our Own*.

Walter, originally destined for the Scottish Bar after reading law at Glasgow University, had settled in to life with the family law firm and as the Town Clerk of Peebles and Procurator Fiscal. Like his brother and sister, he had literary interests. He had already written a life of the Duke of Wellington for Nelson in 1909 and during this period he was busy producing a three volume history of Peebleshire, to which his surviving brother contributed the section on literary figures.

Often Buchan would leave the children with his mother and sister while he and Susan went further north. Almost every year the two of them would stay for a week with Gerard Craig Sellar and his mother at Ardtornish opposite Mull in a house that could only be reached by boat and another week with Ian Nelson at Glenetive. In 1922 they went with the Maitlands to Letterewe on Loch Maree and the following year to Rhiconich and Kinlochbervie in Sutherland. It was during that holiday that Buchan was forced to grow a beard after catching a skin infection while out stalking. As he told Roderick Jones 'I am not allowed to shave, and my appearance soon will be a cross between that of Abraham and Lazarus!'[27]

In 1926 Buchan, Susan and their eldest son went to stay on Unst, the most northerly island in the British Isles, where Charles Dick was the minister. There they fished for sea trout and went bird watching and Buchan gave the address in the church at Uyeasound. Another part of the holidays was spent at an inn in the West Riding of Yorkshire where Buchan tried unsuccessfully to persuade his sons to climb. Sometimes the Buchans, including the Peebles Buchans, would go to Ardura on Mull or Ben More Lodge, a Victorian shooting-box near Tarbet where the family would relax by fishing, going for long walks and collecting shells. It was just such a holiday that gave Anna material for some chapters in her novel *The Day of Small Things*.[28]

Later as the family grew older the Buchans leased a large house at Ffrwdgrech in the Brecon Beacons where they went riding and he would catch up on his writing. He was not an easy holiday companion as even on vacation he needed to keep himself constantly busy. His pleasures needed to be as carefully organized as his work and as his son William has noted he 'could only stand family life, as lived on holidays, in small and varied doses'.[29]

The mark of these holidays was fresh air and exercise. Buchan was essentially a countryman and wished to pass on his love of the wilds to his children.

He enjoyed stalking though not always the kill, could cover large distances on foot each day and loved fishing, a passion he passed in particular to his son Johnnie, who later remembered how his father could easily throw a salmon-fly thirty yards.[30] As William later wrote: 'these were strenuous holidays, with much fishing, shooting, riding and many long, challenging hill-walks. Something strongly masculine was thus brought into our lives, and for that we were grateful, being as I have indicated, generally somewhat overwhelmed by a very positive feminine influence.'[31]

Buchan had long been interested in America and in particular the Civil War. He had written about the early settlers in *Salute to Adventurers*, put Lincoln into his *The Path of the King* and long nurtured the hope of writing the life of General Robert Lee. 'I would rather write that life than do any other piece of literary work I can think of,' he had told the American author Gamaliel Bradford in August 1924.[32] The opportunity to find out more about the United States came with an invitation in the autumn of 1924 to go there on Reuters business and give the yearly address at a boys' school, Milton Academy. Though Buchan had often been invited to make lecture tours of the States he had always turned them down on account of his health. In 1924 he felt able to go.

Alice was sent abroad with Susan's mother and Aunt Blanche while the boys were despatched to Mrs Buchan at Broughton. At the end of August and accompanied by his wife, John Buchan sailed on the *Empress of France* bound for Quebec. From there they went to Ottawa where they stayed in a house pro-vided by Sir Wilfrid Laurier and saw the Prime Minister, Mackenzie King, whom they had met first briefly in May 1919 and then at Chatsworth the pre-vious year, when the Duke of Devonshire had entertained the Dominion Prime Ministers at the Imperial Conference. They then went on to Boston where they saw Ferris Greenslet, a partner in Houghton Mifflin and Buchan's US publisher. After this they headed south by train to Washington where Buchan had 'twenty minutes' talk with the President and found him as gar-rulous as King George V'.[33]

In Washington the Buchans saw the Lincoln Memorial and Lee's house at Arlington before being joined by the historian Samuel Eliot Morison. With him and Greenslet the Buchans then set out in an open car for their tour of the Civil War battlefields, the Shenandoah Valley and to see Jefferson's house, Monticello. As Buchan told Nancy Astor: 'Susy and I both completely lost our hearts to Virginia and its people. It is the only place in the world where you can still find the old English life.'[34] Both Morison and Greenslet were par-ticularly impressed with Buchan's knowledge of the Civil War. He seemed to know, Greenslet later wrote, 'the names of the mountains without looking at the map.' In Richmond they were joined by the editor of the Richmond *News-Leader*, Douglas Freeman. Buchan, realizing he would have neither the time nor the necessary access to papers to write his proposed life of Robert E. Lee, suggested that Freeman should take it over. Freeman agreed and his acclaimed biography appeared ten years later.[35]

The party returned via Washington and New York to Boston where the Buchans stayed with an old friend from Oxford, Roger Merriman now Professor of History at Harvard and head of Eliot House. They dined with the President of Harvard and the poetess, Amy Lowell, whom they thought very self-centred. They saw their first football game and visited Merriman's son, Dan, at Groton. 'The thing that is indelibly impressed on my mind about that afternoon,' Dan Merriman later wrote 'is Mr Buchan's knowledge of and interest in everything he saw. No bird, tree, shrub or flower escaped his eye ... His knowledge was incredible, his powers of observation uncanny, and his supply of information about all branches of natural history inexhaustible.'[36] Finally, after a few days rest at a farm house in New Hampshire, Buchan delivered his address at Milton Academy on 16 October. 'Two Ordeals of Democracy' drew heavily on his Civil War tour and Buchan devoted much of it to an appraisal of Abraham Lincoln. The speech was published the following year in America by Houghton Mifflin and included in his 1926 collection of essays *Homilies and Recreations*.

At the end of October the Buchans returned to Canada where they met the Governor-General, Lord Byng, the wartime Prime Minister, Sir Robert Borden and the Principal of McGill, General Sir Arthur Currie whom Buchan had known when Currie was commanding the Canadian Corps in France during the final stages of the First World War. The Buchans also stayed with Vincent Massey, then about to enter government service after a career in academia and business. The Canadian trip was a great success. Byng wrote to Buchan shortly after his return passing on 'the inundation of nice things said about you, your visit and your speech at the Canadian Clubs here and elsewhere ... Dear John, you said the right thing at the right time, in the right way.'[37]

The reception in Canada gave Violet Markham the idea that Buchan might be a possible candidate to succeed Byng as Governor-General. Mackenzie King seemed in favour of the idea and Markham also enlisted support from the most recent Colonial Secretary, the Duke of Devonshire, but his successor Leo Amery, approached in April 1926, was less keen. He noted in his diary on April Fool's Day 1926: 'I gave Violet to understand, as gently as I could, that he really had not quite the experience or qualifications – much as I loved him and Susie – and that these appointments could not be settled by Dominion PMs' picking out their personal friends.'[38]

Buchan affected to distance himself and refused to lobby for the position. He used his wife to act as an intermediary with Violet Markham, who was told by Susan:

> He can only accept the thing if it was *strongly* put to him as a matter of duty without any attempt on his part to get it. He says the point is theological and that you will understand it![39]

In the end Markham's efforts were unsuccessful for the job went to Viscount Willingdon who had previously been Governor of Bombay and then Madras. Susan wrote to Violet 'I daresay a very good appointment but why did he worry us when he knew that Willingdon was there and eager to go?'[40]

10

NOVELIST

IN the fifteen years between moving to Elsfield and leaving for Canada Buchan wrote sixteen novels, all of them for Hodder & Stoughton. They ranged from a series of 'shockers' recounting the adventures of Richard Hannay, the hero of *The Thirty-Nine Steps* and a children's book to several historical novels and contemporary romances. They can be grouped chronologically within several distinct groups. First, the three post-war Richard Hannay novels, then the three Edward Leithen novels, then the three Dickson McCunn romances and finally Buchan's children's story *The Magic Walking Stick*, the short story collection *The Runagates Club* and *A Prince of the Captivity* a powerful parable set against the rise of the European dictators. The second part of the chapter looks at Buchan's five historical novels.

The Three Hostages (1924) was the first Buchan 'shocker' to be published after the war and it is revealing that he should have waited five years to resurrect his most popular hero, Richard Hannay. Like *The Power House* it is concerned with the fragility of civilization, here given a new emphasis by the uncertainties of the post-war world and Buchan's recently enhanced knowledge about the techniques of propaganda. The book begins, as with so many Hannay stories, with our hero happily settled and more interested in country life than with 'what might be happening in Parliament or Russia or the Hindu Kush.' It is seven years since his adventures in *The Thirty-Nine Steps*. He has married Mary Lamington and they are living peacefully at Fosse Manor in the Cotswolds with their fifteen month old son Peter John when Hannay receives a note from Bullivant, now Lord Artinswell, asking him 'to undertake a troublesome piece of business'.

Hannay is visited by Julius Victor, an American banker whose teenage daughter, Adela, has been kidnapped. He further learns from a Scotland Yard detective, Macgillivray, that two other hostages have also been taken, a Christ Church undergraduate, Lord Mercot and the ten year old son of 'the great soldier and administrator' Sir Arthur Warcliff. These three hostages constitute 'the daughter of the richest man in the world, the heir of our greatest dukedom, the only child of a national hero'.[1]

Hannay's quest to find the hostages, who have been hypnotized in various mind control experiments, takes him from a seedy club off Fitzroy Square to Norway, where he is reunited with the 'good' German Gaudian from *Greenmantle*, and finally to a thrilling climax on the Scottish moors. It also brings him his toughest opponent so far. Dominick Medina is a London MP, a poet and classical scholar, 'the best shot in England after His Majesty', 'and the handsomest thing in mankind since the Greeks'. He is also a man 'utterly and consumedly wicked, with no standard which could be remotely related to ordinary life'. The surprise is that he is also a member of the Thursday Club, a secret dining society consisting of twenty members which had been founded 'after the war by some of the people who had queer jobs and wanted to keep together'. Fellow members include Sandy Arbuthnot, Edward Leithen, now Attorney General, Sir Arthur Warcliff, a Cambridge Fellow who had captained a Bedouin tribe, 'one of the Q-boat VCs and Pugh of the Indian Secret Service'.

The Three Hostages, which was originally called *The Enchanter's Nightmare*, is a state-of-the-nation novel with Buchan attempting to show the underside of the post-war world; what Dr Greenslade calls the 'dislocation of the mechanism of human reasoning, a general loosening of screws'. It is a powerful and prophetic book though not entirely satisfactory in terms of its structure. Instead of the climax of the book coming with the downfall of Medina and the safe release of the third hostage Buchan cannot resist introducing a scene where Hannay stalks Medina across the Scottish moors. Though an exciting climax it does reduce Medina from being a Lucifer figure to a mere mortal. The novel was dedicated to 'A Young Gentleman of Eton College' 'in the hope that in the eyes of you and your friends it may atone for certain other writings of mine with which you have been afflicted by those in authority'. It was published simultaneously in Britain and the United States in August 1924 and serialised in *The Graphic* between 25 April and 9 August 1924 as well as in *All-Story Weekly* in June and July. It received extensive review coverage but it is clear the critics regarded it as a piece of lightweight nonsense.

Stanley Baldwin, an admirer of Buchan's novels, thought *The Courts of the Morning* (1929), in which Hannay makes his next, albeit brief, appearance his best novel so far and on its publication the book drew generally favourable reviews. The *Daily Telegraph*, which serialized it, wrote:

> In this book Mr Buchan shows himself even more skilful than usual. The rapidly changing scene, the prominence given to each character, and the deft touches that make a countryside or a human figure spring into life all proclaim a master of the novelist's art.[2]

Hannay is summoned by the American Embassy, worried about the disappearance of Blenkiron, and subsequently reads his obituary. At the same time he hears from various colleagues in the Thursday Club that Sandy has been sighted around the world behaving mysteriously. The book then moves to the fictional South American republic of Olifa where Archie Roylance is on a delayed honeymoon. There he meets the Gobernador of the rich mineral area, Gran Seco, who plans to take over the rest of Olifa with the help of his Conquistadores. Olifa is fully realized as a country, even though Buchan had never been to South America, to the extent that a detailed map of the country is provided at the beginning of the book. He gives Olifa a history, its own wine and there are extensive descriptions of the racial characteristics of the people, the capital and the interior. The portrait of the country is partly drawn from Buchan's memories of South Africa and particularly the Olifants in Bechuanaland and partly based on his own imagination, though in the book its capital is described as 'a reticent Paris, with a dash of Wall Street'.

Sandy Arbuthnot, who dominates the novel, begins to take on many of the characteristics, particularly physical, of T.E. Lawrence and he adopts the sort of guerrilla tactics used by Lawrence in The Arab Revolt some ten years earlier; the original title of the book was in fact *Far Arabia*. Buchan had just been reading Lawrence's October 1920 article for the *Army Quarterly*, which described various guerrilla tactics and he incorporated much of it into *The Courts of the Morning*. In turn, the military historian Basil Liddell-Hart thought so highly of this aspect of the novel that he put it on the reading list for his own book *The Future of Infantry*.

Mussolini is mentioned in the *Courts of the Morning* and in part the novel is an attempt to warn of the nature of dictatorship. As so often in Buchan it also becomes, as the critic T.J. Binyon has pointed out, an account 'of an individual's voyage towards self-knowledge, a spiritual progress which can end in regeneration and rebirth in life, or in self-sacrifice and transfiguration in death'. Many of the characters reach a degree of self-knowledge in the course of the book. Sandy, who has been feeling listless at the beginning of the novel finds a new purpose and love while Castor the villain becomes a hero and realizes he must regain his soul.[3] Castor hopes to isolate America from international affairs and another of the themes of the book is the importance of America as a bulwark for democracy. 'The era of the Old World is over, and it is the turn of the New World to-day,' says one of the characters. '. . . the difficulties even of Europe must be settled in the West.' The book is dedicated to Buchan's American publisher Ferris Greenslet, there are several American characters including Blenkiron's niece, Barbara Dasent, and the book is studded with references to American history.

On its publication, review coverage was mixed, with some papers failing to understand the complexities of the book. The *Nation & Athenaeum*, while aware of 'the intricacies of motive, the realistic geographical and military fic- tions' argued that 'if the "ideas" grate they need not be taken too seriously'. The *New York Times* in its review noted: 'There is mystery of an unusual kind; there is adventure and plenty of it; there are thrilling and dramatic moments, touches of the humble and bizarre, and at the root of it all, a sharp conflict between two utterly different philosophies of life.' The most perceptive review came from J.B. Priestley in the *Evening News*.

As an old Buchan fan I was slightly disappointed by his new tale *The Courts of the Morning*. It begins very well indeed with a convincing South American republic, mysterious copper mines in the mountains and a first- class villain on the grand scale. Somewhere about halfway through I found myself losing interest. To begin with, there is no longer any mystery. Then the villain begins to change character, and nobody effective takes his place. And the long and involved accounts of guerrilla warfare that take up most of the later chapters seemed to me below the usual Buchan level of interest. In many ways this is a more ambitious tale than most of his old 'thrillers' but it does not seem to me so successful.[4]

Richard Hannay's final adventure, which was serialised in the *Daily Mail*, was *The Island of Sheep* (1936) – a title borrowed from Buchan's 1919 sympo- sium – which was published in America as *The Man from the Norlands*. The book was written during 1933 and was partly based on a fortnight's trip Buchan had made to the Faroe Islands with his son Johnnie in July 1932. The book is dedicated to Johnnie and in the guise of Peter John, Hannay's son, he becomes one of the central characters of the story. Peter John, like Johnnie Buchan, is a fine naturalist with a particular interest in falconry. Indeed, a knowledge of wild life is integral to the plot with a crucial scene dependent on Peter John remembering that pink-foot geese when startled move towards, not away from, an intruder.

One night on a train journey from Victoria to his boat on the Solent Richard Hannay meets Lombard, a businessman whom he had known twenty five years before in South Africa. He is reminded of a skirmish in which he, Lombard and Peter Pienaar took part to protect a gold speculator Marius Haraldsen, which has resulted in a vendetta being passed down to Haraldsen's descendants. Hannay discovers that Haraldsen's granddaughter, Anna, has been kidnapped and, with Lombard, feels honour bound, under a pact made at the time, to come to the Haraldsen family's aid. The two men are joined in their endeavours by Sandy Arbuthnot, who has an old score to settle with one of the villains, the French aristocrat, Jacques D'Ingraville.

As with many Buchan novels the novel is about middle-aged men being shaken out of their complacency by an important mission and the book is filled with a sense of optimism, and plenty of action, including a whale hunt and a car chase along the Great North Road.[5] *The Island of Sheep* received respectful but rather low-key reviews, most notably from C. Day Lewis, writing as Nicholas Blake, in the *Spectator*. As with *The Courts of the Morning*, Buchan had allowed his mysticism and concern with contemporary politics to impede the narrative flow. It was a tendency increasingly evident in the Hannay novels, with the result that the later Hannay books have never been as popular as *The Thirty-Nine Steps*, *Greenmantle* and *Mr Standfast*.

Edward Leithen, briefly mentioned in *The Three Hostages*, moves resolutely centre stage in Buchan's two novels, *John Macnab* and *The Dancing Floor*. In the former Leithen, Lord Lamancha, Secretary of State for the Dominions and banker John Palliser-Yeates are bored with life. At their club they meet Archie Roylance and together they concoct a bet that they cannot kill a stag or a salmon from three different Scottish Highland estates without being caught. Warning is to be given to the owners of the respective estates in a note signed by 'John Macnab'. The book describes the men's attempts to realize their challenge in the course of which there are some marvellous evocations of Scottish field sports and scenery drawn from Buchan's own experience stalking and fishing particularly on Gerard Craig-Sellar's estate at Ardtornish. For once there is no villain, just some love interest and gentle comedy. Though ostensibly a romp about middle-aged, respectable men turning their backs on responsibility and challenging authority, the book is also an examination of the changing nature of society and in particular the life of the Scottish Highlands. Gertrude Himmelfarb has called it 'a parable about authority and property'.

The three landowners are all very different. The Radens, first encountered in the short story *The Far Islands*, have a history going back to Robert Bruce and Flodden, Lord Claybody is a self-made British businessman who believes in the sanctity of property, while Acheson Bandicott is an American and the most prepared of the three to accept fluidity in the social structure. One of the underlying themes of the book is that privilege cannot be justified unless it is earned, what Archie at his political meeting calls 'the doctrine of Challenge'. Janet Raden admits to Archie that: 'The old life of the Highlands is going, and people like ourselves must go with it . . . We've long ago lost our justification.' The Radens have failed to adapt. 'Their only claim was the right of property, which is no right at all.'[6]

Buchan has returned to several favourite themes including the contrast between the freedom of Scotland and the stuffiness of London and the need for successful men to test and cleanse themselves in the wild. It is partly an attempt to articulate his own dilemma, caught between his position as a member of the English Establishment and his more modest Scottish roots, a throwback to the disdain for success of Raymond Asquith and his circle. The book's premise is a Calvinist one: 'You've got to rediscover the comforts of your life by losing them for a little.' There are other undercurrents including the tension between male friendship and love for a woman shown when Roylance, who falls in love with Raden's daughter Janet, finds his sympathies divided in the resolution of the bet.

The idea of the sporting bet was inspired by the exploits of an exact contemporary of Buchan, Captain James Brander Dunbar, who accomplished just that on Lord Abinger's Estate at Inverlochy near Fort William in 1897. Buchan was certainly aware of the story and later inscribed Brander Dunbar's copy of *John Macnab*. While on holiday on Mull the year after publication he was delighted to receive, though unable to accept, a similar challenge to that of 'John Macnab' signed by 'Three Labour MPs'.[6] The novel was published in July 1925 and dedicated to Rosalind Maitland, with whom the Buchans often holidayed in the Highlands. Critical reaction was muted. *The Nation and Athenaeum* for example thought that despite 'Mr Buchan's skill in conveying the atmosphere of moor and Highland forest' the story could not be 'sustained beyond the limits of a short story.' It has however remained one of Buchan's best-loved books.[8]

The Dancing Floor was the expansion of Buchan's short story *Basilissa*, which had appeared in *Blackwood's Magazine* in April 1914, and was in turn based on the Buchans cruise in the Aegean in 1910. Originally contracted as *The Goddess of the Shades*, Buchan began it while returning from a trip to Canada in November 1924. The book was completed in October 1925 and published the following July with a dedication to Henry Newbolt. Once again Buchan was exploring, as in the early short stories, the survival of pre-Christian cults in the present day. Shortly before the First World War Edward Leithen meets a young Oxford undergraduate, Vernon Milburne, who tells him of a strange experience he has every year. On the first Monday in April he dreams that a fire is approaching him, each year the fire moving a room closer to his own. Then in the spring of 1914 Leithen and Milburne are guests on Lamancha's yacht in the Aegean and spend a day on the island of Plakos which, though beautiful, Leithen also finds menacing. It is these two strands which form the crux of the story.

War comes and only at its end are the men reunited when they find themselves in adjacent hospital beds. Leithen is amazed, that given his war experiences, Milburne seems to have led a charmed life and suffered very little injury. He learns too that Plakos has been inherited by a young woman called Kore Arabin. Shortly afterwards Leithen meets Arabin, who asks if he will help her with a legal problem concerning Plakos. He discovers that a curse has been put on the island and the only way of restoring its prosperity is through the sacrifice of a young man and woman. Leithen, the dry lawyer, falls in love with Kore and asks her to marry him. Milburne tells him if he does it will be the end of their friendship. Buchan is again introducing the theme of male friendship jeopardized by romantic love. Kore flees to the island followed by Leithen. Vernon Milburne too finds himself on the island on the crucial first Monday in April in the year that the fire is meant to arrive in his own room. At the climax of the novel all three principal characters are drawn into the pagan ceremonies on 'The Dancing Floor' and forced as a result to face up to their previous lives.

At the centre of the action as in many Buchan novels is a house and a sacred place, here called 'The Dancing Floor'. Similarities can be drawn with a number of the historical novels written at the same time. In its depiction of the power of place over succeeding generations comparisons can also be made with the short story 'The Grove of Ashtaroth'.[9] Contemporary reviewers failed to understand the novel, each drawing their own conclusions from it. The *New York Times* thought it 'a competent and conventional character study that turns after a hundred pages or so into one of the best adventure stories of the year'. The *TLS* felt 'the real theme of the novel is the triumph of courage over fear and of religion over what roughly amounts to devil-worship.' But in *The Nation and Athenaeum* Edwin Muir wrote: 'With a style fitted for excellent work he writes inanities, tries to make us forget everything that is of consequence, showing now and then a touch of hostility one would almost imagine, against thought and sincerity.'[10] Critics were quick to note the book's inspiration in *The Golden Bough* and since then its stature has grown, with the Buchan critic David Daniell calling it 'a subtle and significant book.'[11]

Leithen's next appearance, in a group of related tales called *The Gap in the Curtain*, is significant in charting his move from detached narrator to playing a more introspective role in the development of the story. The book was written between March 1930 and February 1931 and published in Britain in August 1932 and subsequently in America, Italy and France. Buchan dedicated it to old friends Sybil, daughter of Earl Grey, and her husband the banker Lambert Middleton. A house party has been assembled at the home of Sally Flambard in the Cotswolds. Among the guests is Professor Moe, 'the greatest mathematician alive', who has discovered that: 'Time is not a straight line, but full of kinks and coils . . . the Future is here with us now, if we only knew how to look for it.' He suggests that the house guests take part in an experiment. 'To-day is the sixth of June. Four days from now, if you and the others consent, I will enable you to see for one instant of time – no longer – a newspaper of the tenth day of June next year.' *The Times* for the year ahead is produced where the financier sees news of an important merger, the politician discovers the name of the next Prime Minister and two guests see their own deaths. The book then deals with the men's reaction to this knowledge of the future.

The idea of being able to look into the future was hardly a new one but Buchan gave it a new spin from his recent reading of J.W. Dunne's *An Experiment with Time*, Henri Bergson's *Time and Free Will* and *Matter and Memory* and Drayton Thomas's *Some New Evidence for Human Survival*. The book was a satirical look at politics and high finance, reminiscent of Aldous Huxley, within the context of Buchan's fascination with the concept of time and space, already explored in short stories such as 'Space'.

However, there are deeper resonances to the book and Buchan is exploring wider issues such as the redemptive power of love, resurrection and the nature of Free Will and predestination. The action of the story takes place, as in *The Dancing Floor* around Easter. It may be that this is a time when Leithen is likely to be free from his work to have such adventures but it may also be because this is a story, as David Daniell has suggested, about 'the visitation of the Holy Spirit expressed in powers of prophecy and the assurance of the power of the Risen Christ.'[12]

The book is rich in quotations from several languages and writers as diverse as Dickens, Donne, Milton and D.G. Rossetti and full of cross references to other Buchan novels. Anthony Hurrell from *The Runagates Club* reappears while another character, Pamela Brune, is presumably related to the Flora

Brune of another of Buchan's country house novels *The Lodge in the Wilderness*. The novelist Claypole could be Arnold Bennett or Hugh Walpole, Maffit, the explorer of the Bramaputra gorges, is probably Cecil Rawlings and Bunyan's 'The Interpreter's House' here takes the form of a business.

L.A.G. Strong in *The Spectator* called it 'confident, assured, and, within its chosen limits, masterly' but again it was J.B. Priestley who showed himself to be Buchan's most perceptive critic. Reviewing the novel in the *Evening Standard* he wrote:

> Instead of giving us what amounts to a series of short stories Mr Buchan, inspired by such a grand theme, should have flung aside his other interests as politician, publisher, historian, biographer and plunged boldly into a big novel in which all the strands would have been woven together. But I admire gallant versatility (which Mr Buchan has in abundance) and so I must not grumble. His *Gap in the Curtain* can be read with excitement and profit.[13]

It is largely on the strength of this book that Buchan is so highly regarded in France as a master of the supernatural.

Buchan described *Huntingtower*, the first book in the Dickson McCunn trilogy, as 'a Glasgow Fairy Tale' and it certainly has the customary ingredients – a beautiful princess locked up in a tower, a lovelorn suitor who is a poet and who helps rescue her and a mysterious villain who is 'the devil incarnate'. He gave it a fresh twist by setting it in the Galloway landscape he knew so well and adding some unlikely characters, who reappear in subsequent adventures, including a middle-aged Glasgow grocer, Dickson McCunn, and a gang of street urchins from the slums of Glasgow, the sort of boys he might have taught in his father's Sunday School, the Gorbals Die Hards. They include Chief of Staff Thomas Younie, Peet Paairsson, Napoleon, Wee Jaikie and 'Auld Bull'.[14]

The basic premise on which *Huntingtower*, rests is that there is a world-wide conspiracy penetrating to every level of British society and which the forces of organized law and order are powerless to defeat. Here it is because 'There's no' a policeman nearer than Knockraw – yin Johnnie Trummle, and he's as useless as a frostit tattie.' The book was written four years after the Russian Revolution and there was considerable concern that Bolshevism might spread west. In *Huntingtower* Buchan adds to the threat by having Bolshevik agents reach the West of Scotland and including many real place names in the

South-West of Scotland. The house at the centre of the story, Huntingtower, takes its name from a village just outside Buchan's birthplace, Kirkmichael is a village south of Maybole and Dalquharter House is probably based on the neighbouring Dalquharran castle where Raymond Asquith had stayed in August 1904.

Saskia, a princess who has fled the Russian Revolution, has been traced and imprisoned in Huntingtower by Bolshevik agents. McCunn and the Die-Hards stumble upon the conspiracy while on a walking tour and immediately decide to rescue her which they do with the help of Archibald Roylance. The book makes frequent references to fairy tales but Buchan within this ostensibly lightweight romance was also trying to say something about the immediate post war world. The poet John Heritage says he 'learned in the war that civil-isation anywhere is a very thin crust' and Saskia has a long percipient speech where she reflects on what has happened to Russia:

> My country has been broken to pieces, and there is no law in it; therefore it
> is a nursery of crime . . . My people are not wickeder than others, but for
> the moment they are sick and have no strength. As for the government of
> the Bolsheviki it matters little, for it will pass. Some parts of it may remain,
> but it is a government of the sick and fevered, and cannot endure in health.
> Lenin may be a good man – I do not think so, but I do not know – but if
> he were an archangel he could not alter things.[15]

Russia is contrasted with Britain which Saskia thinks 'the safest place in a mad world' and, though there is some gentle satire at Mrs McCunn's expense, the British middle class are seen as the backbone which should prevent any comparable revolution taking place in Britain. McCunn's bourgeois views are shown to prevail over Bolshevik dogma and the synthetic radicalism of Harrow and Cambridge-educated John Heritage. McCunn according to one of the characters 'is the stuff which above all others makes a great people. He will endure when aristocracies crack and proletariats crumble.' The Die-Hards, in spite of their modest backgrounds, have the potential to move up the social scale. Dickson tells them 'There's the stuff in you to make Generals and Provosts – ay, and Prime Ministers . . .'[16]

The book was serialized in *Popular Magazine* between August and September 1921 and dedicated to a friend of the Buchans, W.P. Ker, a Fellow of All Souls, who had been Professor of English at University College, London since 1889. It was published in August 1922.[17] Review coverage was generally kind. The New York Times found the book 'delight-ful' if improbable and concluded 'No one who becomes acquainted with

McCunn, the grocer, will be likely to forget him . . . the story plunges forward, thrill piling on thrill, battle following battle . . . Mr Buchan is undoubtedly one of the best of contemporary light novelists.'[18] Film rights in *Huntingtower* were sold in 1925 to Gainsborough Pictures who filmed it two years later at Bamborough Castle with the Scottish comedian Harry Lauder playing McCunn. Subsequently rights were sold for a play and another film but neither were produced. However the book has proved popular on radio with dramatizations in 1938 and in 1988.

Written between April 1928 and March 1929 and first published in July 1930 *Castle Gay* takes up the story of Dickson McCunn and two of the Gorbals Die-Hards six years after *Huntingtower*. McCunn has become a country laird with five hundred acres on 'the spur of a Carrick moor' and the two slum boys Jaikie Galt and Dougal Crombie have respectively become a Cambridge and Scottish rugby international and a successful journalist on the papers of the newspaper magnate, Thomas Craw. Craw, a satirical mix of Lord Rothermere and Robertson Nicoll, has made his fortune by producing a paper, redolent of the *British Weekly* or ill-fated *Scottish Review*, which is aimed at 'simple folk, who wanted a little politics, a little science, a little relig-ion, set to a domestic tune'.[19]

Jaikie and Dougal on a walking tour of Galloway take refuge one night with a Mrs Catterick and discover their fellow guest is Craw, mistakenly kid-napped by undergraduates involved in a Glasgow University Rectorial elec-tion. The two boys agree to cycle to Craw's nearby rented home, Castle Gay, and deliver a letter to his secretary. Craw is a supporter of the monarchist party in the Central European republic of Evallonia and the boys, joined by McCunn, become involved with Evallonian monarchists and republicans who for various reasons have come in search of the newspaper magnate. Prince John, the Pretender to the Evallonian throne, escapes from the clutches of the Evallonian republicans after several adventures, which appropriately include his dressing as Bonnie Prince Charlie at a fancy dress ball. Craw undergoes a conversion, having been redeemed by his testing in the Scottish wilds, and marries one of the characters.

The Evallonians have attempted to contact Craw because they feel British newspapermen determine Government policy. *Castle Gay* was written during Beaverbrook's Empire Free Trade campaign and one of the themes of the book is concern that newspaper magnates have too much power in government circles. Buchan had always been a strong supporter of a free press and as the guest of the Newspaper Society in May 1929 had praised the present quality of journalism, but he did have anxieties about its possible abuse and these are implicit in the book. Another contemporary concern that Buchan plays on is communism. The Evallonian monarchists are the only bulwark against com-munism and therefore to be supported.

Other Buchan themes are also introduced. One of the subplots involves Jaikie falling in love with Alison Westwater, daughter of Castle Gay's owner Lord Rhynns. The ancient Westwaters with their sense of noblesse oblige are contrasted with the *nouveau riche* Craw, a subject explored at greater length in *John Macnab*. And as always Buchan includes a number of real people and places. The dog Woolworth in the story is Spider, the Buchan's mongrel terrier, Evallonia is based on the Central European republics set up in 1919 and many of the fictitious sites in Galloway are based on real places. Portaway is Newton Stewart, Gledmouth is Dumfries, Castle Gay, supposedly the Castle of Old Risk and Fallatown, is Wigtown. Evelyn Waugh, reviewing the book in the *Graphic*, had only praise for it:

> The climax of the story, when for a moment the succession of events carries the characters away from comedy into sudden, convincing melodrama only to drop them again instantly into a placid half romantic half humorous conclusion is most accomplished literary craftsmanship.[20]

McCunn returns for his final adventure in *The House of the Four Winds*. He is suffering from various aches and pains and is sent to a kurhaus in Rosensee, very similar to one Buchan had himself attended some years earlier. Previous characters in the series also converge on Rosensee including Alison Westwater, Archie Roylance now a PPS to the Under-Secretary for Foreign Affairs, Jaikie Galt on a European walking tour and Dougal Crombie, 'almost the force in the Craw Press', on a fact-finding journalistic mission. There is trouble in Evallonia as a nationalist youth movement, Juventus, with similarities to those in Hitler's Germany, led by the Countess Araminta Troyos intrigues to put Prince John on the throne. McCunn, the Roylances and the Die-Hards are drawn into the internal politics of Evallonia. They are joined by Randall Glynde, the owner of a travelling circus, a secret service agent with a penchant for Latin poetry and disguises and a cousin of Alison Westwater. Glynde is the Aubrey Herbert character in the story, having 'been everything in his time from cowpuncher to film star, not to mention diplomat, and various sorts of soldier, and somebody's private secretary'. Alison and the Roylances are captured by Prince John's principal adversary, Mastrovin, the 'toughest communist in Europe' first encountered in *Castle Gay*. A daring rescue takes place and McCunn, representing age and experience over youth and enthusiasm, saves the day when he impersonates the Evallonian Archduke in a scene reminiscent of Sandy Arbuthnot's success as the prophet

Greenmantle. At the centre of the story, as in the previous two books in the series, is a house. This time it is the home of one of the leading monarchists Prince Odalchini's the House of the Four Winds, so named because winds converged on it down several valleys.

The House of the Four Winds is one of the least popular of Buchan's books, perhaps because of the uneasy mixture of comedy and drama. There are certain similarities with Anthony Hope's classic *The Prisoner of Zenda* but as Janet Adam Smith has pointed out 'Ruritania was not Buchan's country'.[21] Published in August 1935 it received poor reviews. Cyril Connolly writing in the *New Statesman and Nation* thought it 'disappointing, too involved and too ruritarian . . . On the strange curve which has led Buchan from his first appearances in the Yellow Book to the Governor-Generalship of Canada this novel occupies a rather low point . . .' Subsequent critics have not substantially challenged that contemporary view.[22]

Though not strictly speaking a Dickson McCunn story the children's book *The Magic Walking Stick*, published in 1932, can conveniently be grouped with the Huntingtower trilogy given its similar preoccupation with monarchists and republicans. The book is an account of thirteen-year-old Bill's adventures with his magic walking stick, a walking stick which has the power to take Bill, and whoever is holding his hand, to the place of their wishes – 'the blinding white sands of the Solomon Islands . . . the rowans and birches of a wintry Highland glen'. A large part of the story is devoted to Bill's rescue from the republicans of Prince Anatole, the fourteen year old heir to the Balkan throne of Gracia.[23] It was dedicated to Susan's sister Margaret, her husband Jeremy and their daughter Carola and arose out of a game Buchan used to play with his own children. It had first appeared as a short story in a 1927 collection of stories *Sails of Gold* edited by Cynthia Asquith. Buchan expanded it and it was serialized in the magazine St Nicholas between December 1933 and April 1934.

Buchan had known Cynthia Asquith since his time at Oxford. A granddaughter of the Earl of Wemyss and March she had been in love with Raymond Asquith but in 1910 married his younger brother Herbert 'Beb'. The great love of her life, however, was Basil Blackwood, thirteen years her senior, whom she had seen much of after his return in 1910 to become Private Secretary to the Lord Lieutenant of Ireland. Later Cynthia worked as Secretary to J.M. Barrie whose royalties she inherited. Her son Michael and his wife Didy Battye were friends of Buchan's own children.[24]

Both Richard Hannay and Edward Leithen appear in *The Runagates Club*,

Buchan's only collection of post-war short stories, published in July 1928. The book consists of a series of stories told by members of the Thursday Club, a dining society which had appeared briefly in *The Three Hostages* and *The Dancing Floor*.[25] The book is unique in the Buchan canon in including all the major Buchan characters such as Richard Hannay, Sandy Arbuthnot, Edward Leithen, John Palliser-Yeates and Lord Lamancha as well as introducing many new figures such as Francis Martendale, Henry Nightingale, Oliver Pugh, Ralph Collatt, Anthony Hurrell and Martin Peckwether. Whereas his earlier volumes of short stories had often centred on a theme, these stories, as the reviewer in the TLS noted: 'are pleasingly diverse in subject, incident and treatment'. They range from Hannay's eerie tale set in the Transvaal and the Duke of Burminster's comic adventure in the Scottish Borders to Leithen's tangle with South American revolutionaries in central London and Oliver Pugh's journey of discovery in 'the Sachischen Sweitz'. The stories are beautifully self-contained, often end with a twist and demonstrate the usual Buchan themes of the unwitting amateur drawn into adventure and the fragile division between civilization and chaos.[26] The book was not taken very seriously by the reviewers with Raymond Mortimer's review in the *Nation and Athenaeum* indicative of the general approach: 'Mr Buchan has considerable invention, a good narrative style, and a pleasing affection for the aristocracy.'[27]

A Prince of the Captivity is not easily categorized and is among the least known of Buchan's novels. Though one of his last novels it most closely resembles his first contemporary novel, *The Half-Hearted* with its story of a man who only restores his self-esteem by sacrificing himself in a dramatic gesture at a mountain pass. The story is based closely on the experiences of Major Cecil Cameron, a Cameron of Lochiel, who shortly before the First World War was sentenced, alongside his wife, at the Edinburgh High Court for faking the robbery of a pearl necklace to claim the £6,500 insurance money. Though the crime was committed by his wife Cameron was accused of covering for her and remained in prison until 1914 when he emerged as an intelligence officer running agent networks in Belgium for GHQ BEF. It was almost certainly then that Buchan, who was based at GHQ, first met Cameron and learnt of his secret service adventures. In January 1918 Cameron resigned from the GHQ Special Intelligence section and was posted to M12(d), a section of military intelligence responsible for Russia where he later accompanied General Knox, the head of the military mission to Russia. In 1920 Cameron was appointed by Brigadier Ormonde Winter, Director of Intelligence in Ireland, to run a secret recruiting office sending agents into Ireland against the IRA. Four years later he committed suicide.

In *A Prince of the Captivity*, Adam Melfort is an army officer who is forced to resign his commission and serves a two year prison term for a cheque forgery committed by his wife. He earns his passage back into society through intelligence work in the First World War. Melfort's adventures take him to the Greenland ice-cap, the Midland town of Birkpool, the Italian Alps and to post-war Germany where he foils a plot to bring down the Chancellor Loeffler, whom Buchan admitted was based on Bruning.[28] Melfort is pitted against the wealthy Warren Creevey, an economist who has made a reputation as a Government financial adviser and who is supposedly based on Maynard Keynes. Falconet, the American millionaire whom Melfort saves, is probably the philanthropist Edward Harkness to whom the book is dedicated.[29]

Many of the usual Buchan themes and literary devices are here – the opening in a Club, the liberating nature of the Scottish countryside, a hero able to speak several languages, the brotherhood of men drawn from disparate backgrounds, the undercurrent of Calvinism. The kidnapping of Creevey is similar to the capture of Castor in *The Courts of the Morning* while Adam's dream about the Scottish island, Eilean Ban, is reminiscent of that of Colin Raden in the short story 'The Far Islands.' The book is set against a background of the First World War and the rise of Hitler. Buchan, then an MP, introduced many of his current preoccupations – the nature of political leadership, the role of trade unions, the responsibility of the individual. Perhaps he was too ambitious in trying to place all his ideas within the context of an adventure story with the result it never really succeeds either as an adventure story or novel of ideas. The didactic nature of the book has always put off readers as has the poorly conceived characterization. For example Andrew Amos who appears here as a shop steward is a quite different character from his earlier appearance in *Mr Standfast*. Melfort, even by the standard of Buchan heroes, is rather too good to be true. He speaks French, German, Italian, Spanish, Russian, Turkish and is 'a master of the Scandinavian tongues'.[30]

A Prince of the Captivity was published in July 1933 and, at least initially, enjoyed a moderate success being reprinted four times in the first two months of publication. However, the critics were divided. William Plomer writing in the *Spectator* was dismissive: 'It is a British book, for boys of all ages if not of all kinds, and will find a niche in school libraries. It discloses a 'decent', scout-masterly attitude to life, and a wildly romantic view of human nature, especially that of men of action.' The *TLS*, however, in its review noted that the book was highly ambitious in its scope and structure providing 'a Buchanorama of the upheaval, physical, mental and spiritual, of the last twenty years'.[31] *A Prince of the Captivity* is not as easy a book to read as one of those in the Richard Hannay series but it is a fascinating insight into Buchan's mind and times.

The first of Buchan's postwar historical novels was *The Path of the King*, a title and theme in Buchan's mind since writing his Newdigate prize poem on the Pilgrim Fathers twenty three years earlier. The book was serialized in the magazine *Outward Bound* between October 1920 and October 1921, published in March 1921, and dedicated to Susan, the first time he had dedicated a book to her.[32] It follows the unknowing transmission of royal blood in fourteen chapters from the son of a Viking:

> through a Norman knight, the wife of a Flemish burgomaster, a highlyborn French girl whose life was changed by a meeting with Joan of Arc, a French lord who sailed with Columbus on his second voyage and became one of the first Protestants, an adventurer from Devon, one of the 1649 regicides, a professional spy (the Titus Oates plot), a secret agent in 1715, a friend of Daniel Boone, and finally Abraham Lincoln.[33]

The novel reflects Buchan's interest in kingship, later to be explored in *The Blanket of the Dark*, and the chance encounters of history. Indeed, there are many similarities between the two books. Daniel Boone is linked in *The Blanket of the Dark* with the royal Bohuns while the Lovell family, from Minster Lovell in *The Blanket in the Dark*, figure in several of the chapters in *The Path of the King*. Several stories draw on Buchan's knowledge of American history and the book demonstrates his growing interest in America and his desire to show the continuity of the Old World with the New. Many of the characters that appear are Buchan favourites such as Sir Walter Raleigh, some Jacobites, Charles I and Oliver Cromwell. It was G.M. Trevelyan's favourite 'Buchan' but the critics were less enthusiastic. The *TLS* found it 'disappointing':

> Mr Buchan uses the conventional methods of popular romance, and the result is a dimness and uncertainty of impression which is unlike his best work. He relies too much, it seems to us, upon the pseudo-romantic vocabulary, the use of slightly pretentious and unusual words and locutions where commoner and more vigorous ones would serve better.[34]

In May 1921 Vernon Watney, a neighbour of Buchan's at Cornbury Park, sent him a copy of his book *Cornbury and the Forest of Wychwood* which Watney had privately published eleven years earlier. To Buchan, already fascinated by the history of the area, it provided a literary stimulus. He knew the Forest of Wychwood from excursions with his children. Now he discovered Cornbury had sheltered Jacobite fugitives after Prince Charles's retreat from Derby. Buchan had always been interested in the Jacobites and the chance encounters of history, as exemplified in his 1908 short story 'The Company of the Marjorlaine'. He now decided to write an historical novel set in the area, adding to it a character associated with Elsfield – Dr Samuel Johnson. *Midwinter*, subtitled *Certain Travellers in Old England*, was begun at Elsfield in June and written there over the course of the next nine months. Buchan dedicated it to Watney, from whose book he drew much of the background, and after a serialization in the *Daily Telegraph* it was published in August 1923. It marked a return to the historical romances with which Buchan had begun his career some twenty five years earlier and was notable for its portrait of Johnson as an attractive young man rather than the rather crusty old man of legend.

It is 1745 and young Alastair Maclean is sent by Bonnie Prince Charlie on a secret mission to raise support for the Jacobite cause in the West of England. In the course of his travels he meets two quite different men, an impoverished tutor called Samuel Johnson and the mysterious 'Midwinter' leader of a half-pagan gang called the Naked Men or Spoonbills. This nation-wide band of countrymen hark back to another England:

an Old England, which has outlived Roman and Saxon and Dane and Norman and will outlast the Hanoverian. It has seen priest turn to presbyter and presbyter to parson and has only smiled. It is the land of the edge of moorlands and the rims of forests and the twilight before dawn, and strange knowledge still dwells in it.[35]

This was a theme first explored in the collection of short stories *The Watcher By The Threshold* and in particular 'No-Man's Land', and the book is full of contrasts between the order of the country house and the wildness of the countryside beyond. Reviewing the American edition the *New York Times* noted: 'It is a story that has many merits and few faults, the greatest of which is that it tells too little about Midwinter. Can it be that the author is reserving him for another tale?' It is certainly a possibility for *Midwinter* enjoyed some success. The book was reprinted several times, with four different editions by Nelson in 1925 alone, and translated into several languages including Czech and Gaelic.[36]

Buchan's fascination with the conflict between paganism and Christianity is further developed in his next novel *Witch Wood*, originally called *The Minister of Woodilee* and serialised in the *British Weekly* as *The High Places*. The book was dedicated to his brother Walter and published in July 1927. The Reverend David Sempill arrives in the parish of Woodilee, which is based on Broughton, on the 26 August (Buchan's birthday) 1644. He is a Platonist and humanist, a scholar whose ambition is to write the definitive work on the prophet Isaiah 'so that Sempill on Isaiah would be quoted reverently like Luther on the Galatians or Calvin on the Romans'. But there are strange things going on at Woodilee. One of his parishioners tells him he has 'seen visions and spoken with strange voices' in the Wood of Melanudrigill. Sempill decides to investigate and one night sees for himself figures dancing around an altar, 'the women half-naked, but the men with strange headpieces like animals'.[37]

The wood is almost a character in itself, representative of the 'Divided-Self'. It becomes another of Buchan's sacred places which like the dancing floor can be a force for good during the day or bad at night. Here Sempill first sees not just the witches but also the ethereal Katrine Yester with whom he falls in love. Sempill confesses his love and she agrees to marry him but shortly afterwards she dies in the plague which has afflicted the village, thereby fulfilling the sacrificial role of many of Buchan's heroines. The book was written while Buchan was researching his revised biography of Montrose and a secondary, but interrelated, plot is Sempill's involvement in sheltering one of Montrose's colonels. Buchan contrasts Sempill's humanism and support for one of the 'Kirk's oppressors' and the behaviour of some of his congregation, who combine their enthusiasm for pagan rites with a fierce denunciation of those not strictly committed to the Church's teaching. Sempill becomes a heroic victim of the hypocrisy of the period and it is possible, as Christopher Harvie has written, to draw parallels between him and Montrose as 'men destroyed by the society they wish to purify'.[38]

Witch Wood was Buchan's favourite novel. As he later admitted it was drawn from 'the Tweedside parish of my youth at the time when the old wood of Caledon had not wholly disappeared, and when the rigours of the new Calvinism were contending with the ancient rites of Diana'. Buchan had so imbued himself with the spirit and language of the period from his Montrose research that he was able instinctively and naturally to catch the idioms of seventeenth century Scotland.[39] His Montrose research, together with work on several aspects of Church history, had also raised questions of religious tolerance which he wanted to explore in a novel. His own religious position was by now established. Though he still took a keen interest in the affairs of the Church of Scotland, primed by his mother's obsession with the subject, he now worshipped to her disgust at the local Church of England church a hundred yards from his home. The Buchan household had never been narrowly Calvinistic and Buchan's own views had been modified by his studies at Glasgow and Oxford and his thirty years in the South of England. All this shaped this balanced examination of the complexities and paradoxes of Calvinism.

Though certain preoccupations can be traced back through recent books such as *The Dancing Floor* and the short stories *Witch Wood* marked a complete change in Buchan's style. There is still the importance of place, the theme of the frontier, the conflict between 'good' and 'evil' but in David Daniell's words there are 'no great distances, wild escapades, miracles of chance'. Everything takes place in the small parish of Woodilee and irony becomes central to the story. David, determined to expel witchcraft from the church, himself becomes the victim of a witchhunt within it.[40] The novel has come to be regarded as Buchan's masterpiece but even at the time the critics were aware of its significance. The *Spectator* called it 'this powerful, charming and spiritually earnest novel which almost entitles Mr Buchan to be called a modern and terse Walter Scott.' One of the reviews that most pleased Buchan was from a Clydeside MP in the *Glasgow Herald*:

> Whether regarded as an historical novel, a tale of adventure, a romance of the supernatural, or a psychological novel *Witch Wood* must be adjudged the greatest of Mr Buchan's published works. That it concerns the land and history of Scotland, that it makes a brilliant use of braid Scots dialect and that it enshrines many aspects, both admirable and contemptible, of the Scottish character are features that must give satisfaction to Mr Buchan's countrymen.[41]

His friends also liked it. C.S. Lewis, writing from Magdalen Oxford ten years later, claimed it as a favourite and noted the connection with Galt's *Annals of the Parish*. *Witch Wood* was perhaps Buchan's most penetrating response to the kailyard school of writing which he had despised since his days at Oxford and which he felt had stunted the development of Scottish writing since Scott and Stevenson.

Throughout his life Buchan remained fascinated by the 'ifs' of history. Eight years after his first historical novel set in the Cotswolds, *Midwinter*, Buchan returned with another, *Blanket of the Dark*. He set it two centuries earlier against the backdrop of the Reformation a period he had re-created in his preface to a Council for the Preservation of Rural England booklet the *Survey of the Thames Valley*, published in 1929. Peter Pentecost is a clerk at the abbey of Oseney frustrated by his lowly position in life and torn between the attractions of a temporal and secular life. He 'wanted life and power and pride; not in a sinful cause, but for noble purposes . . . He wanted to look the world in the face, to cast a spell over men and make them follow him.'[42] His chance soon comes when he learns he is really Bohun, son of the last Duke of Buckingham, sixth in descent from Edward III and rather than Henry VIII the legitimate King of England. He receives the news with mixed feelings, aware that he is now in danger of acting as the focus of any opposition to the King. When a plan by his supporters to kidnap Henry fails, Pentecost actually saves the King from drowning. He tells Henry who he is; and in return the King offers to make him Abbot of Oseney, but Peter declines. Now that his dreams have the potential to be realized he has lost interest in worldly success. While the usurper to his throne enjoys being King, Peter realizes he would take no pleasure in becoming sovereign.

The book is filled with contrasts between image and reality and between the high born and low life, best represented by Peter's protector Solomon Darking and his followers, here fulfilling the role of the Naked Men in *Midwinter*. Peter, like most of Buchan's heroes and implicitly Buchan himself, is torn between his duties as a citizen and his pleasures as an individual. He must choose between duty and love represented by Sabine Beauforest. She like Katrine Yester, is a creature of myth, 'the very goddess of love, Venus sprung from the foam', but there is a strong suggestion of sexuality, unusual in a Buchan heroine: '. . . her gown was scarcely a covering, for the snow of her neck and bosom was revealed, and, as she moved, the soft supple lines of her body . . . Her every movement was voluptuous . . . the occasional fall of her cloak which revealed more of a white bosom'.[43]

The Blanket of the Dark is a quotation from the first act of Shakespeare's *Macbeth* and it becomes a refrain throughout the book. Buchan uses it specifically to refer to Tudor despotism in England so that after Peter is sentenced to death by Henry the young clerk muses he sees 'the blanket of the dark rolling over all England'. The expression is also imbued with a more symbolic meaning. After he turns his back on the secular world Peter's thoughts are only for Sabine and he asks 'might there not be a world of light under the blanket of the dark?'[44] There is also the same sense as in *Midwinter* of an older England: 'The blanket of the dark lies heavy on it . . . But there is an uneasy stirring, and that stirring may soon be an upheaval that will shake down crowns and mitres. There is a new world coming to birth . . . though men know it not and crave rather to have an older world restored.' The book ends on a note of optimism with the hint the Bohun legacy may be taken up by the American Daniel Boone. 'There is a dark blanket which covers Europe, but beyond it there are open skies and the sun.'[45]

Janet Adam Smith has argued that this 'is Buchan's most deeply felt novel: characters and actions are devised which fittingly embody his sense of a time of drastic change, and his own deep – I would almost say wild – love of his adopted countryside.' The book is a homage to an old England and is rich in lyrical descriptions of the personification of that old England – the country-side near Elsfield. Many of the Buchan preoccupations, particularly from *Witch Woods* appear – 'the lost leader, the magic ground where the girl appears, the crippling fever at a crucial time.' And the book, as with many Buchan novels, is packed with religious symbolism ranging from Peter's surname to chapter headings such as 'the Road to Damascus'.[46]

Buchan was pleased his literary friends appreciated the book. Henry Newbolt wrote after receiving his copy: 'I read the book at two gulps – I am more astonished than ever at your historical and topographical knowledge, your unexhausted vigour and the boldness of your imagination.' Rudyard Kipling called it a '*tour de force*' while Rose Macaulay thought it 'so enchant-ing and beautiful that I often read it for my pleasure'.[47] L.A.G. Strong in the *Spectator* identified one of Buchan's strengths generally as a novelist. 'Mr Buchan's secret is his love of place, and his sense of wonder. He excites his reader because he himself is excited. At his best, he will not let you put the book down: at his worst, he is picturesque, appropriate, and conscientious.'[48]

For his last work of historical fiction, *The Free Fishers*, Buchan moved from the Cotswolds back to Scotland and a new period, the Napoleonic Wars. It is a book more in keeping with his earlier romances and heavily influenced by R.L. Stevenson. The book was dedicated to John Key Hutchinson 'In memory of our boyhood on the coast of Fife.' The hero of *The Free Fishers* is Anthony Lammas, a young Professor of Logic and Rhetoric at St Andrews, who is drawn into a plot to kill the Prime Minister, Spencer Perceval. The Free Fishers, previously smugglers, are a secret organisation and they fulfil the func-tion vital in many of Buchan novels of giving the hero support. Indeed, though an historical novel, many of the ingredients of the contemporary 'shocker' are here. Justin Cranmer, against whom Lammas is pitted, is 'the most dangerous man now alive on earth' and 'an immense perverted genius'.

The action switches from Fife to the Northumberland moors, which Buchan knew from his visits to G.M. Trevelyan. There is a sharp portrait of a Regency buck in Sir Turnour Wyse, some notable action sequences, and Lammas emerges as a sympathetic character who at the end of the book after his adventures turns his back on success to return to his 'little study and the drawer with the manuscripts of his great treatise on the relation of art and morals'. Indeed Buchan put much of one side of himself into 'Nanty' Lammas, the story of a man who prefers his books and the knowledge of secret work to the ambitions of national life. *The Free Fishers* has never been among Buchan's most popular books, even amongst his historical novels, for it lacks the strong narrative pace of the 'shockers' and the complexities of the historical novels, but it has a charm of its own, particularly in its evocation of various types of countryside.[49]

BIOGRAPHER AND HISTORIAN

THE first part of the twentieth century saw the development of 'The New Biography', of which the precursor and most notorious was Lytton Strachey's *Eminent Victorians* published in 1918. It was a departure from the recognized form of biography that was quite alien to Buchan who between 1927 and 1935 produced a revised version of his Montrose biography and lives of Sir Walter Scott, Julius Caesar and Oliver Cromwell – all men with whom he could closely identify. Whereas Strachey chose to satirize public figures and challenge many of the orthodoxies of the period, Buchan found it hard, particularly after the slaughter of the First World War, to be iconoclastic and instead concentrated on producing biographies which were as strong on the period as the subject. His historical work has been over-shadowed by the success of his 'shockers' but it was as a biographer that he wished to be remembered. G.M. Trevelyan, for example, has called Buchan's book on Scott, perhaps his most personal book after his autobiography, the 'best one-volume biography in the language'.[1]

Buchan was himself to write in his memoirs that the:

four books were, indeed, in a sense a confession of faith, for they enabled me to define my own creed on many matters of doctrine and practice, and thereby cleared my mind. They were a kind of diary, too, a chronicle of my successive interests and occupations. They were laborious affairs compared to my facile novels, but they were also a relaxation, for they gave me a background into which I could escape from contemporary futilities, a watch-tower from which I had a long prospect, and could see modern problems in juster proportions.[2]

His apprenticeship as a biographer was a long one stretching back to his 1897 Stanhope Prize essay on Sir Walter Raleigh and early biographical articles most notably gathered in *Some Eighteenth Century Byways* in 1908. After the First World War he had been drawn into a series of elegiac memoirs about his dead friends such as *These For Remembrance, Francis and Riversdale Grenfell* or privately commissioned biographies such as *Lord Minto*. By the late 1920s he felt able to tackle something rather more ambitious. Reviewing Trevelyan's *Clio, a Muse*, Buchan had set out his own view of history.

> History is neither science nor philosophy, though it enlists both in its service; but it is indisputably an art. As a reconstruction of the past it demands precisely the qualities that we look for in the novel or the play. It is primarily a story, and must have the swiftness and cohesion of good narra-tive.[3]

He continued, emphasising the importance of character, 'These protagonists must be made to live again with something of the vigour of reality, and psy-chology must lend its aid to make them credible human beings.'[4]

It was these skills as a novelist that Buchan brought to his historical books, which, even though they may now have been superseded, have a pace often missing in modern biography. He had a trained historical sense and a highly developed historical imagination which meant he was able to see a period of history as a whole and its place in the long sweep of history. He allied this ability to tell an historical story and a sense of drama with dedicated research amongst a wide range of primary and secondary sources, drawing on disci-plines as varied as military science, religion, archaeology and philosophy. Above all he brought to his biographies in particular a genuine interest in, and perception of, human character.[5]

His 1913 life of Montrose had been criticized for its poor research, inaccu-racy and over-romanticized and overly sympathetic view of Montrose. In 1927, after fifteen years of scholarly research and background reading, he returned again to one of his great heroes. He began to research this second book on Montrose during the General Strike and it was completed in March 1928. A.L. Rowse was later to regard it as Buchan's 'chief contribution to his-torical research in the strict sense of the term; it is written wholly from original sources and he had various additions and corrections of his own to offer in writing it . . . It all goes to make a masterly historical biography'.[6]

He had now read more widely in the literature of the period and was able to address more thoroughly the position of the Church and Covenanting pol-itics. He was more measured in tone and judgement and the campaigns, which had tended to dominate the earlier book, were set more firmly in the context of the life. Even so Buchan's treatment of the methods of war, the military tactics and weaponry is one of the highlights of the book. In the new version he devoted more attention to Montrose's political ideas, though as J.D. Mackie in the *English Historical Review* noted 'the author tends to interpret Montrose's political ideas in the light of his own moderate opinions and to apply a severer standard in judging the acts of the covenanters than in judging those of the great marquis.'[7] The book is important in understanding Buchan. As he admitted in letters to both Lord Beaverbrook and Stair Gillon it is not only a 'guide to the topography of nearly all Scotland' but it also 'contains nearly all of my philosophy of life'.[8]

One of its greatest admirers was T.E. Lawrence, then stationed in Waziristan on the North West Frontier, who praised its ability to set a scene and sustain a narrative. 'Its dignity, its exceeding gracefulness, its care for exact ness, and the punctilio of your manners, fits its subject and period like a glove. You've put a very great man on a pedestal. I like it streets better than anything else of yours.' Another supporter was Liddell-Hart, who had checked the proofs and thought it 'a magnificent piece of work.'[9] The critics too recognized its qualities. The *English Historical Review* felt Buchan had 'produced a complete study of his hero inspired by enthusiasm and founded upon a deep and wide research into both original sources and modern authorities'. Its reviewer Mackie thought it 'a valuable contribution to Scottish history' and praised its understanding of the Highland mentality and ability to bring alive the land scape. *The New Republic* concluded: 'It may be recommended highly as good literature and good history' while *The Times* thought it 'likely to remain the standard life'.[10]

Buchan had always been a great believer in the individual's ability to affect the course of history, a view under attack from a more determinist and Marxist school in the years after the First World War. In 1929 he was invited to give the prestigious Rede lecture at Cambridge and took as his theme the chance occurrences that may change the course of history. As he put it, 'when a great event has been determined by some small thing which it is difficult to describe as anything but an accident.' He called his talk The Causal and the Casual in History and it was published later that year under the same title by the Cambridge University Press.[11]

The book drew praise from other historians, including somewhat surprisingly the Labour historian, G.D.H. Cole. G.P. Gooch, recently retired as President of the Historical Association, wrote to Buchan: 'I agree with every word of it and have often told my hearers that from one point of view history is a chapter of accidents.'[12] Buchan had often drawn on historical events for the background to his novels and speculated on what might have happened in other circumstances, most notably in the short story 'The Company of the Marjolaine'. In *The Causal and the Casual in History* he claimed not to be interested in the customary historical speculations about the size of Cleopatra's nose or what might have happened if Anne Boleyn had borne a live male child. Instead he chose to discuss several key episodes in history that might well have had different conclusions. He covered such diverse topics as what would have happened if Henry, Prince of Wales had not died aged eighteen in 1612, whether the 1745 could have succeeded if Prince Charles Edward Stuart had marched on London from Derby, and turning points in the careers of the first Duke of Marlborough, Napoleon, the American Civil War and the Dardanelles campaign. He also stressed the importance of great men in public life such as Alexander, Caesar, Calvin and Lenin. It was an attitude he would bring not just to his writing but also to his own life.

Sir Walter Scott was written for the centenary of Scott's death and was the first full biography since J.G. Lockhart's monumental study of 1838. Buchan had been fascinated by Scott since his youth and had already written extensively on both him and his work. At the Glasgow Scott dinner in 1911 Buchan had called Scott 'the greatest figure that Scotland has given to literature and one of the half-dozen great figures in the literature of the world'. He had proposed Scott's memory at the Edinburgh Sir Walter Scott club in 1923, written an English Association pamphlet on him in 1924 which was reprinted in the 1926 collection *Homilies and Recreations* and included a study of him in a Nelson 'Teaching of English' series booklet in 1925.[13] He admitted in the preface to the biography that 'It is a book I was bound one day to write, for I have had the fortune to be born and bred under the shadow of that great tradition.' As Janet Adam Smith has argued, 'No less than Montrose, Scott stood for an ideal of Scotland. In him also were reconciled the two strains in her history; the aristocratic and Cavalier, the Covenanting and democratic. Buchan would have liked to do what Montrose did; he had in fact done much that Scott did.'[14]

Lockhart's seven volume life had been so thorough that it is initially difficult to imagine what Buchan could add which was new. Theodore Spencer in the *Atlantic* wrote: 'Comparison with Lockhart's great work only increases one's respect for the way in which Mr Buchan has included, in so short a space, nearly everything that illuminates his subject.'[15] Buchan understood Scott because they were similar in upbringing, views and character. In a radio broadcast for the centenary he confessed: 'I share nearly all his principles and all his prejudices. So for me to say what I feel about Sir Walter would be to make an elaborate confession of faith.'[16]

Both men had grown up in the Borders acutely aware of its history, geog-raphy and literature, both had trained as lawyers but made their reputations as writers, both were Conservative romantics who drew inspiration from Scotland's past and both enjoyed the life of a country gentleman. Buchan had known and loved Scott's work since his childhood and had modelled himself in part on his hero. There was the same passion for vigorous exercise, the same interest in preserving Scottish heritage, the same belief that the writer must also be a man of public affairs. Scott's influence on Buchan's writing in both subject matter and narrative technique is obvious. Dickson McCunn is a descendant of Baillie Nicol Jarvie in *Rob Roy* while Richard Hannay and Edward Leithen are firm admirers of Scott. Buchan in his autobiography himself admitted the book was an attempt to state his 'literary credo.'[17]

One of Buchan's skills in the book is to maintain the narrative pace and yet include precis of the novels, evaluations of the characters and analyses of Scott's themes. His judgements are shrewd and perceptive, clearly the result of close and considered reading. He understands plot and character development in a way only a practising novelist can. It was a point stressed by David Cecil in his *Spectator* review.

> Colonel Buchan is the first man to try to give a full and adequate estimate of Scott's work. He is perhaps a trifle over-reverent . . . Still, it is more important to praise rightly than to blame rightly; and Colonel Buchan praises superbly. He looks below the surface; he admires Scott for his intrin-sic not for his superficial merits; he discerns and brilliantly analyses his mag-nificent Shakespearean sympathy with human nature; and he has that wider culture which enables him to assess his merits by comparisons with the great writers of other schools and other countries.[18]

At the same time he is able to cover all aspects of Scott's life from the liter-ary and domestic to the financial and political. The book is as interesting for its portrayal of Scottish Border society as its insights into the man and his writing. It was this sense of being able to place Scott in context which most impressed the *TLS* reviewer who in a long review thought that Buchan 'brings to his study just that trained historical imagination which by placing Scott accurately in his time and place shows us the real man in the comprehensiveness of his genius'.[19] He had checked his tendency to hero worship and shown himself to be aware of Scott's faults: his opposition to Parliamentary Reform, his extravagance, his unfair behaviour to his publisher Constable. The result is a magisterial life that is one of Buchan's great literary achievements.

Immediately *Scott* was published Buchan began research for his next major biography which he regarded as a companion piece to *Montrose*. This was a life of Oliver Cromwell. The book was a return to Buchan's favourite period, the seventeenth century, and assessed one of the most controversial personalities in British history, someone Buchan called 'a mystery to his contemporaries and an enigma to his successors'.[20] It was this enigma that A.L. Rowse felt he had successfully explained. 'With Cromwell himself, that extraordinary man, Buchan had an inner sympathy that makes him at last clear to one. I believe that his view of Cromwell – that character so open to controversy, the subject of so much debate – is essentially right.'[21]

It is on the whole a fair portrait, alive to the atrocities Cromwell's troops committed. One of its themes is the contradiction evident between Cromwell's character and his ruthless actions:

> Paradox is the fibre of his character and career . . . a devotee of the law, he was forced often to be lawless; a civilian to the core, he had to maintain himself by the sword; with a passion to construct, his task was chiefly to destroy; the most scrupulous of men, he had to ride roughshod over his own scruples and those of others; the tenderest, he had continually to harden his heart; the most English of our greatest figures, he spent his life in opposition to the majority of Englishmen; a realist, he was condemned to build that which would not last.[22]

Buchan pays due consideration to Cromwell's religious views, as well as his political philosophy, drawing as he later admitted in his autobiography on the experience of his own Calvinistic upbringing. The book was written with Buchan's eye for the salient and dramatic detail and marked, as with the previous biographies, by extensive primary research. The book was serialized in the *Sunday Times* and published in September 1934, alongside a biography of Cromwell by Hilaire Belloc. Among those who liked it was Albert Schweitzer who wrote to Buchan from Alsace thanking him for the copy he had sent. The *TLS* thought it 'a good and a full biography' while G.M. Trevelyan, in the *Spectator*, called it 'the best book on him that our generation is likely to produce'. A more discordant note, however, was sounded by Ezra Pound in the *New English Weekly*:

> Given the degree of economic sensibility in the more lively contemporary historians one is impatient of a good deal of Buchan's detail . . . John Buchan's historic curiosity is not of the most biting kind, it is not an insatiable curiosity determined to understand all the facts of Cromwell's career.[23]

In April 1932 Buchan wrote a short life of Julius Caesar aimed at a popular market for Peter Davies, one of the boys J.M. Barrie adopted and who became known as 'the lost boys', who had just set up his own publishing firm. Caesar had been an early hero of Buchan and the book was written in four months during the previous autumn. Stanley Baldwin liked it but the *New Statesman and Nation* thought it ill conceived in its execution, being too scholarly in approach for the general reader and yet making too little contribution to scholarship to be of interest to the academic. The *Spectator* was more generous: 'Mr Buchan tells his famous story tersely and well. He makes no parade of high scholarship or pedantic erudition. He was wellinspired; he has given us within a brief compass and in language which – if at times a trifle loaded with cliches – is always vigorous and effective . . .'[24] Several further short books for Peter Davies followed including *The Massacre of Glencoe* in 1933, *Gordon at Khartoum* in 1934 and a collection of essays, *Men and Deeds*, in 1935. This last included the earlier works together with Buchan's 1930 St Andrews University address 'Montrose and Leadership', an essay on Lord Rosebery written for the Proceedings of the British Academy in 1930 and his chapters from *The Kirk in Scotland*.

By education and temperament Buchan was a classicist and from the life of Caesar came one of his finest biographies, *Augustus*, which was published in October 1937 to mark the bimillennium of Augustus's birth. The book was researched during his first two years in Canada where he made use of the libraries in the Ottawa Parliament Buildings and Quebec's Laval University. He was helped in his research by two friends in Oxford, Hugh Last, the Professor of Ancient History, and Roberto Weiss a refugee friend of the Buchan family. Those two years 1935 to 1937 saw the intensification of the International Crisis in Europe and Buchan was aware of the parallels that could be drawn with the dictators and Mussolini in particular. At the end of the book he made this explicit: 'Once again the crust of civilization has worn thin, and beneath can be heard the mutterings of primeval fires . . . In the actual business of administration there is no question of today which Augustus had not to face and answer.'[25] It was a theme picked up by the copywriter for the American publisher. 'The GovernorGeneral of Canada tells how a Republic became a Dictatorship. Americans, has this no message for you?' Buchan also used the book to reflect on the nature of empire, a subject of continued interest to him.

As in his previous biographies Buchan was good at first setting the scene. *Augustus* is not just a portrait of a man he called 'the greatest practical genius in statesmanship that the world has seen,' but also a brilliantly realised portrait of the social life of the early Roman empire covering its politics, literature, daily and business life.[26] One criticism, however, was that Buchan should have included more economic history. He admitted to B.K. Sandwell, the editor of the *Saturday Review*, that he had 'rather scamped the economic background. I am no Marxist but I fully realise its importance. In my *Cromwell* I was engaged principally in stressing the spiritual development of my subject, and the economic background had already been well done by other people. As for *Augustus* we have extraordinarily little data.'[27]

Otherwise the reviews were excellent both in the learned journals and the popular press. The *Classical Journal* praised it as 'a joy to read and a distinct contribution to the literature dealing with Augustus and the Roman Empire' while F.A. Wright in the *New Statesman and Nation* thought it 'nearly a perfect biography, quite perfect if we can agree with the estimate of Augustus's character which it puts forward; well-balanced, vividly written, and beautifully produced, it supersedes all the other English books now existing on its subject'.[28] The *TLS* wrote: 'John Buchan shows a firm grasp of both ancient and modern authorities, works on a broad canvas and approaches his subject as a historian. Some of his interpretations will invite criticism and some need supplement, . . . but his foundations are sound and the superstructure invariably attractive.'[29] H.A.L. Fisher writing in the *Spectator* praised Buchan's 'careful character sketches and literary appreciation'. He noted that 'His wise, eloquent, and sensitive pages everywhere bear traces of a scholar's scrupulous diligence. Augustus . . . deserves a good biography and has got it.'[30]

There were also a number of miscellaneous books. Together with Edward Gleichen, Buchan edited a twelve volume study of the contemporary world *The Nations of Today* published by Hodder & Stoughton between 1923 and 1924. Much of the supervisory work was done by Gleichen – in particular on the volumes on Canada, Italy, The Baltic States – but Buchan wrote the general introduction and introduced old friends, such as Robert Rait and Hilaire Belloc, as contributors.

Buchan had long been interested in Scottish poetry. Many of his poems in *Poems Scots and English* had been written in Scottish Doric and during the First World War he had written a preface to Violet Jacob's *Songs of Angus*. In 1920 when the poet Hugh McDiarmid (C.M. Grieve) edited *Northern Numbers* described by the publishers T. N. Foulis as 'being representative selections from certain living Scottish poets', Buchan was included. The first series consisted of eleven poets including Violet Jacob, Neil Munro and Grieve himself with Buchan as the first contributor. Three poems were chosen – 'Fratri Dilectissimo', 'Fisher Jamie' and 'From the Pentlands Looking North and

South'. The following year a second series was produced with Lewis Spence joining seven of the original eleven. Again Buchan's work was the first selection, this time consisting of 'The Gipsy's Song to the Lady Cassilis', 'The Wise Years' and 'Wood Magic'.

Northern Numbers had been the first attempt to collect and assess the poetry produced by the burgeoning Scottish Literary Renaissance, in which Grieve played such an influential part. Buchan realized the need for a more comprehensive anthology drawing on Scotland's rich poetical past and in the autumn of 1924 he edited for Nelson *The Northern Muse: an Anthology of Scots Vernacular Poetry*. In his introduction he stressed it was very much a personal selection and described the evolution of a Scottish vernacular poetry. Both the introduction and the widely praised commentary of notes at the end showed him to have read and thought deeply about the subject. The two hundred and forty-five poems were divided not chronologically but into eighteen subject areas such as 'Youth and Spring', 'Plaisir D'Amour', 'Sport', 'Death' and 'Divine Philosophy'. There were the obvious inclusions such as William Dunbar, Robert Burns, Allan Ramsay, Sir Walter Scott, Robert Fergusson and R.L. Stevenson but he also introduced younger or lesser-known poets including Christopher Murray Grieve, and a young barrister, later Speaker of the House of Commons, W.S. Morrison. He also included three of his own poems: two war poems 'On Leave' and 'Fisher Jamie' and 'The Fishers' from the Theocritus in Scots translation.

Grieve, who was to form a perhaps surprising friendship with them, was to describe Buchan as 'Dean of the Faculty of Contemporary Scottish Letters' and write of *The Northern Muse* that it stood 'in relation to Scots poetry as Palgrave's *Golden Treasury* to English . . . a definitive book, supplying a long-felt want in a fashion that seems likely to give such an impetus to Scottish poetry that it will stand as a landmark in our literary history . . .'[31] Buchan had come across Grieve a few years previously and had tried to help his career, most notably by writing supporting a job application to Sir John Findley of the *Scotsman*. In 1923 Grieve had dedicated his *Annals of the Five Senses* to Buchan and two years later Buchan repaid the compliment by writing the introduction to Grieve's *Sangschaw*.

The Northern Muse received good and long reviews from St Loe Strachey in the *Spectator* and Robert Graves in *The Nation & Athenaeum*. The latter, praising Buchan 'for the number of balls he keeps in the air at once', thought he had 'achieved the distinction of being the first man to make a comprehensive Anthology of Scottish and Northern English poetry which Southerners can read with real pleasure.' He added 'The notes at the end are copious and scholarly beyond suspicion, and there is a fine introduction, but the most remarkable feat of editorship has been in keeping the Northern Muse within the decent bounds of sentiment.'[32]

The book was dedicated to the former Prime Minister, the Earl of Rosebery, whom Buchan had known for thirty years. He had met Rosebery while at Oxford, most probably through Rosebery's nephew Hugh Wyndham, and he had become an important mentor and inspiration. Rosebery, thirty years older, became a surrogate father, a Scotsman with shared literary and political interests to whom Buchan could turn for advice and help. Buchan had enlisted Rosebery's support at the *Scottish Review* and before the First World War when he had been involved in the moves to organize a memorial to General Wolfe on the Plains of Abraham. It was Rosebery, too, who had written the introduction to the initial 1915 edition of the *Nelson History of the War*. Buchan had based the character Lord Appin in *The Lodge in the Wilderness* on Rosebery and had reissued Rosebery's study of Napoleon while at Nelson.

Buchan was drawn to Rosebery by a shared feeling for history and view on Empire and moved by the sadness of the former Prime Minister's old age and the mourning for his dead son, Neil Primrose. Often, he would visit Rosebery at Durdans, his home near Epsom, and accompany the old man on long drives. In 1921 he had persuaded Rosebery to let him edit a collection of speeches and articles which Hodder published as *Miscellanies, Literary and Historical*. Rosebery insisted that the royalties should go to Buchan who used part of them to restore the little temple at Elsfield and gave the rest to charitable causes. Buchan was later to edit a series of essays under the auspices of the British Academy on Rosebery published in 1930 and included in his 1935 volume *Men and Deeds*.

In 1920 Buchan had been asked by Lady Minto to help her write the life of her husband, who had been GovernorGeneral of Canada 1898–1904 and Viceroy of India 1905–1910. Increasingly he found it easier to take over all the writing himself, though he was hampered by the fact it was a family memoir and the book depended on family cooperation and Minto's own papers.[33] When the book was published in October 1924 he was criticized for taking many episodes at face value and later had to apologize to the former Canadian Prime Minister, Sir Robert Bordern, for failing to see the Canadian point of view or understand much of the Canadian background. The critical reception was better. The *Nation & Athenaeum* thought it 'a most successful piece of work – bright in narrative and in its use of letters and official documents a model.'[34] The *Canadian Historical Review* gave it a two page lead review by Oscar Skelton, the UnderSecretary of State for Canadian External Affairs. Though Skelton thought Buchan had been patronizing in dismissing Canadian politics as 'opportunism', he concluded that Buchan had 'brought to his task an intimate knowledge of the countryside and family background, a sympathetic appreciation of the type to which Lord Minto belonged, and a terse, swinging style . . .'[35]

Of most importance however was that the biography developed Buchan's knowledge and interest in Canada and his understanding of the role of the Governor-General. Lord Lansdowne wrote to Lady Minto about the book:

> Buchan seems to me to have done his work quite admirably. The facts are marshalled with transparent clearness and the writer, without being fulsome in his praise, does justice to Roly's ability, his fine qualities, and to the personal charm which won for him the affection of all with whom he had to deal.[36]

The result too was that Buchan was approached on several subsequent occa-sions to write official lives, most notably of Curzon and Haig. Though he declined the offers he was an obvious choice in 1935 to write the official book to mark the twenty-fifth anniversary of George V's reign, an invitation he did accept.

Buchan had continued to lecture or write for various organizations and magazines and some of his material was collected in an essay collection pub-lished in September 1926 and dedicated to Waldorf Astor. *Homilies and Recreations* consisted of sixteen essays covering a wide range of Buchan's inter-ests – Edmund Burke, Arthur Balfour, the nature of democracy, literature and topography, the judicial temperament, Scots vernacular poetry, Robert Burns, Morris and Rossetti and Catullus. Many of them had appeared elsewhere. 'Two Ordeals of Democracy', Buchan's Milton Academy lecture, had already been published in the States, 'The Literature of Tweeddale' had formed part of Walter Buchan's history of Peebleshire and 'Some Notes on Sir Walter Scott' had originally been an address and then pamphlet for the English Association.[37]

He had always taken a close interest in the work of the English Association and had been President of its Scottish and Oxford Branches. Between 1915 and 1917 he had been Chairman of the Committee and from 1932 on was one of the Association Vice-Presidents. In 1926 he succeeded A.C. Bradley and W.P. Ker in editing their twelfth annual volume of essays, *Essays and Studies*, he himself contributing articles on Canadian Literature and the Scottish Ballads. His Presidential address to the Scottish branch in October 1923, 'The Novel and The Fairy Tale', which stressed his links with the Victorian novel, is one of his most revealing statements about his own literary tastes. Another literary organisation with which he was involved was the Royal Society of

Literature. He had been elected to its Council in 1922 and chaired a number of lectures for both Henry Newbolt and Hugh Walpole. In January 1925 he read the Society a paper, 'The Old and the New in Literature', which was another of the essays in *Homilies and Recreations*.

Buchan's principal income during these Elsfield years – 1920 to 1935 – came from his writing. His output was enormous. Apart from a novel each year he wrote or edited twenty full-length non-fiction books and contributed to a further twenty books and numerous newspapers. Hodder & Stoughton built him up to be one of their five top authors and the Buchan novel each summer was an important event in the literary calendar. Houghton Mifflin in Boston became his principal American publisher and translation rights were sold by his literary agent Alexander Watt in numerous languages including Czech, Spanish, Portuguese, Polish, Russian, Dutch, Serbo-Croat, Danish, Ukrainian, Hungarian, Japanese, Arabic, Flemish, Hebrew, Swedish and Norwegian. Many of his books also generated good serialization or film deals and his stories were included in countless anthologies. His advances and royalty income rose correspondingly throughout these years making him one of the most successful and widely-read novelists of the inter-war years.

For his novels he tended to receive an advance for the British rights of between £750 and £1,000 with the extraordinary royalty rate on some books of 25% rising to 33⅓% of the cover price. (For most authors it was about 15% maximum). His non-fiction was even more lucrative with *Cromwell* and *Augustus* securing a £2,000 advance and his memoirs commanding £3,000. The Houghton Mifflin advances ranged between $3,000 and $5,000 with a royalty rate of 15–20%. The pattern was for Hodder to publish in hardback at 7s. 6d then just over a year later to publish a cheaper edition at 3s. 6d. About three years later Nelson would then publish the book in their uniform series with its distinctive red covers at 4s. 6d. The Richard Hannay 'shockers' sold best followed by the McCunn trilogy (though *Huntingtower* out-performed even some of the Hannay books), the Leithen titles, the historical fiction and finally the short story collections. Janet Adam Smith estimated the total number of books sold by Hodder and Nelson up to 1960 as follows: *Greenmantle* (368,000), *The Thirty-Nine Steps* (355,000), *Mr Standfast* (231,000), *Huntingtower* (230,000), *The Three Hostages* (216,000), *John Macnab* (156,000), *Castle Gay* (151,000), *The Island of Sheep* (122,000), *The Dancing Floor* (122,000), *Midwinter* (112,000), *The House of the Four Winds* (101,000), *The Free Fishers* (100,000), *Witch Wood* (98,000), *The Courts of the Morning* (96,000), *The Runagates Club* (85,000), *A Prince of the Captivity* (83,000), *The Gap in the Curtain* (78,000), *The Path of the King* (75,000), *The Blanket of the Dark* (73,000), *The Watcher by the Threshold* (63,000).

The paperback editions are even more difficult to quantify but Janet Adam Smith thought that total sales for the Pan editions, first published in 1952, and Penguin series launched in 1956 up to the mid 1960s, when her life of Buchan was published, were *The Thirty-Nine Steps* (670,000), *Greenmantle* (330,000), *Prester John* (220,000), *The Three Hostages* (175,000), *The Island of Sheep* (121,000), *Huntingtower* (104,000), *Mr Standfast* (98,000) and *The House of the Four Winds* (84,000). By comparison the biographies sold less well. The most successful was *Sir Walter Scott* (47,000) followed by *Augustus* (36,000), *Oliver Cromwell* (28,000) and *Montrose* (28,000). It is hard to establish the total number of books Buchan sold or his literary income since many of the Watt and Hodder & Stoughton files have been destroyed and the books were published in so many different editions, but an estimate would be that he had an annual income from his writing of about £5,000 when he first moved to Elsfield in 1919 which had doubled by the time he left for Canada sixteen years later.

In an influential essay for the *Spectator* on Buchan's last novel Graham Greene noted that: 'What is remarkable about these adventure-stories is the completeness of the world they describe. The backgrounds . . . are elaborately worked in . . .' He also pointed out 'the vast importance Buchan attributed to success.' This supposed cult of success has been at the heart of much Buchan criticism. Richard Usborne has written 'Success in Buchan is competitive. It was not enough to have done a good job well. You had to have made a name for yourself by doing it better than anybody else. Heroes and villains, they almost all "make big names for themselves."'[38]

At Oxford Vernon Milburne has won the Craven and been runner up for the Hertford, Lewis Haystoun had 'the best first of his year' and Colin Raden had been President of the Boat Club. Richard Hannay, a South African mining engineer, becomes a Major General with a KCB and a manor house in the Cotswolds; Blenkiron is a millionaire from Wall Street; Charles Palliser-Yeates is the 'head of an eminent banking firm' while Lord Lamancha is the son of a Marquis and Secretary of State for the Dominions. Arbuthnot, Roylance, Leithen, Raden, Lamancha, Palliser-Yeates, Haystoun and Lariarty have all been to Eton. Even in the modern romances, such as the Huntingtower trilogy, McCunn the Glasgow grocer becomes a millionaire laird and the Gorbals Die-Hards each achieve great success in their respective fields.

For Buchan's heroes, as Gertrude Himmelfarb has pointed out:

these marks of success are not the ends towards which his heroes – or villains – strive. They are the preconditions of their being heroes or villains at all, much as the characters in fairy-tales are always the most beautiful, the most exalted, the most wicked of their kind. They are the starting-points for romance, not the termination.

In a defence of this cult of success it has been argued that the characters are not 'motivated by desire for rank or position . . . They may have an over-ready admiration for success and tend to calculate worth in these terms, but we are not in the world of C.P. Snow where everybody is calculating his chances of promotion.'[39]
    There is a distinction between the 'shockers', which often had to fit the conventions of the genre, and the historical novels where there is a completely different set of values. Andrew Garvald's Glasgow values prevail over those of Virginia society in *Salute to Adventurers*; David Sempill rejects the life of a laird to continue in the ministry; Peter Pentecost in *The Blanket of the Dark* prefers to remain a clerk rather than join the world of the court and Anthony Lammas in *The Free Fishers* returns after his adventures to academic life at St Andrews. Many of Buchan's literary characters are drawn from the worlds he knew but they are not restricted to the country houses of the Borders and the smoking room of the House of Commons. Even in the thrillers they include a Boer hunter in Peter Pienaar, a Trade Union official in Andrew Amos, a Scottish urchin in Fish Benjie, a Canadian Indian guide in Lew Frizel, a Fusilier batman in Geordie Hamilton, a black preacher in John Laputa and a pacifist in Launcelot Wake. Buchan's own views on success can be gauged from the speech given in October 1924 to Milton Academy and subsequently repeated to several other schools. 'Success, I need not tell you, does not mean making a lot of money or attaining a great position or great fame. A man may do all these things and be a failure. It means doing sound work in which you are happy, and becoming in the doing of it, braver and wiser and kinder people.'[40]
    The case for Buchan's apparent anti-Semitism is a stronger one and has been argued most notably by writers such as Gertrude Himmelfarb, Benny Green and Mordecai Richler. The books are certainly scattered with disparaging comments about Jews. In *The Half-Hearted* 'Europe is a dull place at present, given up to Jews and old women'; Deira in the 1906 story 'The Kings of Orion' is run by 'a brand of Levantine Jew who was fit for nothing but making money and making trouble'; one of the villains in *Mr Standfast* is a Portuguese Jew, who masquerades as a German professor of Celtic languages and who also happens to talk such good Gaelic 'he would have passed for the ordinariest kind of ghillie'. There are several references in *The Three Hostages* where comparisons are made between Jews and Bolsheviks. Dr Greenslade

notices that 'all the places with names like spells – Bokhara, Samarkand (are) run by seedy little gangs of communist Jews' and MacGillivray makes a similar remark to Hannay that among those imbeciles intent on violence are 'the young Bolshevik Jews'. In the book Hannay looks into a night-club where he sees 'fat Jews and blue-black dagos'. There are also mentions in the *Huntingtower* trilogy. The enemies of Saskia are 'the Jews and behind the Jews our unsleeping enemies'; Hermitage is critical of the Bolsheviks because there are 'too many Jews among them'. In *Castle Gay* 'The present mis-governors of our land have no popular following, and no credit except among international Jews' and in *The House of Four Winds* there is mention of Rosenbaum a 'Jew barber out of a job'.[41]

The most celebrated anti-Semitic remark in the Buchan oeuvre is Scudder's at the beginning of *The Thirty-Nine Steps*: 'The Jew is everywhere ... if you're on the biggest kind of job and are bound to get to the real job, ten to one you are brought up against a little white-faced Jew in a bath chair with an eye like a rattlesnake. Yes, sir, he is the man who is ruling the world just now . . . '. Indeed in many of the books stretching back to the turn of the century there is the suggestion that an unholy alliance of sometimes Jews and sometimes financiers is to blame for the country's ills. In *The Half-Hearted* a character talks about the 'whole gang of Jew speculators and vulgarians who would corrupt a great country' though by *The Three Hostages* the threat comes now not from Jews but from criminal profiteers promoting strikes and revolutions to reap speculative profits.[42]

It is difficult to find any evidence of anti-Semitism in Buchan's own personal views. Many of his closest friends such as Lionel Phillips and Moritz Bonn were Jewish and Buchan was deeply troubled by the persecution of the Jews first in Russia and then in Hitler's Germany. His activities in the House of Commons show him to have been a committed Zionist who sought to assert rather than deny the Jewish identity just as he wished to promote the Scottish identity. Indeed, it was the similarities between the two cultures, and in particular their shared respect for education, which formed the basis of his speech to the Jewish National Fund when his name was inscribed in the Golden Book. When the Nazis published their 'Who's Who in Britain', a hit list of British figures who might be imprisoned if the Germans occupied Britain, Buchan was singled out for his 'Pro-Jewish activity'.[43]

If it is not true of the man, is it true of the writer, and if so is there an explanation? Was Buchan pandering to the views of his readership or merely careless in his use of stereotype? It is worth looking at some of the anti-Semitic references in context. For example it needs to be remembered with regard to the often quoted reference in *The Thirty-Nine Steps* that they are the remarks neither of Buchan, nor even Hannay but the crazed Scudder, remarks incidentally quickly dismissed by Bullivant, who considers the American unbalanced. He tells Hannay 'He had a lot of biases. Jews for example made him see red. Jews and the high finance.' The conspiracy turns out to be a German not a Jewish one.

Many of the references are in books published just after the First World War when Jews were associated with popular notions of international upheaval. In Buchan's novels the Jews tend to be revolutionaries, businessmen or financiers and stand in contrast to the gentlemen amateurs of Clubland but then the conflict in Buchan is often between the rootless and the secure and the Jews, like the Scots, are the eternal wanderers. Sandy Arbuthnot, better known on the Baluchistan frontier than in the City of London, is 'the wandering Scot carried to the pitch of genius' and therefore associated with the rootless. In most of his appearances he is ostensibly on the side of the enemy, for example as the false prophet in *Greenmantle*, Kharama in *The Three Hostages* or on the side of Castor in *The Courts of the Morning*.

It is sometimes argued that Buchan's villains are invariably Jewish but in fact it is their foreignness that is the distinguishing feature. Castor in *The Courts of the Morning* is born in Austria with Spanish blood, Makar in *The Half-Hearted* has a German father and Russian mother, Dominick Medina is Irish but the suggestion is that he is Spanish or Portuguese, and Jacques D'Ingraville is French. When the villains are apparently British, as with Andrew Lumley in *The Power House*, we discover they are actually German.

There are Jewish conspiracies and Jewish villains but there are also sympathetic Jewish characters such as Julius Victor in *The Three Hostages*, Mr Macandrew in *A Prince of the Captivity* and Eric Lowenstein, 'a Jewish financier' in *A Lodge in the Wilderness* who is described as a 'modest, gentle soul' and 'one of the first financial geniuses alive'. Later in the novel Mrs Yorke says 'I differ from most of my countrymen in liking Jews . . . they are never vulgar at heart. If we must have magnates, I would rather Jews had the money.'[44]

The attitudes of some of the characters may now offend our sensibilities but they reflect commonly held attitudes of the time. Buchan was no worse and a great deal better than many of his contemporaries such as Dorothy L. Sayers and Sapper. It is important to remember too that the charges of anti-Semitism were not made until Gertrude Himmelfarb's famous article on Buchan in 1960. Six years earlier Richard Usborne had passed over the subject by saying of the books 'They were slightly antisemitic, but no more so than was polite in any author in the pre-Hitler period.'[45]

Another charge made is that Buchan is sexist. Again one has to be constantly aware of the conventions of the period and the genre and that there are differences between his depiction of women in the historical novels and the shockers. For example Buchan's earlier novels tend to portray rather stronger women. In *A Lodge in the Wilderness* women play an active and sensible part in the discussions while Claudia Barriton in the 1909 story 'A Lucid Interval' converses with men as an equal. Women figure rarely in the shockers and when they do they are generally decorative, childlike or behave like men. Janet Roylance is a fine rifle shot while Mary Lamington talks like a member of a schoolboy sports team. Indeed, as one critic has written, Mary Lamington, Janet Roylance, Barbara Dasent and Alison Westwater 'bind themselves to the same values and tasks which the men do and do not see themselves in any different light than the men view themselves.'[46]

It is a man's world in the 'shockers' so that Hannay can admit in *Greenmantle*: 'Women had never come much my way, and I knew about as much of their ways as I knew about the Chinese language.' But that is perhaps not surprising since he has spent most of his life as a mining engineer in South Africa and as he continues 'All my life I had lived with men only, and a rather rough crowd at that.'[47] The point is that it is certain men who feel uncomfortable with women, the products of the public school system and a life in the empire. Lewis Haystoun admits to finding himself equally unprepared for women. 'The ordinary gardener's boy can beat me at making love.' This is not to say, as some critics have, that Buchan's heroes display signs of homosexuality, but merely that they fit into the tradition of Victorian and Edwardian popular fiction. Buchan was always conscious of the weakness of his female characterization. Commenting on one of the characters in his sister's novel *The Setons* he wrote to her 'in Elizabeth you draw a wonderful picture of a woman a thing I could about as much do as fly to the moon.'[48]

One of the interesting aspects of Buchan's characterization is its epicene nature so that Peter Pienar has a face 'as gentle as a girl's' and Sandy Arbuthnot in *Greenmantle* has 'a pair of brown eyes like a pretty girl's'. Even John Laputa at six foot six inches with a deep chest and massive shoulders has slender hands like a 'high-bred woman's, and Von Stumm has 'a perverted taste for soft delicate things'. This characteristic is also apparent in Buchan's non fiction books, such as *Augustus*, where the emperor has 'features so delicately modelled as to be almost girlish.' Girls on the other hand have boyish characteristics so that Mary Lamington is described as having 'the strong, slim grace of a boy' and walking 'with the free grace of an athletic boy'; Kore Arabin is 'like a wild boy'; Saskia has 'eyes as grave and candid as a boy's'; Katrine is 'friendly as a boy' and Janet Roylance looks 'like an adorable boy'. Indeed it seems that boyishness is the defining attractive feature for most Buchan heroes in their relationship with women.

The nature of Hannay's relationship with Pienaar mirrors that later with his wife and there are frequent comparisons between the strength of male friendship and married life. As Hannay admits: 'Women, bless their hearts! can never know what long comradeship means to men ... Even Mary under-stood only a bit of it. I had just won her love, which was the greatest thing that ever came my way, but if she had entered at that moment I would scarcely have turned my head.'[49] According to the writer Susan Hill, Buchan is in fact one of the few thriller writers to appeal to women. As she has pointed out 'mar-vellously evocative and accurate descriptive writing, elegance of expression, simple clear use of language, can indeed go hand in hand with stories of phys-ical exploits and derring-do travel, excitement, violence, mystery, the thrills of the flight and the pursuit'. And she adds 'Buchan is a master at the art of beginning a book, raising at once the pulse of his reader, and making him quite unable to resist reading furiously on.'[50]

Buchan was modest about his abilities as a writer. While he took immense trouble over his historical novels and non-fiction books and was pleased when they were praised he wrote his 'shockers' quickly and for amusement and was embarrassed by their commercial success. In *The Three Hostages* he gives one of the characters, Dr Greenslade, the recipe for writing a thriller:

> ... I begin by fixing on one or two facts which have no sort of obvious connection – an old blind woman spinning in the Western Highlands, a barn in a Norwegian *saeter*, and a little curiosity shop in North London kept by a Jew with a dyed beard. Not much connection between the three? You invent a connection ... The reader ... is pleased with the ingenuity of the solution, for he doesn't realise that the author fixed upon the solution first, and then invented a problem to suit it.[51]

Given that he wrote quickly and at snatched moments his books are often episodic and filled with inconsistencies and coincidences. He explained away some of the coincidences by suggesting that the hand of providence was some-times at work. Hannay in *The Three Hostages* remarks 'then suddenly there happened one of those trivial things which look like accidents but I believe are part of the rational government of the universe.' This Calvinist belief in just retribution was especially evident in the deaths of the villains such as Ivery in *Mr Standfast*. A Calvinistic sense of pervading evil also permeates many of the 'shockers', an evil represented for example by the Kirk elders in *Witch Wood* and Medina in *The Three Hostages*. Buchan is interested, as Eric Ambler and

Grahame Greene would be later, with the world of moral and political
anarchy. The conspiracies are world-wide, the villains are fallen angels rather
than men and the battle one against the elemental forces of evil. This evil may
be world-wide but what makes it particularly frightening is that it has penetrated into everyday lives. The villains are often respectable members of society,
the sort of people with whom one was at school, members of one's club,
people who play tennis with one at the seaside. Danger is not now to be found
only in battle but also on the streets of London and in the Cabinet. Those
drawn in to the conspiracy are ordinary members of the general public. It was
this aspect of Buchan's work that Grahame Greene drew attention to in his
review of *Sick Heart River* in 1940 when he wrote: 'John Buchan was the first
to realize the enormous dramatic value of adventure in familiar surroundings
happening to unadventurous men . . . murder in 'the atmosphere of breeding
and simplicity and stability.'[52]

The characters exhibit a Calvinistic sense of guilt and duty. They feel a
need to be tested in order to prove their worth. Saskia in *Huntingtower* admits
to feeling too secure, Hugh in *The Lodge in the Wilderness* claims 'I never feel
quite happy unless I am a little miserable', while in its classic exposition in *John
Macnab* one character remarks 'You're got to rediscover the comforts of your
life by losing them for a little.' Many of the books begin with the characters
showing signs of ennui and in need of a sense of purpose. *The Power House*
opens with Leithen tired of routine work, *The Thirty-Nine Steps* with Hannay
bored with life, *Greenmantle* with Hannay and Sandy bored by convalescence,
The Courts of the Morning with Sandy depressed and assessing the purpose of
life. This theme is apparent from the early short stories and developed most
obviously in *John Macnab* and *Sick Heart River*. As Himmelfarb puts it: 'All
Buchan's heroes are periodically beset by fatigue and lassitude, a "death-wish"
that is overcome by divesting themselves of their urban identities – success
being an urban condition – and donning the shabby, anonymous clothes of
the countryman.'[53]

Many of Buchan's characters are men of gipsy temperament forced by need,
convention or a sense of duty to take up sedentary occupations and become
lawyers, bankers or cabinet ministers, from which they can only be freed by
exposure to the wilds. It is a further refinement to the continuous border in
Buchan's work between the primitive and the civilized. It was something that
Buchan himself felt strongly. As he admitted in his memoirs his real fear as a
young man was that 'Even a perverse career of action, seemed to me better than
a tippling of ale in the shade, for that way lay the cockney suburbanism which
was my secret terror.'[54]

Few writers are as good as Buchan in describing landscape and weather so that they come alive and become an integral part of the story and the menace. His parliamentary colleague Walter Elliot was later to write: 'He could write about the small hidden green valleys of the Border till they closed round you; he could write of journeys, breathless, cross-country, perilous, while your breath came short and your heart hammered on your ribs.' Throughout Buchan's short stories and novels, most obviously in *Sick Heart River*, nature is shown to have redemptive qualities. In *The Gap in the Curtain* Ottery finds solace in the wilds of Newfoundland for he has the 'idea that if he went into the wilds he might draw courage from the primeval Nature which was all uncertainties and hazards'. This solace comes especially from the Scottish wilds so that even the South African countryside in *Prester John* or Turkish terrain in *Greenmantle* resembles a Scottish moor.[55]

Part of the attraction of the "shockers" rests too in the converse of Calvinism, in Buchan's ability to evoke a degree of sophistication and cosmopolitanism though paradoxically, given the accusations of snobbery and his supposed attachment to the cult of success, he is never good at describing high society convincingly. When he mentions in passing an inn on the Achensee in Tyrol, a fur shop in the Galician quarter of Buda, a club in Vienna and a bookshop off the Rackitzstrasse in Leipzig the reader is immediately made to feel that of course they know these places. He uses lists of places or people in different ways. Sometimes it is to suggest a certain knowledge of the world in the character. Sometimes it is to present the scale of the conspiracy ranged against humanity. In *Mr Standfast* the Wild Birds range from a woman in Genoa and a princess married to a Greek financier to an Argentinian editor and Baptist minister in Colorado. In *The Three Hostages* the gang consists of, among others, 'several fashionable actresses', a Presbyterian accountant, a French count, an American senator and a 'Prince of the Church' of Rome.

Against this evil is massed an equally disparate collection of ordinary people. In *Mr Standfast* Blenkiron's best agents include 'a girl who posed as a mannequin in a milliner's shop in Lyons and a concierge in a big hotel at St Moritz' while in *Greenmantle* Bullivant can report that British Intelligence has reports in the East from among others 'peddlars in South Russia, Afghan horsedealers, Turcoman merchants, pilgrims on the road to Mecca, sheikhs in North Africa, sailors on the Black Sea coasters, sheep-skinned Mongols, Hindu fakirs, Greek traders in the Gulf, as well as respectable consuls who use cyphers'.

Though Buchan chose to write dozens of very different books many of the themes are consistent and can be traced from one to the other. There is what Janet Adam Smith has called 'the root of the matter treatment'. Wake in *Mr Standfast*, Craw in *Castle Gay* and Castor in *The Courts of the Morning* all undergo a spiritual journey in the course of the books in which they appear so that initially unsympathetic characters win our sympathy through some redeeming action. Indeed even many of the sympathetic characters are on a spiritual journey – Lewis Haystoun in *The Half-Hearted*, Dickson McCunn in the Huntingtower trilogy, Adam Melfort in *A Prince of the Captivity*, Edward Leithen in his various adventures, Peter Pentecost in *The Blanket of the Dark* and Lombard in *The Island of Sheep* who sums it up 'every man must discover his own Island of Sheep'.

It is interesting in tracing themes in Buchan's work to see just how many of his own current interests or those of his family are ascribed to characters or are central to the books. They include mountaineering, fishing, birds, walking and the card game patience. As the critic Patrick Cosgrave has put it: 'He did not metamorphose his personality when he came to write adventure stories: he merely relaxed, and indulged some of the whims of his temperament and imagination.'[56]

One of the attractions of reading Buchan is his ability to mix real people and places with fictitious counterparts to create a recognizable world. Many of his names are taken from rivers or places around Peebles such as Leithen, Manor Water, Lamancha, Deloraine and Haystoun. There is a Crask, the name of Roylance's Scottish estate, in the Highlands and Hannay's Fosse Manor on the Fosse Way has a counterpart, now a hotel, just outside Stow-on-the-Wold though in fact William Buchan pinpoints the fictional house's location as between Northleach and Circencester. Glenaicill Forest and Correi na Sidhe figure in both the 1910 short story 'Space' and the 1924 novel *The Three Hostages*.[57]

Both major and minor characters tend to reappear in several stories so that Burminster and Martendale are in *The Courts of the Morning* and *The Runagates Club*, Lady Altrincham is in *The Dancing Floor* and *The Gap in the Curtain*, Captain Arcoll in *Prester John* is mentioned in *Greenmantle* and *The Island of Sheep*, the left-wing politician Toombs is in both *Mr Standfast* and *Castle Gay* and the barrister McGillivray, one of the heads of the Criminal Investigation Department, is in five of the novels. McGillivray is almost certainly based on Ewen McGillivray, a barrister colleague of Buchan's at 3 Temple Gardens. The name of the character Amos, who first appears in *Mr Standfast*, may have come from Thomas Amos a Nelson employee killed during the war, and not, as has been suggested, the Elsfield chauffeur Amos Webb whom Buchan had not at that stage met, while Corporal Hamilton shares the same name as Alastair's batman in the Royal Fusiliers.

Many of the characters seem to be related or their relations have figured in other books. The Clanroydens have been at Glenaicill since the 1900 story

'The Watcher By The Threshold' and Sir Hugh Clanroyden figures in 'Fountainblue' published the following year. One of Kore Arabin's relatives married a Manorwater, a Lady Manorwater is Lewis Haystoun's aunt in *The Half-Hearted* and the Manorwater family are mentioned in the short story 'The Company of the Marjolaine'. No doubt Virginia Dasent in the short story 'The Green Glen' is related to Barbara Dasent in *The Courts of the Morning* and Sebastian Derwent in *The Dancing Floor* has some relationship with Walter Derwent in *Sick Heart River*. Among the characters in *The Lodge in the Wilderness* are Mrs Deloraine, presumably related to Tommy Deloraine from *The Power House*, Marjory Haystoun, no doubt a relative of Lewis Haystoun from *The Half-Hearted*, Lady Amysfort, who later figures in *The Dancing Floor*, Lady Warcliff, whose husband Arthur appears in *The Three Hostages* and *The Runagates Club* and whose son is mentioned in *The Island of Sheep* and *The Three Hostages*. There is a Flora Brune in this book, a Pamela Brune in *The Gap in the Curtain* and a Hugo Brune in *The Dancing Floor*. Mollie Nantley in *The Dancing Floor* is a Brune and a cousin of Leithen. Mary Lamington's cousin is Launcelot Wake and Alison Westwater is related to Janet Raden and Randal Glynde. Barbara Dasent, married to Sandy Arbuthnot, is Blenkiron's niece and her daughter's godmother is Mary Lamington.

It is tempting also to speculate on the originals of various characters. The character probably closest to Buchan himself in terms of temperament and background is Edward Leithen. Both are the same age and had digs in the High at Oxford, both come from the Borders and enjoy mountaineering and fishing but now live in the Cotswolds, both were Colonels in the First World War and are now lawyers and Members of Parliament. Their only difference is that Leithen has reached the Cabinet while Buchan is a successful novelist. Many of the characters are modelled on Buchan's Oxford circle, particularly Hugh Wyndham, Aubrey Herbert and Raymond Asquith. Several of Buchan's characters take the names of his Oxford friends such as Hugh, Archibald (Wyndham's second name) and Sandy or take on their physical characteristics. Compare for example these two descriptions: Lamancha in *John Macnab* is described as 'a tallish man with a long, dark face, a small dark moustache, and a neat pointed chin which gave him something of the air of an hidalgo'; in his autobiography *Memory Hold the Door* Buchan writes of Basil Blackwood that 'with his pointed face and neat black moustache he had the air of a Spanish hidalgo . . .'[58] Raymond Asquith is Lewis Haystoun in *The Half-Hearted*, Vernon Milburne in *The Dancing Floor* and with the Grenfell brothers the inspiration for the central figure in the short story 'Tendebant Manus'. At the Amsforts' ball in *The Dancing Floor* Milburne is described as 'uncommonly handsome after the ordinary English pattern.

What struck me was his poise . . . I have never seen anyone so completely detached, so clothed with his own atmosphere.' In his autobiography Buchan describes how Asquith 'always had the complete detachment from the atmosphere, which we call distinction . . . His manner was curiously self-possessed and urbane, but there was always in it something of a pleasant aloofness, as of one who was happy in society but did not give to it more than a fraction of himself.'

Increasingly critics have become aware of the depth and complexity of Buchan's writing. The hidden subtexts of his work have been explored by Christopher Harvie who has shown how Buchan's sympathies between the civilized and the primitive and his attitude towards England, Scotland and the Empire were much more ambivalent than had been assumed. And yet they have also been confused about how to judge Buchan. They agree in the words of John Raymond that: 'to think of him as a kind of fifth-form entertainer – though he is certainly that at one stage of our lives – is far from the whole truth.'[59] Some critics have felt uncomfortable with the fact he was both a writer and a politician as if they were mutually exclusive; more often though they have felt that he squandered his talents in order to make money. David Daniell, speaking in a radio programme to mark the publication of his study of Buchan's work felt that: 'if he hadn't given that obsessive and conspiratorial theory of evil its head and stuck more to the vision and imagination that he derived from his Scottish background he might have been a really great novelist, because potentially I think he was.'[60] It is debatable whether Buchan could ever really have been a great writer. He combined a rich imagination with strong moral values, thereby giving the stories mythic proportions, but his world view was a limited one. As he himself preferred to say, he was a storyteller, 'the kind of man who for the sake of his yarns would in prehistoric days have been given a seat by the fire and a special chunk of mammoth.' But he certainly deserves to be remembered as a popular writer, one of the most successful and influential of the twentieth century.[61]

12

PUBLIC SERVANT

HAVING been a parliamentary candidate before the First World War it is likely Buchan could have won a seat in the 1918 election and indeed he had considered applying for the Oxford seat in 1914. He was, however, physically exhausted, disillusioned by public service and wanted to spend more time with his young family. He knew he just could not physically manage to represent an ordinary constituency and continue his writing and other activities. He knew too that his writing was likely to bring him a better income to support his family than the salary of a back bench MP. In 1920 he refused to stand again for Peeblesshire and two years later declined an offer from Central Glasgow to succeed Bonar Law as their candidate. However, he maintained his interest in Conservative politics, accepting the job of Senior Treasurer of the Oxford University Conservative Association. It was a role ideally suited to him, bringing him into contact with the rising new political generation and allowing OUCA to attract heavyweight speakers such as Stanley Baldwin.

By 1927 however his writing had given him some financial security and he found his other interests did not take up sufficient of his energies. He had always said 'Publishing is my business, writing my amusement and politics my duty'. The sudden death of Sir Henry Craik, who held one of the three Scottish university seats, in March 1927 gave Buchan his opportunity to re-enter public life. There were twelve university seats in total and their Members were elected in a postal ballot by graduates of the respective universities with what was in effect a second vote. University Members tended to sit loose to party affiliation and take an interest in educational matters. It was the ideal seat for Buchan in that it allowed him to represent a Scottish constituency of which he had once been a constituent and to take a more independent line than his parliamentary colleagues. Given also that there was little electioneering and few constituency engagements it was less physically demanding than a more conventional seat.

He was proposed by Sir Hector Cameron, the Emeritus Professor of Clinical Surgery at Glasgow and in his election address of 11 April stood on a programme of the need for public economy, a common Imperial economic policy and support for the new Trade Union Bill. Polling took place between 26 and 29 April and the results were announced on the 30 April. Buchan had won a majority in all four Scottish universities and beat his opponent, a school-teacher, Hugh Guthrie, who lost his deposit, by 16,903 votes to 2,378. It was a victory as much for Buchan the writer as Buchan the politician. His novel *Huntingtower* had just been filmed with Harry Lauder in the principal role and he admitted to his Glasgow University contemporary, Alec MacCallum Scott, who had written to congratulate him: 'I think a great many people must have voted for Harry Lauder!'[1]

The House of Commons to which Buchan had been elected consisted of 413 Conservatives, 151 Labour and 40 Liberals. Many of them, particularly in the Cabinet, were old friends such as Leo Amery, the Secretary of State for the Colonies, Lord Robert Cecil, Chancellor of the Duchy of Lancaster, F.E. Smith (now Lord Birkenhead) Secretary of State for India and Sir Arthur Steel-Maitland, Minister of Labour. In the three years since taking office in 1924 the Conservative Government had enacted twenty-one bills but the General Strike and then debates over Trade Union reform had tempered its reforming zeal and a selection of by-election defeats over the summer of 1927 had stimulated media calls for a Cabinet reshuffle.

Buchan took his seat on 3 May but did not make his maiden speech until a debate on 6 July on a Labour vote of censure of Government plans to reform the House of Lords. These would have given back to the Lords many of the powers surrendered in the 1911 Parliament Act. Reform of the Lords had been a subject that had interested Buchan throughout his career and it is perhaps not surprising he should choose it as the subject of his maiden speech.[2] What was surprising was the line he chose to take. The vote of censure was moved by Macdonald with Baldwin replying. Buchan had been due to speak fourth after Lloyd George but was thrown by Baldwin's changing his planned speech, Lloyd George swapping to speak after Buchan, and by having to leave to meet his daughter Alice and a tea-party of young ladies on the Terrace during Baldwin's speech.

He rose to make his speech at 5.30 p.m. to an almost deserted chamber. Claiming to speak for the backwoodsman peer who 'may be very close to the life of the country' he criticized both his own Government's plans and the Labour vote of censure. He asked by way of introduction 'why should we give

up the creation of eight centuries in favour of the work of a few hurried and
hustled gentlemen in the year 1927?'[3] He based his argument on the
Conservative attitude that there was no need to change something if it worked.
He was also frightened that the Lords might be dominated by non-elected
Socialists who might upset the findings of the First Chamber, though ironically the initial reasoning behind the legislation had been to act as a counter-
balance should the Socialists dominate parliament. In his memoirs Buchan
admitted that speaking against the Government and his own party 'gave me a
slight fillip' though it has to be added that Baldwin was only too happy for the
ill-considered plans to be defeated.[4]

Buchan described the speech in detail to his mother the following day:

> I spoke for about five minutes rather labouredly, and then I suddenly real-
> ised that the House was full up and packed with people standing below the
> gangway (in itself a great compliment). Then I suddenly seemed to get
> going, and after that I really enjoyed myself. I was cheered to the echo again
> and again, and when I sat down, after speaking for over twenty minutes,
> there was so much applause that it was some minutes before Lloyd George
> could begin. I am sending you *Hansard* with a full report, and you will see
> some references to me later in the debate, which I have marked with a blue
> pencil. I had a ludicrous amount of congratulations, which I must store up
> against the day when I shall make a fool of myself![5]

Speaking immediately afterwards Lloyd George congratulated him on
'making so brilliant, so wise and so eloquent a maiden speech.' It was a view
shared by the Press and many of Buchan's parliamentary colleagues who compared it in brilliance to that of Birkenhead's some twenty five years earlier. The
Daily News noted that: 'An outstanding event of the evening was the quietly
audacious maiden speech of Col. John Buchan, the novelist lately elected
Conservative member for the Scottish Universities. It was delivered in the style
of a Scottish son of the manse with an Oxford education'. The report continued by describing the line he had adopted:

> He maintained stoutly that the existing House of Lords, though an
> anachronism, is sound, representative and capable of good work and that
> to touch it must prove highly dangerous under existing circumstances.
> Why not leave that job to the Labour Party if it must be done at all?[6]

The parliamentary commentator, James Johnston, wrote shortly afterwards
'not only that it was the best maiden speech I had ever heard, but that it was

the best speech I had heard in this Parliament . . . Mr Buchan is not an orator in the special sense in which the name is used in this volume, but he is most certainly to be classed with the eloquent.'[7]

Almost immediately Buchan was seen as a coming man and associated with the younger, abler and more ambitious Conservatives MPs, to many of whom he had acted as mentor in the Oxford University Conservative Association. This reasonably homogeneous group advocated the need to harness the power of the state to aid both industry and social reform and included among others Robert Boothby, Oliver Stanley, Walter Elliot, W.S. Morrison, Lord Hugh Cecil, Lord Balniel, later Lord Crawford, and Harold Macmillan. Buchan had never been a die-hard Tory and had always been open to opposing ideas and views. Some years later he wrote to J.B. Priestley that he was 'delighted to find your political creed very much the same as mine. I believe profoundly in the progressive socialization of the State, but the vital thing must always be the preservation of the spiritual integrity of the individual. That is why I could never call myself a Socialist in the ordinary sense.'[8]

His views had been shaped by his upbringing as the son of the manse and the Scottish belief in the Democratic Intellect, which placed a premium on education and social mobility. His father's ministry had brought him into contact with people living in terrible conditions and had also taught him the importance of the community taking responsibility for its members. A profound influence on his political thinking had been the First World War. Having experienced its horrors at first hand he was determined that Europe should never again go to war and, as after the Boer War, he was anxious to play a part in the process of reconstruction. That was why he was a League of Nations man and had been a firm supporter of the Locarno Pact. He admired those such as Gustav Stresemann and Aristide Briand who were trying to rebuild Europe and was worried, as were many others, by events such as the Russian Revolution and the General Strike which for him were signs of the cracks in civilization.

Whereas many of his Tory colleagues had moved effortlessly from school and university to Parliament, Buchan had had to make his own way in life. He would often quote the words of Sir Walter Scott: 'I was born a Scotsman, and a bare one. Therefore I was born to fight my way in the world.' Buchan strongly believed that privilege had to be earned. His was a progressive, if sometimes rather naive, Conservatism which always sought the common ground and the best in people. Like Baldwin, he accepted the conventions of party discipline but was happiest when members of all parties could work together to find a solution to a problem and as a result enjoyed good relations with members of all parties, even the Red Clydesiders. Men such as James

Maxton, who had served a prison term for inciting a General Strike, David Kirkwood, George Buchanan and Tom Johnston with their radical views were not obvious companions for a Tory Member of Parliament. They appealed, however, to Buchan's wilder and more Scottish temperament. Many of them had been at Hutchesons' or Glasgow University, several were members of the Church of Scotland and they all shared the same language and fierce pride in Scotland. The Clydesiders behaved in a way that the more controlled Buchan must have sometimes envied, touching on the more primitive side of his character that usually either had to be held in check or sublimated in his writing.

Buchan, though he was a regular attender of debates, did not often speak in parliament but when he did so he spoke with authority and was taken seriously. He chose to concentrate on a number of specific areas, principally Scotland, education, defence and the empire but his contributions in parliament also included speeches on such diverse subjects as the role of the press, protection of birds and rural amenities and scientific developments in Newfoundland. Though Scottish Nationalists have claimed him as their own, Buchan was really an enlightened Unionist, prepared to cloak his own views in rhetoric that would appeal to all the Scottish electorate. He was prepared to devolve some power to Scotland but he believed that Scotland's interests lay within the Union. He chose to set out his own position in his second parliamentary speech made on 19 July 1932 during a debate on a new painting in St Stephen's Hall. He defended the 1707 Act of Union and made clear his position about Scottish Home Rule. Then, after dismissing some of the arguments made against a Scottish Parliament, he conceded 'I believe every Scotsman should be a Scottish nationalist in the true sense.' He outlined his concerns about Scotland losing her historic individuality and the declining population, especially in rural areas. He argued for a Scottish Office in Edinburgh – which eventually happened when St Andrew's House opened in Edinburgh in 1939 – a specifically Scottish Government policy, and Scottish MPs working together for the country's rather than party interests.

During his first year in the House he took little part in parliamentary business. He accepted, particularly as someone who had already made a reputation in public life, that he needed to work his passage. Apart from supporting an amendment to the Cinematograph Films Bill in November 1927 and speaking in favour of the Prayer Book in December 1927, he dutifully supported the Government during the spring of 1928 on such disparate measures as the Local Authorities Bill, Equal Franchise Bill and Rubber Export Restriction Scheme. One particular interest was defence. Buchan was one of the first politicians to realize the importance of air power. Through friends such as

Maurice Baring, Bron Lucas and the Head of the Royal Flying Corps during the First World War, David Henderson, he had become aware during the First World War of its effectiveness and had resolved to publicize its virtues which he did in several articles for the *Graphic* magazine. At the beginning of 1928 he had written a joint introduction with Duff Cooper to Rothesay Stuart- Wortley's posthumous *Letters from a Flying Officer*, a book which he argued was 'intended as propaganda to interest the youth of England in the future of the Air'.[9] In March 1928, during the debate on Air Estimates, when the Secretary of State for Air, Samuel Hoare, asked for an increase of £700,000 a year, Buchan was one of those who supported him and also called for more to be spent on Home Defence. He was pleased that savings had been made by the Ministry of Air, but pointed out: 'However you may picture any future war, it seems pretty certain that the first stage will be a conflict in the air for the mastery of the air'.[10]

In March, having been lucky in the ballot, he introduced a Private Member's Bill for the local licensing of dog tracks. It enjoyed all party support as well as approval from the Churches. On 11 May he successfully moved the second reading of his Dog Racing Bill with a majority of 200, but ran into procedural problems in Committee. The Government claimed it could not give it any more time and the bill was lost, though strangely it did find time almost concurrently to introduce measures legalizing the Totalisator on race- courses. Neville Chamberlain's Local Government Act of 1929 was one of the centre pieces of the Government's programme. In Scotland, a similar bill transferred most powers of local government, including those over education, to the county councils partly at the expense of the burgh councils. Buchan took an active part in opposing this Local Government (Scotland) Bill, defending Scottish burghs and supporting plans for educational authorities. Speaking during the third reading on 11 March he explained his credo. 'I am a Tory and so I have not the Whig distrust of State action. I am ready to admit that many activities are better in the hands of the community than in the hands of individuals.'[11]

Reviewing the parliament James Johnston wrote that Buchan had been one of:

the two great discoveries of this Parliament . . . Mr Buchan has spoken only some five or six times, but he has never fallen appreciably below the stan- dard which his maiden speech created for him . . . Mr Buchan has a large, statesmanlike mind, a polished, well-cultivated eloquence such as is seldom heard nowadays. He gives the House of his best, and never debases his stan- dard of speech in order to win applause.[12]

He went on to prophesy that he would achieve high Government office. It was a promising start to Buchan's political career.

Buchan was again selected to represent the Scottish Universities in the May 1929 General Election and topped the poll with 9,959 votes. But the 'Safety First' campaign had not inspired confidence in the country as a whole. Though they had polled more votes than Labour, the Conservatives actually lost 150 seats allowing Labour to take power for a second time. Many Conservatives, such as Harold Macmillan, had been defeated and Buchan's own majority was reduced. Shortly afterwards he was ordered to bed, partly as a result of exhaustion from the election campaign. He was told to cancel all engagements until the autumn and hardly went into the Commons for the rest of the year. In November, he decided to resign his directorship of Nelson's and he even cut back his journalism with only two *Spectator* articles during the period, one an obituary of Gerard Craig-Sellar and the other on progressive Conservatism. It was clear his ill-health was likely to be an impediment to any political ambitions.

The main domestic problem facing the incoming Labour Government was unemployment which had been exacerbated by the American Stock Market Crash of October 1929. By January 1930 there were 1½ million people unemployed and by the end of the year the number had risen by another million. Buchan had long been aware that the principal task facing any government was to deal with unemployment. Six months before the election he had written to Susan: 'I feel pretty certain that unemployment will dish us unless we can get a really big imaginative scheme before the country, and the only scheme I can see is my idea for emigration. Conservative Headquarters seem to be living in a fools paradise.'[13] The idea of empire settlement as a way of reducing domestic unemployment was by no means unique to Buchan. Among its greatest exponents was his mother-in-law, Caroline Grosvenor, who had started the Colonial Intelligence League (for Educated Women) which had become the Society for Overseas Settlement of British Women. It was an idea that had already been explored in John Galsworthy's 1924 novel, *A Modern Comedy*. In the book an idealistic Member of Parliament advocates a scheme called Foggartism to send the youth of Britain's slums to the dominions as a solution to the problems of crime, poverty and unemployment.

In March 1929, Buchan wrote, along with several other MPs, a letter to *The Times* proposing 'A colony in Canada' as a solution to the rising unemployment problem. The letter pointed out that money was available through the 1922 Empire Settlement Act but accepted: 'You cannot move human beings about like bales of goods.' Therefore, they continued: 'It seems to us that emigration cannot be used to solve our unemployment troubles unless the thing is taken up in a different spirit and on a far greater scale – taken up as an urgent administrative duty, as a great enterprise, with the whole weight of the nation behind it.' The signatories suggested that the Government should buy land in Canada to develop, thereby providing a solution to Canada's shortage of labour:

> Now is the chance for a fresh wave – not a driblet, but a wave which might well mark a new stage in the history of Canadian life ... we do not believe that there is one of our greater British problems which can be solved except on the basis of Imperial partnership. Today the Empire is a real partner, ship, an executive alliance of sovereign States. If such a partnership is to have any value it must use the strength of one part to meet the changed conditions in another.[14]

Eight months later Buchan advocated yet another scheme for reducing unemployment. Through Susan's work with the Oxford House settlement at Risca in Wales, he had become fascinated by work camps and now put forward a plan to put unemployed male teenagers in the equivalent of scout camps in order to give them some job training. There they could learn to be stablemen, chauffeurs or gardeners. There they would be properly fed, learn a trade and most importantly, be given hope that society had not abandoned them. Speaking on 21 January 1930 in a debate on unemployment, Buchan criticized the new Labour Government for not having a proper policy to deal with unemployment and hinted that unless government dealt with this, the most important problem facing society, it would lead to supra parliamentary activity: 'In the difficult and intricate conditions under which we live, I believe that it will be necessary in the near future to broaden our executive basis and to bring to an unexampled extent into actual administrative work the right kind of private citizen.'[15]

The speech brought praise from the *Nation*, a Liberal paper:

> Mr Buchan and Mr Boothby followed with two of the best speeches heard from their side in this Parliament. Each of them would have spoken with more appropriateness from the Liberal benches, and each, in attacking the record of this Government, was attacking by implica, tion with even greater force the far more prolonged failure of their own. Mr Buchan was particularly impressive when he warned the House that the ordinary man, if continually disappointed by party leaders, might turn to unauthorized practitioners and dangerous remedies, such as Empire Free Trade.[16]

Buchan had himself become drawn into Beaverbrook's Free Trade Campaign. He wrote to Beaverbrook at the height of the campaign:

> I have meant to write you for some time about your crusade. All we Conservative Members have been talking loosely for years about the neces sity of treating the Empire as an economic unit, and it is high time that we got down to brass tacks. You have done a very great service in forcing this on, and I need not tell you how much I admire your courage and devotion. In the old days of the Chamberlain campaign I was a Tory Free-Trader. Today I think the whole centre of gravity has changed, and we must con template a very considerable advance in the State control of industry and commerce.[17]

Though he confessed to reservations about Beaverbrook's scheme, he had been trying to persuade Baldwin to create 'closer and franker co-ordination' between the Conservatives and Beaverbrook, using the resources of the Conservative Research Department, which had been founded in that year.

As the economic crisis worsened, Buchan began to argue for more drastic solutions. In a letter to *The Times* in October 1930 he wrote:

> . . . it is the primary business of a Government or a party to look at facts and to select the best method of dealing with them. In certain circumstances the solutions may lie in individual effort, in others in the use of the corporate powers of the State. It is a question of fact in each case. To Socialism as a rigid and universal creed the Tory is as much opposed as he used to be to the atomic individualism of the Whigs, for he disbelieves utterly in abstract dogmas. But, as I read the history of our party, we have never shown any narrow jealousy of State action when such action was warranted by the facts. Why should we be asked to resign an important weapon in our armoury merely because some people want to make an extravagant use of it? No dry fly purist will prevent me fishing my fly wet if it is the best way to catch trout.[18]

Later that month, speaking in the debate on the King's Speech at a time when the unemployment levels exceeded two million, he was adamant: 'There is only one problem before the country to-day, and that is the problem of our economic situation. Everything else should be subordinated to its solution.'[19] He went on to call for a National Government:

> The advantage of such a Government would be twofold. It would pool two things – brains and unpopularity. It would bring the best talent in the

nation to the solution of our difficulties . . . More important still, it would saddle every party without distinction with the necessary unpopularity, so that none would have an advantage over any other.[20]

At the end of December in another letter to *The Times* he again called for a National Government; this time it was signed by other prominent public figures such as Beaverbrook, Sir Robert Horne, Walter Elliot and Oliver Stanley.

Meanwhile he continued his campaign to raise the school leaving age when the Education (School Attendance) Bill had its second reading in November 1930. Speaking against James Maxton he played on his roots: 'I have had the inestimable advantage of getting my education in precisely the same way, and at the same school and the same college as my friend the hon Member for Bridgeton.' Reluctantly he voted against the bill, not because he was against it in principle, indeed the opposite. He defended the bill as 'a genuine step in educational progress, a view in which I differ from most Members of my own party.' However, he felt that it would cost £5 million in the first year rising to £8 million and the Government just could not afford it given the economic crisis.[21]

Throughout his second parliament Buchan began to adopt a more independent line. In an adjournment debate in June 1930 about recognising the Bolshevik Government in Russia he admitted: 'I have very little admiration for what seems to be the policy of the present regime in Russia. I do not admire their economics or their public doings. They seem to me to be a return to barbarism.' But he argued that Britain should keep up links with Russia and along with only two other Conservatives, Robert Boothby and Lady Astor, voted in support of the Labour Government's recognition of the Soviet Union.[22] He also tended to take a close interest in the moves towards Indian self-government. In a letter to *The Times* in July 1930 after the Simon Commission had reported, he dealt with the question of Dominion status and argued that in dealing with India, Britain needed to show 'sympathy and imagination . . . a strong sense of reality, a scrupulous candour and a steadfast purpose.'[23]

His range of parliamentary interests was considerable. On 21 February 1930 he spoke in the Rural Amenities Bill, explaining that a balance had to be drawn between protecting the countryside and providing roads and houses. 'Rural England is not an antiquarian museum; it is the home of people, and the interests of the people must come first.' He went on to suggest that National Parks be set up 'partly for the public enjoyment, for holiday camps and such things, and partly also as sanctuaries for wild life.' He concluded that just as everyone was entitled to education and 'to the treasuries of art and letters' it was 'the right of every citizen to have access to the refreshment and peace which is given by the most beautiful countryside in the world.'[24] He also took an interest in matters relating to the Press, as befitted a professional journalist and member of the Reuters Board. On his election he had joined the Parliamentary Press Committee and in December 1930 he spoke on the Press Bill.

> I can speak from long experience of handling the printed word in most of its forms, and I do not believe there is any class of man more worthy of trust, less likely to abuse any privileges given to them than the working journalists of Britain.[25]

When the question of the university vote was raised in the Representation of the People Bill in February 1931, he fought hard to save it as much from personal belief as selfinterest. 'I believe that every citizen in this country is worth one vote, but I believe many of them are worth more. That is to say I believe in plural voting.'[26] He pointed out that Labour supported a form of plural voting by having nonlocal trade union votes on the selection of parliamentary candidates and went on to defend the university franchise, claiming that it brought into parliament MPs who might otherwise not stand, that it gave a vote to those living abroad and that it was important to have someone specifically representing the interests of graduates. It was a subject on which he felt very strongly. In his memoirs he wrote how he 'thought that the rigid territorial basis for elections was out of date. It might continue in part as a framework, but the Universities' precedent should be followed, and there should be additional representation for great economic, cultural and professional interests ...' It was an interesting idea but perhaps more suited to a Second Chamber.[27]

Throughout 1931 Britain's economic crisis had worsened with growing unemployment and industrial depression. In August Sir George May's report on national expenditure was published, advocating huge reductions in government spending, including unemployment benefit. Ramsay MacDonald, unable to secure agreement in his own Cabinet, handed in his resignation but was immediately asked by King George V to form a coalition. It was what Buchan had been calling for for months. The new coalition went to the country in October to secure support for the new arrangements. On doctor's orders Buchan took little part in the election campaign, only speaking at a rally in Stirling and then disappearing for a holiday in Cornwall. There his only political activity was to visit the committee rooms of A.L. Rowse, an undergraduate visitor to Elsfield and the antiNationalGovernment Labour candidate for Penryn and Falmouth.

Buchan became the first member of the new parliament when he was returned unopposed. It was a landslide victory for the National Government which took 556 seats (472 Conservative, 33 Liberal, 35 Simonite Liberal, 13 pro-Government National Labour and a few Independents) to Labour's 46. The Labour party had lost 241 seats and, with the exception of George Lansbury, Clement Attlee and Sir Stafford Cripps, all the Labour Ministers were out of Parliament. When the new Cabinet was formed Buchan again found to his frustration, and that of the *Evening Standard* who thought he should be in the Government, that he had been passed over for office. He had been in the Commons for almost five years and felt he had served his apprenticeship. At fifty-six he recognised time was not on his side. In November, he wrote again to Baldwin:

Some of my friends seem to regard me as mainly pledged to the pursuit of letters. This is not so. Writing has never been more than an occasional hobby. Now that I have retired from business and am a free man and have got back my health I am most ready and willing for any public service that comes my way.[28]

Buchan would write in his memoirs:

When I entered the House I decided that I had no desire for the ordinary *cursus honorum*. A minor post would only have complicated my life, and I was too senior to begin to try for Cabinet office. So I had no reason to put myself forward, and I spoke only on subjects where I had special knowl-edge or a special interest.

The reality was rather different.[29]

In June 1931 Violet Markham had written to Tom Jones suggesting Buchan as President of the Board of Education:

It would be a thousand pities if that appointment is made on the rigid lines of party spoils. John has vision and imagination. He holds a unique place in public life detached from strict party allegiances. He would bring vigour and enthusiasm to that dreary department and I believe might make a great success of the post. It never seems to me that his services and very real abilities have received adequate recognition so far. He never pushes or clamours and so he seems to get left aside – greatly so I think to the public detriment.[30]

After the election Jones raised the matter with Baldwin, then deputy Prime Minister, but without any success. Baldwin told him: 'Buchan would be no use in the Cabinet' and that the number of Liberals supporting Herbert Samuel needed to be kept up. Buchan's opponent at Peebleshire, Donald Maclean, a Samuelite Liberal, went to Education instead.[31] It seems Buchan had already turned one Cabinet post down. He claimed to Basil Liddell Hart at a lunch at the Athenaeum on 12 November 1931 that Ramsay MacDonald had offered to create room for him as Secretary of State for Scotland but he had declined, arguing 'that Samuel Liberals would soon go in any case'.[32]

He continued to devote himself to back-bench parliamentary business. Later that month he became Chairman of the Parliamentary Palestine Committee with Barnett Janner, a Liberal MP, as the Secretary. Buchan had long taken an interest in the subject of a Jewish Homeland, stimulated by Baldwin and before that by Balfour and Milner, and in April 1930 had pub-lished an article, Ourselves and the Jews. He made his own position on the subject clear a few months later speaking in a Colonial Office debate on Supply with reference to Palestine: 'Our attitude, as I see it, should not be pro-Jewish or pro-Arab but simply pro-British.[33] But he went on:

> What is our national obligation of honour? It is not to bring Jews back to Palestine, but it is to prepare and make possible a National Home for such Jews as desire to return. The Zionist ideal does not depend upon the extent of territory over which a national home is created, but upon the chances given for the development of the Jewish national genius.[34]

Perhaps in consolation for being denied a Cabinet post he was made a Companion of Honour in the New Year's Honours List for 'public, educa-tional and literary services'. Beaverbrook wrote immediately to congratulate him, 'It is so much finer than being "Sir John"' but added 'I do think, however, that you might have been given the OM instead.' Buchan, painfully aware of the problems of hitherto obtaining an honour, nonchalantly passed it off with 'I prefer a suffix to a prefix.'[35] Though he had failed to be made a Cabinet Minister there were signs, however, that Baldwin was keen for him to hold some government post. In May 1932 Buchan wrote excitedly to his wife:

> Now here is something important which I want you and Alice to talk over before I come back on Friday. They are going to separate Burma from India, and make it a separate Dominion under a Governor-General, and since the Burmese are a reasonable and docile people, they believe that if self-gov-ernment succeeds there, it will be a model for India. I was sent for last night,

and they asked me to be the first Governor-General. I have been whistling 'Mandalay' while shaving for some weeks, and that seems to have been an omen. What do you think about the old 'Moulmein Pagoda'? This would not be like Canada, a quasi-royal affair, but a piece of solid and difficult work. There is no hurry about a decision, for I have only been sounded, but I wish you would turn it over in your mind. Are we too old for a final frisk?[36]

In the event Burma was not separated and the suggestion came to nothing.

As a result of his activities during the First World War and his writing, Buchan had always taken a close interest in the film industry and when the Sunday Entertainments Bill was being debated in May 1932 he made an imaginative suggestion, that 5 per cent of the money from takings on Sundays should be put aside for 'the assistance and development of British films'. He continued:

What those who are interested in the matter desire to see is something positive, a constructive effort to help in the development of this great medium of instruction and entertainment. We want some kind of link between the trade and the public, something which will help to develop what is best in the films and will relate that to the other interests of the national life . . . The idea is ultimately the creation of a film institute, not a Government Department but a private body with a charter under the aegis and support of the Government.[37]

He went on to propose that it should be 'a school for the study of technique and the interchange of ideas', give advice 'about the educational possibilities of the film . . . advise Government Departments as to the use of films' and help rationalize the development of the British film industry. He argued that the two novelties of the post-war period were the wireless and films. There was already a public body, the BBC, for the former but nothing for the latter. The following month he repeated his hope 'to form a kind of staff college for the study of technique, a clearing house for knowledge of ideas, and to help to exploit the very great assets for film production which we believe Britain and the British Empire possess.'[38]

The result was the formation of the British Film Institute in October 1933. Nine Governors were appointed including Buchan, Alan Cameron and the Editor of the *Listener*, R.S. Lambert, under the Chairmanship of the Duke of Sutherland. Buchan was appointed Chairman of the Advisory Council, which also included a representative from the Board of Education, and several panels were set up covering special aspects of the film industry including scientific research, international relations and amateur cinematography. Most of the films inspired by the British Film Institute were produced by Gaumont British Instructional Ltd under the aegis of H. Bruce Woolf with whom Buchan already had close links.[39]

He also continued to take an interest in Scottish matters, on which he spoke widely throughout the country as well as in Parliament. In June 1932, in a debate on Scottish Records and speaking as President of the Scottish History Society, he claimed: 'in the last half century the interests of Scotland have been shamefully neglected. Our records are in a deplorable condition, uncatalogued, unindexed, in no way properly accessible to the public, and there is a real danger that unless we take care many of them will be destroyed altogether.' He said between £1,000 and £2,000 was needed and some of the profit from the Register of Sasines should be redirected to the Public Record Office.[40] Five months later in a debate on the Address he pointed out that true 'Scottish business is swamped in this House because of the numerical inferiority of Scottish Members' though he admitted the same criticism might be levelled if the Parliament was in Edinburgh, because then the Highlands would be 'at the mercy of an enormous Lowland majority representing different interests'.[41]

One needed to go to the root of the problem he felt. 'What is the exact nature of this sentiment of dissatisfaction which is behind the Scottish movement? What element of substance and of value is there in that sentiment?' He continued in a departure from his speeches of a few years earlier:

I believe that every Scotsman should be a Scottish Nationalist. If it could be proved that a separate Scottish Parliament were desirable, that is to say that the merits were greater than the disadvantages and dangers, Scotsmen should support it.

I would go further. Even if it were not proved desirable, if it could be proved to be desired by any substantial majority of the Scottish people, then Scotland should be allowed to make the experiment, and I do not believe that England would desire for one moment to stand in the way.[42]

He continued to be worried about the falling rural population and the churches losing their influence. 'In language, literature and art we are losing our idiom, and it seems to many that we are in danger very soon of reaching the point where Scotland will have nothing distinctive to show to the world.'[43] The economic problems of the early 1930s, which had affected Scotland more heavily than England, had stimulated the rise of the Scottish nationalist movement which worried Buchan greatly. The National Party of Scotland had been founded in 1928, had already contested several parliamentary elections and in the 1931 Glasgow rectorial election had achieved a notable success with Compton Mackenzie's victory over Sir Robert Horne.

Buchan was a Unionist and a Conservative but he knew that if the Conservatives were to continue to enjoy support in Scotland they needed to be more sympathetic to Scottish aspirations. He genuinely believed in devolving more power to Scotland, partly from a desire to remedy a long standing griev-ance and partly from a belief that some Scottish matters could best be dealt with at a local level. This interest in Scottish affairs was reflected at the same time in his activities outside parliament. Through Lord Rosebery, Arthur Balfour and Lord Crawford he had become involved in the setting up of the National Library of Scotland and had brought in Hugh Macmillan to deal with its legal affairs. Buchan joined the Board in 1925 and continued to serve on it for the next ten years, during which period he presented the Library with his own collection of books on Montrose. He had also become involved in the committee to preserve the site of the Battle of Bannockburn. The seven years he spent in parliament coincided with some of his most important books with a Scottish theme, most notably his biographies of Montrose and Sir Walter Scott and his historical novel, *Witch Wood*.

At the end of September 1932 Snowden, Samuel and Sinclair resigned from Cabinet over the issue of Free Trade. Yet again Buchan was passed over for office as he had been when Donald Maclean had died in June. Sir Godfrey Collins, a former Liberal Chief Whip, was appointed to the post Buchan had expected, Secretary of State for Scotland. He was extremely annoyed that former liberals who now supported the Government, led by Sir John Simon, should take precedence over him. He wrote to Markham:

What is the good of kow-towing to the Simonites, who are indistinguish-able from the ordinary Tories, except that they are more reactionary and who would not exist for a moment in Parliament except by our permission? I gather that the excessive attention paid to them was not Ramsay's doing, but SB's, who is apt to make a fetish of magnanimity. But my real objec-tion is to their second-rate ability. If the National Government means any-thing, it should be a pooling of the best talents . . . Scotland is going to be a very difficult post in the near future, and Godfrey Collins, the Scottish Secretary, is simply preposterous.[44]

On the same day he wrote to Baldwin in terms very similar to his letter of a year before:

I feel that somehow I have managed to acquire the wrong kind of political atmosphere. Most of my friends seem to think that I am a busy man whose life is completely filled with non-political interests. But that is not the case. I gave up business three years ago in order to devote myself to politics. I do not speak overmuch in the House – there is no need for it – but I do a great deal of speaking up and down the country, especially in Scotland, where I think I have a good deal of influence. Politics have always been my chief interest, and I have a good deal of administrative experience . . . I am very well in body now, and, as you know, I can work pretty hard. So I would like to be considered when posts are being filled, for I am no longer as young as I was, and I want to do some useful public work before the Guard comes to take the tickets! I am not asking for anything, please – I never asked for anything in my life. But I should like my leader to know that I am a free man and really anxious for definite work, so that I may be considered when the occasion arises.[45]

Though he was not in the Cabinet, Buchan did exercise considerable influence as an adviser to both Stanley Baldwin and then Ramsay MacDonald. He helped them with drafting speeches, gave them moral support during early morning walks around St James's Park and provided assessments about both personalities and policies. When a dinner was given by 700 Scots in London for MacDonald shortly after the election of the National Government, Buchan made the principal speech of the evening. His links with Baldwin in particular stretched outside parliament. When Baldwin was installed as Chancellor of St Andrews University in 1930 Buchan on his nomination was given an Hon LLD. That same year the American financier Edward Harkness, who had made a fortune from the Standard Oil Company, donated £2 million to set up The Pilgrim Trust. The money was to be devoted to conserving Britain's heritage and alleviating social distress. Baldwin was elected Chairman and Buchan, together with Sir Josiah Stamp, Sir James Irvine, the Principal of St Andrews, and Hugh Macmillan were appointed trustees with Tom Jones as a full-time Secretary based at 10 York Buildings in Adelphi Terrace.

The trustees were free to spend the capital and interest as they wished and they interpreted their brief widely. Large sums were given to the Oxford and Cambridge Preservation Societies, the McMillan experiment in nursery education in Deptford, the Old Vic, the History of Parliament project, the Rowett Institute of Biological Research for its work on nutrition, the National Trust for Scotland, the Scottish Youth Hostel Association, the establishment of the Scott Polar Research Institute in Cambridge, Talking Books for the

Blind, Lincoln Cathedral and to a study of LCC slum clearance estates. Buchan relished the opportunity to do something specific about the social problems of the day and to find important preservation work. Many of his own interests benefited from the Pilgrim Trust, such as the Risca settlement in the Rhondda valley, the Oxford Exploration Club, Toynbee Hall, the Society for Army Historical Research and the Bodleian.[46]

As a result of his interest in broadcasting he was asked to join Lord Rankeillour and Lord Gorell on an inter-party consultative committee to advise on controversial political talks and in February 1935 became a member of the BBC General Advisory Council under the Chairmanship of William Temple, the Archbishop of York. The Council replaced the Central Council for Broadcast Adult Education and its purpose was to advise the Corporation on policy matters and act as a link between the BBC and particular sections of the community. The other members of the BBC Advisory Council included Lloyd George, Sir William Beveridge, Hugh Macmillan, Sir Robert Rait, Bernard Shaw and Dame Sibyl Thorndike.

One of Buchan's main interests in parliament was the School Age Council. This had been created by MPs and community leaders in July 1934 to lobby for the raising of the school leaving age to fifteen. It was chaired by Buchan and its supporters included the Archbishops of Canterbury and York, the Moderator of the Church of Scotland, the Chief Rabbi and Directors of Education, Trade Unionists and industrialists. The following February, Buchan led a deputation from the Council to 10 Downing Street. This included among others Viscount Astor, the Archbishop of York, the Wardens of Toynbee Hall and All Souls, Herbert Morrison from the London County Council and representatives of the National Union of Teachers, various Education Committees and a host of voluntary organizations. The Council were anxious to extend the leaving age for educational reasons, but also felt there were benefits at a time of high unemployment in extra training and taking people off the job market. Eventually it achieved its aim in 1936, though the actual implementation was to take effect only from 1 September 1939.

As late as February 1934 Buchan continued to hold out hope of gaining government office. He told Max Nicholson, a member of the Oxford Exploration Club, that he had been led to believe he might be given the Home Office and after lunching with Lady Londonderry he wrote to his wife: 'The idea apparently is to get John Davidson out of the Chancellorship of the Duchy and put me in. I don't think that possible, for Baldwin would certainly resign, in spite of his friendship for me. The only other alternative would be to create an extra Minister without portfolio.'[47] The following week he brought his wife up to date on the intrigue:

Circe is living in a whirlwind. She saw SB, who was most cordial, but thought that the PM would be difficult to ginger up to putting me in the Cabinet straight away. He was rather inclined to suggest that I should be made a Privy Counsellor and attached to the PM as a sort of first lieutenant till he saw how things went. The PM was dining at Londonderry House last night and Circe meant to speak winged words to him.[48]

Circe was Edith, Marchioness of Londonderry, the leading Conservative hostess of the period, and a great friend of Ramsay MacDonald. Both Buchan and MacDonald were social romantics who enjoyed tradition, colour and pageantry and soon they became regulars at her parties. Indeed MacDonald was so close to the Marchioness that it was often suggested he had exchanged the Red Flag for the Londonderry Air. Many of Circe's parties revolved around her 'Ark', a group of men prominent in the arts and politics, which she had founded during the First World War and which after the war met each Wednesday at 9.30 p.m. in the great ballroom. By the time Buchan, known as the Buck, had stepped inside the Ark it numbered some fifty people who included Churchill (Winston the Warlock), Edward Wood, Lord Halifax (Edward the Woodpecker), Lady Astor (Nancy the Gnat), Sir William Orpen (Orpen the Ortolan), Sir Edward Carson (Edward the Eagle), Arthur Balfour (Arthur the Albatross) and Harold Macmillan (Harold the Hummingbird).

Though never a great socialite Buchan welcomed the opportunity the parties provided to meet writers such as George Bernard Shaw and Edmund Gosse and painters such as Sir William Orpen and Sir John Lavery. As Circe's biographer has put it: 'Half-amused by, half-disapproving of Edith's flamboyance, grandeur and insouciance, he was romantically drawn to the aura of history and tradition emanating from Londonderry House, and fascinated by the glamour of the whole glittering scene.'[49] When Edith Londonderry decided to write a memoir of her father, Henry Chaplin, Buchan spent a few weeks at the Londonderry family home at Mount Stewart helping her with the research and writing. The book was published in October 1926 by Harold Macmillan's family publishing firm.[50]

The question has to be asked why, given his undoubted talents and friendship with leading political figures, was Buchan not asked to join the Cabinet? There are a number of possible explanations. One was his age and lack of political experience. Buchan had been elected to parliament at the age of fifty one and in comparison with the other members of the Cabinet had only been in the House of Commons for a comparatively short time, but Neville Chamberlain had been elected at a similar age and within five years had become Minister of Health. Another suggestion is that because he had so many commitments outside politics, including a newspaper column on the *Sunday Times*, he was seen as a dilettante. Though generally liked by his colleagues, the fact that he continued to work as a journalist undermined his political credibility. Yet a number of leading politicians, such as Winston Churchill, wrote extensively on a wide range of subjects without any hindrance to their career. Another possibility that has been raised is that Buchan could be indiscreet, which made both Baldwin and then MacDonald wary of entrusting him with particularly sensitive information. All the evidence, however, suggests that it was because of his very discretion that he was trusted as a confidential adviser and 'fixer' by both men.[51] A more important factor was his health, which was still uncertain. It was felt he might not have the strength to run a department. Another was his temperament. Buchan was just not suited to the complex government decision-making process. He liked to organise his own time carefully and was impatient of the slow compromises needed in committee work. His previous administrative experience in South Africa and during the First World War had required him to make decisions quickly and he felt frustrated by the demands of peacetime government.

Where the Conservative Party did make use of his talents was in the area of political education and developing a youth wing. As a parliamentary candidate before the First World War he had been critical of the Conservative Party machine and in an article in *Blackwood's* in January 1911 had argued in favour of a strong Party Chairman running Conservative Central Office like a business, pre dating Lord Woolton's efforts by thirty years. Shortly after his election as an MP he was asked to revive the Conservative Party's educational efforts. The Chairman, John Davidson, felt Buchan was the ideal candidate, given his long associations with the adult education movement and the close links he had maintained with both schools and universities. The fact that for many years before his election to Westminster Buchan had been Senior Treasurer of the Oxford University Conservative Association also helped.

The Education Department at Central Office was closed and replaced with a semi-independent body to be called The Conservative and Unionist Educational Institute. The idea was to offer political education, much as the Labour Party had been doing for some time, but with a Conservative slant along the lines of the burgeoning groups like the Workers' Education Association. The Institute would be a charitable trust with its own endowment fund and governed by trustees under a trust deed.[52] He explained: 'its aim is to give to young men and women leaving public and secondary schools a short course of a university standard in economic science, political thought and history, British Imperial development, foreign relationships and national and local government.'[53]

Baldwin was asked to be President, John Davidson Vice-President and Buchan was chairman of the executive committee. The Council included Lady Astor, Walter Elliot and Harold Macmillan with Hugh Williams as Director. The Institute was named Bonar Law College and based at Ashridge, formerly the home of Lord Brownlow. As *The Times* reported: 'the work hitherto carried on by the educational department of the party organisa-tion will be developed considerably, and a large number of new study circles, lecture courses, and correspondence courses are being formed.' The Bonar Law College was one of the great success stories of the inter-war years, sub-stantially improving the political knowledge and techniques of a generation of Conservative activists.[54]

Buchan was also asked to draw up plans for a Students' Unionist Federation along the same lines as the Liberal and Socialist Federations. This was an attempt to strengthen links with younger Conservatives, particularly in the newer universities, to help create a route into the Party for students and to give them an opportunity to mix and attend courses at Ashridge. He became the first President of this Federation of University Conservative and Unionist Associations, which consisted of about a dozen university conserv-ative associations. The Federation's initial conference was held in Birmingham in January 1931. Buchan spoke of youth's responsibility to replace the lost generation of the War, a theme he was to return to in speeches and his writing throughout the 1930s. Further conferences under his patronage followed over the next four years in Liverpool, Oxford, Manchester and Edinburgh.

It was an ideal appointment for him. He had already taken a close interest in OUCA and many aspiring politicians would come to Elsfield for tea. One was the present Lord Longford, then a Conservative, who remembered him as 'the kindest man I ever met'. Buchan had often toured the country speak-ing to schools and universities and he enjoyed the intellectual curiosity of young people and the opportunity it gave him to be a mentor.

This was where his talents could best be utilized. Though an assiduous attender at Westminster, staying late night after night to vote in debates, he was never really a House of Commons man. Perhaps his speeches were just that bit too polished, the comments too balanced, the tone ironic rather than sar-castic for him to make a real impression on the floor of the House. He lectured rather than debated, drew on historical analogy rather than contemporary allusion and approached each problem more as an intellectual exercise to be solved than as a party political point to be made. Lord Birkenhead was later to write: 'there was a suggestion of the lecturer, a hint of the dominie, and a whiff of some by-gone Calvinism in his speeches which was alien to the House of Commons.' While William Brown, a parliamentary colleague who sat first for Labour and then as an Independent, thought he 'had a curious sing-song way of speaking in the House. His intonation was rather like that of the music-hall parody of a curate, but his matter was always first rate.' Indeed Buchan's voice was so quiet that a heckler supposedly once called out 'Let us pray' in the middle of one of his speeches, speeches perhaps were more suited to the columns of the *Spectator* or the benches of the House of Lords than the floor of the House of Commons. Buchan's qualities were not necessarily those of an effective politician. Essentially he was a thoughtful, courteous and sensitive man; in politics these characteristics are not always regarded as assets.[55]

At the beginning of April 1933 Buchan wrote to his wife: 'Ramsay has just offered me the Lord High Commissionership and I have accepted. It must be kept desperately secret until the King has assented. Don't even tell Nan.' Three days later it was announced in *The Times* and Buchan began to make arrangements for his term of office.[56] The Lord High Commissioner acts as the Sovereign's representative during the annual meeting in May of the General Assembly of the Church of Scotland. His job is to address the Assembly at its opening and close and preside over its discussions. Increasingly, however, the job of Lord High Commissioner had developed into representing Scottish national identity within the Union. An important part of the job was to entertain local worthies and, though the Commissioner is given an allowance, it was this aspect of the job that most concerned Buchan. Only after he had agreed the level and cost of hospitality expected of him did he accept the job.

It was a post that traditionally went to a Scottish peer, though Ramsay MacDonald had appointed the Scottish miners' leader and MP for South Ayrshire, James Brown, in 1924. Buchan was not the first choice but he turned out to have been an inspired one. He was the first Lord High Commissioner whose father had been a minister. As he professed in his initial address: 'I have in my bones the tradition of Scottish Presbyterianism.' He had been an active member of the Church of Scotland all his life and an elder of St Columba's, the principal Scottish church in London, since just after his marriage. His mother religiously attended the Assembly each year and Buchan, himself, had been as an elder representing St Columba's in 1929 and as a guest of James Brown when he was reappointed in 1930.

When the Established and the United Free Church had amalgamated again in 1929 Buchan had been asked to deliver an address during the General Assembly on the subject by the Home Mission Committees of the Church of Scotland and the United Free Church. This was published later that year as the pamphlet *What the Union of the Churches means to Scotland*. He followed this up the next year with a rather longer book, giving the historical background, called *The Kirk in Scotland*, which he wrote with the biblical scholar George Adam Smith.[57] Buchan knew the Church of Scotland in a way few of his predecessors had, able equally easily to converse with theological scholars and parish ministers. Above all, MacDonald knew that it would appeal to Buchan's sense of history and love of ceremony. He might not be suitable Cabinet material but this was one job he could discharge and discharge very well.

The Buchans arrived in Edinburgh on 22 May, 1933 he suitably dressed in the uniform of a Deputy Lord Lieutenant for Peebles, for the ceremonial presentation of the keys to the city. His party included Baldwin, Sir Godfrey Collins, the Secretary of State for Scotland, the Duchess of Hamilton and Duchess of Atholl MP and Lord and Lady Elgin. Most of his entourage, however, consisted of close family or friends. His schoolboy friend Charles Dick, now a minister in Shetland after a spell in Barbados, was his chaplain while his sister Anna and old Oxford friend Caroline Johnston-Douglas, now Lady Kinross, acted as ladies-in-waiting. Alice was one of the maids of honour and the three boys Johnnie, now an undergraduate at Brasenose, and William and Alastair, still at Eton, paid brief visits.

Susan's mother came for the whole week as did his mother, a regular attender with her devotional books. Helen Buchan had always dreamed of seeing her son preside over a General Assembly, and seemed resigned to the fact it would now only be as Lord High Commissioner rather than as Moderator itself. She assiduously attended the debates during which she knitted furiously and made occasional asides to her neighbour. Her wide knowledge of the affairs and personalities of the Church of Scotland proved invaluable to Buchan who at the end of the week presented her with a photographic record of his stint inscribed 'To my dearest Mother, this record of what was as much her show as mine.'

Over the course of the next few days he addressed the Women's Guild in the Usher Hall, opened the new Edinburgh Castle War Museum and spoke at the Royal Infirmary Thanksgiving Service. He also took the opportunity to visit the Free Church Assembly – his father had originally been a minister of that church – which remained outside the union of 1929. For his speech on the last day he took as his theme the Scottish Church and Empire. In it he expounded on the spiritual dimension to the empire, an implicit theme of much of his fiction as well as non-fiction: 'The true bond of Empire is the spiritual bond. Its cohesion is in its ideal and not in its form of government . . . The true empire is a spiritual thing based essentially upon Christian ideals . . . It is a union in far more than the functions of government.'[58]

Buchan loved all the tradition and trimmings that went with the week of ceremonies – living in the Palace of Holyroodhouse, having a military guard of honour, the twenty-one-gun salute from the Castle, the aides-de-camp with their aiglets on the right shoulder to distinguish them from the ADC's to the Sovereign. He could reflect how the post had been held by scions of the Scottish aristocracy and even by a member of the Royal Family, Albert, the Duke of York, who had graced the position in 1929. His new surroundings appealed to his romantic and historical imagination and his sense of the mystic. In his memoirs he wrote how:

> I shall not soon forget those dinners in the great gallery of the Palace, where sometimes a hundred sat at table – the lingering spring sunshine competing with the candles, the dark walls covered with portraits of the Kings of Scotland (daubs two hundred years old, but impressive in the twilight), the toast of the King, followed by the National Anthem, and that of the Church of Scotland, followed by Old Hundred, the four pipers of the Argylls, who strutted round the table and then played a pibroch for my special delectation. On those nights old ghosts came out of secret places.[59]

One unexpected consequence was that on the last night Alice announced her engagement to one of the ADCs, Brian Fairfax-Lucy. Brian Fairfax-Lucy at thirty five was ten years older than Alice. The second son of a baronet he had been educated at Eton from where he had gone into the Cameron Highlanders. After service in the First World War, in which he had been severely wounded, he had spent six years in India, three of them as ADC to the GOC Madras District. After a year with the Army in Germany he had returned in 1927 for a three year posting as Adjutant of the 2nd Battalion Cameron Highlanders. There his career seems to have stalled and for the previous two years he had been acting as ADC to the Lord High Commissioners. Alice, recovering from a broken love affair, was keen to settle down and adamant that she wanted only a short engagement. Three months later the couple were married at St Columba's, she in a white satin dress and Fairfax-Lucy in his Highland dress. The Marquess of Douglas and Clydesdale, who had been a fellow ADC at Holyrood, was the best man and the honeymoon was spent at Violet Markham's home in Kent.

Buchan returned as Lord High Commissioner the following year, again with Charles Dick as his chaplain and Lady Kinross and Alice as Ladies in Waiting. Apart from Walter, Anna and Mrs Grosvenor he had invited G.M. Trevelyan and his wife, his publisher Percy Hodder-Williams and the Unionist MPs Victor Cazalet and William 'Shakes' Morrison. An invitation was also extended to the eccentric poet Ezra Pound with whom Buchan was now engaged in a regular, if rather bizarre, correspondence.[60] Pound, then living in Rapallo in Italy, had first written to Buchan at the beginning of 1934 commenting on Buchan's writing and the current world political scene. When Buchan became Lord High Commissioner Pound wrote to congratulate him on being a 'very great pot indeed (Ld High Admiral of the Free Kirk (or the other one) etc.)' Buchan hastened to tell him 'I am not much of a "pot"'. After receiving a volume of Pound's essays and a torrent of invective about world politicians Buchan diplomatically replied: 'I feel that in all these matters I do not differ from you *except in opinion* (and in that I differ violently). But opinion does not seriously matter. I greatly admire your vigour and courage and often unholy insight.' The two kept up a correspondence until the end of 1935.[61]

Though he had enjoyed this second experience as Lord High Commissioner he was determined not to do it a third year running and instead claimed to have pushed for the Duke of Kent to take over from him. In 1935, shortly before going out to Canada, however, he wrote to Charles Dick: 'I should like to be Lord High Commissioner again, when I come back for good. But it would not do, I am afraid, to attempt it in the middle of my tenure of office.'[62] To their neighbours in Oxfordshire the job had meant little. 'So you've been to Hollywood,' a puzzled country neighbour supposedly said. But to Ramsay MacDonald and Stanley Baldwin it showed that Buchan did have a role to play in public life as he was shortly to discover.

13

THE ELSFIELD YEARS

B Y the 1930s the Buchans had settled into Elsfield and a regular routine. He tended to spend the week in London on parliamentary business staying first with relations of his wife, such as Blanche Firebrace in Buckingham Palace Road, or later at the St Stephens Club in Cannon Row. If he was at Elsfield he would breakfast alone then return to say goodbye to his wife who liked to breakfast in bed. He would select his buttonhole, his silver cigarette case, heavy leather, brass-locked briefcase with Royal cipher and large umbrella with its engraved gold band and tortoiseshell handle. Then he would be taken to the station by the family chauffeur, Amos Webb. Buchan loved cars and during the fifteen years the Buchan family spent at Elsfield there was a succession of them, mostly American. First there was an Overland 'open tourer', then several Dodges built to his own specifications and finally a series of Wolseleys. In spite of this passion Buchan never learnt to drive nor ever showed any interest in the workings of the internal combustion engine. He was quite happy to leave all that to Webb.[1]

Susan was happiest remaining in the country, involving herself in social work and in particular the Women's Institute. Buchan would joke that if he saw a dozen women in Egyptian costume on the stairs he would know there was a meeting of the local branch. It was through the Women's Institute drama group that Susan had first met the novelist Elizabeth Bowen who, together with her husband Alan Cameron, became a close friend of the Buchan family. It was for the Oxfordshire Women's Institute in 1926 that Buchan took the part of the Prior of St Frideswide's Community in a pageant held in Worcester College gardens depicting the life of Oxford City. A few years later Bowen played George Eliot to Buchan's Cardinal Newman for another pageant organised by the same drama group. Elizabeth Bowen and

Susan would often go to each other's houses to write. Bowen's story 'Reduced', written at Elsfield, and her novel *To The North* (1932) are both dedicated to Susan, while it was to Elsfield that she sent duplicates of *The Heat of the Day* for safekeeping during the Second World War.

In June 1932 Buchan had accepted the post of Atticus columnist on the *Sunday Times* and he continued to write for the paper for the next three years. Few knew the identity of Atticus and Buchan would sometimes add to the mystery by including his own activities in the column. At the same time he took on responsibilities in several organizations such as acting as Honorary Treasurer to the British Institute of Philosophy.

The three Buchan sons had been sent to the Dragon School in Oxford, the first two as weekly boarders and Alastair as a day boy. In turn they had all then gone to different houses at Eton. It was the school of their maternal grandfather and family and also a convenient distance from Elsfield and London. A further link was that the headmaster, Cyril Alington, had married a cousin of Susan and therefore was already known to the family. Alice, together with several other girls from the area such as Beatrice Spencer-Smith, was educated at home by two governesses, Kathleen Claxton and Harriet Smeaton. An intellectual child, with a passion for history and English, Alice deeply regretted that she had not been given the opportunity of going to university like her three brothers. Buchan may have been deeply interested in widening education provision but that belief did not extend to his own daughter. Though she managed to take some classes at the Ruskin School of Art in Oxford, she was being prepared to be brought out as a debutante with a view to finding a husband as quickly as possible.

Alice shared her aunt Anna's love of the theatre and during the annual visit of the Peebles Buchans, *en route* to visit Alastair's grave each April, the two women would pay frequent visits to the theatre in Stratford. Later in the 1930s she would study at RADA and tour in repertory with Sir Donald Wolfit's company. She had a beautiful speaking voice and a feel for poetry and in the summer of 1938 won the national verse-speaking competition judged by John Masefield and Walter de la Mare. In 1931 she published a one-act play, *St George and the Dragon*, and two years later her play *The Fifth of November* won her first place in the Oxford Drama Festival. The play was produced at Elsfield with Buchan playing the part of Sir Francis Tresham and Alice, 'the slightly vixenish Countess of Hatfield.' She inherited the family literary talent and in 1931 published a novel, *The Vale of Menalus*. She also worked with her father on a play about the American Civil War and would occasionally help him with his articles.

Buchan was a busy and sometimes distant father but he was proud of his children and tried hard to take a close interest in their affairs. When they were young he often sat and read to them aloud and later when they had gone to school he wrote regularly and encouraged them in their activities. William from an early age showed a particular aptitude for English, winning the Eton English verse prize and publishing short stories and poetry. When he became editor of a school magazine, *Masquerade*, in the spring of 1933 his father wrote enlisting support from his friends for articles and publishers for advertisements. As a result of his efforts the magazine was able to include contributions from J.M. Barrie, Harold Nicolson and Henry Newbolt. At the same time he persuaded the publisher Peter Davies to take a book from Alice and pushed the head of the B.B.C., John Reith, to give her a poetry slot on radio. For Johnnie's twenty-first birthday in November 1932 he hosted a dinner in the House of Commons with his own closest friends. They included Ramsay MacDonald, Stanley Baldwin, Viscount Grey of Falloden, Lord Cecil of Chelwood, Henry Newbolt, Roderick Jones, Harold Baker and Lord Howard de Walden.

Each of the Buchan sons would go up to different colleges at Oxford. Johnnie had never been particularly academic at school and had obtained poor results in his School Certificate. It was only at his second attempt that he became a member of his father's old college, where he took up rowing, founded the Falconry Club and in 1934 came down with a Fourth class degree. He then joined the Colonial Administrative Service and was posted to Uganda as an Assistant District Commissioner. William spent only a short time at New College, where he became editor of the university magazine *Isis*, before being asked to leave, whereupon his father secured him a job with Alfred Hitchcock. Alastair, the most academic of the sons, would take a Second in History at Christ Church, where he was Master of the Christ Church Beagles, before going on to spend a year at the University of Virginia.

Elsfield Manor always seemed to be full of people. Susan's sister Margaret, who lived only thirty miles from Elsfield at Wendover Dean, near Amersham, had been widowed in 1929 and her three children would often come and stay at Elsfield. Margaret had originally trained to be a singer and had joined her uncle Reggie Talbot when he was appointed Governor of Victoria in Australia. Her singing career had not flourished but she had found work as secretary to Dame Nellie Melba. Later she had become involved in running an antique business in Mayfair. The Buchans, too, saw something of Jack Stuart-Wortley's widow and her new husband, the painter William Nicholson. Another relation through marriage who came to stay was Geoffrey Dawson, now editor of *The Times*.

The Buchans mixed comparatively little with writers. Enid Bagnold, the author of *National Velvet*, would come and stay but only because she was married to Roderick Jones of Reuters. Walter de la Mare, a contact through Nelson, had long been a family friend and another was John Galsworthy, whom Buchan called Bilgeworthy. Robert Graves lived five miles away at Islip and the two families often saw each other. Graves dedicated his *The Meaning of Dreams* published in 1924 to Buchan and his wife. Susan remained close to her childhood friend, Virginia Woolf, who in July 1935 came to stay for a few days. They dined with Isaiah Berlin, a Fellow of All Souls, and then the two women paid a visit with William to the Necromancer of Snowshill. Mr Wade was an eccentric London businessman who liked to wear eighteenth century clothes and had retired to a William and Mary manor house which he proceeded to fill with assorted artefacts ranging from a stuffed crocodile to a collection of flowered silk waistcoats and a model railway.

T.E. Lawrence was another visitor to Elsfield. He would turn up either on a pushbike or on his motor-cycle, Boanerges, whose performance much impressed the Buchan boys. Many of these visits were unexpected and on one occasion, announcing himself as Aircraftman Shaw, he was turned away by the new Buchan butler in the belief his employers would not wish to be disturbed by an aircraftman in the RAF. There is some confusion about when the Buchans first met Lawrence. Buchan claimed in his memoirs to have heard of Lawrence from D.G. Hogarth before the First World War and then learnt of Lawrence's exploits in the Middle East from friends such as Aubrey Herbert and Alan Dawnay, but that he did not actually meet him until the summer of 1920.[2] However, in a broadcast in Canada in 1936 he claimed to have seen Lawrence either in 1915 or 1918 and Susan said that they had met through Lionel Curtis in the spring of 1919, when both men were Fellows of All Souls. She leaves this description of their meeting: 'He was silent, keeping his eyes veiled by heavy lids, but occasionally opening them widely and disconcertingly and letting me look into their deep procelain-blue. I thought that they were of the most wonderful colour and depth that I had ever seen in a human head.[3]

Part of the attraction, as Buchan admitted, was that 'there seemed to be reborn in him all the lost friends of my youth.' Lawrence appealed to Buchan's innate sense of adventure and romance. They shared similar literary enthusiasms, for example for the work of Charles Doughty, and had comparable views about politics, especially the Empire. Lawrence had written to Buchan: 'I think there's a great future for the British Empire as a voluntary association, and I'd like to have treaty States on a big scale attached to it ... We are so big a firm that we can offer unique conditions to small businesses to associate with us'.[4] Lawrence was, like many of Buchan's fictitious characters and biographical subjects, most notably Montrose, the introspective man of action. Buchan later wrote of Lawrence words that could easily have been used about himself: 'There was a fissure in his nature – eternal war between what might be called the Desert and the Sown – on the one side art and books and friends and leisure and a modest cosiness; on the other, action, leadership, the austerity of space.'

It had been Buchan who indirectly had been responsible for drawing the world's attention to Lawrence during the First World War. Now during the 1920s he helped propagate the legend. Reviewing the Oxford edition of *Seven Pillars of Wisdom* in 1926 he described it as 'one of the most remarkable works of our time' and remembered how when he first read the book in manuscript 'it seemed to me to have more of the raw stuff of genius than anything I had read for years'. Lawrence wrote gratefully from Karachi after reading Buchan's introduction to the American edition: 'It is tactful and interesting and gives nothing away. So it pleases me.'[5] Buchan was asked to write Lawrence's obit-uary for the *New York Herald Tribune* and devotes eight pages to him in *Memory Hold The Door*. Lawrence called him JB; Buchan called him 'the only man of genius I have ever known'.[6]

Buchan's *Julius Caesar* is dedicated to Lawrence and the two had planned jointly to edit a collection of the Gadarene poets. Lawrence was a great admirer of Buchan's work, especially *Montrose*, though he remained puzzled by some of the novels, most notably *A Prince of the Captivity*. In turn Buchan claimed to admire Lawrence's writing. 'When you do not get inundated with adjectives,' he told him, 'you are the best living writer of English prose.' Lawrence was unconvinced, writing to Edward Garnett: 'He does not mean it, but I take all praise at its face value.'[7]

In 1925 Buchan helped secure Lawrence's transfer from the Tank Corps to the RAF by writing to Baldwin. Lawrence remained grateful to both and sent two copies of the limited edition of *Seven Pillars of Wisdom* to Buchan in 1927 – one for him and the other for Baldwin. Seven years later he wrote to Buchan: 'the return to the Air Force secured me by him (on your initia-tion) has given me the only really contented years of my life.'[8] When in May 1930 Baldwin was installed as Chancellor and Buchan received an Hon LLD from St Andrews University Lawrence was offered, through the offices of Baldwin and Buchan, a Doctor of Laws. Lawrence 'concluded it was a student leg-pull, and sent it cheerfully back to the address given'. In his letter to 'JB' he attempted to excuse himself from the ceremony on the grounds it was difficult to reach St Andrews from Plymouth where he was stationed, that as a member of the Services he was forbidden to wear plain clothes and would have to accept in uniform and he was worried about the publicity. 'The Labourites think I'm an unpaid spy and Die-Hards thought I was a bolshie and Lord T. says I'm a self-admiring mountebank. So it would be better for me if the matter could quietly drop.' He was however grateful to Buchan. 'It was exceedingly nice of you. I don't think I have ever been so surprised in my life.'[9]

On his discharge from the RAF in February 1935 Lawrence sent Buchan a typescript of his experience as an airman, *The Mint*. 'The story has more shadow than sunlight in it,' he explained. 'Its language is often grossly obscene for it is the language of the troops. And besides I have a fear that in it I have given away my limitations more bluntly than I would wish.' He added 'Retirement without plans is rather a daunting state, and I am a little fright-ened of being completely my own master.'[10] Buchan was impressed by it and suggested now that Lawrence had left the Services he should write. Four years earlier he had suggested a biography of Alexander the Great but Lawrence had declined since 'no literature rises out of contentment'. Now, though reluc-tant to write a novel, Lawrence was considering a biography of Sir Roger Casement, a subject that was abandoned when he could not secure access to the Casement diaries. In a letter to Buchan shortly before his death he wrote from his cottage at Clouds Hill: 'I am back here again in precious peace and liking a life that has no fixed point, no duty and no time to keep.'[11]

Both Susan and John Buchan integrated easily into the local community, seeing much in particular of the Gaskells at nearby Kiddington Hall. The gardens at Elsfield were often opened to local charities and in November 1932 the house and garden featured in the magazine *Homes and Gardens*. Buchan took a keen interest in the husbanding of the countryside, sat on the Council for the Preservation of Rural England and was one of the founders and the first President of the Oxfordshire Branch. The Oxford Preservation Trust was another organization with which he became involved. It was for the Trust he wrote a prologue, printed in *The Times*, for a fund-raising event in February 1930. Among those appearing was Edith Evans while a young Peggy Ashcroft sold souvenir programmes. Another fund raising effort was *Oxford Prologizes* which consisted of a collection of verse and prose contributions from old Oxonians such as Ronnie Knox, Charles Morgan and Philip Guedalla. A.P. Herbert updated *Romeo and Juliet* to a nightclub while Evelyn Waugh wrote an open letter with his own views on the preservation of Oxford:

> Would it not be better to pursue a policy less of Preservation than of judi-cious destruction? A very small expenditure on dynamite should be enough to rid us for ever of the clock tower at Carfax, the Town Hall, the Indian Institute, the High Street front at Oriel, the Holywell front of New College and the whole of Hertford, thus changing Oxford from a comparatively ugly city to a comparatively beautiful one.[12]

The Buchans mixed widely in University circles aided by the fact that Buchan held several positions within the University administration. Between 1924 and 1930 he served on the University Chest responsible for the University' finances and in 1934 he was elected chairman of the University's senior Conservative Committee, whose main function was to choose the candidates to represent the University in Parliament. Particular friends in the academic world included H.A.L. Fisher, the Warden of New College; Francis Pember, the Warden of All Souls and G.N. Clark, a Fellow of Oriel and Editor of the English Historical Review and the author of a history of Elsfield commissioned by Buchan. Another friend made in the period was another Fellow of Oriel, the historian G.M. Trevelyan. The two men, who were almost exactly the same age, had met before the First World War and were drawn to each by a shared love of the Border country and a strong historical imagination. Both combined scholarship and accessibility in their writing and were great admirers of the other's work. Buchan would dedicate his biographies of Scott and Augustus to Trevelyan and in turn Trevelyan would dedicate two of his books to Buchan. In 1921 Buchan became a godfather to Trevelyan's daughter Mary, then aged sixteen, and four years later tried to persuade Baldwin to make Trevelyan the Regius Professor of Modern History at Oxford. He failed but Trevelyan, in 1927, secured the Regius Professorship at Cambridge.

Mary Trevelyan was just one of the many members of the University who would walk or drive to Elsfield for tea each Sunday during term. Buchan was involved in a number of undergraduate societies, often filling in if a speaker from outside Oxford had to cancel at the last moment, and therefore was well known in student circles. Many of the undergraduates who came were the children of friends such as Tommy Nelson's sons, Lord Cromer's son Evelyn Baring, and J. St Loe Strachey's son John. Others who came for tea were active in student politics, either at the Union or in the Conservative association. Among those who visited Elsfield were future Cabinet Ministers such as Frank Pakenham, then a Conservative but later as Lord Longford a Labour peer, and John, later Lord, Boyd-Carpenter. Buchan had continued to stay in touch with his First World War Intelligence contacts and he occasionally would pass on the name of a suitable recruit for the Intelligence Services. Among those possibly recruited this way was Christopher Pirie-Gordon and A.E.W. Mason's nephew Michael Mason.

One of the student societies in which Buchan took the greatest interest and whose members were often at Elsfield was the Oxford Exploration Club which had been founded in December 1927 by Max Nicholson, a Hertford undergraduate. Its original purpose was to mount each Long Vacation an expedition of graduate and undergraduate members to some remote part of the world. Over the years it expanded its activities to work closely with the Public Schools Exploring Society and include on its trips members of other universities. Its expeditions included Greenland (1928), British Guiana (1929), Lapland (1930), the Hudson Strait (1931), during which its under-graduate organizer Christopher D'Aeth was killed, and three trips in 1933 – Spitzbergen, the New Hebrides and Abyssinia led respectively by Alexander Glen, John Baker and Wilfred Thesiger. With Thesiger in particular, Buchan became extremely friendly. He went to hear him speak at the Royal Geographical Society in November 1934 and agreed to address a private dinner to mark Thesiger's return. After Thesiger had spent a summer holiday on an Icelandic trawler operating out of Hull, Buchan persuaded his son Johnnie to follow suit another year. Later, one of the Gorbals Die-Hards would spend his summer in the same fashion in *The House of the Four Winds*. Thesiger was later to claim that *Prester John* had inspired him more than any other book and called one of his adopted African boys Laputa.

Buchan agreed to act as President of the Club and continued to support its activities even after he left Elsfield. In Max Nicholson's words he was used to 'unlock doors and find facilities for expeditions'. Buchan took his duties seri-ously; for example, writing to Rajah Brooke and helping to raise money for Tom Harrisson's 1932 Sarawak expedition. The Club also benefited from grants made by organizations in which he had influence such as the University Chest and the Pilgrim Trust.[13] He wrote the introduction to Nicholas Polunin's book about life on a timber boat in the White Sea, *Russian Waters* (1931) and the introduction to Eddie Shackleton's book *Arctic Journeys* based on Shackleton's 1934 trip to Ellesmere Land. Polunin was to write later that he owed him 'more probably than anyone else outside my own family.'[14]

Throughout his life Buchan remained fascinated by exploration, especially Everest. He had been on the advisory council of Sir Francis Younghusband's pre-war attempt from the Tibet side and made several of the publishing arrangements for the 1921 expedition through his contacts with the Royal Geographical Society. It was Buchan who helped the expedition's medical officer, Alexander Wollaston, sell his account to the American papers and who put Younghusband in touch with Sir William Jury, who had been Director of Cinema Propaganda at the Ministry of Information, when Younghusband was putting together an expedition in 1921.

In 1933 when Lady Houston sponsored a flight over Everest it was Buchan who brought in a parliamentary colleague, the Marquess of Douglas and Clydesdale, to actually do the flying and then wrote the introduction to Peregrine Fellowes' book on the expedition *First Over Everest*, which was published in December 1933. He was also involved with a film of the flight, *Wings Over Everest*, which was produced by Gaumont-British in the summer of 1934.[15] The expedition inspired him to draft a film script for the film director and brother of Raymond, Anthony Asquith. The plot of the thriller revolved around the escape of an American, an Englishman and English girl with important secret documents from China which culminated in a flight over Everest and eventual safety in Kathmandu.

Buchan had been interested in films since his time at the Ministry of Information and had made it one of his subjects in the House of Commons. Through Anthony Asquith, who had produced their first sound film, *A Cottage on Dartmoor*, Buchan had become involved with British Instructional Films and had subsequently been appointed to their Board of Directors. British Instructional Films was a documentary film company specializing in educational and geographical programmes run by Harry Bruce Woolfe until he resigned in 1933 and set up Gaumont-British Instructional Films. Woolf, who was five years younger than Buchan, had taken an active part in the Educational and Cultural Films Commission which had eventually led to the British Film Institute and it was he who was probably instrumental in stimu-lating Buchan's own interest in the Institute.

When the Admiralty and Navy League sponsored a silent film in 1927 reconstructing two 1914 naval triumphs, 'The Battles of Coronel and Falkland Islands', Buchan was brought in to write the script under the aus-pices of British Instructional Films. The following year he was involved in writing the commentary to a film about the battle of Gallipoli directed by Asquith called *Tell England*. And in 1932, he and Bruce Woolfe directed a British Instructional Films half-hour film, *England Awake*, on 'achievements in science, engineering, and industry in Britain and the Empire'. There had also been discussions on a film on a South African theme and another to be called *Conquest* on the history of Britain from the Norman Invasion to the Great War but both were abandoned after Buchan had written part of the script.

The first of his own books to be optioned was *Prester John* by H.L. Locque in December 1913 and then by African Film Productions, who wanted to call it *The Ruby Snake*, in March 1919. It was, however, *Huntingtower*, bought by Gainsbrough Pictures in November 1925, that was to be the first Buchan novel actually filmed. Harry Lauder was paid £10,000 to play McCunn, which was about the total cost of the average British feature of the time, and a genuine Russian exile, Vera Veronina, played Princess Saskia. In 1934 Gaumont Pictures had bought a seven year option for the film rights to *The Thirty-Nine Steps* for £800 and the following year it was filmed by Alfred Hitchcock. It was the making of both Hitchcock and Buchan. Hitchcock had long been influenced by Buchan and some of this influence is reflected in his film, *The Man Who Knew Too Much*. He had first considered optioning *Greenmantle* but then decided on a 'smaller subject' which he felt was 'a literary masterpiece'. Part of the book's attraction too was that it neatly broke up into a series of separate episodes which made it ideal for filming.[16]

Hitchcock introduced several changes strengthening the comic and satirical element in the story and inventing a witty and sophisticated romance. There had been no female character in Buchan's novel; indeed, part of its menace was the picture of a man alone in the wilds, pitted against both Scotland Yard and the Black Stone. Now Hannay, played by Robert Donat as a Canadian, had the actress Madeleine Carroll handcuffed to him for part of the film, Scudder was replaced by a beautiful woman and the villain has part of a finger missing rather than 'hooding his eyes like a hawk'. Another change was to update the story from 1914 so that the conspiracy was to steal the design of a new aircraft engine rather than the battle disposition of the British Home Fleet. An essential new element was the introduction of Mr Memory, who when asked by Hannay cannot help blurting out the truth about the thirty-nine steps. The character was based on a real music-hall performer called Datas who would answer questions posed by the audience including trick questions such as 'When did Good Friday fall on a Tuesday?' The answer being 'Good Friday was a horse running at Wolverhampton race track and he fell on Tuesday, June 21 1864.' Hitchcock also added a scene where Hannay takes shelter with an old man and his sexually frustrated wife beautifully played by Peggy Ashcroft.

The Hitchcock film is a classic and by far the best of the three versions made of the book. The script was written by Charles Bennet with extra dialogue by Ian Hay. Hitchcock added to the pace of the book with rapid scene transitions and expertly built up the suspense. Events are seen through Hannay's eyes with the camera perspective his perspective, for example when he sees the two gang members waiting for him outside his flat. The sense of danger everywhere is expertly captured so, for example, when on his flight to Scotland he sees a policeman the image we have is of the man looking straight at the camera. Hitchcock later worked on a film version of *The Three Hostages*, a novel he felt that had many similarities with *The Thirty-Nine Steps*. In the end he dropped it because he could find no convincing way of conveying hypnotism on the screen; but Buchan's novel remained an important influence on Hitchcock's *North by Northwest*. One of the most memorable scenes in the later film is the aeroplane hunting the lone protagonist in the wilderness and there is the same preoccupation with disguise.

At the beginning of June, Gaumont gave a dinner for the Buchans at the

ABOVE LEFT: Alice and Johnnie Buchan with their uncle Alastair killed at Aras on 9th April 1916. *Reproduced by permission of Lord Tweedsmuir.*
ABOVE RIGHT: J.B. on leave from the front at Checkendon, the home of his friend F.S.Oliver. *Reproduced by permission of Lord Tweedsmuir.*
BELOW LEFT: Tommy Nelson, J.B.'s business partner killed at Arras the same day as Alastair Buchan. *Reproduced by permission of Lord Tweedsmuir.*
BELOW RIGHT: Stair Gillon, an Oxford friend and J.B.'s personal assistant at the Department of Information. *Reproduced by permission of John Dobie.*

ABOVE: Elsfield taken from the garden. *Reproduced by permission of Lord Tweedsmuir.*
BELOW: The Buchan family *c.* 1934. *Reproduced by permission of Lord Tweedsmuir.*

ABOVE: A holiday party at Glen Etive. J.B. is standing extreme left. *Reproduced by permission of Lord Tweedsmuir.*

BELOW: Ardtornish where the Buchans often went on holiday and which formed the backdrop for *John Macnab. Reproduced by permission of Faith Raven.*

ABOVE: J.B. as Lord High Commissioner of the Church of Scotland 1933. *Reproduced by permission of Lord Tweedsmuir.*

BELOW: J.B. on board the *Berengaria*, returning from the United States in 1934. He, Beverley Nichols and J.B. Priestley are gathered together around Hugh Walpole, in bed with arthritis. *Reproduced by permission of Brown University.*

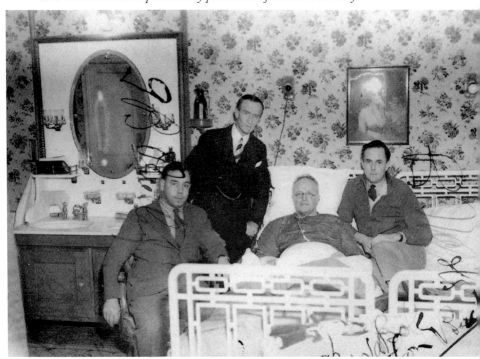

ABOVE: Sir Harry Lauder as Dickson McCunn in *Huntingtower* (1928). *Reproduced by permission of the British Film Institute.*
BELOW: Robert Donat in a scene from *The Thirty-nine Steps* (1935). *Reproduced by permission of British Gaumont/Rank.*

ABOVE: Rideau Hall in the snow. *Reproduced by permission of The National Archives of Canada.*

BELOW: F.D. Roosevelt and J.B., probably April 1937. *Reproduced by permission of Lord Tweedsmuir.*

ABOVE: The Royal Visit of King George VI and Queen Elizabeth, 5 May 1939. *Reproduced by permission of The Royal Archives.*
BELOW LEFT: J.B. with his two sons, Johnnie and Alastair, on the outbreak of the Second World War. *Reproduced by permission of Lord Tweedsmuir.*
BELOW RIGHT: J.B. in Red Indian Chief head-dress as "Teller of Tales". *Reproduced by permission of Lord Tweedsmuir.*

ABOVE: J.B.'s funeral cortège, February 1940. *Reproduced by permission of The National Archives of Canada.*
BELOW: Elsfield Church with J.B.'s grave. *Reproduced by permission of Solange Lownie.*

Piccadilly Hotel preceding the first showing of *The 39 Steps* – the film title was spelt differently from the book – at the New Gallery. William, who had taken a close interest in the filming, was there along with old friends of the Buchan family such as Sir John Simon, the Marchioness of Londonderry and the two principal stars, Robert Donat and Madeleine Carroll. Hitchcock is reputed to have slept through the showing. Susan hated the introduction of a heroine but her husband, whether through modesty or honesty, claimed to prefer Hitchcock's version and be intrigued to know what happened next. The film received rave reviews and most critics agreed that Hitchcock had 'improved' the book. *Variety* thought it 'more original than the book from which it was derived' and Sydney Carroll in the *Sunday Times* wrote 'In the *Thirty-Nine Steps* the identity and mind of Alfred Hitchcock are continually discernible, in fact supreme. There is no doubt that Hitchcock is a genius. He is the real star of the film.'[17]

The filming of *The Thirty-Nine Steps* had heightened interest in Buchan's writing. In February 1935 he had told Johnnie: 'I am besieged by film magnates just now. The purity crusade in America has driven them to all my books, which combine the decent with the dramatic! I ought to make a certain amount of money before I am done.'[18] Among the film magnates was Alexander Korda, who had just bought the film rights to T.E. Lawrence's *Revolt in the Desert*. He was interested in *Prester John* and, as Buchan told his eldest son, wanted 'to send out an expedition to Africa for the purpose – perhaps to Ruwenzori'.[19] Another projected venture revolved around Douglas Fairbanks, who had just set up a film company and wanted to discuss making a film about the life of Bonnie Prince Charlie. Buchan had also been giving help to Robert Graves in his negotiations with Korda over a film of Graves' book *I Claudius*. Though over the coming years a number of other Buchan novels were optioned none of them were made, which is surprising given Buchan's popularity and that the books lend themselves easily to filming.[20]

The Buchans had made plans for a long trip later in 1934 from the Cape to Cairo and to see Johnnie *en route* now that he had been posted by the Colonial Office to Uganda. This would be the first trip by Buchan to the continent for thirty years. As he admitted to Johnnie: 'You ask me if I never long for Africa. Indeed I do. I have never got Africa out of my bones'. However events were to conspire against his returning there as perhaps the greatest challenge of his life was offered him.[21]

In January 1934 Mackenzie King had noted in his diary that Buchan was being mentioned, along with Vincent Massey – who instead went as Canadian High Commissioner to London – as a candidate for the

Principalship of McGill University in Montreal. Shortly afterwards Lord Bessborough made it known that on account of his wife's ill-health he had no wish to extend his term of office as Governor-General of Canada and speculation began to grow on who might succeed him. After a Canada Club dinner in July Buchan reported to his wife that the President of the University of Toronto 'told me that everybody in Canada was hoping I would succeed Bessborough as Governor-General,' adding 'Not for me!' Two days later he was asked to represent Britain at some Canadian celebrations in September but refused because he didn't want to interfere with Alastair's school holidays. H.A.L. Fisher went instead.[22]

In mid October Mackenzie King discussed with Sir Clive Wigram possible successors to Bessborough. Athlone was the leading candidate but the Earl of Airlie, Lord Halifax, Lord Linlithgow, Lord Lothian, Lord Cromer, Lord Astor and the writer J.A. Spender were also mentioned. The following week Mackenzie King floated the idea of Buchan as Governor-General with Churchill who 'belittled him very much as insignificant etc'.[23] In November, Mackenzie King, prone to receiving mystic advice, claimed to have had a vision in which he realized that he had not properly argued for Buchan as Governor-General and resolved to push for him again.

He is the style of Governor-General who would greatly appeal to University men and women and students, to authors, poets, artists & the like – the Intelligentsia – who are becoming a controlling factor in government – brains, not wealth & position (by artificial means) but what he has of both by work & worth. I feel strongly he may be the right person to appoint . . . all may yet work out.[24]

Buchan had by now returned from his successful trip to America where he had opened the Harkness Library at Columbia and won plaudits for his skills at diplomacy and his understanding of America. Baldwin had been particularly impressed with Buchan's political reporting on American isolationism and his suggestions, among which had been the need for British consulates in Chicago and San Francisco.[25]

Since the 1930 Imperial Conference, the appointment of the Governor-General had been made after consultations with the appropriate Dominion rather than with British ministers. The following February, the Canadian political leaders Mackenzie King and R.B. Bennett therefore began serious discussions on the next Governor-General. Bessborough had suggested Linlithgow but it could not be arranged. Then the Earl of Athlone was mentioned but the King was reluctant that his relation should give up his lucrative directorships. The Earl of Airlie for some reason was counted out on the grounds he was a Christian Scientist. It was clear there was no obvious candidate. One important qualification, given the number of Scots in Canada, was that the new Governor-General should be Scottish. Bessborough reported to Clive Wigram, George V's Private Secretary, on 28 February: 'I believe that Mr Mackenzie King, though he never told me so himself, for some time had Lord Elgin in mind. His ancestry and Scottish blood no doubt also appealed to him.' Lord Elgin, a descendant of two previous Governors-General, was keen to come; his qualities included, according to Bennett, his ability 'to preach a sermon and sing songs.' However he was judged unsuitable.[26]

Mackenzie King then threw Buchan's name into the ring again, pointing out he had experience as a politician, was an 'author of great distinction', would appeal to journalists and he had just successfully acted as Lord High Commissioner, a job that had many similarities to that of Governor-General. Bennett agreed he was ideal and that the journalist J.A. Spender should be kept in reserve.[27] In particular Mackenzie King was drawn to Buchan because of his Scots Presbyterian background and because he was a commoner who had achieved prominence through his own efforts. On 13 March it was agreed Wigram should approach Buchan with the offer of the Canadian Governor-Generalship. Buchan's reaction was unexpected. Reporting a few days later to the King, Wigram wrote:

> Colonel Buchan went on to say quite openly and frankly that he would really like to be appointed Governor-General of South Africa, as he loved the country, knew the people and could talk Dutch. I explained to him that the Governor-Generalship of that Dominion was not vacant until next January and that at present there had been no preliminary conversation . . .[28]

It was also revealed that Mackenzie King had already approached Buchan the previous summer about the possibility of his appointment. The Palace gave some thought to satisfying Buchan's wish to go to South Africa, of which they had been unaware, but in the end pressed him to take the job in Canada. At first he could not decide whether or not to accept. He told his eldest son Johnnie he would have preferred the Washington Embassy if not the Governor-Generalship of South Africa but admitted: 'I can scarcely refuse Canada on the chance of these other things.'[29]

He wrote to Susie on 20 March: 'I talked to Baldwin and Ramsay yesterday about Canada. They knew nothing about it, for of course the business is entirely in the King's hands. Baldwin was rather inclined to urge me to go, but both of them reserve their judgment until they have thought it over.' The next day Buchan made up his mind to go and it was officially announced on 27 March, a day earlier than planned since the papers had already run the story in their editions of the day before. He was immediately made a Privy Councillor and awarded the GCMG. As he told his eldest son: 'I am a hopeless adventurer, and cannot resist the challenge of a new thing.'[30]

Buchan was to become the thirtyfifth GovernorGeneral of Canada, a job despite his disclaimers that he had always hankered after, and the first commoner to be appointed to the post. As Gilbert Murray wrote in his congratulations: 'the great Canadian plan has come off!' The appointment was generally warmlyreceived in Canada, though there were concerns in some papers about the secrecy in which the soundings had been taken and that a Canadian, such as the former Prime Minister Sir Robert Borden, had not been chosen. John Buchan and his sister were both wellknown and popular as writers. His Scottish background, especially as a son of the manse, was appealing; he was respected as a politician and administrator and known as a fine public speaker. Above all he had an extensive knowledge of Canadian history.[31] He had taken an interest in Canadian affairs for over thirty years, regularly attending the Dominion Day dinner in London and building a good relationship with each Canadian High Commissioner in Britain. He had written about the country in the *Spectator* and *Scottish Review*, had penned a life of a previous GovernorGeneral and, together with Edward Grey, collected money for the Wolfe Memorial as far back as 1908. 'A Canadian Statesman', Wakefield, had been a key figure in his *A Lodge in the Wilderness*.

Another advantage was that Buchan had known the Prime Minister, Mackenzie King since 1919. After Buchan had stayed with Mackenzie King at Laurier House in 1924 the Canadian politician had written to Violet Markham: 'I can honestly say that I know no man whose companionship I would rather be privileged to share, to me he is truly a man after God's own heart, so full of all the qualities most to be admired and so utterly devoid of any flaw of character.'[32] The following year he had suggested to her that 'it might be possible to have Buchan succeed Lord Byng in the GovernorGeneralship of our Dominion . . . In dealing with the problems with which we are faced, I should find the association with a man like Buchan an ideal one . . . .'. But for the constitutional crisis involving Mackenzie King and the GovernorGeneral Byng, the details of which Buchan had closely followed, Buchan might well have become GovernorGeneral in 1926.[33]

Congratulations poured in from among others John Masefield, Lloyd George, J.M. Barrie, L.B. Namier, Peter Fleming, who had read it in a three months-old copy of *The Times*, Ezra Pound, the Chief Rabbi, Chaim Weizman, Robert Graves, Lord Bessborough, Sir Robert Borden and even from Colonel Brander-Dunbar in Elgin who addressed his letter to 'My dear John Macnab'. The Secretary of the Jewish Agency for Palestine wrote:

> To us Zionists, I need hardly say that your departure from London will come as a personal loss, and we shall miss very greatly your deep under-standing of our cause, and your ready help and advice in the house.[34]

Buchan had hesistated before accepting for several reasons. He knew that Susan was settled in Oxfordshire and would be unhappy about being thrust into the public eye and separated from the children. He himself felt he should be near his mother. Above all his health had not been good. Since the begin-ning of the year he had been 'rather seedy' and had been seeing a Hungarian refugee doctor, Dr Plesch, on the recommendation of his mother-in-law. Plesch, a close friend of Albert Einstein, had married a champagne heiress and lived in a penthouse on Park Lane from where he dispensed medical advice, undaunted by the fact that he actually had no medical qualifications. Plesch put him on a strict regime which included a number of inoculations from a nurse at 8.30 each morning.

The Canadian job was a great opportunity and as he admitted to Johnnie: 'If I am going to do anything of this kind in my life, I must do it before I am too old to enjoy it.' It was also an honour which might lead to other things. Lord Cottenham touched on it when he wrote: 'After Canada, John, there is South Africa. After South Africa, there is India, not to mention a small arid spot called Australia. And why stop at that? I feel you will probably be the person to inaugurate Dominion status in Elysium.' It was a view echoed by Cosmo Lang, whose enthronement as Archbishop of Canterbury Buchan had attended seven years earlier: 'The Viceroyalty of India or possibly a Dictatorship of the British Empire may be in your view.'[35] In fact Buchan saw the job in Canada as a stepping-stone to the job he really wanted, British Ambassador in Washington.

His parliamentary colleagues seemed genuinely sad to see him go. Clement Attlee wrote: 'We shall miss you very much in the House for although you spoke seldom, your influence was pervading and you will leave a gap which will not be easy to fill in the scanty ranks of those who are to a large extent above the battle.'[36] The appointment also meant that Buchan had to give up his job as Atticus on the *Sunday Times*. The Editor of the paper was sorry to lose his columnist but added his good wishes: 'There have been several appointments of which it could be said that there was no damned merit about them. But under the new order you go to Canada because Canada wants you – and wants you because you are John Buchan.'[37]

The question of whether Buchan would go as a commoner or a peer was his first experience of controversy. Both Mackenzie King and Violet Markham, who had done so much to secure him the job, were against his taking a title because, as she put it, 'you have a name that is world wide'. Buchan claimed not to care one way or the other. In response to a letter of congratulation from Vernon Bartlett, then on the *News Chronicle*, he wrote somewhat disingenuously: 'I have always disliked titles, and have so far managed to avoid them. But in this matter I am rather in His Majesty's hands, for it is not like accepting a peerage in the New Year or Birthday Honours. If he thinks his personal representative ought to be a peer, it is hardly for me to gainsay him.'[38]

King George V was adamant that his representative must be a peer and so Buchan spent the next few weeks trying to decide on a title. He preferred it to be Scottish, but among the possibilities discussed were Lord Elsfield or Otmoor. On 2 April he wrote to Johnnie: 'We are still arguing about the title. If I take a territorial name, I think Tweedsmuir seems best. But it might be wise to keep my own name, in which case the alternatives of Buchan of Tweed, Buchan of Tweeddale and Buchan of Fruid present themselves.'[39] Two weeks later he had changed his mind again. 'If I have to be a peer I have decided to call myself Lord Manorwater.' On 16 May the Barony was announced. John Buchan was henceforth to be Lord Tweedsmuir of Elsfield, a title which combined his Border and Oxford links. The following month he finalized his coat of arms. He wrote to his son and heir: 'I saw the Lord Lyon in Edinburgh and have settled the supporters for our arms – a stag out of compliment to me, and a falcon to you – both noble animals. The alternatives were Spider and Duggie!'[40]

Alan Lascelles, Bessborough's Secretary, sent a confidential fourteen page memo full of shrewd advice about the country and the job. In it he stressed the role of the Governor-General 'to represent the English to the Canadians', the need 'to know when the Viceroy should become the Man' and he emphasized how the Governor-General has to be all things to all men:

Any GG with a certain amount of personal charm, a conversational knowledge of French, and a store of patience, can win the province of Quebec without much trouble. British Columbia is quite satisfied if it gets an English gentleman and sportsman, while the ideal of the Prairie Provinces is 'a regular fellow with no frills' and some understanding of Agriculture.[41]

There was advice about when to wear a top hat and how to dress warmly, the importance of 'pomp and circumstance', the need to fraternize with a wide range of people in informal circumstances and the complexities of the Canadian character. Lascelles also pointed out the 'almost universally low standard of education' but singled out for praise the Royal Military College, the Mounted Police and the Winter Fair at Toronto. Buchan was also given a memo on features of the British Cabinet Office introduced in Canada and a note on 'The Prime Minister's Responsibilities'.[42]

Further honours followed. His old Inn of Court, the Middle Temple, made him an Honorary Bencher, he was given the Freedom of Edinburgh alongside the Prime Minister of Australia. On 9 July he took his seat in the Lords supported by Hugh Macmillan and Lord Strathcona. That evening Brasenose held a dinner in his honour at Claridges, presided over by Sir Richard Lodge, the Brasenose Fellow who had become the first Professor of History at Glasgow while Buchan was there. The dinner was attended by over 200 past and present members of the College, their matriculation dates spanning almost seventy years, and included his old tutor Francis Wylie. It was Lodge who had written to Brasenose when Buchan was taking the Oxford entrance exam urging them 'not to pay excessive attention to Buchan's Latin Prose or even to his translations, but to read carefully his Essay and General Paper, and if they were really good, to elect him in spite of possible defects in his other papers'. One of the outcomes of the evening, at Buchan's suggestion, was the formation of the Brasenose College Society whose responsibility was to organise, among other events, an annual dinner.[43]

One sadness that summer had been T.E. Lawrence's death in a motorbike accident in May. The Buchans had seen much of him since his leaving the RAF earlier in the year and only six weeks earlier he had turned up one Sunday at Elsfield on his motorcycle. As Buchan told Johnnie:

We had him for the whole day and he has become one of the most delightful people in the world. He has lost all his freakishness, and his girlish face has become extraordinarily wise and mature. He relies a good deal on my advice, but I don't know what can be done with him, for he won't ever touch public life again, and yet he is one of the few men of genius living.[44]

Lawrence's death put paid to a scheme dreamt up by Buchan and supported by Archie Wavell and Basil Liddell-Hart to set up under Lawrence's auspices a youth movement called 'Lawrence's Bands'. These bands, inspired by the Boy Scouts, were to give young boys a focus to their lives teaching leadership and Outward Bound type skills.

It was also a worrying time in Buchan's private life. Johnnie was not happy in the Colonial Service and had contracted amoebic dysentery in Africa, while Brian Fairfax Lucy was still without a job. There were signs too of teenage rebellion from Alastair, still at Eton. He wrote to his eldest brother at the beginning of August about their father, who had just had all his teeth removed in the hope that somehow that might help his gastric trouble: 'The colonel also makes life very difficult. He is so cantankerous and one notices his filthy eating and his eternal boasting more than ever now. I hope things will be different in Canada and don't answer for anybody's sanity if it isn't. Given half a chance I would take the first airplane to Uganda.'[45] Buchan's irritability was principally due to his health which continued to worry him. He was now on a drastic diet and medication; smoking and alcohol had been forbidden. Both he and Susan had suffered from bouts of depression, particularly during the summer of 1934, and he was now apprehensive about what the future might hold.

Throughout the summer there was a series of lunches and dinners in his honour given by the Canada Club, the Royal Empire Society and various other organizations devoted to fostering links between Britain and Canada. Buchan was occupied with the question of staff and particularly, the post of Private Secretary. Tommy Lascelles had suggested Percivale Liesching, a thirty-nine year old official in the Dominions Office, who had been with the High Commissioner in Canada and was now Political Secretary in Cape Town, but Wigram was against a Home Civil Servant being appointed. Buchan then suggested Eric Mieville, who had been secretary to the Viceroy of India, or Alan Dawnay, a Coldstream officer who had served with T.E. Lawrence during the First World War and had briefly acted as John Reith's deputy at the BBC, but neither was possible. In the end Shuldham Redfern, then under forty and a rising star in the Sudan Civil Service having been appointed Governor of Kassala Province the previous year, was appointed. Meanwhile, Harold Nicolson had unsuccessfully pressed Buchan to give a job to James Lees-Milne, then in his twenties, who had been working for Sir Roderick Jones. 'He is a quiet, hard-working, tactful and very precise person and combines great personal and social charm with a hard head and a real passion for routine work.'[46]

Buchan's principal Canadian ADC was to be Lt Colonel Willis-O'Connor, who had served as an ADC to the Governors General for twenty five years and whom Buchan had first met during the First World War while Willis-O'Connor was on the staff of Sir Arthur Currie. The other ADCs were to be Captain Michael Adeane of the Coldstream Guards, Lieut S.G. Rivers-Smith of the Royal Navy and Lieut P.J.S. Boyle of the Royal Scots

Fusiliers. Adeane, then aged twenty five and with a First class history degree from Cambridge, was an unusual choice for such a ceremonial post. On leaving Canada he would become Assistant Private Secretary to George VI in 1937 and eventually Private Secretary to Queen Elizabeth II.

There were emotional partings with Baldwin and MacDonald and an afternoon with the Prince of Wales and, just before they left, the Buchans lunched with the King at Buckingham Palace. Buchan had known and liked the King since his work during the First World War. He had written speeches for him and earlier in the year had written an account of George's reign, *The King's Grace*, to celebrate the Silver Jubilee. One of his last parliamentary duties was to draft the address from the Commons to the King, which was delivered in May in Westminster Hall.

On 25 October the Buchans, accompanied by Alice, Brian and William, were seen off from Euston on the Liverpool boat train by Lord and Lady Bessborough and J.H. Thomas, the Secretary of State for Dominion Affairs. One of the ladies in waiting, Beatrice Spencer-Smith, noted in a letter to her mother: 'The whole thing feels rather mad – Susie cried most of the way to Crewe.' And she added 'John made no attempt to console her but left her to Brian and me.' From Liverpool the Buchans set sail on the *Duchess of Richmond* via Belfast and Greenock for Canada and a new chapter in their life together.[47]

14

PROCONSUL

AFTER a stormy journey the Buchans arrived in Wolfe's Cove, Quebec on the evening of Saturday 2 November. There they were met by Mackenzie King who pointedly addressed the new Governor-General as John Buchan. Buchan remembered 'a flaming West Highland sunset behind the dark line of the Citadel and every ship in the harbour whistling, and our drive by torchlight with a cavalry escort through the old cobbled streets'.[1] He reviewed the red-coated troops in the old Square then was officially sworn in as Governor-General. Instead of staying at the official residence in Quebec, the Citadel, the party then boarded the Governor-General's train for Ottawa. The Sunday was spent in a railway siding fifteen miles out of Quebec, from where Buchan and the Comptroller of the Household, Eric Mackenzie, drove down the St Lawrence to spend part of the day watching snow geese.

After this short rest, the Buchans continued their journey, arriving in Ottawa on the afternoon of the 4 November where there were more troops to review, a levee of several hundred people, a nineteen gun salute from Parliament Hill and a carriage drive with a cavalry escort through the streets. Buchan estimated the crowd lining the streets at 30,000.[2] Two days later, wearing a blue and scarlet uniform with gold epaulettes and gold braid, a cocked hat with a cascade of white feathers, black half-boots, white kid gloves and carrying an ivory-handled ceremonial sword, he opened parliament.

Life in Canada was not entirely new. The Buchans had taken several of the Elsfield staff with them – James Cast the butler as valet, Annie Cox the housekeeper as Susan's personal maid and Amos Webb to drive the family Wolseley. They had also brought a Siddeley Special adapted so that the occupants could be clearly seen by the public and with doors high enough to allow those in top hats to enter or leave in a dignified manner. Beatrice Spencer-Smith, a family friend who had been a lady-in-waiting the previous year when Buchan was Lord High Commissioner, and Lilian Killick, who had been his Secretary since his Nelson days, completed the party.

Most of the time the Buchans lived at Rideau Hall, a plain stone mansion in a wooded park a few minutes drive from the Parliament Buildings in Ottawa. Built in the 1830s it had become Government House in the 1860s. James Cast thought it 'something after the Windsor style'. Buchan's own description of Rideau as 'like a very big, comfortable English country-house' was rather closer to the mark.[3] One entered through the centre into a large hall from which a broad marble staircase led to suites of rooms, including on the second floor the bedrooms of Buchan and his wife. On either side of the main block were lower wings, one the throne-room and ballroom and the other the Chinese Gallery which was used for informal dances. Beyond the drawing-room with its two huge fireplaces, green brocade curtains and bright yellow chintzes was Buchan's sitting-room and beyond that his study. Susan also had a sitting-room on the ground floor. The ADCs shared a room in one corner of Rideau Hall, noticeable for the 'Men at Work' notice outside which Shuldham and Alastair Buchan had persuaded a railway company to donate. The Buchans also spent part of the year at the Citadel in Quebec with its dramatic views over the St Lawrence. Here the Governor-General's private rooms looked on to a square where each morning they would be serenaded by a band. Buchan also had an office in the East Block of the Parliament Buildings in Ottawa where three mornings a week he made himself available to any Canadian politician who wanted a confidential discussion.

Since 1926, the Governor-General had had little responsibility for British Government business, which was now channelled through the British High Commissioner in Ottawa. Instead he was the King's representative in Canada and assumed many of the Sovereign's duties. It was the Governor-General who opened Parliament, delivered the speech from the Throne, summoned the party leader to form a government and gave his assent to legislation. That however did not prevent Buchan using his position to act as a conduit between Britain and Canada. In a report written two months after arriving he defined his job as 'two-fold – to interpret Canadian opinion in Britain, and to interpret British opinion to Canada'.[4]

The Governor-General communicated directly with the King. Buchan, wrote regular long and chatty letters to the King apprising him of the political situation but always leavening the letters with jokes and anecdotes. On Buchan's first report in November the King approvingly added 'Most interesting and charmingly written as one would expect.'[5] Among the matters covered in the report was Roosevelt's invitation to Mackenzie King, then on a visit to Washington, to go swimming in the presidential pool. Buchan noted: 'these two eminent men, neither of whom possesses an elegant figure, wallowing in the White House swimming-bath would have been an excellent subject for an historical painting!' He concluded: 'The Ottawa people are most cordial and I do not think I have yet become a victim of the celebrated Ottawa gossip, though I do not know with what private vices I may presently be credited.'[6] Much of the Governor-General's work involved attending functions where invariably there were speeches. Complaining to the King about them soon after his arrival Buchan added 'I had much in my mind the answer of the English schoolboy who was asked a question about America and wrote "America is a country where people are put to death by elocution."'[7]

In his biography of Lord Minto, written some ten years earlier, Buchan had written: 'A Governor-General in an autonomous Dominion walks inevitably on a razor edge. His powers are like those of a constitutional monarch, brittle if too heavily pressed, a shadow if tactlessly advertised, substantial only when exercised discreetly in the background'.[8] It was a lesson he was to learn himself only gradually. Though he tried to confine himself to 'Governor-Generalities' there were often moments of tension with the notoriously sensitive Mackenzie King who combined great political shrewdness and an interest in spiritualism with a mother-fixation and passion for the works of J.M. Barrie. Mackenzie King had written to Buchan shortly before the latter left for Canada: 'I have not the least doubt that your appointment will be one of those historic milestones which help to mark by pleasant, rather than painful, transition, the path of a new order.' Relations, however, between the Prime Minister and the Governor-General were initially difficult. Mackenzie King had been keen that Buchan come as a commoner, was upset at being overruled by the King and was determined to make sure that Buchan knew his place. One of his first actions was to explain to him the background to his appointment and make quite clear to whom he owed his good fortune.[9]

There were further conflicts over titles. Buchan had proposed after dinner on the day of his arrival that a knighthood be conferred on Howard Ferguson, the outgoing High Commissioner in London, and suggested the creation of the Order of St Lawrence, as a Canadian equivalent of the Star of India, in order to reward civil servants. At one point he had unconsciously said to Mackenzie King: 'I would advise you to consider.' Mackenzie King had noted icily in his diary: 'It is not the business of the Governor-General to advise, but to accept advice.' He reflected on the evening's discussion that 'It confirms the view that where a man is a Tory, Tory instincts are apt to be stronger than almost anything else, no matter how democratic in utterance and appearance one may be.'[10]

On his arrival Buchan decided immediately to address the long-standing problem of Canadian unity, which he felt was largely the result of ignorance about the different groups living in the country. Shuldham Redfern succinctly summed up the problem:

> Those who lived in Eastern Canada knew little and understood less of the difficulties which beset the Prairie farmers. The great chain of the Rocky Mountains was not only a physical barrier; it was also an obstacle to the interchange of knowledge between the West Coast and the rest of the country. But the greatest differences of all existed between the Canadians of French origin, strongly imbued with the Roman Catholic faith, who formed a third of the total population, and their fellow-citizens elsewhere.[11]

'I feel more and more that my chief usefulness here lies in visiting the remoter places,' Buchan told the King on New Year's Eve. 'Canada's real problem is how to counteract the difficulties of her enormous size and bind together her scattered population with a uniform national spirit.' This need for national unity, which was important in the immediate aftermath of Canada's new Dominion status after the Statute of Westminster, became imperative as the situation in Germany and Italy increasingly made war likely.[12] He described his task in a letter to Anthony Eden six months after his arrival. 'Canada has never yet thought out her position vis-à-vis the Empire and international affairs, and is monopolized with her own domestic problems . . . One of my chief tasks is to try to make Canada a little more conscious of her international obligations, for a good deal of the worst dynamite in the world is steered near her Western borders on the Pacific.'[13]

Buchan's working day would begin about 9.00 a.m. in his office in Rideau Hall where there would be invitations to accept, speeches to write, documents to sign. He worked efficiently and with great concentration, was a good delegator and always well-prepared with the result that he was able to discharge his official duties quickly and then turn to his biography of Augustus. He had started to write this soon after his arrival and increasingly he began to draw analogies between the Roman Emperor and the current Italian leader. He wrote to Baldwin in March 1936: 'It is extraordinary how that great man, the only dictator who ever kept his head, anticipated so many things in the modern world. A good deal of Mussolini's Corporative State comes straight out of his policy – only badly misinterpreted.'[14] In Canada he continued his routine from Oxford and Elsfield of spending the afternoons taking exercise. He had taken up skiing, skating and curling and he would go for long walks in the grounds of Rideau Hall or in the nearby Gatineau Hills. Then between tea and dinner he would meet journalists or other opinion formers. As far as possible he tried to cut down on official evening functions which he did not enjoy, preferring informal lunch parties instead, so after dinner he would read or play patience.

One of the reasons that Mackenzie King had been so keen on Buchan was his reputation as a writer and consequent appeal to the intelligentsia. Soon after he arrived, Buchan had been approached by the Canadian Authors' Association, asking him to be their Honorary President, an invitation he was happy to accept. For many years the Association had tried unsuccessfully to set up Confederation Medals, each with substantial cash prizes, for the best books of the year. Shortly after his arrival the matter was raised with Buchan who agreed to lend the title of Governor-General to the awards, but stipulated that there could be no cash payment from the Government and they must be administered by the Association. The first prizes were awarded in 1936 and its recipients since then have included Margaret Atwood, Michael Ondaatje, Robertson Davies, Brian Moore and a fierce critic of Buchan, Mordecai Richler. Though the Governor-General's Literary Awards have become the most prestigious of the Canadian literary awards, Buchan's decision not to support them financially has been criticized for delaying their development. Many commentators have since felt it was a sadly missed opportunity to stimulate Canadian literature and thereby create the sense of national identity that he had claimed to be such a priority.[15]

The month after his arrival Buchan, at Mackenzie King's prompting, prepared a note on how the Prime Minister's office might be reorganized. One of his suggestions was the appointment of a *chef du cabinet* who would be 'head of the PM's office, intelligence officer and liaison officer'. He claimed that in January 1934 MacDonald had discussed creating such a role for him, making him 'a member of the Cabinet without portfolio to act as his personal assistant'. In the end he had done the work privately and without a Cabinet position.[16]

In February 1936, Buchan made his first tour of the country when he visited the gold-mines of Northern Ontario and the next month his wife joined him for a week in the Eastern Townships of Quebec, where he delivered thirty-two speeches in English and seventeen in French. The trip gave him the opportunity for his first Canadian holiday when he spent three days at a fishing camp in the Laurentian Hills with Johnnie, where between them they managed to land over 150 trout. Then in July, just as he was about to start his important Western Tour, his old gastric problems returned. He was immediately taken

to the Royal Victoria Hospital in Montreal for a series of tests conducted by
the Professor of Medicine at the University, Jonathan Meakins. As Buchan
explained to his mother:

> for four days I went through the most elaborate examination a man could
> have. I was x-rayed at least forty times in every conceivable attitude, and I
> can tell you it is no light task to defy the laws of gravity and take a bismuth
> meal standing on one's head! . . . As I lay naked on the slab with these grave
> faces around me in the uncertain light, I was very much reminded of
> Rembrandt's picture 'The Anatomist'.

His stomach was drained and then by artificially inflating it with a pump it
was discovered 'the trouble came from a thickening of the mucous membrane
– a functional and not an organic mischief.' He was told to rest after meals and
put on a strict diet of milk and Vichy water.[17]

A possible element in Buchan's ill health was his increasing concern about
both his wife and his children. In the spring, Johnnie was invalided home from
Uganda. Beatrice Spencer-Smith confided to her mother there might be more
to the situation than first apparent: 'I darkly suspect that the Uganda authorities are grasping at any chance of getting rid of him as they have already complained that he never does any work . . .'[18] There were reports that William
had run up debts and he too had become seriously ill. Perhaps most importantly Alice's marriage was in difficulty. She had become engaged within days
of meeting her husband and married only nine weeks later. Marriage provided
her with an escape from her family but she soon discovered that neither she nor
Brian were ideally suited. 'You can't go into 2 Upper Grosvenor St without
being set on and taken into little rooms for private talks,' Beatrice Spencer-
Smith confided to her mother in November. 'There is no doubt Alice is a bad
wife but as neither of them want a divorce what is the good of talking.'[19] One
of the principal problems was Brian's inability to find a job. On his marriage
in 1933 he had left the Cameron Highlanders and become a Stipendiary
Steward of the Greyhound Racing Club but that had now ended. He had
taken the job originally on a temporary basis in the hope of becoming a Jockey
Club Steward but no job was forthcoming. Attempts by his father-in-law to
try and secure a job through Clive Wigram at the Royal Stud had also come
to nothing.

Later that summer Buchan made his postponed Western Tour visiting
Winnipeg, Regina, Saskatchewan, Edmonton and the small towns of
Alberta until eventually reaching Vancouver. He was made a Chief of one of
the Indian tribes with the name 'Teller of Tales' and met the naturalist and

writer Grey Owl. Buchan enjoyed these opportunities to meet ordinary Canadians. Though not always entirely easy with his own family he had a gift for making people feel at ease. Partly this came from his own warmth and interest in other people, partly as a result of his wide sympathies and knowledge. For example he surprised his travelling colleagues by breaking into Icelandic, which he had taught himself as a student, when visiting the Icelandic settlements between Lake Winnipeg and Lake Manitoba. The purpose of the Western Tour was not only to meet the people but also to investigate the agricultural conditions of the Prairies. Many of the lessons he had learnt in South Africa about making agricultural improvements to develop the rural economy, he was able to put into effect again. Writing to the King after his tour he confessed that: 'of all the parts of Canada I have yet visited Alberta has most taken my fancy. There is something tannic in its air, not only physically but spiritually, for it has the feeling of a Borderland.'[20]

Much as he enjoyed his time in Canada, Buchan did feel cut off from the centre of events. He had regular correspondents such as Lord Crawford, Violet Markham and Leo Amery and throughout 1936 he was visited by among others Philip Kerr, Charles Dick, Edmund Ironside, Cynthia Asquith, the Astors and the Duke and Duchess of Atholl but as he told Baldwin in the spring of 1936: 'I feel rather like a Scots laird at the end of the eighteenth century, who cultivated his estate in the wilds of Sutherland, while Pitt and Fox and Burke were hard at it in the House of Commons and the Revolution was blazing away in France. It is uncommonly easy to slip into the parochial habit of mind.'[21]

There certainly was a revolution of sorts in Britain. In January, George V's life had 'moved peacefully to its close' and he was succeeded by his son who became Edward VIII. Edward's relationship with an American divorcee, Wallis Simpson, had been the subject of Society gossip for some time. By the summer it had been mentioned in various American papers and Mrs Simpson even named in the House of Commons. Throughout the autumn of 1936 the issue of whether Edward could be King and marry Mrs Simpson began to develop into a constitutional issue. Buchan, who had been privy to inside information from high level friends in Britain as well as his own reading of the Canadian and American press, was now drawn into the matter in his role as Governor-General. According to the 1931 Statute of Westminster, which had given the self-governing Dominions such as Canada full autonomy, any alteration in the royal succession required the assent of the Parliaments of all the Dominions.

On 15 October, Hardinge, worried by coverage of 'the King's domestic affairs' in the foreign press, had written to Buchan asking for a summary of

Canadian opinion. Buchan was in a difficult position, caught between his loyalty to the reigning sovereign and duty to the institution of monarchy. He replied on 27 October that he thought Canadians were 'irritated, shocked and genuinely alarmed' by events and that the King's behaviour threatened to weaken the Empire.[22] In response to another letter from Baldwin on 26th October, after the Prime Minister had broached the subject with the King, and which asked for a more detailed report he reported:

> Canada is the most puritanical part of the Empire and cherishes very much the Victorian standards of private life . . . She has a special affection and loyalty for the King, whom she regards as one of her own citizens. This is strongly felt particularly by the younger people, who are by no means strait-laced; and they are alarmed at anything which may take the gilt off their idol. Canada's pride has been deeply wounded by the tattle in the American Press, which she feels an intolerable impertinence.[23]

He added that if an official reaction was required that was best left to the Prime Minister, Mackenzie King.

One area of concern was the way Beaverbrook, a supporter of Edward, claimed in his papers to be interpreting Canadian opinion. Leo Amery told Buchan: 'The line he is taking is that a ruthless and dictatorial Government, wishing for a thoroughly tame monarch, have suddenly put the King into an impossible choice between his inclinations and his Throne and are prepared to "bump him off" without giving him any time to look around and reflect on the situation.'[24] Mrs Simpson's divorce at the end of October, thereby freeing her to wed the King, initiated the final part of the crisis. At the end of November Baldwin saw the Canadian High Commissioner, Vincent Massey, who repeated much of what Buchan had said. Advice from other Dominion leaders, including Mackenzie King on 30 November, was unanimously against Edward and in favour of Baldwin. On 2 December, the Dominions' rejection of a morganatic marriage was confirmed by the Cabinet.

Still the crisis dragged on with Buchan writing to his mother on 7 December 'No settlement yet! It cannot be much prolonged for the Australian Parliament is in special session waiting for news. I am desperately sorry for everyone concerned. Baldwin's speech in the House yesterday seemed to me excellent. Winston is surely making a blazing fool of himself.'[25] Matters finally came to a head when Edward abdicated in favour of his brother, George, on 11 December, though Buchan claimed to have been informed of the King's decision by secret wire on 9 December. He was sad to see the King go but was also rather relieved. As he wrote to his mother: 'this is the first case of a British

Admiral who has become third mate to an American tramp.' Violet Markham summed up the general mood when she noted to Buchan: 'What will history say of a man who held an American harlot of more importance than the welfare of the nation or Empire?'[26]

In a letter to Baldwin, Buchan mused: '. . . like you, I was very fond of him, but always a little uneasy about what might happen. Now I cannot get him out of my head. I cannot see any happiness in the future for one with no purpose in life, and very few interests . . .'. He went on:

> we have gained something out of our perplexities. In the first place we have got a new king who is in the direct tradition of George V. He has not the personal charm of his brother, or his gift of imagination, but, from what I know of him, I think he has got solid brains and the highest sense of duty. He has also got a wife and a family of exactly the right sort. I cannot but hope that his accession will mean the going out of fashion of this miserable jazz-night-club atmosphere, which has been the worst bequest of the War, and a return to something of the old Victorian seriousness . . . A third gain is, I hope, that the power for mischief in Winston and his like has now been killed.[27]

One of Buchan's priorities had been to strengthen relations between Canada and America. Partly this was a realization that Canada's future lay with her North American neighbour and partly it was an attempt to act as an interpreter for relations between America and the British Empire as events turned more ominous on the European continent. Soon after his arrival he had suggested that he and Roosevelt have a series of informal meetings but George V would not countenance it. Wigram wrote on his behalf in February 1936: 'Your successors (who will probably be less eloquent and may be less politically discreet than you) would not bless you for exposing a flank that has always been jealously guarded.'[28] Buchan persisted and plans were made for the two men to meet in June, in Ottawa, but Congress adjourned late and the meeting had to be cancelled. Instead Roosevelt took the opportunity of a sailing trip off Nova Scotia with his sons at the end of July to see Buchan in Quebec. Amazingly, it was the first official visit of an American President to Canada.

The visit was judged a success though the large number of Secret Service men with their special requirements and even a machine-gun upset the Controller of the Household, Eric Mackenzie, and Buchan was intrigued by FDR's personal bodyguard, an ex New York 'cop' whom he described to the King as 'a sort of American Sam Weller'. Susan wrote to her children immediately afterwards: 'I must say I liked the President very much indeed. He does not tell you things; but listens to what you have to say, and gives you the impression of being a most attractive and intelligent human being.'[29] Roosevelt and Buchan struck an immediate rapport. Though the President was a few years younger than the Governor-General they shared similar interests and temperament. Both regarded themselves as intellectuals in politics, both had always taken a close interest in military and foreign affairs, both had been dogged by ill health and they shared common interests in bird watching, golf and fishing. A further link was that Roosevelt had taken his honeymoon in the Dolomites and Venice only two years before Buchan and had fought his first election the year before Buchan stood in Peebles.

Immediately afterwards Buchan reported to the King that Roosevelt was keen to issue 'an invitation to the leaders of the Great Powers to confer, before it is too late, not on any particular question, but on the need of doing something to safeguard civilization before it crashes'.[30] At the same time he wrote to Mackenzie King:

> the key to the future is in the relations between Britain and the United States, and that Canada is the strategic point . . . I am wholly of your mind that if trouble in Europe does come to a head, if possible we must keep the British Empire out of it. The situation is wholly different from that of 1914, and if we can achieve an honourable detachment and so restrict the area of conflict it would be by far our best contribution to the cause of ultimate peace.[31]

He repeated the sentiment two weeks later to Susan's mother Caroline:

> Canada has no interest in this miserable struggle of Communism and Fascism in Europe and no more has Britain. I am very clear that except for a direct threat to the Low Countries, which are an external British interest, or an unprovoked attack on France Britain should not accept any challenge.[32]

Two weeks after that he expanded on his world view to Mackenzie King:

> The Empire, if it remains detached and keeps its head, can play a great part in pacification; but that part will be impossible if we are once dragged into the European dog-fight. What Europe is witnessing at present is not a conflict of genuine principles so much as the wrangling of ambitious mob-leaders, who have behind them nations who have lost their nerve. In this wrangling we have no real interests, except as peace-makers.[33]

In December he told his brother Walter:

> I am really more anxious about the situation in the Far East than about
> European conditions. There is a great deal of gunpowder lying about on
> the Asiatic shores. Canada is beginning to realize this and is thinking
> gravely about the matter. Two advantages spring from the situation; one is
> that she is no longer inclined to an isolationist creed, which is impossible
> today; and the other is that she and the United States are being compelled
> more and more to think together. This does not mean in any way a weak-
> ening of the imperial tie, but it does mean that Canada may be the motive
> power towards that closer understanding between the United States and the
> Empire, on which I believe the future of the world depends.[34]

In the spring of 1937, it was the Buchans' turn to go south for discussions
in Washington on the international situation and more local concerns such as
the Alaska Highway. They were met at Union Station early in the evening of
the 30 March by the Secretary of State, Cordell Hull, and driven to the White
House where Buchan was delighted to be given Lincoln's study as his sitting-
room. After a dinner honouring the actress Katherine Cornell, Buchan and
the President retired for a private chat about the world situation. The next day
there was a visit to Mount Vernon on the Presidential yacht, Buchan inspected
a squadron of cavalary at Fort Meyer, lunched with Woodrow Wilson's
widow and laid a wreath at the tomb of the unknown soldier at Arlington
before returning for a State Dinner at the White House. Recapping on the trip
to his family he wrote: 'After it we had a group of negro singers, who sang very
beautifully a number of negro spirituals and plantation songs. After that I
talked to the President until far into the night.'[35]

   The following day he gave an address at the Naval Academy at Annapolis,
lunched at the British Embassy and then addressed Congress – the first British
person ever to do so. The Buchans caught a midnight train back after dinner
at the Canadian Legation. The visit had been a success, though Harold Ickes
noted in his diary that Mrs Roosevelt had been told by her husband: 'that
notwithstanding what protocol said or what might have been done in the past,
no one was going to do any curtsying in the White House to any foreign
visitor.'[36] Buchan was impressed with Cordell Hull, the Chairman of the
Senate Foreign Relations Committee, but most especially with Roosevelt.

> His vitality oxygenates all his surroundings, and his kindliness diffuses a
> pleasant warmth about him wherever he goes. His reception out of doors
> was unbelievable. He is a real leader of the people. What impressed me

most was his extraordinary mental activity. I have never met a mind more
fecund in ideas. And these ideas are not mere generalities, for he has an
astonishing gift of worming his way into a subject. His thought is not only
spacious, but close-textured.[37]

The compliment was returned. Roosevelt told their mutual friend Arthur
Murray that Buchan 'is the best Governor-General that Canada has ever
had'.[38]

The purpose of the visit had been to discuss Roosevelt's suggestion of a
European peace plan brokered by the Americans. In a memo summing up
his impressions of the talks Buchan told Roosevelt: 'The more I think over the
matter, the more I feel that no conference can be a success except under your
direct personal supervision.' At the same time he wrote to Stair: 'I am one of
those people who have a natural liking for Americans . . . I am more and more
convinced that the future of civilisation lies in the co-operation of Britain and
the USA.' Unfortunately it was not a view shared by the new British Prime
Minister, Neville Chamberlain, and an opportunity to possibly avert the
Second World War was lost.[39]

Apart from the international situation, Buchan faced problems in Canada.
The costs of relieving unemployment and underwriting the national railway
system had meant an unbalanced budget. There was confusion as a result of
the British North America Act over the division of revenues between the
Dominion and the Provinces, while many Provinces could not support them-
selves without extra Federal funding. Buchan proposed a new Constitutional
Conference chaired by Stanley Baldwin on the relationship between the
Federal and Provincial Courts. The Conference did meet, but under the
Chief Justice of Ontario rather than under Baldwin. There was also a resur-
gence of French nationalism in Quebec and Buchan feared 'with the present
increase in their population, in fifty years there may be a French majority in
Canada'. He realized that much of the blame rested with 'a truculent Orange
element in Ontario, and in Montreal, where the whole business is run by the
English . . . My job is to try and foster the larger loyalty. That is why I have to
be constantly on the road, for, as I have said, I am the only *trait d'union* between
the Atlantic and the Pacific, the St Lawrence and the North Pole.'[40]

Susan had never been keen on uprooting herself and moving to an
unknown life in Canada, far from friends and family. Already at Elsfield she
had been lonely and the problem intensified in Canada and especially during
the 1936 Western Tour. Part of the problem was there was very little for her to
do as the Governor-General's wife. She took no interest in the running of
Rideau Hall and spent much of her time either shopping or going for long,

meaningless drives. She tended to stay in bed late and was prone to bouts of deep depression, accentuated by worries over her family and her husband's health. By the beginning of 1937 Beatrice Spencer-Smith reported that Susie had accepted that Brian and Alice might divorce. 'Being a Governor-General's wife hasn't so far made me loud voiced and commanding (at least I don't think so),' Susan wrote to her old friend Virginia Woolf in April 1937. 'It rather makes me feel like a card Queen, one dimensional with no back to me – It's a queer life. I always seem to be dressing and resting and receiving bouquets and talking endlessly to people.'[41]

Never popular with the staff, especially Redfern, there was concern that she had to be given an interest. She had already become involved in the Canadian Women's Institutes. Now mindful of the need to raise standards of education and literacy she inaugurated a scheme to supply books to the Prairie Provinces. She reported on the scheme to Queen Mary: 'I have sent nearly five thousand books to the Prairie Provinces, and I hope before I leave Canada to have collected about three times that number.' In the event, through help from the Carnegie Trustees in New York, some 40,000 books were distributed under the scheme.[42] Another interest was writing books. In 1928 Susan had written *The Sword of State*, a book on Wellington after Waterloo, and this had been followed in 1932 by a biography of one of her ancestors Lady Louisa Stuart. Then shortly before coming out to Canada she had published a children's book, *Arabella Takes Charge* and, through Leonard and Virginia Woolf's Hogarth Press, *Funeral March of a Marionette*, a study of Charlotte of Albany. Now she embarked on a novel, *The Scent of Water*, which was published later that year.

In June 1937, the Buchans made their delayed tour of the Maritimes returning again that October to visit Prince Edward and Cape Breton Islands. The tour, however, which most appealed to Buchan and generated considerable interest in Canada was his tour to the Arctic in the summer of 1937. In July he had written to his brother Walter:

> There is one card I mean to play for all it is worth. The future of Canada lies in the North. There lie the great mineral riches, not to speak of unexplored wealth in timber and fishing . . . My job is to arouse an enthusiasm for our North which would be a binding force, for the North is common to practically all the Provinces and to all our different race stocks. That is why I am going to the Arctic this year.[43]

It was an important trip not just because it was an area Buchan personally wished to explore, but because he realized he needed to publicize the North,

PROCONSUL   263

which was little known even in Canada. There had always been a tendency for Canadians to look to their powerful southern neighbour. He hoped that by highlighting the problems and activities of the North he could generate a greater sense of national spirit and unite the country in trying to solve them. Though the Mintos had travelled north to the Yukon in 1900, no previous Governor-General had gone to the Arctic. Now with improved communications it was possible to do so. This Arctic Tour would be the longest continuous trip ever made by a Governor-General. The party was to consist of the Buchans accompanied by Alastair Buchan, Shuldham Redfern and his wife, a young widow, Joan Pape, who had succeeded Beatrice Spencer-Smith as a lady-in-waiting in January 1937, and two ADCs, Lieutenant Gordon Rivers-Smith and an officer from the Black Watch, Pat Campbell-Preston, who Buchan had told Stair 'is curiously like Tommie Nelson both in face and manner'. Mrs Killick was to join them en route.[44]

The party left Quebec on 3 July travelling via Winnipeg and Calgary to begin the principal part of the journey at Edmonton on 20th July. From there the party travelled by train, the 'Muskeg special', 'through a tangle of fir-weed, goldenrod and flaming wild flowers' to Waterways, the railhead for the North. Here the Buchans parted, with Susan going on to British Columbia and the rest of the party catching a Hudson's Bay steamer, the *Athabasca River*. *En route*, the group stopped at Fort Norman so that a small party led by two native guides could climb Bear Rock. Buchan elected to take the most difficult route but while he made it to the top sustaining only torn trousers the two much younger men Rivers-Smith and an Edmonton doctor George Macdonald, who had just joined the party, became stuck and had to be rescued by a couple of Indians with ropes.[45]

A new addition to the party was an American photographer from *Life* magazine, Margaret Bourke-White, who had flown up from New York to join the party. She has left this portrait of Buchan:

From the very start there was a kind of affectionate friendship between His Excellency and myself. I found him a wiry, astute man of few words. He was indexing the manuscript of a biography of Augustus that he had recently completed, and he spent the greater part of the day at the stern of the boat, an excellent place to write undisturbed. A long narrow table had been contrived for him with a couple of planks, and there he sat with the fluttering little white paper markers of his index all over the place. Our cargo almost swallowed him up. His spare form was all but lost in the midst of the pig crates, the cage of chickens, the tractor, the assortment of agricultural implements which surrounded him.[46]

In turn he was charmed by her, calling her Maggie, taking an interest in her collection of butterflies and lending her books to read, including *Greenmantle* and *The Thirty-Nine Steps*. Susan had found her 'most fashionably dressed and very self-possessed', but was surprised that though she claimed to be taking landscapes she was continuously taking pictures of the Buchans.[47]

Just before the end of July the party crossed the Arctic Circle, where they were joined by Santa Claus and Buchan was admitted to the Sanctuary of the Arctic with the Eskimo blessing: 'May you have warmth in your igloo, oil in your lamp and peace in your heart.' On their return by plane the Buchans stopped at the national reserve established by the British Columbia Government in March 1936 and named Tweedsmuir Park. There for ten days they camped and trekked, swam their horses across the Ootsa River and fished for salmon and rainbow trout. As Buchan reported to Stair immediately on his return: 'In the last two months I have been a tramp on a grand scale, for I have covered about four thousand miles by train, two thousand by steamer, a thousand by camel and pack-horse, and well over three thousand by air.'[48]

The trip had given Buchan an opportunity to see the country and meet a wide range of people. It had allowed him to highlight both the problems and strengths of the North. In his reports on the trip to the Hudson Bay Company and the Prime Minister he had stressed the importance of air transport, the need to extend farming and ranching much further north and the opportunities for tourism. And he had skilfully turned the trip into a huge public relations exercise for Canada as much as for himself. The party had included a journalist from the Canadian Press, Guy Rhoades; another member of the party, the composer Thomas Wood, had written two articles for *The Times* and Susan had contributed an article on Tweedsmuir Park to the *National Geographic*, which was published in April 1938. The result was that the tour was followed avidly around the world and gave Buchan an opportunity to return to his theme of Canada's need to take an active part in international affairs.[49]

Six weeks after the completion of the tour he raised the issue in a speech at the anniversary dinner of the Canadian Institute of International Affairs. He stressed the importance of an informed electorate that was prepared to take an active interest in both domestic and international affairs and continued: 'From this duty no country is exempt. Certainly not Canada. She is a sovereign nation and cannot take her attitude to the world docilely from Britain, or from the United States, or from anybody else. A Canadian's first loyalty is not to the British Commonwealth of Nations, but to Canada and to Canada's King.'[50] The speech caused a storm. Loyalists thought he had gone native, constitutionalists thought he had strayed too far from Governor-Generalities, nationalists adopted his words as a slogan while Mackenzie King, who had cleared the speech, made no comment at all. Buchan had succeeded in focusing Canadian minds on the implications of the Statute of Westminster and in redefining the role of Governor-General. He had always argued that people could hold a series of loyalties, drawing on his own experience as a Borderer, a Scotsman and a supporter of both the British Empire and of close ties with America. It was a mark, however, of how far he had come to love and understand Canada that he felt able to make such a bold statement. This speech two years after he had first arrived in Canada was to be a watershed in his own approach to his job and in public perception of him and his role. For two years he had worked his passage, meeting a huge range of people across the country and carefully listening to their views, earning their trust and respect and risking his own position to defend Canadian interests. Buchan had always been a chameleon able to adapt quickly to his surroundings. Nowhere was this clearer than now in Canada.

15

NATIVE

AT the beginning of November 1937 Buchan found himself nominated as Chancellor of Edinburgh University by a Professor of Clinical Medicine at the University, Edwin Bramwell. He unwittingly accepted to discover that he would have to fight the Marquess of Lothian in a contested election. He was placed in a difficult position, especially by the King, since it would be unseemly if he lost and it was felt that he could not properly discharge his functions while in Canada if he won. *The Times* reported that Lothian had been put forward as the official candidate because 'the office of Chancellor carried duties and responsibilities which could not be fulfilled by a man who was to be absent from this country for the next few years, and for the appointment of an absentee such as one holding high office in one of his Majesty's Dominions there was no precedent.'[1]

Having accepted the nomination Buchan felt bound to continue. In any case as he wrote to his mother:

I receive endless wires of encouragement. So I will go to the poll. I really ought to beat Lothian. Meantime I have received an invitation to be Lord Rector of St Andrews, but have asked them to postpone it, since I would not be able to deliver my rectorial address during my term of office. One reason why I am standing for the Edinburgh Chancellorship is that Canada is very keen about it.[2]

The King was less keen, and his suspicion of Buchan was intensified when he discovered that Buchan had written several articles for the *Sunday Times* about his travels. Buchan explained he was only trying to raise the profile of Canada and change many people's preconceptions about it. Wigram, claiming to

speak for the King was quite blunt: 'I do not like the idea of His Majesty's personal representative being, as someone put it to me, a Publicity Agent for
boosting a particular Dominion.'[3]

Buchan was becoming increasingly frustrated by the constraints his position brought. In September 1936 Gaumont-British had proposed to send
Hitchcock out to see him and discuss a film with a Canadian background but
he had been reluctantly forced to reject the offer as incompatible with his role
as Governor-General. It was only the first of a series of offers, many of them
lucrative or prestigious, he felt obliged to turn down because of his official
position. However, several film deals were concluded on his existing books. In
1937 a seven year licence on *Huntingtower* was sold for £800 to be followed in
1938 by a £2,000 deal with Korda for a seven year licence on *Greenmantle* and
the following year, again to Korda, a £3,000 contract for a seven year licence
on an unnamed Canadian film.

Another frustration was his health which throughout 1937 continued to be
bad. In November he wrote to Walter:

> My stomach is a most ridiculous thing. I am perfectly well in everything else
> except that. Like a baby with no teeth I swallow air with my food. The
> diagnosis has now established that beyond a question. This trouble of wind
> all began after my teeth were pulled. The only thing is to eat very slowly
> and to eat with my mouth shut. I am much better, but every now and then
> I have a baddish day. It is a ludicrous affliction to suffer from.[4]

On 18th December, Susan learnt from Walter of Helen Buchan's death at
the age of eighty. She immediately broke the sad news to her husband. 'He was
so good and took it so bravely but I can see that he feels that something big and
interesting has gone out of life and I expect that's what we all feel,' she wrote
to her eldest son. 'Gran for such a tiny person filled up a big space and I can't
imagine life without her.'[5] It was indeed a big shock for Buchan. His relationship with her had been unusually close. He later wrote: 'Not many sons and
mothers can have understood each other better than she and I.' They had
written to each other almost every day they were apart and after the deaths of
his father and two brothers and as the eldest child he had felt particularly
responsible for her.[6]

In many ways hers had been a sad life. Three of her children had died
young and for over twenty five years she had been a widow. The death of her
youngest child, in particular, had been traumatic. Anna remembered how on
the day she died her mother 'woke from a short sleep with a look on her face
of utter content, the look we had seen long years before when she held the

youngest of us in her arms. When I leant over her she said, "It was Alastair, he came and lay down beside me," and we wondered if she were being given back all she had lost.'[7] Her life had increasingly revolved around her family and the Church. Her husband, a kind and intelligent man, had had little ambition so it is perhaps not surprising she had placed all her hopes in her children. She had lived for them and, to an extent, they had in return tried to excel for her sake. It was she who had always kept the faith, certain of her eldest son's potential and of the world's reluctance to recognize and reward his many talents. She had been a nuisance and created torn loyalties, but she had also been a conscience and a stimulus, keeping him in touch with his roots and encouraging him in his endeavours.

She had, however, never been one of his greatest literary fans. Anna later described her reaction to Buchan's books:

> Each one was sent to her with a suitable inscription, and was a treasured possession. The Lives of Scott and Montrose she read with delight, and she gazed with respect at Cromwell and Augustus, but it was a trial to her that she could make so little of his adventure stories. She always kept the new one on her table, announcing that she was going to enjoy it when she could get a really undisturbed time ... (but) after a few pages she would murmur, 'Tuts, they're beginning to swear already.' ... Presently, with a discouraged sigh, she would lay down the book, remarking, 'Now he's got them into a cave, and it's so confusing, I think I'll knit a little.'[8]

His mother's death further weakened Buchan's already poor constitution and he was forced to spend several afternoons in bed resting. His thoughts were for her but also for Walter and Anna and he had turned to Anna's autobiographical novel *Ann and Her Mother*. He admitted to his sister he was 'getting great comfort from it. I am so glad you wrote that, for it is a wonderful record.'[9]

Since Beaverbrook had first raised it in February 1930 there had been speculation about Buchan being sent as British Ambassador to Washington. It was a job he was known to want and his close relationship with Roosevelt further fanned the rumour mills. At the end of 1937 the rumours surfaced again and continued, for example, in private reports to Reuters in London, until the summer of 1938. Buchan claimed to his brother Walter: 'that both Roosevelt and Cordell Hull have shown a most unpleasing desire to ask the British and Canadian Governments to have me transferred to Washington as Ambasador in order to see through the trade treaty and the debt settlement'. He added: 'I simply won't go. I will never desert Mr. Micawber. My work in Canada is only just beginning.'[10] However, he did little to check such speculation and rather disingenuously wrote to Alan Lascelles at the beginning of the year:

> The papers, here and in the States, have been full of idiotic rumours that I was going to be transferred to Washington. There has been this much in them that the President and Cordell Hull keep on saying they want me. But only his Majesty and the Canadian Government can move me, and the Canadian Government certainly won't agree . . . My big job is to try and interest Canadians more in Canada, which means, of course, incessant travelling and mixing with all kinds of people. I feel I am making real headway in this job in the West, and also in French Canada; but I have only made a beginning.[11]

Any official job was beginning to lose its attraction as Buchan certainly felt increasingly frustrated by his inability to pursue activities related to his other interests. He was continually being asked to address American universities, approached by film companies or asked for interviews, all of which he had to decline for fear of cheapening his official position. One direct consequence was that at the same time as his expenses increased as Governor-General his income from writing fell. His literary earnings dropped from £7,000 in 1937 to £3,000 in 1938 and halved again in 1939. Though he was paid a salary of almost $50,000 a year, from that he had to provide many of the running costs of his official position including his cars and gifts to visiting dignitaries. The result was that he could not live on his salary and he had to borrow money from Sir Alexander Grant, a friend who had made a fortune as Chairman of the biscuit manufacturers, McVities, and whom Buchan had known through their involvement with the National Library of Scotland.[12]

He continued to be plagued by ill health with recurrent bouts of nausea and chronic gastritis. In April he admitted to Johnnie, now working in Winnipeg for the Hudson's Bay Company: 'I have had a pretty uncomfortable winter, for I have had four days free from discomfort since August. Meakins is now giving me a powdered extract of liver, which is perfectly beastly to take.'[13] Another concern was the anti-British attitude of the returning Rhodes Scholars, many of whom as academics and journalists were in influential positions to shape public opinion. 'It is very much the point of view of that lowest of created things, the Irish-American,' he told the King. 'I think something will have to be done to discover a better type of Canadian Rhodes Scholar.'[14]

In early June, he spent a week travelling by boat through the lakes of Eastern Ontario followed by a visit to New York with Johnnie where they lunched with the Morgans and saw the playwright Edward Sheldon. Later in the month he received an Honorary Degree at Yale with Thomas Mann and Walt Disney and then the next day attended the Harvard Commencement ceremony, where he spoke on a favourite subject, the role of education. These would be the only two occasions where he was allowed to speak outside the confines of his job in the United States while Governor-General.

Shortly afterwards he left for a three month visit to Britain. The primary reason for his return was his installation as Chancellor of Edinburgh University in succession to J.M. Barrie but he also took the opportunity to see his doctor, Lord Dawson of Penn, and have talks with the Prime Minister and members of the Cabinet. On the 20 July, after first clearing it with the King, he gave his speech on the role of the university, drawing on *Pilgrim's Progress* for his title, *The Interpreter's House*. In it he spoke of the role of the University basing what he said on his experience of the Canadian and American systems.[15] Among those honoured with him at Edinburgh were the sculptor and engraver Eric Gill, the Viceroy of India, Lord Linlithgow, the Governor-General of Australia, Lord Gowrie and four of Buchan's own nominations – Violet Markham, the Principal of Brasenose, Professor Hugh Last, the Minister for Agriculture, 'Shakes' Morrison and the Canadian financier Sir Edward Peacock. He had however failed to secure the honorary degrees he had wanted for Anna, Harold Baker, Lord Halifax and the recent Secretary of State for the Dominions, Ramsay MacDonald's son, Malcolm.

He then immediately checked in to Sir Edmund Sprigg's clinic at Ruthin Castle in North Wales for a month. Susan after an early visit wrote to Alastair: 'The good news is that Daddy is looking so wonderfully well. He has put on two and a half pounds, and has much more colour. He has lost that slightly yellow, rather anaemic look that he had, and his lips have got colour now, which they have not had for ages.'[16] Anna, Walter and William also came to see him, staying at an inn at the Castle gates. They would drive him to local sights or have tea together in the Castle garden where Buchan would read extracts from his current book, a proposed volume of memoirs. Apart from drafting a speech for the King at the launching of the *Queen Elizabeth* he did no work. Much of his time was spent reading everything from Laurence Sterne and Sydney Smith to thrillers by A.E.W. Mason and Michael Innes.

Buchan was in Britain during the Munich Crisis and spent the last week of the crisis in September in long talks with Chamberlain, Halifax and other ministers. His own view, as he admitted to B.K. Sandwell of the *Toronto Saturday Night*, was 'that Chamberlain took the right course. The mistake he made was to represent the result as anything in the nature of a triumph, for it was merely a miserable acceptance of the lesser of two evils'.[17] At the end of September he stayed with the King at Balmoral. He wrote afterwards to his brother Walter: 'I had a most affecting meeting with the king on Monday. We talked for about two hours, and at the end we held each other's hands. He really is a great man, and a wonderfully attractive one.'[18]

The international situation was becoming more critical in the last months of 1938. Moritz Bonn, to whom the Buchans had recently offered to let Elsfield, wrote gloomily to him about Chamberlain. He 'evidently does not understand the type of people against whom he has to play. He may be a first-rate bridge player when playing with gentlemen. He is playing poker with card-sharps, and evidently does not want to see them in this light.'[19] Buchan was being kept well informed of the international situation, especially in Germany, by a number of other correspondents, most notably Lord Crawford. His close contacts with America made him all too aware of the Nazi persecution of the Jews and he was shocked to learn from Walter that the Member of Parliament for Peebles, Archibald Maule Ramsay, had been spreading anti-Semitic propaganda. 'It is abominable, at a time when the wretched Jews are suffering almost the cruellest persecution in history, that Englishmen should give currency to these silly libels, which are all invented in Germany.'[20] He tried to do what he could to help the German refugees, for example, bringing a group of 500 skilled glassworkers from the Sudetenland to Alberta and British Columbia. Other groups followed the glassmakers including glove-makers, potters and some Austrian ski-experts. Though driven by a sense of compassion the policy also appealed to his belief in the need for imported skilled labour in Canada which might also provide a check on the growing French Canadian population. Ironically, it was Hitler who had done more than Baldwin to allow him to put into operation his plans for imperial emigration.

Viewing the situation from Canada, Buchan still regarded war as avoid-able – perhaps because he could not countenance it happening again in his life-time. In September he had written to Walter: 'my considered impression (not opinion, for I cannot give reasons) is that there will not be war.' In December he had told Baldwin: 'I am still fully convinced that every month that war is postponed it becomes less likely.' And by the following month he was report-ing to Bessborough:

I have a feeling, quite illogical, that things may go better in international politics this year. I feel that the universal disapproval of the dictatorships everywhere, except in Japan, must have some effect upon them. It seems to me that, besides our defence preparations, we ought to have a pretty stiff commercial policy towards the new German methods of international trading which are simply a form of bullying.[21]

Buchan began 1939 weighing nine stone. Violet Markham was delighted to hear he was 'looking like a Reubens instead of an El Greco'. This was a noticeable improvement for at times he had been scarcely more than eight stone. However, as he pointed out to Stair: 'I have to continue a fairly strict regime. I never touch alcohol, and my smoking is limited to a maximum of six cigarettes a day. Thank God I enjoyed my vices when I had them!'[22]

One new worry on the horizon was the Royal Tour scheduled for May but already actively in preparation. Buchan had first suggested the tour to the King in December 1936, Mackenzie King had repeated the invitation when he was in London for the Coronation in May 1937 and once accepted Buchan had discussed the arrangements when he saw the King in September 1938. There were several purposes to the trip. First it was to restore confidence in the monar-chy in Canada after the traumas of the Abdication. The Duke of Windsor had been much loved in Canada, and his younger brother was totally unknown. Secondly it was an attempt to strengthen Canada's allegiance to the Crown after the Statute of Westminster. It was important, given the increas-ing influence of a French Canadian separatist movement, to show the Canadians that George VI was their king as much as Britain's. Buchan hoped that the popular Royal couple might do more to unite Canadians and make them feel they were an integral part of the Empire than any political activities might achieve. It was a symbolic act that appealed to his sense of history and theatre. Equally importantly, the tour would also include the United States, where it was hoped it would bring home to the American public the need for the English-Speaking Peoples to stand together to defend democracy and the balance of power in Europe. Violet Markham neatly summed up the situa-tion:

> . . . the three days in the United States is of more value than the three weeks in Canada. You know that as well as I do, and though you may look down your official nose as you read this, you will send me a transatlantic wink at the same time! To have engineered that visit to the President was a real stroke of genius on your part and may have incalculable consequences for the world . . .[23]

In order to avoid raising suspicions about the purpose of the trip among American isolationists and upset Canadian sensibilities, Buchan suggested that Mackenzie King in his capacity as Canadian Minister for External Affairs accompany the King to Washington, rather than the British Foreign Secretary, Lord Halifax. One problem was that Mackenzie King felt that as Prime Minister he should greet the King and Queen on arrival in Quebec and

Buchan then meet them in Ottawa. Raising the matter with Alex Hardinge, private secretary to the King, Buchan wrote: 'I do not myself think that there is a great deal in the Constitutional point one way or another. It is only important if my Prime Minister chooses to think it so.'[24] Hardinge did however think it was important and he and Buchan came up with a possible compromise. Buchan would meet the Royal couple either on board ship or at the point of embarkation and 'surrender his charge' to Mackenzie King. The Canadian Prime Minister would have nothing of it and proceeded to quote the British North America Act that, as the elected representative, he must first meet the King. Eventually Hardinge backed down, deeming it not worth an argument and it was agreed Buchan would see the Royal couple in Ottawa.

There were many details to sort out, some of which Buchan regaled the King with in their regular correspondence. One woman had assumed she would be presented to the Royal Couple because her name was in Burke's Peerage, another offered to give the Queen a massage on reaching Victoria. A couple in New Brunswick called George and Elizabeth who were the same age as Their Majesties made a gallant gesture. As Buchan explained to the King: 'They offer their services as doubles and if Their Majesties, in the course of their arduous tour, would like a day's rest, this couple would be happy to impersonate them.' He added: 'It seems to me a brilliant suggestion.'[25] As the clouds of war gathered there was discussion about whether or not the Royal Tour should continue. Buchan was adamant: 'I think their Majesties should come however dark the outlook is in Europe – come in any case unless war has actually broken out. If war came about when they were here it might be a good thing, for the emotional reaction on this continent would be tremendous.'[26]

The Royal Tour did go ahead, the first by a reigning Sovereign to a British Dominion. King George VI and Queen Elizabeth arrived at Wolfe's Cove, Quebec on 17 May to be met by Mackenzie King before spending three days at Rideau Hall with the Buchans. The stay included an eight mile drive in an open state carriage, a State Dinner at Government House, a Trooping the Colour and a garden party for 5,000 people. The tour began to take on a momentum of its own with a crowd cheering the Royal party when they appeared on a floodlit balcony of the Chateau Laurier after a parliamentary banquet and the Queen endeared herself to the six or seven thousand veterans, who had gathered for the unveiling of the war memorial in front of the Chateau Laurier, when she dived into their midst followed by her husband and the Buchans. As they left from the station by the war memorial, the bands played 'will ye no come back again.'

Buchan's role was now over as Mackenzie King had insisted on escorting

the King and Queen on their tour of the country. 'Poor King and poor Rex
tied up to each other for three weeks,' wrote Violet Markham to Buchan.
'They will bore each other to tears before the end of the time. I wonder who
will weary first.' Mackenzie King was, however, delighted with the success of
the Royal visit, sending a telegram: 'Words cannot begin to describe triumphal
nature of Royal Tour. To date it has surpassed all expectations.' At the end of
the visit Buchan joined the royal train at Truro where he was awarded the
GCVO though the ceremony was prolonged after it took the King ten
minutes to open the case even with the help of a knife.[27]

It had been 'Canada's own show' but it had also been Buchan's show. He
had written the King's four principal speeches delivered at Quebec, Ottawa,
Vancouver and on departure from Halifax. He had been closely involved in
the preparations over the space of six months and he had found that the tours
had done much to cement his own popularity. There were awards for other
members of his staff who had been closely involved with the Royal Tour
though not as many as Buchan had originally hoped. He had recommended
either a KCMG or KCVO for both Mackenzie and Redfern, which he knew
would help Redfern in securing a governorship after his tour of duty in
Canada, and asked for an MVO for Joan Pape.

On June 8 the King and Queen arrived in Washington. Buchan felt the trip
had been a success. He wrote to Neville Chamberlain:

> It will take a long time to realize the full effects. Some are obvious. French
> Canada has gone slightly mad on the subject, for its deep-seated traditional
> royalism has now been given a concrete object about which to centre. The
> Canadians have been made to feel their essential unity as a people, and this
> will do much to break down the stubborn provincialism which is our beset-
> ting sin. But most important, the new status of the Empire had been made
> clear to everybody. The Statute of Westminster is now much more than a
> mere piece of paper, for we have been give a visual revelation of its
> meaning.[28]

He put it more simply to the King himself: 'It is a pleasant saying in the United
States at the moment that you have taken the 'g' out of kingship.'[29]

Buchan was impressed with the new King and his wife. He wrote to Anna:
'We have all fallen deeply in love with their Majesties. She has a kind of gentle,
steady radiance which is very wonderful, and he is simply one of the best
people in the world. I never thought that I should feel the romantic affection
for my sovereign that I feel for him.' To Victor Cazalet he confessed of his long
chats with the King: 'I daily get more impressed by his sagacity and balance.

It is very nice to feel for one's monarch not only an intellectual loyalty but a personal affection.'[30] So pleased was Buchan with the tour as a means to fostering national unity that he proposed to Mackenzie King that he, Buchan, write a pamphlet for children on the significance of the Royal Visit. He estimated an edition of 20,000 copies of 8,000 words with twelve photos could be produced for £70 and the decision was given to go ahead and sell the pamphlet through the Government Stationery Department. However there is no record that the pamphlet was ever produced.

As GovernorGeneral Buchan, who had always taken a close interest in education, realized that it was essential to improve the educational system. In December 1938 he had proposed to the President of McGill, Dr Lewis Douglas, the setting up of a Universities Commission because 'there is a great deal of duplication, and there is a real need of a levelling up in certain directions.' Soundings were taken from headmasters to ensure that pupils were taught to common university entrance standards and proposals made that certain universities should specialize in particular subjects.[31]

During the spring there were visits from Gertrude Lawrence, Carola Oman and Stanley Baldwin and in the summer from Anna and Walter who then went north to greet Johnnie, now fully rid of the dysentery amoeba, on the completion of his year's posting at the Hudson Bay Company, Cape Dorset. 'I expected someone jungly and burly', Buchan told Lord Crawford, 'but found an elegant young man in a respectable flannel suit with an OE tie.'[32] Throughout that summer war grew ever closer. Two of the ADCs, Robin Scott and David Walker, left. Scott joined the Navy and Walker, who had just married, rejoined his regiment the Black Watch. WillisO'Connor thought it best that Walker travel back under a civilian identity in case he was captured and, accordingly, he was despatched to Perth as a salesman of ladies underwear.

As German troops moved into Poland at the beginning of September, Buchan wrote to Stair: 'The skies seemed to have darkened and today it does not look as if war could be averted. Hitler, both from his behaviour and his words, seems to have become a purely pathological case – a certifiable lunatic. What a tragedy that the world should be at the mercy of an inflamed and crackedbrain peasant.' He continued: 'I suppose my principal duty will be to consult with my Prime Minister and to fly about the country reviewing troops . . . We are paying the penalty of our blind idealism of twenty years ago; but after all, it is better to be a fool than a rogue!'[33] When he heard that Hugh Macmillan, his former wartime assistant, had been appointed head of the Ministry of Information he offered the benefit of his experience and American contacts. He stressed the importance of facts rather than propaganda, the need to fight the military and naval 'passion for babyish secrecy', and suggested that Ferris Greenslet among others be given a watching brief on American opinion. He also pressed the services of his son William, who had been working for a newsgathering service, The Imperial Policy Group, claiming the boy had been recently doing semi-official Intelligence work in Europe. The general worries of the war were amplified by having three sons eligible for military service. Both Johnnie and Alastair had enlisted and been made temporary ADCs, John in the Guards and Alastair in the Cavalry though, in fact both were working in the Intelligence Department. On 11 September, Buchan was awakened after midnight to formally declare war, on behalf of Canada, on Germany. He wrote resignedly to Edward Harkness: 'this is the third world war I have been in, in a comparatively short life, and no one could hate the horrible thing more than I do.'[34]

Frustrated with his principal roles of 'reviewing troops, visiting industrial plants and presiding over various patriotic funds and organizations', Buchan suggested to Roosevelt that he slip down to Hyde Park while getting medical advice in New York. He added: 'I greatly sympathize with the difficulties of your own position at the moment.' Roosevelt waited a month to reply and then wrote that he was 'torn between a great personal desire to have you and Lady Tweedsmuir visit us at Hyde Park and the problem of the position of the United States in regard to the so-called neutrality laws.' He pointed out that Buchan could not 'slip down inconspicuously' and added 'I am almost literally walking on eggs and, having delivered my message to the Congress, and having good prospects of the bill going through, I am at the moment saying nothing, seeing nothing and hearing nothing.'[35]

In mid-October the call came when his old friend Philip Kerr, now Lord Lothian and British Ambassador in Washington, asked if the two could meet secretly. They did so when Buchan was in New York for medical treatment the following week. Buchan took the opportunity to sound out opinion about America's attitude towards the war in political, financial and media circles. He was keen to keep Canadian morale high and help Roosevelt in his dealings with Congress and he therefore proposed to Alec Hardinge that the Queen make a monthly broadcast to the Empire and to Chamberlain that Britain issue a 'solemn appeal' about the purpose of the war. Shortly after war broke out Buchan had attempted to do that himself in a speech to the Canadian Legion at the Chateau Laurier:

we are fighting for more than democracy. Democracy is only a system of Government, a system of Government which happens to suit us exceedingly well and which we want to perpetuate. But we are fighting for something greater than a system of Government. We are fighting for the liberties of the individual, the right to live freely. We are fighting for the morality and religion in which we have been brought up. We are fighting for human decencies. There never was a war entered into with a more solemn purpose.[36]

Chamberlain was reluctant however to commit himself to a statement of war aims given the rapidly changing events. Buchan persisted, pointing out that: 'America does not want any statement of detailed war aims, which is impossible at the moment; but a general statement of purpose would have an enormous effect, and would greatly strengthen the hands of our sympathizers.' He went on to propose the setting up of 'a federal system, which would begin by including all the Powers who accept the Reign of Law', but Chamberlain was not having it.[37]

It was a theme Buchan had already raised with Roosevelt and now took up with the King. In a letter of 8 November he wrote:

I should like to see a declaration by the Allies that any peace would not be a dictated peace, but one negotiated with the assistance of the best neutral opinion. Indeed, I should be inclined to go further and suggest the need of some federation of all countries that accepted the reign of law – a true federation, not like the League of Nations, which was a jumble of the most diverse politics involving no surrender of any national sovereignty. Such a declaration would give some comfort to the wiser elements in Germany, and it would greatly impress the United States, who regards herself as the chief expert in federation.[38]

In reply, Alexander Hardinge, the King's private secretary, expressed his surprise that Buchan was 'flirting with the idea of a Federation as one of our peace aims, which will involve some surrender of National Sovereignty! You are indeed a great idealist! I have little doubt that this is the right solution for Europe, but I am afraid that there is little chance of it being accepted in our life-time.'[39] Buchan was less than candid in his response, claiming:

I am not really a federation enthusiast. I think that something of the kind will be necessary in certain parts of Europe, particularly the Danube basin, and we may work our way towards ultimate federation with the Western Democracies. But it will take a long time, and it will have to be gone about with great discretion. I am very much against any attempt to specify details now.[40]

In fact he had already been in touch with the American lawyer Grenville Clark, whose ideas on federation he had adapted, and had circulated a memorandum to among others Gilbert Murray. These proposals for a federal Europe were but extensions of his youthful suggestions of a federated empire now given a new impetus by the declaration of war.

Under the strains of war Buchan's health began to deteriorate. His food was now being carefully weighed and he returned to New York for treatment in mid November. There he continued his talks with important opinion formers, including lunch with journalists on the *New York Times* and an evening with John D. Rockefeller. Meanwhile Susie went to the Metropolitan, the Natural History Museum and saw two plays; 'an amusing Philadelphia farce with Katharine Hepburn' and 'a very grim and Ibsenish affair with Miss Tallulah Bankhead'. They both returned to entertain two old friends at Rideau, Duff Cooper and his wife Diana.[41] One ray of sunshine that autumn was the announcement of William's engagement to Nesta Crozier. The wedding was held at Elsfield at the end of October with Brian Fairfax-Lucy as best man and Anna, Walter and 'Tin' Grosvenor as guests. Buchan wrote to his sister when he heard the news: 'They are a touching little pair, but Nesta seems to be the right kind of person for a poor man's wife and I am certain her companionship will make a great difference to William who is a lonely soul.'[42]

Buchan had increasingly given some thought to his future. He told Charles Dick:

There has been a great deal of talk of my doing another five years out here, and a great deal of pressure, but I have decided against it. I talked to the King on the matter when he was here, and he was of my view. My term of office has been so individual and idiomatic that I do not want my doings to become precedents, for that would seriously embarrass my successor. So unless the bottom goes out of the world I will be going home about September 1940.[43]
His writing projects were now almost complete. He told Violet Markham at the end of November: 'I have been amusing myself with writing a kind of spiritual autobiography – a record of how different stages in my life have affected me.' By 14 December he was able to tell Walter: 'I have finished my book of Reminiscences and shall very soon finish my Canadian Puck of Pook's Hill and also my novel. Early in the New Year I must begin the sad business of touring the country and saying farewell.'[44]

During January 1940 he worked hard to enlist the support of Gilbert Murray, Viscount Cecil and others for a post-war federation which he stipulated should have a simple and easily understood working mechanism, a common political philosophy and in which the United States of America would take a leading role. He took as his models the British Empire and America in what could be argued was a forerunner of NATO and the European Community. At the same time he was attempting to interest the millionaire head of General Motors, Sam McLaughlin, in creating a new centre of film making in British Columbia. This scheme for a Hollywood of the North had the support of among others the actors Cedric Hardwicke, Ronald Colman and Charles Laughton. The war and Nazi threat had concentrated Buchan's mind on certain basic values and brought him back to his Liberal roots. After reading Morley's *Life of Gladstone* he wrote to Gilbert Murray, H.A.L. Fisher and Stair Gillon that he was becoming 'a Gladstonian Liberal'. Having revolted against what he saw as 'platitudes' he now admitted 'it is just those platitudes about which the world must be again convinced.'[45]

Thought was now actively being given to his successor as Governor-General. The subject had been discussed the previous May when a number of candidates had been broached including the present Lord Chamberlain, the Earl of Airlie, and Lord Athlone, the Governor-General of South Africa. On 26 January Buchan again put forward Athlone, who had been considered for Canada five years previously. 'The work would be very light in time of war,' he wrote to Hardinge. 'He and Princess Alice have a great reputation for their work in South Africa, and in Canada's present mood of exuberant royalism a connection of the King would be especially welcome.'[46]

There were some encouraging signs too that Buchan's health was improving and he had hopes that when he returned to Britain there might be a new official role for him, perhaps to do with propaganda. He told his eldest son at the end of January: 'I think my own health is a little better, and I am putting on a certain amount of weight. It is a slow business, but I have little to complain of, compared with many people.'[47] On 5 February he wrote to Anna: 'have finished my novel and my autobiography, and am almost at the end of my children's book about Canada. This will leave me with a clear field for farewells this summer.' It had been intended that he would begin his farewell tour in March but it was not to be.[48]

While taking his morning bath the next day, a Tuesday, he slipped and struck the back of his head on the side of the bath. For an hour he lay undiscovered, bloody and unconscious. It appeared a clot had formed on his brain due to low blood pressure. After he was found he immediately underwent emergency surgery in Government House. Within twenty four hours he had regained consciousness and the use of his paralysed arm and was able to talk to family and friends but a secondary development of pressure had taken place.

At 6.00 p.m. on the 8th Redfern sent a cypher telegram to Hardinge: 'Governor-General's condition very serious. His doctors do not expect him to last more than a few hours.'[49] The next day an emergency trepanning of the skull was carried out at Government House by a brain surgeon, Dr Wilder Penfield, assisted by Buchan's personal physician, Dr Gordon Gunn, and Dr Jonathan Meakins, the latter having driven in a snow storm from Montreal. A channel in the skull was cut and fluid drained to relieve pressure on the brain. That afternoon a special train took Buchan to the Neurological Institute in Montreal where a second cranial operation was performed that evening.

Redfern cabled Hardinge at 6.00 p.m. that evening 'Condition of Governor-General substantially unchanged although there is slight movement of extremities this morning after paralysis had become general yesterday. Head operation being performed now to relieve pressure if any. Heart strong. Temperature normal.' The next day, Saturday, Redfern was able to tell Hardinge there had been a slight improvement in Buchan's condition and there was a chance of recovery.[50] On the Sunday afternoon a third operation, lasting four hours, took place with blood donated by Alastair, a McGill medical student and a Montreal policeman. By this time Buchan's accident had become public knowledge and the country was being kept informed of his medical progress. Flowers, which Susan asked to be distributed in the public wards, had begun to arrive in large quantities. The initial prognosis was good. Penfield later recounted how 'after the third desperate operation he was again beginning to move the extremities of both sides and we thought we saw him entering a safe harbour. Then came the embolism from an unsuspected source and with it a sudden end to it all.'[51]

The telegram sent to Bank House at 8.10 p.m. that night said it all – 'John died in perfect peace at 7.13 this evening.' The King, who had been kept informed of every development and had been told of Buchan's death, immediately telegraphed Susan: 'His loss will be widely mourned and his name, both as an eminent author and a distinguished Governor-General long remembered and esteemed.'[52] Seven days of State mourning were declared and flags were flown at half-mast. Buchan's body was brought back by special train to Ottawa on the Tuesday, where it was met by Mackenzie King. On 14 February two services were held. The first at the Montreal Neurological Institute was led by the doctors who had fought to save the Governor-General's life. Jonathan Meakins in his address spoke of how 'I have often heard it said that he was frail – yes, perhaps frail as a rapier is, compared to a battle axe. There was that fineness of quality of Toledo steel in things physical, mental and spiritual.'[53]

Buchan's state funeral was at St Andrew's Church where only the week before he had read the lesson. Some of his favourite hymns and music were played – the Dead March from Handel's *Saul*, 'O God of Bethel' to the Salzburg tune, 'I vow to thee my country', the psalm 'To the Hills' and Beethoven's *Marche Funèbre*. In his sermon, the Reverend Alexander Fergusson recalled: 'When, just over four years ago, Lord Tweedsmuir stepped ashore at Quebec he was to us an official . . . Today all Canada mourns him as a friend. There is not a home amongst us that is not saddened by his passing, nor a heart that does not sorrow with his gracious wife and family because so rare a spirit has fled.'[54] Outside the church as the bands played 'Abide With Me' the coffin was placed on an open gun carriage and drawn by ratings of the Royal Canadian Naval Volunteer Reserve the funeral cortege walked to Union Station. As the train pulled out for Montreal there was a nineteen-gun salute in what the *Ottawa Journal* called 'a fitting end to Lord Tweedsmuir's splendid life'.[55]

In a small grey stone building overlooking the Mount Royal cemetery he was cremated. Only Susan, Alastair, Redfern and a few private mourners were present. At the end of February his ashes were returned to Britain on board HMS *Orion* where they were met by Vincent Massey and Johnnie and William Buchan. They were taken to Elsfield and buried in a corner of the churchyard. They lie under a headstone designed by Herbert Baker with a Latin inscription of Dougal Malcolm roughly translated as: 'Here, in his own earth, lies a man of letters, who served his country and enjoyed the affection of countless friends.' Nearby lies buried the loyal Amos Webb who had suffered a stroke at almost exactly the same time as his master.

> Grant me the happy moorland peace;
> That in my heart's depth ever lie
> That ancient land of sea and sky
> Where the old rhymes and stories fall
> In kindly soothing pastoral.
> There in the hills grave silence lies,
> And Death himself wears friendly guise;
> There be my lot, my twilight stage,
> Dear city of my pilgrimage.
>
> John Buchan 1898.

16

BUCHAN'S LEGACY

BUCHAN'S literary estate for the purposes of death duties took some time to sort out. There were twenty six books currently in print with Houghton Mifflin and over thirty with Hodder. Outstanding Hodder contracts included five novels (advances of £750 each), another untitled biography (£2,000), a book on William the Conqueror (£2,000) and *The Delight of Fishing* (£700). His literary agent Alexander Watt, on the basis of his earnings over the previous three years, estimated the literary estate to be worth just under £20,000 but this figure was then lowered to £11,000.[1]

In his will prepared at Ardura on the Isle of Mull, and dated 31 July 1927, Buchan had made over half of his estate to Johnnie with the rest divided between Susan and the three other children. There were a number of special requests. The National Library of Scotland were to have all his books dealing with the Marquis of Montrose and Anna money due under a life assurance policy taken up in 1901. An addendum was added ten weeks later giving copyright of his books to Johnnie and another in October 1933, a few months after Alice's marriage, whereby her annual annuity of £400 was to be replaced on Buchan's death by a lump sum of £10,000 and she was to have no further claim on his estate. When finally calculated the estate came to £24,513 which rose to £28,685 when account was taken of his shares, copyrights and the household furnishings at Elsfield.

Susan returned to Elsfield and lived there until 1954 when the house was sold and she moved to Burford. Over the next fifteen years she published a series of historical novels, including *Cousin Harriet* (1957), *Dashbury Park* (1959) and *A Stone in the Pool* (1961), some children's books, a social history *The Edwardian Lady* (1966) and several volumes of memoirs such as *The Lilac and the Rose* (1952) and *A Winter Bouquet* (1954). She died in 1977 aged ninety five. Anna and Walter Buchan continued to live at Bank House until their deaths in 1948 and 1953.

All the Buchan children inherited their father's literary gifts but perhaps only after his death did they feel able to exploit them. The second Lord Tweedsmuir had a distinguished war career, commanding the Hastings and Prince Edward Regiment in Sicily and Italy where he was wounded and dec' orated for gallantry. In 1948 he married Priscilla Grant, a war widow who eventually became a Minister of State at the Scottish Office. He himself held a number of distinguished posts including the Rectorship of Aberdeen University and the Chairmanship of the Advertising Standards Authority and published several volumes of memoirs. William Buchan served as a Squadron Leader in the RAF during the war, wrote several well'received novels and held a variety of jobs in public relations and publishing. Alastair Buchan took part in the Dieppe Raid and after the war became a journalist on the *Economist* and *Observer*. After heading the Institute for Strategic Studies and the Royal College of Defence Studies he was appointed Professor of International Relations at Oxford in 1971 and died five years later at the early age of fifty seven. In 1944 Brian Fairfax'Lucy inherited Charlecote, which had been in his family since the twelfth century, and he and Alice devoted the rest of their lives to restoring it. He established a career as a writer of children's books while she wrote several books about the house as well as a biography and two historical novels. They died respectively in 1974 and 1993.

It is sometimes assumed because it was completed only shortly before his death and published posthumously that Buchan began to write his autobiography, *Memory Hold'the'Door* only when he realized he was dying. In fact he had started it in the spring of 1938 and signed a contract with Hodder for both it and a book of angling memoirs during his visit to Britain that July. The fishing book was never finished but the two completed chapters were included at the end of the autobiography as 'Pilgrim's Rest'. He explained in the preface: 'It is not a book of reminiscences in the ordinary sense, for my purpose has been to record only a few selected experiences.' He was writing the book away from his papers and his family and his memory was sometimes faulty. Though broadly in chronological order he also adopted a thematic approach, paying tribute for example to his parents and dead brothers almost at the end of the book.[2]

He chose only to write of the dead. So there are marvellous portraits of Alfred Milner, R.B. Haldane, T.E. Lawrence, Philip Snowden, Douglas Haig, Arthur Balfour and vivid memoirs, often taken directly from *These For Remembrance*, of his dead contemporaries Auberon Herbert, Basil Blackwood and Raymond Asquith. Friends such as Harold Baker, John Edgar, Charles Dick, Stair Gillon and Violet Markham, however, are not mentioned, nor is there more than a brief reference to Baldwin. Ten pages are devoted to his mother and father but there is hardly a reference to his wife and nothing on his daughter. The Cocoa Tree club figures but not 'The Club'. *The Pilgrim's Progress* has several mentions but there is nothing on The Pilgrim Trust. *The Thirty Nine Steps* is passed over in a sentence while the biographies receive four pages. David Daniell has called it 'a curiously oblique book'. That said it is a very revealing one, both consciously and unconsciously. There is much on the influences on his life and work – the Border country, his favourite authors, the Calvinism of his youth, his views on Empire, the joys of mountaineering, his discovery of and love for America, and many of the best passages are descriptions of the Border, Oxford and Canadian countryside and people. There are some witty and amusing anecdotes and some interesting offbeat information. For example he tells of how he tried to persuade Herbert Asquith to write as a rejoinder to Strachey's *Eminent Victorians* a study of John Stuart Mill, Herbert Spencer and John Morley to be called *Three Saints of Rationalism*.

In the preface Buchan described the book as 'a diary of a pilgrimage, a record of the effect upon one mind of the mutations of life' and later added: 'These chapters are meant as a record of how the surface of life has appeared to one pilgrim at different stages.' This sense of pilgrimage was recognized in America where the book was called *Pilgrim's Way* and became J.F. Kennedy's favourite book. In Britain it was published at the end of August 1940 as *Memory Hold The Door*, after being serialized in the *Sunday Times* for the then huge sum of £2,500.[3] The *TLS* devoted a whole page to the autobiography and P.M. Jack in the *New York Times* called it 'a book of great beauty and strength, the book of the year in autobiography, and a distinguished addition to the few first-rate autobiographies in the English language'. Dougal Malcolm, reviewing the book in the *Spectator*, singled out Buchan's 'amazing genius for friendship' which explains the 'wonderful exhibition of portrait sketches' and Hugh Walpole in the *Sunday Times* likewise praised 'its fine ordered and rhythmic prose, its omission of everything extraneous, its sense of atmosphere, and above all . . . its remarkable pictures of the men' he had known. Not all the reviews, however, were good. *The Yale Review* found it 'as dull as any book could be . . . a gallery of unrelated portraits, much incidental description of landscape; and sundry moral reflections.'[4] The book's initial print run of 46,000 copies was almost immediately sold out and it was reprinted nine times in the five months to the end of the year. There were a further nineteen reprints up to the end of 1945, giving some idea of Buchan's continuing popularity for the six years after his death.[5]

At the same time Hodder published *Canadian Occasions*, a collection of forty speeches Buchan had delivered in Canada and which had been scheduled to mark his retirement as Governor-General. The collection included his controversial speech on the importance of Canadians recognizing they were a sovereign people and that they must adopt distinctively Canadian responses to international problems. To coincide with Hodder's publication of *Memory Hold the Door* and *Canadian Occasions* Nelson published a selection of his contributions to The *Scottish Review* under the title *Comments and Characters*. Though some of the essays by then were rather dated they are important in revealing his views, in particular about foreign affairs, in the years preceding the First World War.

'His Excellency is writing a very odd book,' Mrs Killick had told Susan Buchan in the autumn of 1939, 'so unlike him, so introspective.' Buchan's last novel, *Sick Heart River*, is perhaps his most personal and profound, allowing him to articulate his own feelings and doubts in a manner otherwise not open to him. The religious undertones always present in his previous books are here made much more explicit.[6] Sir Edward Leithen is told he has tuberculosis and has only a year to live. At the same time Blenkiron enlists his help in tracing Francis Galliard, his niece's husband and a partner in a New York banking-house. Leithen's journey takes him from New York to Quebec and from the Arctic to the shores of the Mackenzie River. Accompanied by a half-Scots, half-Indian guide, Johnny Frizel, he discovers the French-Canadian Galliard has returned to his roots in flight from worldly success. At the same time Leithen realizes he must find the banker's former travelling companion, and incidentally the brother of Johnny, Lew Frizel. Lew has gone to the Sick Heart, a pastoral sanctuary of green meadows amongst snow-covered mountains, which he believes is a paradise that can save his soul rather like the Garden of Eden. Leithen brings Lew out of Sick Heart River and then collapses. Both men are forced to examine the purpose of their journey into the heart of darkness and both regain the will to live from the experience. On their return they come across an encampment of dying Hare Indians. At first Leithen is unmoved by their plight but the outbreak of war acts as a catalyst and he now feels his duty is to save their lives, even at risk to his own. The book ends with the curing of the Hare Indians and the death of Leithen.

Sick Heart River is Buchan's only Canadian novel and into it he channelled his experiences there over the previous four years. Much of the scenery and a number of characters, such as the Scottish-Indian half-breeds, Hare Indians, Oblate Mission Fathers and Eskimos, were all drawn from his own travels in the country and in particular his trip in the summer of 1937 to the Arctic. The Galliard farm in Quebec in the book was inspired by a similar spot glimpsed from an aeroplane and the descriptions of the Arctic in winter came from Johnnie Buchan's own time with the Hudson Bay Company.[7] Many of the ubiquitous Buchan themes are present – the power exerted by place, the redemptive quality of the wild, the happy band of brothers here dedicated to saving individual lives rather than the Empire, the notion that privilege must be earned. One of the strongest themes of the book is success and the purpose of life. At the beginning of the book Leithen attends a dinner party that is remarkable for the distinction of the guests. Leithen as Attorney General is ostensibly among the most successful present but his terminal illness forces him to reconsider his priorities. His experiences in the wilds have shown him that 'man is nothing and God is all' so that his journey becomes, like that of many of Buchan's characters, a spiritual as well as physical one. Lewis Haystoun found redemption through death on the North-West Frontier, Leithen now finds it in the Canadian North.

The emptiness of success was a theme that Buchan had been exploring in his writing since his time at Oxford and which formed the basis of his short story 'Fountainblue' published in 1901. It was something that had always perplexed him, divided as he was between his romantic Covenanting nature and his Calvinist upbringing, between his sense of duty and his instinctive distrust of ambition. It was a subject that had particularly exercised him after the death of his mother and as he realized his health would not now permit him to continue to serve in government at the highest level. It has always been assumed that the fictitious character most closely resembling Buchan himself is Leithen and this is particularly true in *Sick Heart River* where the ascetic and introspective Leithen becomes more and more like his creator in character, upbringing and physique. Leithen's memories of the Borders, Oxford, holidays on Exmoor and the Dolomites are those of Buchan and it is a Buchan poem that Leithen quotes as his own.[8] *Sick Heart River* was serialized in *Blackwood's Magazine* between October 1940 and its publication in April 1941. The American edition, with an introduction by Howard Swiggett, was published under the title *Mountain Meadow*.[9]

Buchan's own enthusiasm for Canada and its history was something he wanted to share with Canadians. *The Long Traverse*, published as *Lake of Gold* in Canada and America and originally to be called *La Claire Fontaine*, was an attempt to give Canadian children a more vivid picture of their country's past than they generally received in the classroom, what he described as a Canadian *Puck of Pook's Hill*. The Long Traverse is a journey into Canada's past by a young boy, Donald, guided by an old Indian guide who is able to make the boy see historical events. Donald witnesses the hardships of the early explorers and settlers, the activities of the Hudson's Bay and North-West

Companies, the lives of the fur-traders and Eskimos. Buchan started writing
it at the beginning of 1938 and it remained unfinished at his death so Susan
added an epilogue. The book was published in 1941 but had only sold 15,000
of the 25,000 print run by the following spring when the price was reduced.
In 1964 part of it was adapted and set to music as an 'orchestral-choral fanta-
sia'.

At the beginning of 1942 Susan wrote to John Edgar asking for copies of
letters from her husband. 'I have had several requests from publishers for a life
of John to be written sometime, because *Memory-Hold-the-Door* left so much
unsaid. 'The result was *The Clearing House: A Survey of One Man's Mind*, a
selection of Buchan's writings arranged by Susan, with an introduction by
Gilbert Murray and which Hodder published in 1946. It consisted of almost
a hundred extracts from his essays, novels, poems and biographical works and
while giving a flavour of his work was rather unsatisfying.[10] Susan followed
this in 1947 with two books. The first, a sixty page booklet, *Life's Adventure*,
consisted of another collection of extracts from Buchan's writings grouped
under subject headings such as 'Youth', 'Courage' and 'The End of the
Road'. The second, *John Buchan By His Wife and Friends*, included a long essay
about their married life with contributions from A.L. Rowse, G.M.
Trevelyan, Catherine Carswell and Alastair Buchan, on different facets of
Buchan's life. Over 30,000 copies were printed and it sold reasonably well,
though a rueful note on the Hodder royalty ledger admitted the print run may
have been too high. 'It was embarked on in a wave of enthusiasm and there is
some indication that the reign of books about Buchan may be petering out.'[11]
Anna Buchan's own account of their childhood, *Unforgettable, Unforgotten*,
had appeared in 1945 and a short biography, based on a doctorate, by Arthur
Turner followed four years later but otherwise critical interest in Buchan
seemed to have lapsed.

The publication of Richard Usborne's *Clubland Heroes* in 1953 was the
beginning of the critical reaction to Buchan. In it, Usborne considered the
nineteen 'shockers', equating them with the prewar jollies of Dornford Yates
and Sapper. Usborne, writing with irony, levelled many of the charges that
would come to stick, in particular accusing Buchan of worshipping success
and portraying women as boyish.

In October 1955 the John Buchan collection at Queens University,
Kingston, Ontario was formally opened. It had come to Queens, after the sale
of Elsfield, through the intervention of the Rector Dr Leonard Brockington.
The gifts included a bronze bust of Buchan, his writing desk and library step-
ladder and some 3,500 of his books. The following year Penguin marked its
twenty first birthday by reissuing ten Buchan novels with an unattributed

introduction by William Buchan – *The Three Hostages, The Thirty–Nine Steps, The Island of Sheep, Greenmantle, Huntingtower, Mr Standfast, John Macnab, Castle Gay, House of the Four Winds, Prester John.* Critical reaction was generally favourable, though Robertson Davies writing in *Saturday Night* struck a jarring note: 'Frankly, I never liked these books very much when I first read them as a boy, and looking them over again I like them even less . . . the characters are thin and elusive; I cannot care what happens to them because I am never permitted to know them.'[12]

Gertrude Himmelfarb published an important article in *Encounter* in September 1960 entitled: 'John Buchan: an untimely appreciation,' which she later modified as 'John Buchan: the last Victorian' in her 1968 book *Victorian Minds.* In her two essays Himmelfarb argued that Buchan was 'the last articulate representative of the old England', citing such tell-tale signs as the casual bravery of his heroes and the implicit view that 'looks upon politics, espionage, and war alike as an opportunity to practise good English sportsmanship'.[13] She argued, as Buchan had himself admitted in his memoirs, that he was out of touch with the post First World War mood in both politics and literature. But she expertly defended Buchan against the various charges made against him – the cult of success, imperialism, racism and anti-Semitism. She concluded that the unpopularity of Buchan's work in intellectual circles was 'the sense of a temperament and mentality that is inimical to the prevailing "liberal imagination" . . . Buchan – Calvinist in religion, Tory in politics, and romantic in sensibility – is obviously the antithesis of the liberal.'[14]

The Oxford don, M.R. Ridley's 'A misrated author?' in his collection of essays *Second Thoughts*, published in 1965, was another crucial stage in the rehabilitation of Buchan as a serious literary figure. In it Ridley stressed Buchan's ability to describe scenery, his excellent prose style, the quality of his biographies as well as his novels, his strength as a writer about Scotland.

The first and only full biography of Buchan appeared twenty five years after his death. Its author, Janet Adam Smith, had already written an acclaimed life of R.L. Stevenson and was herself steeped in the world Buchan had known. Her father had collaborated with Buchan on his history of the Church of Scotland and as a student she had come up to Elsfield. She brought to her biography an instinctive sympathy for Buchan and his work and, understandably given her friendship with Susan, who helped her extensively, the book was highly favourable to him. There are hints between the lines of tensions within the family and the unremittingly high expectations Buchan had of his children but her main emphasis was on Buchan the public servant and story teller rather than the family man. The book draws on the memories of his contemporaries and for that alone the book would be highly valuable. Buchan was lucky in his biographer for Adam Smith wrote with great perception, in particular, about Buchan's debt and contribution to Scotland. Her literary judgements are sensible, her narrative pace good and her central thesis clear. She took six years researching and writing the book and within the limitations of what was then known about Buchan it is a highly impressive work which remains fresh and authoritative thirty years after it was published.

Raymond Mortimer in the *Sunday Times* thought it 'scholarly and sympathetic, though not uncritical', *Punch* 'a very good book indeed' while the Earl of Birkenhead in the *Daily Telegraph* called it 'an admirable book, carefully researched and readable at every point throughout its 500 pages.' John Gross in the *Observer* argued that she had been too sympathetic in particular in differentiating between careerism and honourable ambition and had taken Buchan too seriously. '. . . one of the main reasons for enjoying Buchan is because he is so preposterous. The tuppence-coloured rhetoric and the bluff characterisation are an essential part of the appeal.' Gross personally was more interested in the books than in the minor statesman for 'they continue to tantalise while his more solemn achievements fade.'[15]

One of the most interesting and thoughtful reviews of the book came from Simon Raven in the *Spectator* who thought Adam Smith had been too defensive about her subject. He admitted it was easy to criticize Buchan's 'smugness, his cult of the open air, his do-gooding and his self-deception' and also 'his devout biographer, with her wholesome approval, her earnest chronicle of endeavour, and her glum evasions when anything nasty needs to be said.' He felt that the biography's significance was as 'a fascinating study in cultural ambiguity: for the first Lord Tweedsmuir . . . was a very odd fish indeed.'[16] Raven thought:

> the most bizarre and entertaining of all Buchan's characteristics (was) his obsessive love-hate of the Devil . . . residual Calvinism gave strength to Buchan's vision, while a classical education lent an additional and highly personal insight: the trouble was that this Evil was often beautiful, damned but genuinely beautiful, and therefore insidiously attractive even to solid citizens like John Buchan.[17]

Adam Smith's biography did much to change the perception of Buchan as a writer at a time when Hannay looked very unfashionable in comparison with the anti-heroes of John Le Carre and Eric Ambler. When Ambler wrote an article in *Books and Bookmen* in 1962 claiming 'John Buchan wrote little better than Boys'-Own-Paper stuff' people were quick to come to Buchan's defence.[18] Buchan, however, remained a writer easily if affectionately

sent up as he was in Beachcomber's story 'The Queen of Minikoi' and Alan
Bennett's highly successful 1968 satirical play *Forty Years On*. Leithen, Sandy
and Hannay are discussing the villain:

> Sane? He is brilliantly sane. The second sanest in Europe. But like all sane
> men he has at one time or another crossed that thin bridge that separates
> lunacy from insanity. And this last week the pace has quickened. Else
> explain why a highly respected Archbishop of Canterbury, an interna-
> tional hairdresser and a very famous king all decide to take simultaneous
> holidays on the Black Sea.[19]

Alan Sandison's *Wheel of Empire*, published in 1967, was subtitled 'A
Study of the Imperial Idea in some Late Nineteenth and Early Twentieth-
Century Fiction'. In the book Sandison looked at four writers – Rider
Haggard, Rudyard Kipling, Joseph Conrad and John Buchan – whose books
he argued had reflected and shaped the popular perception of the British
Empire. He identified how the imperial idea appealed to Buchan with its
concept of 'service and sacrifice, duty and trust, clear purpose and exemplary
conduct.' Far from being outdoor relief for the younger sons of the aristocracy
it became the Church of Scotland on safari. He argued that Buchan's view of
empire changed, increasingly investing it 'with an altogether ecclesiastical significance'.[20]

Richard Usborne returned to the fray with a revised version of *Clubland
Heroes* in 1974, in which he modified many of his initial charges. On the
centenary of Buchan's birth in 1975 the National Library of Scotland
mounted an exhibition on him and Nelson published David Daniell's *The
Interpreter's House*, the first detailed study of Buchan's novels. He was the first
critic to analyse Buchan's debt to the literature of the seventeenth century and
to demonstrate the recurring themes throughout the Buchan oeuvre. Daniell
skilfully demonstrated Buchan's ability to evoke landscape and how he assimilated his wide reading, 'developing into the writer of a clean, bare, narrative
style where literary references have been truly assimilated.'[21]

Some commentators, however, still remained unconvinced about Buchan's
merits as a writer. The jazz musician, Benny Green, used the opportunity of a
review of Daniell's book in the *Spectator* to mount a spirited attack on Buchan,
arguing he was a snob, parochial, had little understanding of women and was
weak on narrative:

> Like Churchill, for instance, he believed in the sanctity of the Anglo-
> Saxon mission; like Macaulay, he was utterly sincere and indomitably pro-

vincial in foisting off English culture on the locals, whoever they happened to be; like Belloc, he suspected Jews of subversion; like half the games masters in the Empire, he thought that cold baths and long walks in the heather were better calculated to boost a fellow's religiosity than a roll in the clover.[22]

Bernard Richards, in a shrewd essay 'John Buchan's Aesthetic Consciousness' published in 1976 in the Brasenose College Magazine, drew attention to Buchan's fascination with the motif of the Scholar Gipsy, his associations with the *Yellow Book* and interest in Walter Pater to argue that an important undercurrent in Buchan's writings up to and especially in *Sick Heart River* is a 'critical, dispassionate even alienated aesthetic consciousness'.[23]

In March 1979, the Buchan Society was formally inaugurated with a one day seminar at Edinburgh University. It consisted of a series of lectures on Buchan's life and work followed by a showing of *The Thirty-Nine Steps*. The Society was the brainchild of Eileen Stewart, who had just completed a PhD thesis on the themes of frontiers in Buchan's work and quickly drew the support of members of the Buchan family. The Society saw its role as encouraging interest in Buchan's life and art and specifically as working towards reissues of Buchan's books and if possible a complete annotated edition. It produces a scholarly journal and amongst its activities organizes an annual dinner and weekend conference. In the same year two new books appeared on Buchan. Buchan's daughter Alice produced a memoir, *A Scrap Screen*, which shed new light on his relationship with his family and Janet Adam Smith compiled a picture book *John Buchan and his World*.

Daniell's two volumes of Buchan's short stories, published in 1980 and 1982, were another important step in the re-evaluation of Buchan as a writer. All the short story collections had hitherto been out of print, the early volumes for over fifty years. Hugh Greene, reviewing the first of the collections, was surprised to discover that only four Buchan titles were in print and wondered why 'Buchan's books are so neglected today, in spite of films and television'.[24] He singled out *The Power House*, *Greenmantle*, *Prester John* and *Salute to Adventurers* as 'among the best of their kind ever written. There are others nearly as good. Buchan's writing provides a touchstone by which to judge the thriller writers of today and very few pass the test.' He added: 'I wish I could believe that the appearance of this book heralds, and will encourage, a return of interest in Buchan's work. But I doubt it.' Alan Bold, writing in the *Scotsman* about the second volume was equally puzzled. 'As time passes it is increasingly obvious that Buchan is a classic whose work does not date but deepens in retrospect.'[25]

The publication in the same year of 'a memoir, a personal recollection' of his father by Buchan's son William helped sustain the recovery in Buchan's fortunes. This was particularly so, given the affection and warmth with which William Buchan depicted his father, whom he succeeded in portraying as a man and father rather than the successful politician and writer of Janet Adam Smith's biography. Paul Scott, writing in the New Edinburgh Review thought it 'a delightful and rewarding book, which gives a fresh and indelible picture of John Buchan as a man.'[26]

Throughout the 1980s, with the growth of Scottish studies and expansion of Scottish publishing, Buchan's work came to be both re-evaluated and more widely available, helped by the fact that the Scottish Arts Council were prepared to subsidize the publication of indigenous literature. In 1985 Janet Adam Smith's biography was reissued by OUP with a new preface stressing the success of his Canadian sojourn and later that year, to mark the fiftieth anniversary of his appointment as Governor-General, the National Library in Ottawa held an exhibition devoted to his time in Canada. The fiftieth anniversary of Buchan's death in February 1990 was marked by extensive coverage. Michael Coren in the *Sunday Times* admitted that in the years since his death 'Buchan's reputation has suffered badly at the hands of success and successors. Risible adaptations of his books in famous feature films, a miasma of anti-Semitic accusations surrounding his opinions and theories, and indifference from the literary *savants*, have left us with a portrait of a somewhat misanthropic hack writer with political aspirations.'[27] In *The Times*, Dudley Fishburn argued he was 'a writer whose time has come again', while William Deedes thought his novels had eternal fascination. 'Buchan's favourite theme, repeated in several of his novels, was how thin our protective layer of civilization is. That strikes me as wholly contemporaneous.'[28]

In the years after his death Buchan's work continued to be adapted for both radio and television, much of it for children's programmes. In May 1950 the BBC proposed to produce a radio portrait of 'John Buchan: the man and his books' followed by an adaptation of *Midwinter* aimed at children of 13 to 15; but nothing seems to have come of the proposal. In June 1952 C.A. Lejeune adapted *The Three Hostages* for six weekly half hour television episodes. Two years later 'a radio impression' of *Witch Wood* was produced with Ian Cuthbertson as Will Rollo alongside a television adaptation of the book. In the spring of 1955 a biographical portrait of Buchan, 'Border hills and African veldt', was put together by Margaret Miller. Two years later *Huntingtower* was adapted for television in six episodes and in February 1960 *The Three Hostages* transmitted as a reading serial for radio in an adaptation by R.J.B. Sellar. In November 1962 the BBC produced 'The Childhood of John Buchan'.

The publication of Janet Adam Smith's biography in the autumn of 1965 stimulated a new interest. In January 1966 Stewart Conn produced eight hour long weekly episodes of *The Island of Sheep* for the radio, and that was followed later in the year by a two part radio programme on Buchan's life. In April 1967 there was a radio programme on 'The John Buchan Country: Up Manor Water and Down Tweed' and the next month five readings from *The Runagates Club*. In November 1972 Joan Bakewell talked to Susan Buchan, then aged eighty four, about Buchan for a programme, 'Times Remembered', and the following year Alastair Buchan paid his own radio tribute.

There were a number of programmes in August 1975 to mark the centenary of Buchan's birth and the publication of the first critical study of Buchan's writing, David Daniell's *The Interpreter's House*. Susan, Alastair and Johnnie appeared alongside Janet Adam Smith and Owen Dudley Edwards in a Radio 3 programme, there was a biographical portrait entitled 'The Archetypal Lad o'Pairts', Benny Green appeared on 'Stop the Week' to discuss 'John Buchan's Snobbery', Radio 4 dramatized *Witch Wood* and the 'Book at Bedtime' was *The Power House*. In 1977 *The Three Hostages* was produced for BBC Television with a script by John Prebble and the following year there was a television adaptation of *Huntingtower*. In 1978 Don Sharp directed the third cinema version of *The Thirty-Nine Steps* with Robert Powell as Richard Hannay; the 1950s version starred Kenneth More in the central role. Though closer than the two earlier versions to the book the Powell film still managed to introduce some new plotlines including a climax at Big Ben. Powell subsequently starred in a Thames Television series of Hannay's adventures.

Since then there have been a number of radio adaptations, including a Radio 4 production of *The Island of Sheep* in January 1983, a three part dramatization of *Huntingtower* as the Classic Serial in January 1988, a three part adaptation of *The Thirty Nine Steps* in December 1989 and productions of *Witch Wood* in 1992 and *The Courts of the Morning* in 1993. David Jackson Young's excellent documentary 'In Richard Hannay's Footsteps' was broadcast in the summer of 1992. Several Buchan novels are now available on spoken word cassette, most notably *The Thirty-Nine Steps* and *Witch Wood*. John Buchan was one of the two main themes chosen for the 1991 Borders Festival and five different Buchan productions were mounted – a lecture on 'Buchan in the Borders' by Professor Christopher Harvie, a performance of three of the early short stories, a one man play, *Buchan of Tweedsmuir*, and a dramatization of *Witch Wood*.[29]

'When psychoanalytical novels are cluttering the cellars of secondhand booksellers I am sure that you will live as the supreme storyteller of the age,' wrote Basil Liddell Hart to Buchan from Paris in 1926. Seven years later T.E. Lawrence confided in a letter to Edward Garnett discussing Buchan's novels: 'For our age they mean nothing: they are sport, only: but will a century hence disinter them and proclaim him the great romancer of our blind and unde-serving generation?'[30] The answer seemed to come quicker than even Lawrence realized. Reviewing the 1956 Penguin reissues, Anthony Hartley posed and then answered the same question. 'Will Buchan continue to be read? It seems very doubtful. In the Scandinavian social democracy for which this country is heading, will not the foiling of plots to destroy civilization and the assumption of the white man's burden in spots as far remote as the republic of Evallonia . . . seem impossibly exotic amusements.'[31]

For the next thirty years Buchan remained in critical disfavour but he con-tinued to be read by the public. It seemed that a post-war generation were only too happy to read of the pre-war exploits of Richard Hannay, Edward Leithen and other members of The Thursday Club. Penguin continued to keep many of the titles in print and in the 1990s began to reissue some of the less well-known books. The top seller, out-selling much of their new fiction, was *The Thirty-Nine Steps* at just over 10,000 copies a year followed by *Greenmantle*, *Island of Sheep*, *The Three Hostages* and *Mr Standfast*. The *TLS*, analysing the latest Public Lending Right figures in January 1994, noted that Buchan still managed over 100,000 loans a year, putting him in the same category as Charlotte Bronte, Arthur Conan Doyle, George Eliot, Somerset Maugham, and Virginia Woolf. He had now also become a highly collectable author with first editions of his early books selling for hundreds of pounds and his auto-graph alone worth about £100.[32]

Since his death, Buchan's reputation has continued to grow. His books are now more available than at any time since 1940 and important bibliograph-ical, biographical and critical studies are being carried out on his life and work. Part of this renewed interest in his writing has come not just from liter-ary critics but also from cultural historians studying 'the political linkages they disclose between the late-Victorian novel of imperial adventure and the twentieth-century spy thriller.'[33] He is now regarded as one of the founders of the modern spy story and an influence on subsequent writers such as Ian Fleming and John Le Carré. The latter has scattered several Buchan references in his own novels. In *Tinker, Tailor, Soldier Spy* Jim Prideaux reads Buchan novels, a quotation from *Mr Standfast* is the epigraph to a section in *The Looking Glass War*, while Smiley in *The Honourable Schoolboy* calls himself Mr Standfast. Two of the staples of the spy story, 'the hunted man' and 'the mole within', through ideas that go back to Classical Literature, were popularized in this century by Buchan.

David Daniell has argued that Buchan wrote 'novels with a mixture of surface pace of action, and a deeper density of content which have a timeless quality'. Though the end of the Cold War has reduced interest in the subject of espionage there will always be a market for well-written and exciting stories of adventure. Buchan had a rich imagination and a gift for narrative which combined to create powerful mythical books which have a wide and sustained appeal. The huge sales of his thrillers have, however, tended to overshadow his other literary and political achievements and he has never enjoyed the critical esteem he deserves. As Chesterton once wrote of Stevenson, good writers come in many disguises, even in those of popular and successful ones.[34]

In its obituary of Buchan the *New York Herald Tribune* noted: 'History will have a tough time grading this extraordinary man's many different contributions to the life of his generation, in the order of their importance and excellence . . .' That process of evaluation has been going on for over fifty years and only now, as new papers are being released, are many of his activities as a public servant becoming apparent. Only now in hindsight is the prophetic nature of much of what he wrote being appreciated.[35]

John Buchan was a highly complex and private man who may not always himself have understood his own motivations and abilities. More than most people he was full of contradictions. There are few photographs of Buchan smiling and the popular impression is of a stern, repressed Calvinist driven by a Scottish ambition to rise to the very top of the English Establishment. He seems to be always totally controlled, and a German psychiatrist claimed never to have met anyone before so free of neuroses. Yet Anna Buchan could write of how, every so often, he would start singing songs and tell ridiculous stories. 'We knew him well in this mood. All his life, after long concentration, writing for hours, he would suddenly take what Mother called a "daft turn" and pour forth a stream of nonsense which reduced us all to helpless laughter.' 'What surprised me here was the confiding recklessness of his comments,' the biographer Catherine Carswell later wrote, after lunching with Buchan in the 1930s. 'He stated his personal preferences and distastes with entire lack of caution . . . There was in him a strong spring of youthful imprudence.'[36]

He enjoyed the company of young people and wrote marvellous stories for and about them. Numerous men and women owe much to his support, financial or otherwise, as they were growing up. Perhaps he found in them the lack of cynicism he himself enjoyed, perhaps too he found in them the respect he was denied by some of his own contemporaries. Yet for all the interest he showed other children he often ignored his own. They seemed to disappoint

him and none of them displayed, while he was alive, the talents that subsequently emerged after his death. All four children went on to write books,
some of them exercises in filial piety and devoted to championing the reputation of a father of whom in their youth they had been so critical.

A son of the Manse with strict views on morality, Buchan nevertheless displayed wide and often liberal sympathies. Together with Vera Brittain, T.S.
Eliot, E.M. Forster, Victor Gollancz and Bernard Shaw he signed a letter pro-
testing against the banning of Radclyffe Hall's lesbian novel *The Well of
Loneliness*. Contrary to public perception, he enjoyed alcohol and strong
Turkish cigarettes until ill health forced him to move to a diet of milk and
steamed fish. In spite of the debilitating ulcer from which he suffered for the
last twenty five years of his life, and which would confine him to bed for days
on end, he had enormous physical energy. He loved the outdoors and even in
his sixties could outwalk and outclimb men far younger than himself. As well
as his love of rock climbing and fishing he counted flower arranging, collecting Wedgwood pottery and amateur dramatics among his interests.

In a speech in February 1939 he claimed that if there were six categories
'from highbrow to solid ivory' he placed himself in the third — 'high-
lowbrow.' His literary tastes stretched from Marcel Proust and Sir Walter
Scott to P.G. Wodehouse and Margaret Mitchell's *Gone With The Wind* which
he described to his mother in 1937 as 'the most considerable work of fiction
that has been published in recent years — an astonishing achievement for a first
novel.' In his youth he had been an admirer of the Aesthetic Movement and
contributor to *The Yellow Book*. In middle-age he had been one of the cham-
pions of the Scottish literary revival and admired by among others Hugh
MacDiarmid and Lewis Spence. His literary friends included such different
writers as Henry James, Ezra Pound, Elizabeth Bowen, Virginia Woolf,
Henry Newbolt, J.B. Priestley and Hugh Walpole.

The myth has grown up of Buchan as a successful careerist, a man who rose
from humble Scottish roots to become one of the great imperial servants of his
day. In fact, his background was prosperous middle-class and his life, it could
be argued, was marked not by success but the failure fully to realise the potential of his youth. At Oxford he was already listed in *Who's Who*, was tipped
as a future Prime Minister and had published eight books by the time he left
university. Yet he failed to gain the All Souls Fellowship on which he set his
heart, was unsuccessful first time in his Bar exams, did not secure the posting
to Egypt with Cromer he might have expected, seems to have made little
impact at the Bar and was out-manoeuvred as a wartime civil servant, failing
to receive any award for his work. He was over fifty before he went into
Parliament, bypassed not just by his own contemporaries but also by many of

the undergraduates whom he had helped after he settled at Elsfield. His books brought him financial but not critical success. Desperate to be acknowledged as a politician and biographer he is now principally remembered for books he dismissed as 'tusheries' and largely wrote to put his children through school.

Part of his failure can be ascribed to his ill health, which meant he was often in pain and confined to bed, but there may be two other explanations to account for the fact he never seemed to realize his potential. Firstly that he spread his talents too thinly without sufficient concentration in any one area because he was caught between opposing parts of his personality – the roman- tic and the practical – and secondly that he remained an outsider all his life. In his own writing, Buchan made much of the frontier between romance and realism. It was a frontier he knew well from his own experience. Brought up in Scotland he soon found himself like Richard Hannay as the outsider who had penetrated the English Establishment. He had left his Peebles family when he went to Oxford but the call of the north was always present, often in the still small voice of his mother. Some of his most personal work, most notably his poetry and the biographies, reflect this Scottish side. G.M. Trevelyan thought Buchan's 'divided self' was most evident in the biographies, noting 'the loyal, pious and self-disciplined child of the Manse, and the romantic lover of Scottish history and of the Border country.'

Buchan emerged from the First World War physically and emotionally shattered. Many of his closest friends had been killed and this loss of his immediate circle reinforced his sense of being displaced. He had never been part of fashionable social or literary circles, he had not been a good party polit- ical man and he had found himself regarded as a Scotsman in England and an Englishman in Scotland. In spite of his chameleon nature and ability to adapt to his surroundings he was always seen as the outsider, a characteristic which he gave to many of his fictional heroes. Richard Hannay is a South African mining engineer, Peter Pienaar a Boer hunter, Dickson McCunn a Glasgow grocer – not the conventional heroes of thrillers. Even his historical characters such as Peter Pentecost and Anthony Lammas – the symbolic names are important – reject high positions to return to their modest lives.

At Oxford Buchan was drawn to men who affected a disdain for the very signs of success he craved and in later life he became friendly with figures such as T.E. Lawrence who had turned his back on fame for the quiet life. Many of his characters are successful but are uncomfortable and unhappy with their position. It was a dilemma he himself wrestled with and which may well have, even sublimely, held him back. The range of his interests and abilities meant that he never fully concentrated on one thing with sufficient application. Speaking at a dinner for Ramsay Macdonald in November 1931 he said: 'We

Scots are a strange folk. We despise incompetence, but we do not greatly admire success. Our sentimental allegiance has usually been given to heroic failures, as if we had an instinct that material and worldly standards were not the true measures of value.'

Like his heroes he was constantly torn between public life and private contemplation. Few men or women have equally distinguished themselves in politics and literature because essentially they require different temperaments. Buchan managed partly because he was both a man of action and thought, the scholar gipsy, the scholar adventurer, the Philosopher King. Men like T.E. Lawrence appealed to him because he saw much of himself in Lawrence, as he had seen part of himself at Oxford in Aubrey Herbert. A Calvinist drawn to paganism, an admirer of both Plato and Theocritus, a Romantic Conservative who felt towards the end of his life that he had become a Gladstonian Liberal, Buchan was full of paradoxes. Many of these contradictions he suppressed in his own life and attempted to reconcile in his writing and much of his own personality and views can be found by judicious reading of his books, for as he wrote in his memoirs 'a writer must inevitably keep the best of himself for his own secret creative world.' Any life of Buchan must inevitably turn the reader back to his books which remain as fresh today as when they were first written, almost a century ago.

CHRONOLOGY OF JOHN BUCHAN'S LIFE

1875 John Buchan born at Perth 26 August
1876 Buchan family move to Fife
1877 Anna Buchan born
1880 William Henderson Buchan born
1882 Walter Buchan born
1888 Violet Buchan born and Buchan family move to Glasgow
1888–92 At Hutchesons' Grammar School
1892–95 At Glasgow University
1893 Violet Buchan dies
1894 Alastair Buchan born
1895–99 At Brasenose College, Oxford
1899 President of the Oxford Union and obtains a 'First'
1901 Called to the Bar
1901–03 Lord Milner's Private Secretary in South Africa
1906 Joins Nelson Publishers
1907 Marries Susan Grosvenor
1908 Alice born
1911 Selected as the Unionist Candidate for Peebleshire and Selkirk.
     Reverend John Buchan dies and John Norman Stuart Buchan born
1912 William Henderson Buchan dies
1915 Becomes a war correspondent for *The Times* and *Daily News*
1916 William Buchan born
1917 Appointed Director of Information. Alastair Ebenezer Buchan and
     Tommy Nelson are killed
1918 Alastair Francis Buchan born
1919 Buys Elsfield Manor near Oxford

1923 Becomes Deputy-Chairman of Reuters
1927 Elected Member of Parliament for the Scottish Universities
1932 Created Companion of Honour
1933,1934 Lord High Commissioner to the General Assembly of the
   Church of Scotland
1935 Governor-General of Canada and ennobled as Lord Tweedsmuir of
   Elsfield. *The Thirty-Nine Steps* filmed by Alfred Hitchcock
1937 Elected Chancellor of Edinburgh University and made a Privy
   Councillor. Helen Buchan dies
1939 Invested GCVO after the Royal Tour of Canada
1940 Dies on 12 February

FAMILY TREE OF JOHN BUCHAN

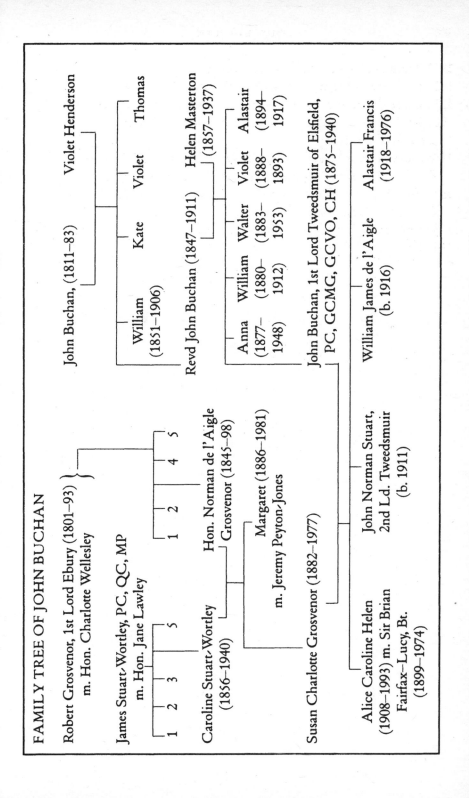

Robert Grosvenor, 1st Lord Ebury (1801–93)
m. Hon. Charlotte Wellesley

John Buchan, (1811–83)
Violet Henderson

William (1851–1906) Kate Violet Thomas

Revd John Buchan (1847–1911)
Helen Masterton (1857–1937)

James Stuart-Wortley, PC, QC, MP
m. Hon. Jane Lawley

1 2

Hon. Norman de l'Aigle Grosvenor (1845–98)

Anna (1877–1948) William (1880–1912) Walter (1883–1953) Violet (1888–1893) Alastair (1894–1917)

Caroline Stuart-Wortley (1856–1940)

1 2 3 4 5

Margaret (1886–1981)
m. Jeremy Peyton-Jones

John Buchan, 1st Lord Tweedsmuir of Elsfield,
PC, GCMG, GCVO, CH (1875–1940)

1 2 3 5

Susan Charlotte Grosvenor (1882–1977)

John Norman Stuart, 2nd Ld. Tweedsmuir (b. 1911)

William James de l'Aigle (b. 1916)

Alastair Francis (1918–1976)

Alice Caroline Helen (1908–1993) m. Sir Brian Fairfax-Lucy, Bt. (1899–1974)

SELECTED LIST OF
JOHN BUCHAN'S BOOKS

(The American title, if different, is given in square brackets.)

1894   – *Essays and Apothegms of Francis Lord Bacon* (edited with introduction)

1895   – *Sir Quixote of the Moors*

1896   – *Scholar Gipsies* (essays): 'Scholar Gipsies', 'April in the Hills,' 'Milestones,' 'May-Fly Fishing', 'The Men of the Uplands,' 'Gentlemen of Leisure,' 'Sentimental Travelling', 'Urban Greenery', 'Nature and the Art of Words', 'Afternoon', 'Night on the Heather', 'On Cademuir Hill', 'An Individualist', 'The Drove Road', 'Nuces Relictae,' 'Ad Astra'.
       Musa Piscatrix (fishing poems and songs)

1897   – *Sir Walter Raleigh* (Stanhope Prize Essay)

1898   – *John Burnet of Barns;*
       The Pilgrim Fathers (Newdigate prize poem)
       Brasenose College

1899   – *Grey Weather* (stories and poems): 'Ballad for Grey Weather', 'Prester John', 'At the Article of Death', 'Politics and the May-Fly', ' A Reputation', 'A Journey of Little Profit', 'At the Rising of the Waters', 'The Earlier Affection', 'The Black Fishers', 'Summer Weather', 'The Oasis in the Snow', 'The Herd of Standlan', 'Streams of Water in the South', 'The Moor Song', 'Comedy in the Full Moon'.
       A Lost Lady of Old Years

1900   – *The Half-Hearted*

1901   – *The Compleat Angler* (edited with an introduction)
       The Book of the Horace Club
       The Book of the Jubilee

1902   – *The Watcher By The Threshold* (stories): 'No-Man's Land', 'The Far Islands', 'The Watcher by the Threshold', 'The Outgoing of the Tide', 'Fountainblue'

1903   – *The African Colony*
1905   – *The Law Relating To The Taxation of Foreign Income*
         The Empire and the Century (chapter on 'The Law and the Constitution)
1906   – *A Lodge in the Wilderness*
1908   – *Some Eighteenth Century Byways* (essays and articles): 'Prince Charles
         Edward', 'Lady Louisa Stuart', 'Mr Secretary Murray', 'Lord Mansfield',
         'Charles II', 'The Making of Modern Scotland', 'Castlereagh', 'A Comic
         Chesterfield' (the 11th Earl of Buchan), 'A Scottish Lady of the Old School'
         (Lady John Scott), 'The Victorian Chancellors', 'The First Lord Dudley', 'Mr
         Balfour as a Man of Letters', 'John Bunyan', 'Count Tolstoi and the Idealism of
         War', 'The Heroic Age of Ireland', 'Rabelais', 'Theodor Mommsen', 'The
         Apocalyptic Style'.
1909   – *Brasenose College Quatercentenary Monographs Vol. 2 Pt. 11*
1910   – *Prester John [The Great Diamond Pipe]*
1911   – *Sir Walter Raleigh*
1912   – *The Moon Endureth* (stories and poems): 'From the Pentlands, looking
         North and South', 'The Company of the Marjolaine', 'Avignon 1759', 'A
         Lucid Interval', 'The Shorter Catechism (Revised Version)', 'The Lemnian',
         'Atta's Song', 'Space', 'Stocks and Stones', 'Streams of Water in the South',
         'The Gipsy's Song to the Lady Cassilis', 'The Grove of Ashtaroth', 'Wood
         Magic', 'The Riding of Ninemileburn', 'Plain Folk', 'The Kings of Orion',
         'Babylon', 'The Green Glen', 'The Wise Years', 'The Rime of True
         Thomas'.
1913   – *The Marquis of Montrose*
         Andrew Jameson, Lord Ardwall
1915–19 – *Nelson's History of the War*
1915   – *Britains' War By Land*
         The Achievement of France
         The Thirty-Nine Steps
         Salute to Adventurers
         Ordeal By Marriage
1916   – *The Power House*
1916   – *The Battle of Jutland*
         Greenmantle
         The Battle of the Somme, First Phase
         The Purpose of War
1917   – *Poems, Scots and English*
         The Battle of the Somme, Second Phase
1919   – *Mr Standfast*
         – *These For Remembrance*: memoirs of Tommy Nelson, Bron Lucas

(Auberon Herbert), Cecil Rawling, Basil Blackwood, Jack Stuart Wortley and
Raymond Asquith

        The Island of Sheep 'by Cadmus and Harmonia' (with Susan Buchan)

        The Battle-Honours of Scotland 1914–1918

1920   – *The History of the South African Forces in France*

        Francis and Riversdale Grenfell

        The Long Road to Victory (editor)

1921   – *The Path of the King*

        Great Hours in Sport (editor)

1921–22 – *A History of the Great War*

1922   – *Huntingtower*

        A Book of Escapes and Hurried Journeys: 'The Flight to Varennes', 'The
Railway Raid in Georgia', 'The Escape of King Charles after Worcester',
'From Pretoria to the Sea', 'The Escape of Prince Charles Edward', 'Two
African Journeys', 'The Great Montrose', 'The Flight of Lieutenants Parer and
M'Intosh across the World', 'Lord Nithsdale's Escape', 'Sir Robert Carey's
Ride to Edinburgh', 'The Escape of Princess Clementina', 'On the Roof of the
World'.

1923   – *The Last Secrets*: 'Lhasa', 'The Gorges of the Brahmaputra', 'The
North Pole', 'The Mountains of the Moon', 'The South Pole', 'Mount
McKinley', 'The Holy Cities of Islam', 'The Explorations of New Guinea',
'Mount Everest'.

        Midwinter

        Days to Remember

1923   – *A History of English Literature* (editor)

1923–24 – *The Nations of Today* (editor)

1924   – *Some Notes on Sir Walter Scott*

        The Three Hostages

        Lord Minto

        The Northern Muse (editor)

        The Scottish Tongue (contributor)

1925   – *The History of the Royal Scots Fusiliers*

        John Macnab

        The Man and the Book: Sir Walter Scott

        Two Ordeals of Democracy

1926   – *The Dancing Floor*

        Homilies and Recreations (essays and addresses): 'Sir Walter Scott', 'The
Old and the New in Literature', 'The Great Captains', 'The Muse of History',
'A Note on Edmund Burke', 'Lord Balfour and English Thought', 'Two
Ordeals of Democracy', 'Literature and Topography', 'The Judicial

Temperament', 'Style and Journalism', 'Scots Vernacular Poetry', 'Morris and Rossetti', 'Robert Burns', 'Catallus', 'The Literature of Tweeddale', 'Thoughts on a Distant Prospect of Oxford'

> *Essays and Studies* (editor)
> *The Fifteenth-Scottish-Division 1914–1919* (with John Stewart)
> *Modern Short Stories* (editor)

1927   – *Witch Wood*

1928   – *The Runagates Club* (stories): 'The Green Wildebeeste', 'The Frying-Pan and the Fire', 'Dr Lartius', 'The Wind in the Portico', '"Divus" Johnston', 'The Loathly Opposite', 'Sing a Song of Sixpence', 'Ship to Tarshish', 'Skule Skerry', 'Tendebant Manus', 'The Last Crusade', 'Fullcircle'

> *Montrose*
> *The 'Teaching of History' Series* (editor)

1929   – *The Courts of the Morning*
> *The Causal and the Casual in History* (Rede Lecture)
> *What the Union of the Churches Means to Scotland*

1930   – *The Kirk in Scotland 1560–1929* (with George Adam Smith)
> *Montrose and Leadership*
> *Castle Gay*
> *Lord Rosebery 1847–1930*

1931   – *The Blanket of the Dark*
> *The Novel and the Fairy Tale*
> *The Poetry of Neil Munro* (editor)

1932   – *Sir Walter Scott*
> *The Gap in the Curtain*
> *Julius Caesar*
> *The Magic Walking Stick*
> *Andrew Lang and the Borders*

1933   – *The Massacre of Glencoe*
> *A Prince of the Captivity*
> *The Margins of Life*

1934   – *The Free Fishers*
> *Gordon at Khartoum*
> *Oliver Cromwell*
> *Six Stories From Shakespeare* (contributor)

1935   – *The King's Grace*
> *Men and Deeds*
> *The House of the Four Winds*

1936   – *The Island of Sheep [The Man from the Norlands]*

1937   – *Augustus*

SOURCES AND REFERENCES

'I also like the absence of footnotes. I never see why one should put the jottings of one's laboratory at the bottom of the page.'

John Buchan to Liddell Hart,
commenting on the latter's *Scipio* 26th October 1926.

ABBREVIATIONS

BWAF Susan Buchan, *John Buchan by his Wife and Friends* (1947).
BBC British Broadcasting Corporation Written Archives Centre, Caversham.
DD David Daniell, *The Interpreter's House* (1975).
JAS Janet Adam Smith, *John Buchan* (1965).
JBJ *John Buchan Journal.*
MHTD John Buchan, *Memory Hold The Door (1950 edition)*
NLS National Library of Scotland, Buchan Family Papers.
QUEENS Buchan Family Papers, Queens University, Kingston, Ontario.
UU Anna Buchan, *Unforgettable, Unforgotten* (1945)
WB William Buchan, *John Buchan* (1982).

INTRODUCTION

1   WB, pp. 255, 258.
2   Lord Lothian, *The American Oxonian*, April 1940.
3   P.L. Scowcroft, 'The railway journeys of Sir Richard Hannay and other transport references in the novels of John Buchan', *JBJ* Winter 1988.

PROLOGUE

1   GM. Trevelyan to Susan Buchan, 19 February 1940, NLS Mss 315.

CHAPTER ONE: A SCOTTISH YOUTH

1 Quoted in WB, p. 61.
2 Ibid., p. 64.
3 MHTD, p. 14. See also p. 15.
4 JAS, p. 16. (cf. MHTD p. 15).
5 Ibid., pp. 249, 246.
6 Ibid., p. 246.
7 Ibid., p. 31.
8 Ibid., p. 16.
9 Ibid., p. 19.

CHAPTER TWO: THE GLASGOW YEARS

1 *The John Knox Magazine* 1942, quoted by Martin Green, *A Biography of John Buchan and his Sister Anna* (1990), p. 59.
2 *The Hutchesonian* 1920 (cf. Buchan's comments on Caddell quoted in *The Hutchesonian* 1954).
3 The book is in NLS Mss 314.
4 MHTD, p. 33.
5 Scott Diary, 10 July 1928, 1465/27.
6 MHTD, p. 35.
7 Scott, 8 July 1928, op, cit.
8 Scott, 12 July 1928, op. cit.
9 Ibid. 30 April 1927, 1465/22.
10 *The Student*, 8 February 1928.
11 JB to Dick 6 June 1893 & 13 June 1893, NLS Mss 310.
12 Ibid. 5 July 1893, NLS Mss 310.
13 Ibid. 6 October 1893, NLS Mss 310.
14 JB to Gilbert Murray, 8 October 1895, NLS Mss 303.
15 Ibid. 14 October 1895, NLS Mss 303.
16 *Glasgow University Magazine* 13 November 1895.
17 Ibid.
18 DD, p. 46.

CHAPTER THREE: THE SPELL OF OXFORD

1 The *Bookman* December 1895, p. 85.
2 JB to Charles Dick, 11 October 1895, NLS Mss 304.

3 MHTD, p. 47.

4 *The Brazen Nose*, November 1949.

5 MHTD, p. 49.

6 JB to Gilbert Murray, 14 October 1895, NLS Mss 303.

7 Quoted, JAS, p. 48.

8 JB to Charles Dick, 22 October 1895, NLS Mss 304.

9 Ibid. November 1895, NLS Mss 304.

10 For more information see Ingoldsby Essay Club Book B1 a53, Brasenose College Archives.

11 JB to Gilbert Murray, 3 March 1896 QUEENS Box 1, 2110.

12 For more information see in Brasenose College Archives Battels Books 1895–96 B5c 56; Pupils Battels 1893–1905 B4 d10; Buttery Books 1895–99 B6 a 17–31; removals 1885–1900 B1 c16; Inventory & Valuation of Rooms 1891–97 B1c 10.

13 JB to Charles Dick, 26 April 1896, QUEENS Box 13, 2110.

14 JB to Anna Buchan, 3 June 1896, QUEENS Box 1, 2110.

15 Quoted, Norman Flower, *The Journals of Arnold Bennett 1896–1910* pp. 10–11. See also Dudley Barker, *Writer by Trade: A View of Arnold Bennett* (1966), p. 67.

16 JB to Benjamin Boulter, 16 July 1896, NLS Mss 303.

17 *The Nation*, 7 January 1897; *The Bookman*, January 1897.

18 The Oxford JCR. 2 February 1897.

19 New later designed one of JB's book plates.

20 JB to Charles Dick, 30 December 1896.

21 Ibid. 7 May 1897, NLS Mss 304.

22 *The Oxford Magazine*, 8 December 1897.

23 See JB to Charles Dick, 9 August 1897.

24 Ibid. 1 November 1897, NLS Mss 304.

25 Ibid. 10 February 1898, NLS Mss 304.

26 *The Isis*, 19 February 1898.

27 MHTD, p. 54.

28 Subsequent arbiters were York Powell, Francis Bussell, Aubrey Herbert, Cuthbert Medd, Harold Baker and Raymond Asquith.

29 Ibid. p. 58.

30 *The Isis*, 18 June 1898. See also 'John Buchan's Newdigate' in *The Brazen Nose* June 1940.

31 *The Oxford Magazine*, 8 March 1899.

32 *The Oxford JCR*, 14 June 1898.

33 JB to Charles Dick, 26 July 1898.

34 Ibid. 18 July 1898; BW was *The British Weekly*.

35 JB to Gilbert Murray, 8 July 1898, NLS Mss 303.

36 *The Oxford JCR*, 7 June 1898; *Labour Leader*, 11 June 1898. See also 1978

Canongate and 1993 B&W editions. Anne Paterson re-creates John Barnet's journey in *JBJ*, Summer 1985.

37 Green p. 87; John Buchan, *These for Remembrance* (1987 edition), p. 11.

38 *The Isis*, 8 May 1897; *The Oxford JCR*, 11 May 1897.

39 *The Isis*, 5 June 1897.

40 Ibid. 4 December 1897.

41 Ibid. 19 February 1898.

42 *The Oxford JCR*, 22 February 1898.

43 *The Oxford Magazine*, May 1898.

44 Ibid.

45 *The Oxford JCR*, 22 November 1898.

46 *The Isis*, 19 November 1898; *The Oxford Magazine* 23 November 1898.

47 UU, p. 80.

48 *The Oxford JCR*, 14 June 1898.

49 *The Isis*, 28 January 1899.

50 *The Oxford Magazine*, 1 March 1899.

51 *The Oxford JCR*, 29 November 1898.

52 *The Isis*, 19 November 1898.

53 *The Oxford JCR*, 9 May 1899.

54 JB to Dick, 27 January 1900 NLS Mss 304; *Blackwoods* published 'The Far Islands' in November 1899 and would bring out 'The Watcher by the Threshold' in December 1900 and articles on Lord Chesterfield and Prince Charles Edward in April and October 1900.

55 JB to Helen Buchan, 3 November 1899, NLS Mss 303.

56 Francis Wylie to JB, 3 November 1899, NLS Mss 303.

57 JB to Gilbert Murray, 5 November 1899, NLS Mss 303; JB to Reverend John Buchan, 7 November 1899 NLS Mss 303.

58 Quoted John Jolliffe, *Raymond Asquith: Life and Letters* (1980), p. 62.

59 MHTD, p. 51; Bussell in *The Brazen Nose* June 1940.

60 MHTD, p. 86.

61 Ibid. p. 52.

62 See NLS Acc 6975 (1).

63 MHTD, p. 87.

CHAPTER FOUR: LONDON INTERLUDE

1 JB to Charles Dick, 27 January 1900, NLS Mss 304.

2 Ibid.

3 Ibid.

4   'Andrew Lang and the Border' would be the subject of a JB lecture at the University of St Andrews in 1932 and be published the following year by Humphrey Milford at the Oxford University Press.

5   JB to Charles Dick, 27 January 1900, NLS Mss 304.

6   JB to Reverend John Buchan, 23 May 1900, NLS Mss 303.

7   MHTD, p. 93.

8   Ibid. p. 91.

9   JB to Lady Mary Murray, 27 September 1900, NLS Mss 303.

10 Ibid. 15 December 1900, NLS Mss 303.

11 MHTD, pp. 92–3.

12 Ibid. p. 93.

13 *Spectator*, 3 November 1928. Graves wrote a poem about Buchan and Belloc called 'The Two Bs'.

14 JB to Charles Dick, 9 June 1901.

15 JB to Helen Buchan, 9 August 1901, QUEENS Box 1, 2110.

CHAPTER FIVE: THE CRECHE

1   JB to Anna Buchan 17 September 1901, QUEENS Box 1, 2110.

2   JB to Charles Dick, 8 October 1901, NLS Mss 310.

3   Ibid.

4   JB to Reverend John Buchan, 7 October 1901, QUEENS Box 1, 2110

5   Lionel Curtis, *With Milner in South Africa* (1951), p. 323

6   JB to Anna Buchan, 8 October 1901, QUEENS Box 1, 2110.

7   MHTD, pp. 108–109.

8   JB speech, 7 December 1933, H of C Deb col 1895.

9   JB to Charles Dick, 8 October 1901, NLS Mss 310.

10 JB to Stair Gillon, 18th October 1901, NLS Mss 303.

11 JB to Anna, 7 October 1901, QUEENS Box 1, 2110.

12 JB to Lady Evelyn Malcolm, 17 October 1901, QUEENS Box 1, 2110.

13 *Spectator*, 22 June 1901.

14 JB to Lady Mary Murray, 16 January 1902, QUEENS Box 1, 2110.

15 JB to Charles Dick, 13 January 1902, NLS Mss 310.

16 JB to Walter Buchan, 9 January 1902, QUEENS Box 1, 2110.

17 JB to John Edgar, 2 July 1902, NLS Mss 303.

18 JB to Anna Buchan, 21 April 1902, NLS Mss 303.

19 JB to Charles Dick, 20 September 1902, NLS Mss 310.

20 JB to Charles Dick, 23 November 1902, NLS Mss 310.

21 JB to Charles Dick, 13 January 1903, NLS Mss 310.

22 JB to Anna Buchan, 21 April 1902, NLS Mss 303.

23 Ibid. 7 November 1902, NLS Mss 303; Ibid. 21 December 1902, NLS Mss 303.

24 Ibid. 21 December 1902, NLS Mss 303.

25 Ibid. 4 January 1903, NLS Mss 303.

26 Quoted, JAS, p. 121.

27 JB to Stair Gillon, 10 January 1903, NLS Mss 310.

28 JB to Anna Buchan, 15 February 1903, NLS Roll 1.

29 JB to Helen Buchan, 22 February 1903, NLS Mss 303.

30 JB to Anna Buchan, 5 April 1903, NLS Mss 303.

31 For an account of the trip see Robert Brand to his mother, 5 April 1903 Brand Papers.

32 For material on the Inter-Colonial Council see PRO CO 549 1.

33 JB to Anna Buchan, 9 May 1903, NLS Mss 303.

34 JB to Charles Dick, 16 May 1903, NLS Mss 310.

35 JB to Anna Buchan, 26 June 1903, NLS Mss 303. It seems JB became an officer in the Royal Mounted Rifles in November 1901.

36 JB to Helen Buchan, 1 February 1903, NLS Mss 303; JB to Charles Dick, 13 January 1903, NLS Mss 310.

37 Ibid. 16 May 1903, NLS Mss 310.

38 The Times, 5 January 1903.

39 'Lord Milner and South Africa' Quarterly Review July 1905, p. 285.

40 Ibid. p. 282.

41 Ibid. p. 285.

42 JB to Charles Dick, 16 May 1903, NLS Mss 310; MHTD, p. 115.

43 JB to Charles Dick, op. cit.

44 'Lord Milner and South Africa', p. 376.

45 Ibid. p. 388.

46 MHTD, p. 130.

47 David Daniell, The Best Short Stories of John Buchan, volume 2, (1982), p. 197.

48 JB to Gilbert Murray, 30 January 1902, Box 126 Murray Papers, Bodleian.

49 JB to Anna Buchan, 17 February 1902 NLS Mss 303.

50 Robert Brand to mother, 20 December 1903, Box 185 Brand Papers, Bodleian.

51 The Oxford Magazine, 16 March 1904; for the Cromer letter see C to JB, 20 December 1903 QUEENS Box 12, 2110.

52 The Oxford Magazine, op. cit.

CHAPTER SIX: SETTLING DOWN

1 John Buchan, The Law Relating to the Taxation of Foreign Income (1905).

2 Susan Buchan, The Lilac and the Rose (1952), p. 146.

3   MHTD, pp. 95–6.

4   Quoted, JAS, p. 143.

5   See Violet Markham, *Return Passage* (1953), and Violet Markham, *Friendship's Harvest* (1956).

6   JB to Anna Buchan, 13 November 1903, NLS Mss 303.

7   St Loe Strachey to JB, 21 May 1904, NLS Mss 303.

8   St Loe Strachey to JB, 21 January 1906, NLS Mss 303.

9   On joining Nelson JB returned to 3 Temple Gardens where he kept a flat until 1921.

10 MHTD, pp. 132–3.

11 For a copy see NLS Mss 324.

12 *The Bookman*, February 1907.

13 *The Lodge in the Wilderness*, chapter 13.

14 Ibid., chapter 10.

15 Ibid., chapter 1. For a fuller discussion of the novel see Jefferson Hunter, *Edwardian Fiction* (1982).

16 Anna claims they had first been there together in 1900. See UU, pp. 91–2.

17 MHTD, p. 140 and p. 139.

18 *Blackwoods*, May 1905.

19 They are 'Half Hours in the Club Library', vol. 12 1913; 'Knees of the Gods' vol. 9 1906–7 and 'Pan' and an unsigned piece, vol. 11, 1907. Walter Buchan joined two years later, again proposed by Stair Gillon.

20 *The Scottish Mountaineering Club Journal*, vol. 22, 1942 pp. 200–205; See also Leo Amery's appreciation in *The Alpine Journal* May 1940 pp. 122–123 and that by WSL in *The American Alpine Journal* vol. 4 1942 pp. 273–278.

21 See W.R. Irwin *An Anthology of the Literature of Mountaineering* (1950) and Donald Orr, 'Mountaineering aspects in the novels of John Buchan', *JBJ*, no. 9.

22 WB, p. 119.

23 The house was sold in 1922 to Lord Leverhulme and eventually became a golf club. It figures in John Betjeman's 'Metroland'.

24 Vesci married Georgina Wellesley in 1906 but they divorced 1919; JB to Susan Grosvenor, 21 October 1905, NLS Mss 9058 1/1.

25 Susan Grosvenor to JB, 5 November 1905, NLS Mss 9058 1/4.

26 Ibid. 14 April 1906, NLS Mss 9058 1/4.

27 JB to Susan Grosvenor, 18 April 1906, NLS Mss 9058 1/1.

28 BWAF, p. 34.

29 Quoted, JAS, p. 162.

30 JB to Helen Buchan, 14 November 1906, private collection.

31 Markham to JB, 6 December 1906, NLS Mss 303.

32 Helen Buchan to Susan Grosvenor, 17 November 1906, NLS Mss 9058 7 /3; WB, p. 123–124.

33 Anna Buchan to Susan Grosvenor, 21 November 1906, NLS Mss 9058 7/3.

34 Brand Papers Box 182.

35 For more on his activities with Nelson see Allistair Candlish, 'John Buchan – Literary Adviser', *JBJ*, Summer 1985.

36 Susan Grosvenor to Caroline Grosvenor, 14 May 1907, NLS Mss 9058 1/6.

37 Ibid. 16 May 1907, NLS Mss 9058 1/6.

38 Ibid. 17 May 1907, NLS Mss 9058 1/6. See Stair Gillon's letter to Arthur Murray dated September 1947 for his adverse reaction to the engagement. Janet Adam Smith papers.

39 William Buchan to JB, 10 June 1907, QUEENS Box 12, 2110.

40 Susan Buchan to Caroline Grosvenor, 7 August 1907, NLS Mss 9058 1/6.

41 Ibid. 18 August 1907, NLS 9058 1/6.

42 BWAF, p. 40.

43 Ibid. p. 72. The house was destroyed by a bomb during World War Two.

44 For more on Charles Masterman see Samuel Hynes, *The Edwardian Turn of Mind* (1968), pp. 57–8.

45 Introduction by Forbes Gray in *Comments and Characters* (1940), p. xiii.

46 Ibid. pp. ix–x.

47 Ibid. p. xix.

48 JB to Forbes Gray, 31 December 1908, quoted in *Comments and Characters*, p. xxxii.

CHAPTER SEVEN: WRITING AND POLITICS

1   *The Records of the Chatham Dining Club 1910–14* (1915).

2   Susan Buchan to JB, 19 February 1910, NLS Mss 9058 1/5.

3   *Peebles News*, 1 April 1911. (cf. *Peebles News* 11 March 1911).

4   MHTD, p. 152.

5   WB, p. 133.

6   William Buchan to JB, 12 December 1911, NLS Mss 304.

7   JB to Susan Buchan, 12 November 1912, NLS Mss 303.

8   Quoted, UU, p. 137.

9   BWAF, p. 46.

10 John Buchan, *Homilies and Recreations* (1926), Introduction.

11 The connection with Swift's novel was first made by Christopher Daniell DD, p. 117.

12 *Prester John*, chapter 7; DD p. 92.

13 Hunter op. cit., p. 122.

14 *Prester John*, chapter 22.

15 Ibid., chapters 11 and 1.

16 JAS, p. 144.

17 *Prester John*, chapter 21.

18 Himmelfarb, pp. 258 and 260.

19 For literary criticism of *Prester John* see Brian Street, *The Savage in Literature: Representations of 'primitive' society in English fiction 1858–1920* (1975); T.J. Couzens 'Towards Interpreting Buchan's *Prester John*' *English Studies in Africa*, vol. 24, no. 1. 1981; David Ogilvie 'Prester John: David Crawfurd's Journeys', *JBJ*, Autumn 1992; David Daniell's 'The Black General' in David Dabydeen's *The Black Presence in English Literature*, pp. 135–53 and Daniell's introduction to the 1994 OUP edition of the book.

20 *Athenaeum*, 27 April 1912.

21 *The Bookman*, December 1912, p. 140.

22 Ibid. p. 142.

23 *TLS*, 18 September 1913; G.M. Trevelyan to JB, 21 September 1913, NLS Mss 303.

24 *British Weekly*, 12 February 1914; *Scottish Historical Review*, October 1913.

25 JB to Charles Dick, 30 April 1910, NLS Mss 310

26 MHTD, pp. 141–2.

27 BWAF, p. 48.

28 John Buchan, *Andrew Jameson, Lord Ardwall* (1913), p. 87.

29 JB to George Brown, 4 August 1914, Nelson Papers B/5/73; David Daniell (in 'At the foot of the Thirty-Ninth Step', *JBJ*, Spring 1991) speculates on the purpose of the Grey meeting.

CHAPTER EIGHT: TRIUMPH AND TRAGEDY

1 JB to George Brown, 25 July 1914, Nelson Papers B/5/67.

2 JB to George Blackwood, 7 December 1914, quoted JAS, p. 194.

3 It was also serialised in *All Story Weekly* in nine parts that summer.

4 *Athenaeum*, 13 November 1915; *TLS* 21 October 1915. See also the review in *The British Weekly*, 1 July 1915.

5 15 December 1915 in *Lady Cynthia Asquith Diaries 1915–18* (1987), p. 112.

6 Trafalgar Lodge is thought to be St Cuby now divided into flats. See correspondence, *JBJ*, Winter 1987. Debate continues on the actual inspiration of the thirty nine steps with the Norfolk and Fife coasts as other locations apart from Broadstairs. William Buchan claims Alice counted thirty-nine steps at Broadstairs and shouted them to her father. In fact there are 105 steps to the beach in front of St Cuby. For background on the Black Stone see Ronald Knox 'John Buchan, the Black Stone and the University of Glasgow' *JBJ*, Winter 1989.

7 *John O'London's Weekly* 1926; For more information on Childers and Buchan see

Bruce Wilkinson *The Zeal of the Convert* (1978), p. 68, and Andrew Boyle *The Riddle of Erskine Childers* (1977) p. 154.

8   Lord Ironside to the author, 27 April 1994.

9   For a discussion of Hannay's identity see Kate Macdonald 'Who was Richard Hannay?', *JBJ*, Winter 1987 and Geoffrey Pavell 'John Buchan's Richard Hannay' in *History Today* (August 1987).

10 Christopher Harvie in the introduction to the 1993 OUP edition. The mythical elements are developed by noting the similarities with Tolkien's work in Robert Giddings and Elizabeth Holland, *JRR Tolkien: The Shores of Middle-Earth* (1981); See also JA and Russell Paterson's 'The Thirty Nine Steps' in *JBJ* Winter 1987 which retraces Hannay's journeys; David Daniell's detailed critique of the book, calling it Buchan's 'confession of faith', in 'At the Foot of the Thirty-Ninth Step', *JBJ*, Spring 1991, and his 'That Infernal Aeroplane', in *JBJ*, Spring 1992.

11 Susan Buchan to JB, 27 October 1914, NLS Mss 9058 1/5.

12 JB to George Brown, 16 October 1914, Nelson Papers B/5/118.

13 Leo Amery to his wife, 7 June 1915, *The Leo Amery Diaries*, pp. 117–18.

14 Charteris to Newton, 15 July 1916, PRO FO 395 51.

15 PRO FO 395 51.

16 For an account of the first visit see Vladimir Nabokov *Speak Memory* (1951) pp. 186–187.

17 Details of Buchan's work at GHQ can be found in PRO FO 395 51, FO 395 53 and FO 395 54.

18 A copy of *The Battle of Picardy* can be found in PRO FO 395 54.

19 Peter Butenhuis *The Great War of Wars* (1987), p. 94.

20 John Buchan, *The Battle of the Somme: Second Phase* (1917), p. 21.

21 See JB to Basil Liddell Hart, 10 February 1917, Liddell Hart Papers 1/124.

22 James Marshall-Cornwall *Rumours of Wars*, (1984), p. 25.

23 Howard Spring, *In the Meantime* (1942), p. 11.

24 Ibid.

25 For more on 'The Fight for Right Movement' see Patrick French *Younghusband* (1994), pp. 295–303. Buchan addressed The Movement in December 1915 and his address was published the following year as 'The Purpose of War'.

26 Milner to Lloyd George, 17 January 1917 Lloyd George Papers F38/2/2; Leo Amery to Milner, 26 January 1917, *Leo Amery Diaries* p. 140.

27 T.L. Gilmour was a former leader writer on the *Morning Post* and Private Secretary to Lord Rosebery.

28 More background on the Department of Information can be found in PRO INF 4/1B.

29 PRO INF 4/9.

30 Andrew Causey, *Paul Nash* (1980), p. 68.

31 Lina Waterfield, *Castle in Italy* (1961), p. 170.

32 JB to Susan Buchan, 23 May 1917, quoted JAS p. 204; MHTD p. 179.

33 JB to Sir Edward Carson, 6 November 1917, Rylands Papers.

34 Burnham to Donald, 31 July 1917, PRO INF 4/7.

35 *The Times*, 7 August 1917.

36 20 August 1917. *The Leo Amery Diary*, p. 167.

37 JB's September 1917 report to Carson reveals the department's Budget was £1,300,000 drawn from Secret Service funds.

38 See also Trevor Wilson, *CP Scott* p. 293.

39 'Inquiry into the extent and efficiency of propaganda reports on various branches of propaganda and recommendations' 4 December 1917, PRO INF 4/4B. See also Donald's comments to C.P. Scott in PRO INF 4/7.

40 See JB's responses to Carson on the Donald and Arthur Spurgeon reports 21 and 28 December 1917 in PRO INF 4/1B.

41 Memo, 1 December 1917, PRO FO 395/235.

42 JB to Alastair Buchan, 10 June 1916, QUEENS Box 12, 2100

43 Quoted, *The Book of Remembrance of Tweeddale*, p. 305.

44 *UU*, p. 150. He is buried at the cemetery at Duisans. An account of a visit to the grave is given by Dee Thomas, *JBJ*, Autumn 1992.

45 *The Book of Remembrance for Tweeddale*, p. 304.

46 BWAF, p. 85.

47 John Buchan, *These For Remembrance*, op. cit. pp. 3–4; JB's obituary of Nelson appeared in *The Times* 14 April 1917 alongside that of Alastair Buchan and the poet Edward Thomas who had also been killed at Arras.

48 Quoted, JAS p. 211.

49 Roderick Jones to Susan Buchan, 15 January 1944, Jones Papers, Reuters Ms 2526 (11) ff. 35–7.

50 Box 55, fol. 157–160 Simon Papers, Bodleian.

51 Beaverbrook to JB, 31 October 1917, NLS Mss 305.

52 Arnold Bennett, *Journals*, vol. 2, p. 242; JB to Charles Masterman 15 December 1918, QUEENS Box 34, 2110.

53 *The Times*, 4 January 1919.

54 JB to Gilbert Murray, 17 December 1918, NLS Mss 305.

55 See Box 40 Brand Papers and League of Nations Union Papers, London School of Economics.

56 For an overall view see J.W.H. Buchan, 'John Buchan and the Great War', *JBJ*, Winter 1987.

57 For more on 'The Club' see *Annals of the Club*' (1914). The President after the First World War was T.E. Lawrence's mentor D.G. Hogarth.

58 JB to Hugh Walpole, 30 March 1913, NLS Mss 304.

59 See Anthony Quinton's introduction to the 1984 Dent edition, repeated in the 1993 B&W edition.

60 *The Power House*, chapter 3.

61 Ibid., chapter 5.

62 Ibid., chapter 7.

63 *The Bookman*, October 1916.

64 The historical background is given in Peter Hopkirk, *On Secret Service East of Constantinople* (1994).

65 Herbert and Arbuthnot were both the second sons of peers, educated at Eton and Oxford, officers of yeomanry and honorary attaches at British Embassies. See Margaret Fitzherbert, *The Man who was Greenmantle* (1983), and James Buchan 'Greenmantle: John Buchan and the Near East', *JBJ*, Autumn 1992.

66 *Greenmantle*, chapter 1.

67 According to a *New York Times* article in May 1940 a Baroness von Einem was put on trial *in absentia* for trying to organise a Fifth column in France as a personal emissary of Goebbels. A General von Einem appears in the first volume of Buchan's *A History of the War*.

68 JB to Helen Buchan, 27 October 1917, quoted JAS p. 208.

69 See also *The Bookman*, October 1916, *Punch* November 1916 and Kate Macdonald's introduction to the 1993 OUP edition.

70 *Punch*, 21 March 1962.

71 *Spectator*, 31 May 1980.

72 See William Buchan's introduction in the 1993 OUP edition and for a study of Buchan's use of Bunyan's *The Pilgrim's Progress* see George Parfitt, *Fiction of the First World War* (1988), pp. 14–20.

73 *Mr Standfast*, chapter 3.

74 Ibid., chapter 22.

75 *The Times*, 22 May 1919

76 *The New York Times*, 17 August 1919.

77 For a recent critique see Alan Massie, 'Buchan's Testament', *New Edinburgh Review*, no. 46, May 1979.

78 The 1936 edition was expanded to include several new poems.

79 DD p. 202; *TLS*, 5 July 1917.

CHAPTER NINE: COUNTRYMAN

1 Balfour to Beaverbrook, 13 December 1918, Beaverbrook Papers.

2 JB to Beaverbrook, 20 December 1918, op. cit.

3 See conveyancing documents Misc Cooper 111/3 Oxfordshire County Archives.

4   WB, p. 25.

5   One of the first guests was Edmund Ironside who came to stay in September 1920 soon after his return from commanding the Allied Forces in Northern Russia.

6   William Buchan, *Rags of Time* (1990), p. 106.

7   Ibid., p. 107.

8   Speech by JB as Governor-General quoted by Peter Vansittart in introduction to *These For Remembrance* (1987).

9   Lloyd George, *War Memoirs*, vol. 3, quoted, JAS, p. 230.

10 *Edinburgh Review*, January 1923; an edition was abridged by Victor Neuburg in 1991 and reviewed in *JBJ*, Spring 1992. See also Keith Grieves 'A History of the Great War', *JBJ*, Winter 1993.

11 JB to Beaverbrook, 3 October 1921, BBK c/314 Beaverbrook Papers.

12 JB to Roderick Jones, 18 November 1926, Misc Correspondence 1926–27 Box 12 Jones Papers Reuters.

13 Quoted, JAS, p. 226.

14 JB to Beaverbrook, 1 February 1922, Beaverbrook Papers.

15 JB to Beaverbrook 5 March 1922, op. cit.

16 Beaverbrook to John Davies, 9 March 1922, op. cit.

17 JB to Beaverbrook, 11 and 13 May 1922, *BBK*.

18 Horne to JB, 18 May 1922, op. cit.

19 JB to Beaverbrook, 19 May 1922, op. cit.

20 Beaverbrook to JB, 7 June 1920, op. cit.

21 See Agreement, 22 January 1907, NLS Mss 9058 6/4.

22 JB to Ian Nelson, 16 July 1923, B/11/158 Nelson Papers.

23 Ian Nelson to JB, 21 July 1923, B/11/158 Nelson Papers.

24 See the two books of study notes published by Louis Herrman and Thomas Palmer.

25 NLS Mss 9058 6/4.

26 *Reuter Review*, January 1938.

27 BWAF, p. 98.

28 For an account of these summer holidays see Lord Tweedsmuir, 'Back Casts' *JBJ*, Winter 1989.

29 WB, p. 171.

30 Lord Tweedsmuir, *Always A Countryman* (1953) p. 38.

31 William Buchan *Rags of Time*, p. 103.

32 JB to Gamaliel Bradford, 27 August 1924, NLS Mss 310.

33 JB to Nancy Astor, 7 October 1924, Astor Papers Reading. Supposedly JB and Coolidge discussed Latin poetry.

34 Ibid.

35 Quoted, JAS, p. 247.

36 BWAF, p. 110.
37 Byng to JB, 7 November 1924, NLS Mss 306.
38 Amery, p. 448. Amery noted on 10 May that the King had thought the suggestion that Buchan become Governor-General 'ridiculous'.
39 Susan Buchan to Violet Markham, 1 June 1926, NLS Mss 306.
40 Ibid.

CHAPTER TEN: NOVELIST

1 *The Three Hostages*, chapter 2. See also Karl Miller's introduction to the 1995
   OUP edition.
2 *The Daily Telegraph*, August 1929.
3 Tim Binyon, introduction p. 2, 1983 Dent edition; see also Andrew Lownie
   introduction, 1993 B&W edition.
4 *The Nation & Athenaeum*, 23 November 1929; *The New York Times*, 11 August
   1929; *Evening News* 20 September 1929.
5 This is traced by David Ogilvie 'The Island of Sheep', *JBJ*, Winter 1988 and
   Thomas Holland Jr, 'Bentley v Stultz', *JBJ*, Winter 1993.
6 *John Macnab*, chapter 8.
7 For more information see James Brander's letter to *The Field*, 17 November 1951,
   Alexander Dunbar's letter to *The Field*, January 1979 and Angus Fairrie's article
   'The Real John Macnab', *The Queen's Own Highlander*, Summer 1993 which
   names three possible candidates. See also David Daniell's introduction to the
   1994 OUP edition.
8 *The Nation & Athenaeum*, 19 September 1925.
9 Certain similarities can also be drawn with John Fowles's *The Magus*.
10 The *New York Times*, 12 December 1926; *TLS*, 12 August 1926; *The Nation &
   Athenaeum*, 23 August 1926.
11 Mary Butts 'Uses of the Supernatural in English Fiction', *Bookman* February
   1933. See also Christopher Harvie, 'For Gods and Kittle Cattle: JG Frazer and
   John Buchan', *JBJ*, Winter 1989.
12 DD, p. 165.
13 *Spectator*, 6 August 1932; *Evening Standard* 7 July 1932. *The Gap in the Curtain* was
   reissued by B&W in 1992.
14 For a biographical sketch see Ranald Laing, 'Dickson McCunn', *JBJ*, Summer
   1985.
15 *Huntingtower*, chapter 11.
16 Ibid., chapter 16.
17 See Andrew Lownie, introduction to 1993 B&W edition.
18 *New York Times*, 28 January 1923.

19 *Castle Gay*, chapter 2. See also JB to Beaverbrook, 28 August 1930, BBK c/314. And 'I would send a copy to Rothermere if I were not on good terms with his secretaries.' Beaverbrook to JB, 17 August 1930, NLS Mss 306.

20 *The Graphic*, 26 July 1930. See David Daniell's introduction in the 1983 Dent edition and for further associations Anne and Russell Paterson, 'Castle Gay', *JBJ*, Spring 1991.

21 JAS, p. 269.

22 *The Nation & Athenaeum*, 3 August 1935; see also Simon Ree's introduction in the 1984 Dent edition.

23 *TLS*, 24 November 1932.

24 See Nicola Beauman, *Cynthia Asquith* (1987).

25 The title is taken from the 68th Psalm:
>   He is the God that maketh men to be of one mind,
>   and bringeth the prisoners out of captivity,
>   but letteth the runagates continue in scarceness.

The name of The Thursday Club may come from Walter Scott's Friday Club, The Tuesday Club, a parliamentary dining society of which Aubrey Herbert was a member or the Cecil Club which met regularly at the St Stephens Club.

26 *TLS*, 12 July 1928.

27 *The Nation & Athenaeum*, 28 July 1928.

28 Bruning's economic adviser was JB's friend Moritz Bonn.

29 Falconet was the title of Disraeli's last novel.

30 There are a number of resemblances between JB and Melfort, among others they both lived in the Temple.

31 *Spectator*, 21 July 1933. It was reissued by Pan in 1962 and Hamlyn in 1981; *TLS* 6 July 1933.

32 She later dramatized two of the stories 'The Maid' and 'The Wife of Flanders' and they were published in French's acting editions in 1933 and 1936.

33 JAS, p. 272.

34 *TLS*, 31 March 1921.

35 *Midwinter*, chapter 1.

36 The *New York Times*, 16 September 1923. See Allan Massie, introduction to the 1993 B&W edition.

37 *Witch Wood*, chapter 4. There is a Woodhouselee nearby.

38 Christopher Harvie introduction to the 1988 Canongate edition p. xi. See also James Greig's introduction to the 1993 OUP edition.

39 MHTD, pp. 196–7.

40 DD, p. 183.

41 *Glasgow Herald*, 28 July 1927.

42 *Blanket of the Dark*, chapter 2.

43 Ibid., chapter 6.
44 Ibid., chapter 16.
45 Quoted, JAS, pp. 278, 279.
46 JAS, p. 278; DD, p. 186. See also David Daniell's introduction to the 1994 B&W edition
47 Margaret Newbolt, *Later Life and Letters of Sir Henry Newbolt* (1942), pp. 375–6; Rose Macaulay to JB, 13 March 1933, NLS Mss 307.
48 *The Spectator*, 8 August 1931.
49 David Daniell, introduction to the 1994 B&W edition.

CHAPTER ELEVEN: BIOGRAPHER AND HISTORIAN

1 BWAF, p. 16.
2 MHTD, p. 209.
3 *Blackwoods*, January 1914; cf. his historical creed in MHTD, p. 204.
4 Ibid.
5 Vivian Newport, 'The Biographical Writing of John Buchan', MA University of Arizona 1961.
6 BWAF, p. 182.
7 *English Historical Review*, July 1929.
8 JB to Beaverbrook, 15 October 1928, BBK c/134. Quoted, JAS, p. 233.
9 Lawrence to JB, 28 December 1928. Quoted, JAS, p. 236.
10 *English Historical Review*, July 1929; *New Republic*, 31 July 1929; The *Times* 28 September 1928.
11 *The Causal and the Casual in History* (1929), p. 42.
12 Gooch to JB, 4 December 1929, NLS Mss 306.
13 24 February 1911, NLS Mss 311.
14 *Montrose*, (1928), p. 7; JAS, p. 354.
15 *The Atlantic Monthly*, October 1932.
16 BBC 1932 broadcast transcript.
17 MHTD, p. 209; For further comparisons Ellen Stevenson 'The Influence of Sir Walter Scott on John Buchan', MA thesis Toronto 1950.
18 *The Spectator*, 19 March 1932.
19 *TLS*, 3 March 1932.
20 *Oliver Cromwell* (1934), p. 19.
21 BWAF, p. 183.
22 *Oliver Cromwell*, p. 20.
23 *TLS*, 6 September 1934; *Saturday Review*, 15 September 1934; The *Spectator*, 7 September 1934; *New English Weekly*, 6 June 1935.
24 *The Spectator*, 16 April 1932.

25 *Augustus*, chapter 6; the Italian edition omitted the chapter on dictators.

26 JB to Amery, quoted JAS p. 434.

27 JB to Sandwell, 4 December 1937, QUEENS?

28 *Classical Journal* see NLS Mss 315; *New Statesman*, 13 November 1937.

29 *TLS*, 30 October 1937.

30 The *Spectator*, 29 October 1937.

31 *Scottish Educational Journal*, 19 June 1925, p. 648, reprinted in *Contemporary Scottish Studies* (1926).

32 The *Spectator*, 20 September 1924; *The Nation & Athenaeum*, 20 September 1924; JB contributed an essay on 'Some Scottish Characteristics' to a series of lectures published as *The Scottish Tongue* (1924).

33 In May 1921 JB declined an offer from Leo Amery to write a history of the Amery family.

34 *The Nation & Athenaeum*, 20 November 1924.

35 The *Canadian Historical Review*, March 1925.

36 Lansdowne to Minto, 31 December 1924, NLS Mss 306.

37 One of the essays 'The Great Captains' was quoted by Lord Longford, then Leader of the House of Lords, when paying tribute to Churchill on his death.

38 Graham Greene 'The Last Buchan' in *The Lost Childhood and Other Essays* (1951), pp. 104–5; quoted, JAS p. 282.

39 Himmelfarb p. 252; The *London Magazine*, June/July 1993, p. 69.

40 It is reprinted as 'Two Ordeals of Democracy' in *Homilies and Recreations* (1926). Gertrude Himmelfarb *Victorian Minds* (1968), pp. 258, 260.

41 For further references see H.D. Ziman's letter to the *Daily Telegraph*, 18 June 1956.

42 *The Thirty-Nine Steps*, chapter 1.

43 See also JB's article, 'Russia and the Jews', *Spectator*, November 1905.

44 *The Lodge in the Wilderness* (1906), chapter 1.

45 Richard Usborne, *Clubland Heroes* (1974), See also Bryan Cheyette *Constructions of 'the Jew' in English Literature and Society* (1993), pp. 55–72 and *TLS* correspondence January to March 1988.

46 Leroy Panek, 'John Buchan' in *The Special Branch'* (1981), p. 46.

47 *Greenmantle*, chapter 14.

48 Quoted, JAS, p. 284.

49 *Mr Standfast*, chapter 15.

50 Susan Hill, *The Lighting of the Lamps* (1987), pp. 195, 196.

51 *The Three Hostages*, chapter 1.

52 Graham Greene, op. cit. p. 104.

53 Himmelfarb, op. cit. p. 253.

54 MHTD, p. 89.

55 BWAF, p. 133.

56 Patrick Cosgrave, 'John Buchan's Thrillers: The Ideology of Character', *Round Table*, July 1972, p. 386.

57 For other Buchan associations see Leland Schubert, 'Almost Real Reality: John Buchan's Visible World', *Serif*, September 1965, pp. 5–14.

58 MHTD, p. 108.

59 The *Scotsman*, 15 April 1989; John Raymond, *England's on the Anvil* (1958), p. 176.

60 BBC, Kaleidoscope, August 1975.

61 MHTD, p. 203.

CHAPTER TWELVE: PUBLIC SERVANT

1 JB to Scott, 4 May 1927, NLS Mss 306.

2 See for example, 'Mr Churchill's Second Chamber', 4 March 1907; 'The Position of the House of Lords', 22 August 1907, and 'the Reform of the Upper Chamber', 10 December 1908, all in the *Scottish Review*.

3 H of C Deb column 1313.

4 MHTD, p. 225.

5 JB to Helen Buchan, 7 July 1927, NLS Mss 310.

6 H of C Deb column 1317; *Daily News*, 7 July 1927. Robert Sanders was surprised that JB should take 'the old-fashioned Tory line'. See John Ramsden (ed), *Real Old Tory Politics* (1984).

7 James Johnston, *Westminster Voices*, p. 251.

8 JB to Priestley, 26 May 1937, NLS Mss 310.

9 Rothesay Stuart-Wortley, *Letters from a Flying Officer* (1928), introduction. See also JB's articles in *The Graphic* 21 June 1930 and 5 July 1930.

10 12 March 1928, H of C Deb column 1576.

11 11 March 1928, op. cit. columns 874–875.

12 Johnston 29 June 1929.

13 JB to Susan Buchan, 7 November 1928, NLS Mss 306.

14 The *Times*, 6 March 1929.

15 H of C Deb column 108.

16 Quoted, JAS, p. 315.

17 BBK, JB to Beaverbrook, 30 January 1930.

18 The *Times*, 3 October 1930.

19 28 October 1930, H of C Deb column 122.

20 H of C Deb column 123.

21 6 November 1930, op. cit. H of C Deb, columns 1127, 1128.

22 6 June 1930, op. cit. H of C Deb, column 2612.

23 *The Times*, 4 July 1930.

24 21 February 1930, H of C Deb, columns 1790, 1792.

25 5 December 1930, H of C Deb, column 2578.

26 2 February 1931, H of C Deb, column 1515.

27 MHTD, p. 230.

28 *Evening Standard*, 10 November 1931; JB to Baldwin, 4 November 1931 Baldwin Papers 45 f. 200.

29 MHTD, p. 226.

30 29 June 1931, quoted Tom Jones *A Diary with Letters 1931–50* (1954) pp. 42–3.

31 Ibid., p. 44.

32 Diary note, Liddell Hart Papers 1/124/35.

33 22 April 1932, H of D Deb, column 1816.

34 H of C Deb, column 1817.

35 BBK c/134, 2 January 1932.

36 JB to Susan Buchan, 31 May 1932, NLS Mss 6975/15.

37 27 May 1932, H of C Deb, column 740.

38 29 June 1932, H of C Deb, column 1833.

39 For BFI see PRO DO 204/5; JB was asked in 1935 to be Chairman of the Scottish Film Council but had to decline.

40 28 June 1932, H of C Deb, column 1718.

41 24 November 1932, H of C Deb, column 259–260.

42 H of C Deb, column 260–261.

43 Ibid.

44 JB to Violet Markham, 4 October 1932, NLS Mss 306.

45 JB to Baldwin, 4 October 1932, NLS Mss 306.

46 See Pilgrim Trust Annual Reports.

47 JB to Susan Buchan, 13 February 1934, NLS Mss 307.

48 Ibid., 21 February 1934, NLS Mss 307.

49 Anne de Courcy, *Circe* (1992), p. 197.

50 For correspondence see Nelson Papers D/LO/f 626).

51 Leo Amery claimed in his diary that JB had told him in February 1924 Macdonald was the illegitimate son of Lord Dalhousie.

52 JB first proposed a Conservative Research Department but his proposals were watered down. J.A. Ramsden, 'The Organisation of the Conservative & Unionist Party in Britain 1910–1930' (D Phil Thesis 1974 Oxford).

53 The *Times*, 30 October 1927?

54 Ibid., 15 February 1928. JB contributed several articles to The *Ashridge Journal*.

55 W.J. Brown, *So Far* (1943), p. 168; The *Daily Telegraph*, 16 September 1965; the dominie was the village schoolmaster in Scots.

56 JB to Susan, 4 April 1933n NLS Mss 307.

57 The most recent edition by Labarum Press in 1985 was reviewed in *JBJ*, Summer 1985.

58 *The Scottish Church and Empire* (1934).

59 MHTD, pp. 244–5.

60 JB to Pound, 28 March 1934, Yale Papers. The correspondence is in 'Letters to John Buchan 1934–35', *Paidemma*, Winter 1979/80.

61 Pound to JB, 18 March 1934; JB to Pound, 18 October 1934.

62 JB to JNS Buchan, 12 February 1935, NLS Mss 9058 2/2; JB to Charles Dick, 17 September 1935, NLS Ms 310.

CHAPTER THIRTEEN: THE ELSFIELD YEARS

1   See Ralph Roney, 'JB and the Motor Car', *JBJ*, Summer 1985.

2   MHTD, p. 222.

3   BWAF, p. 193.

4   MHTD, p. 212.

5   Lawrence to JB, June 1927, NLS 310; *Sunday Chronicle*, 19 December 1926.

6   MHTD, p. 224.

7   David Garnett (ed), *The Letters of T.E. Lawrence* (1938), p. 533.

8   Lawrence to JB, 20 December 1934, NLS Mss 307.

9   Ibid., 21 March 1930, NLS Mss 306. JB was unsuccessfully nominated as Rector of St Andrews in 1925 along with George Bernard Shaw, John Galsworthy and Arthur Conan Doyle and again in 1928 with Shaw, Galsworthy, Sir Walford Davies and Mussolini. The students chose Fridjof Nansen and Sir Wilfred Grenfell.

10 Ibid., 25 February 1935, NLS Mss 307.

11 Ibid., 22 August 1931, NLS Mss 306; see Lawrence to JB, 1 April 1935, Garnett p. 862.

12 NLS Mss 324.

13 Nicholson to the author, 13 May 1994.

14 Polunin to the author, 4 May 1994.

15 See also James Douglas-Hamilton, *Roof of the World* (1983), especially Lord Tweedsmuir's introduction.

16 See Francois Truffaut, *Hitchcock by Truffaut* (1986), p. 122 and Jocelyn Camp, 'John Buchan and Alfred Hitchcock', *Literature/Film Quarterly*, 1978, pp. 230–240.

17 *Variety*, 19 June 1935; *Sunday Times*, 9 June 1935.

18 JB to JNS Buchan, 19 February 1935, NLS Mss 9058 2/2.

19 Ibid., 26 February 1935, op. cit.

19 Ibid., 26 February 1935, op. cit.

20 Graves to JB, 27 March 1935, NLS Mss 307.

21 JB to JNS Buchan, 12 February 1935, NLS Mss 9058 2/2.

22 JB to Susan Buchan, 2 July 1934, NLS Mss 304.

23 Mackenzie King diary, QUEENS 26 October 1934.

24 Ibid., 15 November 1934.

25 JB's shipmates had included Hugh Walpole, Beverley Nichols and J.B. Priestley which had occasioned Walpole to quip that if the boat sank four of Britain's most successful authors would be drowned; cf Baldwin Papers CUL 122 f94–8.

26 Bessborough to Wigram, 28 February 1935, RAGV L2463/41.

27 A full account can be found in MK's diary, 21 February 1935.

28 Wigram to George V, 19 March 1935, RAGV L2463/50.

29 JB to JNS Buchan, 19 March 1935, NLS Mss 9058 2/2.

30 JB to Susan Buchan, 20 March 1935, NLS Mss 307; JB to JNS Buchan, 26 March 1935, NLS Mss 9058 2/2.

31 Murray to JB, 27 March 1935, NLS Mss 307.

32 King to Markham, 24 September 1924, quoted, Joy Esberg *Knight of the Holy Spirit* (1980) p. 164.

33 Ibid., p. 165.

34 28 March 1935, NLS Ms 307.

35 JB to JNS Buchan, 26 March 1935, NLS Mss 9058 2/2; Cottenham to JB, 28 March 1935, NLS Mss 307; Lang to JB, 28 March 1935, NLS Mss 307.

36 29 March 1935, NLS Mss 307.

37 28 March 1935, NLS Mss 307.

38 Markham to JB, 16 April 1935, NLS Mss 307; Bartlett to JB, 10 April 1935, Bartlett Add Ms 59500 f46.

39 JB to JNS Buchan, 2 April 1935, NLS Mss 9058 2/2; Buchan was about to inherit 4,000 acres near Fruid in the Borders from his Masterton relations.

40 JB to JNS Buchan, 16 April 1935, NLS Mss 9058 2/2; Ibid., 11 June 1935.

41 It can be found in NLS Mss 307.

42 Ibid.

43 The Lodge speech is reprinted, *The Brazen Nose*, November 1935.

44 JB to JNS Buchan, 5 March 1935, NLS Mss 9058 2/2.

45 Alastair Buchan to JNS Buchan, 1 August 1935, NLS Mss 9058 7/6.

46 Nicolson to JB, 23 August 1935, NLS Mss 307.

47 Beatrice Spencer-Smith to mother, 28 October 1935, private collection.

CHAPTER FOURTEEN: PROCONSUL

1   JB to Baldwin, 16 November 1935, NLS Mss 307.
2   For accounts see the *Times*, 6 November 1935, and JB to JNS Buchan, 5 November 1935, NLS Mss 9058 2/2.
3   JB to Helen Buchan, 5 November 1935, NLS Mss 307; quoted, JAS, p. 376.
4   January 1936, NLS Mss 310.
5   JB to George V, 18 November 1935, RAGV P633/345.
6   Ibid.
7   Ibid., 11 December 1935.
8   *Lord Minto* (1924), pp. 121–2.
9   Mackenzie King to JB, 19 July 1935, NLS Mss 307.
10 Mackenzie King diary, 5 November 1935.
11 BWAF, p. 234.
12 JB to George V, 31 December 1935, RAGV P633/351.
13 JB to Eden, 23 March 1936, Eden Papers AP 14/1/626.
14 JB to Baldwin, 24 March 1936, NLS Mss 307.
15 For more background see Watson Kirkconnell, *A Slice of Canada* (1967), p. 298; John Bell 'Tweedsmuir as Patron', *JBJ*, Autumn 1986.
16 31 December 1935, NLS Mss 307.
17 JB to Helen Buchan, 14 July 1936, NLS Mss 9058 2/1.
18 Beatrice Spencer-Smith to mother, 17 February 1936, private collection.
19 Ibid., 10 November 1936.
20 JB to Edward VIII, 10 September 1936, RAGV1 048/019.
21 JB to Baldwin, 24 March 1936, Baldwin Papers, CUL 97 f.166.
22 JB to Hardinge, 27 October 1936, NLS Mss 307.
23 Ibid., 9 November 1936, NLS Mss 307.
24 Amery to JB, 7 December 1936, NLS Mss 307.
25 JB to Helen Buchan, 7 December 1936, NLS Mss 9058 2/1.
26 Ibid., 17 December 1936, NLS Mss 9058 2/1; Markham to JB, 21 December 1936, NLS Mss 307.
27 JB to Baldwin, 12 December 1936, CUL 172 f. 164.
28 Wigram to JB, February 1936, RAGV1 048/004.
29 JB to Edward VIII, 5 August 1936 048/017; Susan Buchan to children, 4 August 1936, NLS Mss 307.
30 JB to Edward VIII, 5 August 1936, RAGV1 048/017.
31 JB to King, 31 August 1936, NLS Mss 307.
32 JB to Caroline Grosvenor, 16 September 1936, NLS Mss 307.
33 JB to King, 29 September 1936, NLS Mss 307.

34 JB to Walter Buchan, 17 December 1936, NLS Mss 9058 8/2.

35 'Notes on the Washington Visit', NLS Mss 9058 8/2.

36 Harold Ickes, *Diary*, p. 112.

37 'Notes on the Washington Visit'; JB to George VI, 7 April 1937, RAGV1 011/66.

38 Quoted Arthur Murray, *At Close Quarters* (1946), p. 98.

39 JB to FDR, 8 April 1937, QUEENS Box 13, 2110; JB to Stair Gillon, 9 April 1937, NLS Mss 308.

40 JB to Walter Buchan, 1 July 1937, NLS Mss 9058 8/2.

41 Susan Buchan to Virginia Woolf, 10 April 1937, Leonard Woolf Papers SxMs B11D5a.

42 Susan Buchan to Queen Mary, 5 June 1937, NLS Mss 308.

43 JB to Walter Buchan, 1 July 1937, NLS Mss 9058 8/2.

44 JB to Stair Gillon, 20 February 1937, NLS Mss 308.

45 For a full account see R.H.G. Bonnycastle 'Lord Tweedsmuir as a Mountaineer', *Canadian Alpine Journal*, No. 2, 1943 and JB to Stair Gillon, 7 September 1937, NLS Mss 308.

46 Margaret Bourke-White, *Portrait of Myself* (1964), p. 156.

47 Susan Buchan to JNS Buchan, 22 July 1936 NLS Mss 308; for another version see Bourke-White, op. cit., chapter 13.

48 JB to Gillon, 7 September 1937, NLS Mss 308.

49 The *Times* articles appeared on 12 and 13 October 1937.

50 'Canada's Outlook on the World' 12 October 1937 reprinted in *Canadian Occasions* (1940).

CHAPTER FIFTEEN: NATIVE

1 The *Times*, 26 November 1937.

2 JB to Helen Buchan, 1 November 1937, NLS Mss 9058 2/1; the poll went ahead with Buchan beating Lothian 4,802 to 2,582 votes.

3 Clive Wigram to JB, 20 December 1937, RAGV1 048/055.

4 JB to Walter Buchan, 1 November 1937, NLS Mss 9058 8/2.

5 Susan Buchan to JNS Buchan, 18 December 1937, NLS Mss 9058 371.

6 MHTD, p. 249.

7 UU, p. 211.

8 Ibid., p. 159.

9 JB to Anna Buchan, 21 December 1937, NLS Mss 308.

10 JB to Walter Buchan, 29 November 1937, NLS Mss 9058 8/2.

11 JB to Alan Lascelles, 1 January 1938, NLS Mss 308.

12 By the end of 1939 JB's deficit in the Commercial Bank of Scotland was £2,000.

See PRO DO 28 124 for the 1939/40 Departmental Report for the costs of running Rideau Hall and the Buchan's expense account.

13 JB to JNS Buchan, 29 April 1938, NLS Mss 9058 2/3.

14 JB to George VI, 24 May 1938, RAGV1 048/069.

15 Later published as *The Interpreter's House* (1938).

16 Susan Buchan to Alastair Buchan, 13 August 1938, NLS Mss 6975/16.

17 JB to B.K. Sandwell, 26 November 1938, NLS Mss 310.

18 JB to Walter Buchan, 28 September 1938, NLS Mss 9058 8/4.

19 Moritz Bonn to JB, 15 December, NLS Mss 309.

20 JB to Walter Buchan, 7 November 1938, NLS Mss 308; Ramsay was imprisoned during the war under the 18b Regulations.

21 JB to Walter Buchan, 28 September 1938, NLS Mss 9058 8/4; JB to Stanley Baldwin, 12 December 1938, NLS Mss 309; JB to Bessborough, 4 January 1939, NLS Mss 309.

22 Markham to JB, 17 January 1939, NLS Mss 309; JB to Stair Gillon, 7 January 1939, NLS Mss 309.

23 Markham to JB, 17 January 1939, NLS Mss 309.

24 JB to Alexander Hardinge, 10 January 1939, NLS Mss 309.

25 JB to George VI, 1 February 1939, RAGV1 048/082.

26 JB to Neville Chamberlain, 11 March 1939, NLS Mss 309.

27 Violet Markham to JB, 17 January 1939, NLS Mss 309; King to JB, 30 May 1939, NLS Mss 309.

28 JB to Neville Chamberlain, 19 June 1939, NLS Mss 309.

29 JB to George VI, 28 June 1939, RAGV1 048/089.

30 JB to Anna Buchan, 19 June 1939, NLS Mss 309; JB to Victor Cazalet, 23 May 1939; the Queen wrote on 28 June 1939 thanking the Buchans for the visit and asking for a picture of JB in his Indian headdress, private collection.

31 JB to Lewis Douglas, 13 December 1939, NLS Mss 309.

32 JB to Lord Crawford, 31 August 1939, NLS Mss 309.

33 JB to Stair Gillon, 1 September 1939, NLS Mss 309.

34 JB to Edward Harkness, 11 September 1939, NLS Mss 309.

35 JB to Walter Buchan, 7 September 1939, NLS Mss 9058 8/6; JB to FDR, 8 September 1939, NLS Mss 309; FDR to JB, 5 October 1939, NLS Mss 309.

36 18 September 1939, NLS Mss 313.

37 JB to Neville Chamberlain, 2 November 1939, NLS Mss 309.

38 JB to George VI, 8 November 1939, RAGV1 PS4518.

39 Alexander Hardinge to JB, 21 December 1939, NLS Mss 309.

40 JB to Alexander Hardinge, 20 January 1940, NLS Mss 309.

41 Susan Buchan to family, 11 November 1939, NLS Mss 309.

42 JB to Anna Buchan, 30 October 1939, NLS Mss 309.

43 JB to Charles Dick, 3 November 1939, NLS Mss 310; It seems that Buchan had originally envisaged staying no more than five years in Canada. When his membership of the Royal Society of Literature lapsed in 1937 he wrote to say he would be returning in the autumn of 1940 and he would renew it again then. Killick to Wagstaff, 19 April 1937, RSL Papers.

44 JB to Markham, 27 November 1939, NLS Mss 9058 8/6.

45 Cf. JB to Fisher, 17 January 1940, Fisher Papers 78 fol. 15.

46 JB to Hardinge, 26 January 1940, NLS Mss 309.

47 JB to JNS Buchan, 31 Janaury 1940, NLS Mss 9058 2/3.

48 JB to Anna Buchan, 5 February 1940, NLS Mss 309.

49 Redfern to Hardinge, 8 February 1940, RAGV1 PS4518.

50 Ibid.

51 Penfield's speech at the memorial service, Neurological Institute, 14 February 1940, NLS Mss 316.

52 George VI to Susan Buchan, 11 February 1940, RAGV1 PS4518.

53 The address can be found in NLS Mss 316.

54 Ibid.

55 *Ottawa Journal*, 14 February 1940.

CHAPTER SIXTEEN: BUCHAN'S LEGACY

1 He had also intended to write a book on the Apostle Paul; cf. James Greig, 'In Journeyings often . . .', *JBJ*, Spring 1992.

2 MHTD, p. 5.

3 Ibid., pp. 5, 301.

4 *TLS*, 1 September 1940; The *Spectator*, 30 August 1940; *Sunday Times*, 10 March 1940; *Yale Review* Winter 1941.

5 See David Daniell's introduction to the 1984 Dent edition.

6 See J.D. Sutherland, 'John Buchan's Sick Heart: Some Psychological Reflections', *Edinburgh Review* (1988) pp. 83–101.

7 JB also drew from *The Golden Grindstone: The Adventures of George Mitchell* by Angus Graham (1935); cf. David Daniell introduction to 1994 OUP edition.

8 See however Paul Scott's review in The *Scotsman*, 27 June 1981, which argues that 'there is as much of Buchan in Galliard as in Leithen'; cf. Ranald Laing, 'Sir Edward Leithen', *JBJ*, Autumn 1984.

9 *Mountain Meadow* and *Sick Heart River* were two of four proposed titles. The others were *Pride's Purge* and *The Winepress*; cf. Trevor Royle, introduction to the 1981 Macdonald and 1993 B&W editions.

10 Susan Buchan to John Edgar, 12 January 1942, Box 23 NLS Mss 316; cf. *TLS* 26 October 1946.

11 Hodder & Stoughton Archives. See Stair Gillon's criticism of *John Buchan by His Wife and Friends* in his letter to Arthur Murray dated September 1947. Janet Adam Smith papers.

12 *Saturday Night*, 21 July 1956.

13 Himmelfarb, p. 250.

14 Ibid.

15 *Sunday Times*, 19 September 1965; *Punch*, 29 September 1965; *Daily Telegraph*, 16 September 1965; *Observer*, 19 September 1965; cf. *TLS*, 16 September 1965 and VS Pritchett, *New Statesman*, 17 September 1965.

16 *Spectator*, 1 October 1965.

17 Ibid.

18 See *Books & Bookmen* October & November 1962; Ambler's own *Journey into Fear* has certain similarities with Buchan.

19 Alan Bennett, *Forty Years On* (1991), p. 83.

20 Alan Sandison, *Wheel of Empire* (1967), pp. 149, 179.

21 Janet Adam Smith in the *New Statesman*, 29 August 1975.

22 *Spectator*, 30 August 1975.

23 Bernard Richards, 'John Buchan's Aesthetic Consciousness' *Brazen Nose*, vol. XVI, no. 2 p. 41.

24 The *Listener*, 24 July 1980.

25 Ibid; The *Scotsman*, 29 May 1982.

26 *New Edinburgh Review*, Summer 1982.

27 The *Sunday Times*, 11 February 1990.

28 The *Times*, 12 February 1990; The *Daily Telegraph* 19 February 1990.

29 See John Shedden, 'Playing Buchan of Tweedsmuir', *JBJ*, Spring 1992.

30 Liddell Hart to JB, 30 October 1926, NLS Mss 310; Lawrence to Edward Garnett, 1 August 1933, quoted, JAS p. 280.

31 *Spectator*, 25 May 1956.

32 See *The Book Collector*, December 1984, April 1988, June 1992, October 1995 for articles on collecting Buchan.

33 Norman Etherington, 'Imperialism in Literature: The Case of John Buchan' unpublished paper p. 1.

34 DD, p. 209.

35 *New York Herald Tribune*, 15 February 1940.

36 BWAF, p.160.

BIBLIOGRAPHY

1. MANUSCRIPT COLLECTIONS

Janet Adam Smith, National Library of Scotland
Lady Astor, Reading University Library
Stanley Baldwin, Cambridge University Library
Vernon Bartlett, British Library
Lord Beaverbrook, House of Lords Record Office
EC Bentley, Duke University, North Carolina
William Blackwood, National Library of Scotland
Brasenose College Records
R.H. Brand, Bodleian Library
Anna Buchan, National Library of Scotland
John Buchan, National Library of Scotland
John Buchan, Queen's University, Kingston, Ontario
John Buchan Correspondence, Brown University Library
John Buchan Correspondence, Houghton Library, Harvard
Susan Buchan, National Library of Scotland
Jonathan Cape, Reading University
Victor Cazalet Diaries, private collection
Conservative Central Office, Bodleian Library
Lord Curzon, India Office Library
J.C.C. Davidson, House of Lords Record Office
Geoffrey Dawson, Bodleian Library
Richard Denman, Bodleian Library
Anthony Eden, Birmingham University
Richard Feetham, Rhodes House, Oxford
H.A.L. Fisher, Bodleian Library
Sir Ralph Furse, Rhodes House, Oxford

Glasgow University Archives
Edmund Gosse, Brotherton Library, Leeds
Grosvenor Estate Holdings, Westminster City Archives
Hall Brothers Records, Oxford City Archives
Thomas Hardy, Dorset County Museum
Tom Harrison Correspondence, Royal Geographical Society
Basil Liddell Hart, King's College, London
Aubrey Herbert, (Pixton Papers), Somerset Record Office
Hodder & Stoughton Archives, Guildhall Library, London
Hutcheson School Archives
Roderick Jones, Reuters
W.L. Mackenzie King, Public Archives of Canada
David Lloyd George, House of Lords Record Office
Londonderry Papers, Durham County Record Office
Lord Lothian, Scottish Record Office
Macmillan Publishers Archive, British Library
Hugh Macmillan, London University Library
Violet Markham, London School of Economics
Lord Milner, Bodleian Library
Gilbert Murray, Bodleian Library
Thomas Nelson, Special Collections, Edinburgh University
Max Nicholson/Oxford Exploration Club, Royal Geographical Society
Oxford Union Society Records
J.B. Pinker, Baker Library, Dartmouth College
Ezra Pound, Yale University Library
C.G. Rawling Correspondence, Royal Geographical Society
Reuters Archives
Royal Society of Literature Archives
Rylands Collection, Manchester University
Alexander MacCallum Scott, Glasgow University
Sir John Simon, Bodleian Library
Beatrice Spencer-Smith correspondence, private collection
J. St Loe Strachey, House of Lords Record Office
University College Archives, Oxford
Arthur Willert Papers, Beinecke Library, Yale
Basil Williams, Rhodes House, Oxford
Leonard Woolf, University of Sussex
Francis Brett Young, Birmingham University
Francis Younghusband, India Office Library
Alfred Zimmern, Bodleian Library

2. PUBLIC RECORDS

BBC Records, Caversham
British Film Institute
India Office Library
Public Record Office, Kew
Royal Archives, Windsor

3. NEWSPAPER AND PERIODICALS

United Kingdom
Aberdeen Press & Journal
Alpine Journal
Athenaeum
Biography
Blackwoods Magazine
The Bookman
Bookseller
Books in Scotland
The Brazen Nose
British Annual of Literature
British Book News
Cencrastus
Classical Journal
Country Life
Daily Telegraph
Encounter
English
English Historical Review
Foreign Affairs
Glasgow Herald
Glasgow University Magazine
The Graphic
The Guardian
Illustrated London News
Isis
Jewish Chronicle
Library Journal
Listener
London Magazine
London Quarterly Review

Nation
Nation & Athenaeum
National Review
New Edinburgh Review
New Statesman
Observer
Oxford JCR
Oxford Magazine
Oxford Times Centenary Supplement
Punch
Radio Times
Round Table
Scotland's Magazine
Scotland on Sunday
Scots Magazine
Scotsman
Scottish Educational Journal
Scottish Historical Review
Scottish Mountaineering Club Journal
Spectator
Student
Studies in Scottish Literature
Times
Times Literary Supplement
Twentieth Century

United States
American Alpine Journal
American Scholar
Atlantic Monthly
Books at Brown
Columbia University Forum
Literature Film Quarterly
Living Age
Minneapolis Tribune
Newsweek
New Republic
New York Review of Books
New York Times
New York Tribune
New York Herald Tribune Books
New Yorker

Saturday Review of Literature
Time
Virginia Quarterly Review
Yale Review

Canada
Canadian Alpine Journal
Canadian Forum
Canadian Historical Review
Globe & Mail
Maclean's Magazine
Ottawa Citizen

Europe
L'Europe Nouvelle

4. PUBLISHED SOURCES

AMBLER, ERIC, *To Catch a Spy* (The Bodley Head, 1964)

AMERY, LEOPOLD, *Diaries* vol 1 & 2 (Hutchinson, 1980, 1988)

AMERY, LEOPOLD, *My Political Life vol. 1* (Hutchinson, 1953)

AMERY, LEO, *The Times History of the War in South Africa vol. 1* (Sampson, Low, 1900)

ANGELL, NORMAN, *After All* (Hamish Hamilton, 1951)

ANNAN, NOEL, *Our Age* (Weidenfeld, 1990)

ASQUITH, MARGOT, *Autobiography vol. 2* (Thornton Butterworth, 1922)

ATKINS, JOHN, *The British Spy Novel: Styles in Treachery* (Calder, 1984)

ATTENBOROUGH, JOHN, *A Living Memory: Hodder & Stoughton Publishers 1868–1975* (Hodder & Stoughton, 1975)

BALL, IAN & MARION MACMILLAN, *May We Recommend* Book 4 (Longmans, 1959)

BALL, IAN & MARION MACMILLAN, *May We Recommend* Book 5 (Longmans, 1960)

Balliol College Register 1832–1914 (1914)

BARING, MAURICE, *The Puppet Show of Memory* (Heinemann, 1922)

BARKER, DUDLEY, *Writer by Trade: A View of Arnold Bennett* (Allen & Unwin, 1966)

BEAUMAN, NICOLA, *Cynthia Asquith* (Hamish Hamilton, 1987)

BELOFF, MAX, *Britain's Liberal Empire 1897–1921* (Macmillan, 1987)

BENNETT, ALAN, *Forty Years On and Other Plays* (Faber, 1991)

BLAKE, GEORGE, *Barrie and the Kailyard School* (Arthur Barker, 1951)

BLAKISTON, GEORGINA, (ed), *Letters of Conrad Russell 1897–1947* (John Murray, 1987)

BLANCHARD, ROBERT, *The First Editions of John Buchan* (Archon, 1981)

BOLD, ALAN, (ed.), *The Letters of Hugh MacDiarmid* (Hamish Hamilton, 1984)

BONN, MORITZ, *Wandering Scholar* (Cohen & West, 1949)

BORDEN, HENRY (ed), *Letters to Limbo* (University of Toronto Press, 1971)

BOURKE-WHITE, MARGARET, *Portrait of Myself* (Collins, 1964)

BOYLE, ANDREW, *The Riddle of Erskine Childers* (Hutchinson, 1977)

Brasenose College Register, vol. 1 (1910)

BRIDIE, JAMES, *One Way of Living* (Constable, 1939)

BRIGGS, ASA, *The History of Broadcasting in the United Kingdom vol. 2* (OUP, 1965)

BROWN, W.J., *So Far* (Allen & Unwin, 1943)

BUCHAN, ANNA, *Unforgettable, Unforgotten* (Hodder & Stoughton, 1945)

BUCHAN, J.N.S., *Always a Countryman* (Hale, 1953)

BUCHAN, J.N.S., *Hudson's Bay Trader* (Clerk & Cockeran, 1951)

BUCHAN, J.N.S., *One Man's Happiness* (Hale, 1968)

BUCHAN, SUSAN, *Carnets Canadiens* (1938)

BUCHAN, SUSAN, *The Edwardian Lady* (Duckworth 1966)

BUCHAN, SUSAN, *John Buchan By His Wife And Friends* (Hodder & Stoughton, 1947)

BUCHAN, SUSAN, *The Lilac and the Rose* (Duckworth, 1952)

BUCHAN, SUSAN, *A Winter Bouquet* (Duckworth, 1954)

BUCHAN, WILLIAM, *John Buchan: A Memoir* (Buchan & Enright, 1982)

BUCHAN, WILLIAM, *The Rags of Time: A Fragment of Autobiography* (Ashford, Buchan & Enright, 1990)

BUITENHUIS, PETER, *The Great War of Words* (University of British Columbia Press, 1987)

BUTTS, DENNIS, 'The Hunter and the Hunted: The Suspense Novels of John Buchan' in Clive Bloom (ed.), *Spythrillers: From Buchan to Le Carré* (Macmillan, 1990)

CADOGAN, EDWARD, *Before the Deluge* (John Murray, 1961)

CADOGAN, MARY & PATRICIA CRAIG, *Women and Children First: The Fiction of Two World Wars* (Gollancz, 1978)

CAIRNS, DAVID, *An Autobiography* (SCM Press, 1950)

CAMPBELL, IAN & PETER GARSIDE, *Talking about Scott* (Sir Walter Scott Club, 1994)

CAMPBELL, SHELAGH, *Resident Alien* (Hale, 1990)

CANNADINE, DAVID, *G.M. Trevelyan: A Life in History* (Harper Collins, 1992)

CANNING, JOHN, *Adventure Stories for Girls* (Octopus, 1978)

CARNEGIE, R.K., *And the People Cheered*, (Macmillan, 1940)

CARSWELL, DONALD, *The Scots Weekend* (Routledge, 1936)

CARTLAND, BARBARA, *Ronald Cartland* (Collins, 1943)

CAUSEY, ANDREW, *Paul Nash* (Clarendon, 1980)

CAWELTI, JOHN, 'The Joys of Buchaneering' in Joseph Waldmer (ed.), *Essays in Honor of Russell B Nye* (Michigan State University Press, 1978)

The Records of the Chatham Dining Club 1910–1914 (Constable, 1915)

CHEYETTE, BRYAN, *Constructions of 'the Jew' in English Literature and Society* (Cambridge University Press, 1993)

CHISHOLM, ANNE & MICHAEL DAVIE, *Beaverbrook* (Hutchinson, 1992)

CLARK, G.N., *The Manor of Elsfield* (1927)

CLAYTON, ANTHONY, *Forearmed: A History of the Intelligence Corps* (Brasseys, 1993)

CORNWALL MARSHAL, JAMES, *Wars and Rumours of Wars* (Leo Cooper, 1984)

CRAIGIE, WILLIAM (ed.), *The Scottish Tongue* (Cassell, 1924)

CRIPPS, ARTHUR, *Africa* (OUP, 1939)

CURTIS, LIONEL, *With Milner in South Africa* (Blackwell, 1951)

DANIELL, DAVID, *The Intrepreter's House* (Nelson, 1975)

DANIELL, DAVID (ed), *The Best Short Stories of John Buchan vols 1 and 2* (Michael Joseph, 1980, 1982)

DANIELL, DAVID, 'Buchan and the Popular Literature of Imperialism', in *Literature and Imperialism*, ed. Bart More-Gilbert, (Roehampton, 1983)

DANIELL, DAVID, Introduction in John Buchan *Memory Hold-the-Door* (Dent, 1984)

DANIELL, DAVID, 'Buchan and the "Black General"', in David Dabydeen (ed.), *The Black Presence in English Literature* (Manchester University Press, 1985)

DAVID, HUGH, *Heroes, Mavericks and Bounders* (Michael Joseph, 1991)

DE COURCY, ANNE, *Circe* (Sinclair Stevenson, 1992)

DENNING, MICHAEL, *Cover Stories: Narrative and Ideology in the British Spy Thriller* (Routledge, 1987)

DONALD, MILES, 'John Buchan' in Clive Bloom (ed.), *Spythrillers: From Buchan to Le Carre* (Macmillan, 1990)

DOUGLAS, O, *Farewell to Priorsford* (Hodder, 1950)

DOUGLAS-HAMILTON, JAMES, *Roof of the World* (Mainstream, 1983)

EASTWOOD, JAMES, *General Ironside* (Pilot Press, 1940)

ELLIS, E.L., *TJ: A Life of Dr Thomas Jones* (University of Wales Press, 1992)

ESBERG, JOY, *Knight of the Holy Spirit: A Study of William Lyon Mackenzie King* (University of Toronto Press, 1980)

FAIRFAX-LUCY, ALICE *A Scrap Screen* (Hamish Hamilton, 1979)

FERGUSSON, THOMAS, *British Military Intelligence* (Arms & Armour, 1984)

FITZHERBERT, MARGARET, *The Man Who Was Greenmantle* (John Murray, 1983)

FLOWER, NORMAN (ed.), *The Journals of Arnold Bennett 1896–1910* (Cassell, 1932)

FLOWER, NORMAN (ed.), *The Journals of Arnold Bennett 1921–28* (Cassell, 1933)

FORRESTER, WENDY, *Anna Buchan and O Douglas* (The Maitland Press, 1995)

FRENCH, PATRICK, *Younghusband* (Harper Collins, 1994)

GARNETT, DAVID (ed.), *Letters of TE Lawrence* (Cape, 1938)

GASKEL, PHILIP, *Morvern Transformed* (Cambridge University Press, 1968)

GIDDINGS, ROBERT & ELIZABETH HOLLAND *JRR Tolkien: The Shores of Middle-Earth* (Junction Books, 1981)

GLEICHEN, EDWARD, *A Book of Recollections* (Blackwell, 1932)

GLEICHEN, EDWARD, *A Guardsman's Memoirs* (Blackwood, 1932)

GOLLIN, ALFRED, *Proconsul in Politics* (Anthony Blond, 1964)

GRAHAM, ANGUS, *The Golden Grindstone* (1935)

GRAY, FORBES, (ed.), *Comments and Characters* (Nelson, 1940)

GRAY, MARTIN, *The Thirty-Nine Steps: York Notes* (Longman, 1980)

GREEN, MARTIN, *A Biography of John Buchan and His Sister Anna: The Personal Background of Their Literary Work* (Edwin Mellen Press, 1990)

GREEN, MARTIN, *Dreams of Adventure, Deeds of Empire* (Routledge, 1980)

GREENE, GRAHAM, *The Lost Childhood and Other Essays* (Eyre & Spottiswoode, 1951)

GREENSLADE, WILLIAM, 'Fitness and the Fin de Siècle' in John Stokes (ed.), *Fin de Siècle: Fears and Fantasies of the Late Nineteenth Century* (Macmillan, 1992)

GREENSLET, FERRIS, *Under the Bridge* (Houghton Mifflin, 1943)

GRIEVE, C.M., *Contemporary Scottish Studies* (Leonard Parsons, 1926)

GRIEVES, KEITH, 'Early Historical Responses to the Great War: Fortescue, Conan Doyle and Buchan' in Brian Bond (ed), *The First World War and British Military History* (OUP, 1991)

GRUNDY, G.B., *Fifty-Five Years at Oxford* (Methuen, 1945)

HAMMERTON, J.A., (ed.), *The Masterpiece Library of Short Stories* vol. 20 'The War' (Educational Book Company, n.d.)

HAMILTON, W.W., (ed.), *Holyrood: A Garland of Modern Scots Poems* (Dent, 1929)

HANNA, ARCHIBALD, *John Buchan: a Bibliography* (Shoe String Press, 1953)

HARPER, RALPH, *The World of the Thriller* (Western Reserve University, 1969)

HART-DAVIS, RUPERT, *Hugh Walpole* (Macmillan, 1952)

HARVIE, CHRISTOPHER, *The Centre of Things: Political Fiction in Britain from Disraeli to the Present Day* (Unwin Hyman, 1991)

HARVIE, CHRISTOPHER, 'Political Thrillers and the Condition of England' in Arthur Marwick (ed.) *Literature and Society* (Methuen, 1989)

HARVIE, CHRISTOPHER, 'Second Thoughts of a Scotsman on the Make: Politics, Nationalism and Myth in John Buchan' in Horst Drescher & Herman Volkel (eds) *Nationalism in Literature: Literature, Language and National Identity* (Verlag Peter Lang, 1989)

HASELL, JOCK, *British Military Intelligence* (Weidenfeld & Nicolson, 1973)

HAYNES, E.S.P., *The Lawyer*, (Eyre & Spottiswoode, 1951)

HAYNES, WILLIAM & JOSEPH LEROY HARRISON (eds), *Fisherman's Verse* (Duffield, 1919)

HENDERSON, THOMAS, *A Scots Garland* (Grant & Murray, 1931)

HENSON, HENSLEY, *Retrospect of an Unimportant Life, vols. 1–3* (O.U.P., 1942–50)

HERBERT, AUBREY, *Mons, Anzac and Kut* (privately published 1919)

HERBERT, AUBREY, *Ben Kendim* (Hutchinson 1924)

HILL, SUSAN, *The Lighting of the Lamps* (Hamish Hamilton, 1987)

HIMMELFARB, GERTRUDE, 'The Imperial Responsibility' in Robin Winks (ed.) *British Imperialism* (Holt, 1963)

HIMMELFARB, GERTRUDE, *Victorian Minds* (Weidenfeld & Nicolson, 1968)

HOLMES, COLIN, *Anti-Semitism in British Society 1876–1939* (Edward Arnold, 1979)

HOPKIRK, PETER, *On Secret Service East of Constantinople* (John Murray, 1994)

HOWARTH, PATRICK, *Play Up and Play the Game* (Eyre Methuen, 1973)

HOWE, SUZANNE, *Novels of Empire* (Columbia University Press, 1949)

HUNTER, JEFFERSEN, *Edwardian Fiction* (Harvard University Press, 1982)

HYNES, SAMUEL, *The Edwardian Turn of Mind* (OUP, 1968)

ILLINGWORTH, JOHN (ed), *Reginald Farrer*, (Lancaster University, 1991)

INGRAMS, RICHARD, (ed.), *Beachcomber: The Works of J.B. Morton* (Muller, 1974)

IRWIN, W.R., *Challenge: An Anthology of the Literature of Mountaineering* (Columbia University Press, 1950)

RHODES JAMES, ROBERT, *Rosebery* (Weidenfeld & Nicolson, 1963)

JOHNSTON, JAMES, *Westminster Voices* (Hodder & Stoughton, 1928)

JOHNSON, R.B., 'John Buchan' in R.B. Johnson, *Some Contemporary Novelists* (Parsons, 1922)

JOLLIFFE, JOHN, *Raymond Asquith: Life and Letters* (Century edition, 1987)

JONES, L.E., *Edwardian Youth* (Macmillan, 1956)

JONES, RODERICK, *A Life in Reuters* (Hodder & Stoughton, 1951)

JONES, TOM, *A Diary with Letters 1931–1950* (OUP, 1954)

JONES, TOM, *Welsh Broth* (W. Griffiths, 1951)

KENDLE, JOHN, *The Round Table Movement and Imperial Union*, (University of Toronto Press, 1973)

KEYNES, MAYNARD, *Two Memoirs* (Hart-Davis, 1949)

KIRKCONNELL, WATSON, *A Slice of Canada: Memoirs* (University of Toronto Press, 1967)

KRUSE, JUANITA, *John Buchan and the Idea of Empire* (Edwin Mellen Press, 1989)

KULIK, KAROL, *Alexander Korda* (W.H. Allen, 1975)

LAMBERT, GAVIN, *The Dangerous Edge* (Barrie & Jenkins, 1975)

LAMBERT. R.S., *Ariel and all his Quality* (Gollancz, 1940)

LANCTOT, GUSTAVE, *The Royal Tour of King George VI and Queen Elizabeth in Canada and the United States* (E.P. Taylor Foundation, 1964)

LOCHHEAD, JOHN, *A Reach of the River* (Blackmore Press, 1955)

LOCKHART, J.G., *The Feet of the Young Men* (Duckworth, 1929)

LOEB, KURT, *White Man's Burden* (Lugus, 1992)

LONDONDERRY, EDITH, *Henry Chaplin: A Memoir* (Macmillan, 1926)

LOVELACE, LADY, *Ralph, Earl of Lovelace* (Christophers, 1920)

LOW, RACHEL, *The History of the British Film 1929–39* (Allen & Unwin, 1985)

LOW, RACHEL, *Films of Comment and Persuasion in the 1930s* (Allen & Unwin, 1989)

LOWNIE, ANDREW, (ed.), *John Buchan: The Complete Short Stories vols 1–3* (Thistle, 1996, 1997)

LOWNIE, ANDREW, (ed.), *John Buchan: The Watcher at the Threshold and Other Stories* (Canongate, 1997)

LOWNIE, ANDREW & WILLIAM MILNE, (eds), *John Buchan's Collected Poems* (Scottish Cultural Press, 1996)

LOWNIE, ANDREW, 'John Buchan, The Round Table and Empire' in Andrea Bosco & Alex May (eds), *The Round Table Movement, the Empire, Commonwealth and British Foreign Policy* (Lothian Foundation Press, 1997)

MACKENZIE, JOHN, (ed.) *Imperialism and Popular Culture* (Manchester Univesity Press, 1986)

MACKIE, J.D., *The University of Glasgow 1451–1951* (Jackson, 1954)

MACLEOD, R. & R.D.L. KELLY (eds), *The Ironside Diaries 1937–40* (Constable, 1962)

MACMILLAN, HUGH, *A Man of Law's Tale* (Macmillan, 1952)

MANGAN, J.A. & J. WALVIN (eds), *Manliness and Morality* (Manchester University Press, 1987)

MARBLE, ANNIE, *A Study of the Modern Novel* (Appleton, 1928)

MARKHAM, VIOLET, *Friendship's Harvest* (Reinhardt, 1956)

MARKHAM, VIOLET, *Return Passage* (OUP, 1953)

MASSEY, VINCENT, *What's Past is Prologue* (Macmillan, 1963)

MASTERMAN, LUCY, *C.F.G. Masterman* (Nicholson & Watson, 1939)

MASTERS, ANTHONY, *Literary Agents: The Novelist as Spy* (Blackwell, 1987)

MECHIE, STEWART, *The Office of Lord High Commissioner* (Saint Andrew Press, 1957)

MERRY, BRUCE, *Anatomy of the Spy Thriller* (Gill & Macmillan, 1977)

MESSINGER, GARY, *British Propaganda and the State in The First World War* (Manchester University Press, 1992)

MIDDLEMAS, KEITH & JOHN BARNES, *Baldwin* (Weidenfeld & Nicolson, 1969)

MONAGHAN, DAVID, *The Novels of John Le Carre* (Blackwell, 1985)

MURRAY, ARTHUR, *At Close Quarters* (John Murray, 1946)

WOLFE MURRAY, GEORGE (ed.) *Tweeddale Shooting Club: A Sesquicentennial Memoir 1790–1940* (Oliver & Boyd, n.d.)

NABOKOV, VLADIMIR, *Speak Memory* (Gollancz, 1951)

NEATBY, H. BLAIR *William Lyon Mackenzie King vols 1 and 2* (University of Toronto Press, 1963, 1976)

NEWBOLT, MARGARET, (ed.), *Later Life and Letters of Sir Henry Newbolt* (Faber, 1942)

NIMCOCKS, WALTER, *Milner's Young Men* (Duke University Press, 1968)

O'BRIEN, TERENCE, *Milner* (Constable, 1979)

OLIVER, F.S., *Ordeal by Battle* (Macmillan, 1915)

OLIVER, F.S., *The Anvil of War* (Macmillan, 1936)

PANEK, LEROY, *The Special Branch: The British Spy Novel 1890–1980* (Bowling Green University Press, 1981)

PARFITT, GEORGE, *Fiction of the First World War* (Faber, 1988)

PARRITT, B.A.H., *The Intelligencers* (Privately published, nd)

PARRY, J.P., 'From the Thirty-Nine Articles to the Thirty-Nine Steps: reflections on the thought of John Buchan' in Michael Bentley (ed.) *Public and Private Doctrine* (CUP, 1993)

PARSONS, COLEMAN, *Witchcraft and Demonology in Scott's Fiction* (Oliver & Boyd, 1964)

PHILLIPS, LIONEL, *Some Reminiscences* (Hutchinson, 1924)

Pilgrim Trust Annual Reports 1930–40

RAMSAY, ALLAN, *Nelson the Publishers* (Nelson, 1981)

RAMSDEN, JOHN, (ed), *The Political Diaries of Sir Robert Sanders 1910–35* (The Historians Press, 1984)

RAYMOND, JOHN, *England's on the Anvil* (Collins, 1958)

READ, DONALD, *The Power of News: The History of Reuters* (OUP, 1992)

REEKIE, A.G. et al, *Farewell to Priorsford* (Hodder & Stoughton, 1950)

REEVES, NICHOLAS, *Official British Film Propaganda During the First World War* (Croom Helm, 1986)

REITH, JOHN, *Into the Wind* (Hodder & Stoughton, 1949)

RICHLER, MORDECAI, 'James Bond Unmasked' in Bernard Roseberg and David White (eds) in *Mass Culture Revisited* (Van Nostrand Reinhold, 1971)

RIDLEY, M.R., *Second Thoughts* (Dent, 1965)

RITCHIE, ANNA, *Perceptions of the Picts: From Eumenius to John Buchan* (Croom House Museum Trust, 1994)

ROWSE, A.L., *The English Past* (Macmillan, 1951)

RUTHERFORD, ANDREW, *The Literature of War* (Macmillan, 1989)

RYALL, TOM, 'One Hundred and Seventeen Steps Towards Masculinity' in Pat Kirkham and Janet Thumin (eds) *You Tarzan: Masculinity, Movies and Men* (St Martin's Press, 1993)

SABATINI, RAFAEL, (ed), *A Century of Historical Stories* (Hutchinson, 1936)

SANDERS, M.L. & PHILIP TAYLOR, *British Propaganda During the First World War 1914–18* (Macmillan, 1982)

SANDISON, ALAN, *Wheel of Empire* (Macmillan, 1967)

SCOTT, SHEILA, *John Buchan* (privately published, 1992)

SCOTT, SHEILA, *J. Walter Buchan* (privately published, 1983)

SCOTT, SHEILA, *O. Douglas* (privately published, 1993)

SELDON, ANTHONY & STUART BALL, *Conservative Century: The Conservative Party since 1900* (OUP, 1994)

SHAW, CHARLES, *John Buchan 1847–1911* (privately published, 1911)

SHAW, CHRISTOPHER, 'The Pleasures of Genre: John Buchan and Richard Hannay' in Christopher Shaw and Malcolm Chase (eds), *The Imagined Past: History and Nostalgia* (Manchester University Press, 1989)

SMITH, HERBERT, *Reminiscences of a Tweeddale Laddie* (privately published, 1987)

SMITH, JANET ADAM, *John Buchan* (Hart-Davis, 1965)

SMITH, JANET ADAM, *John Buchan and His World* (Thames & Hudson, 1979)

SMITH, JEAN & ARNOLD TOYNBEE (eds), *Gilbert Murray: An Unfinished Autobiography* (Allan & Unwin, 1960)

SMITHERS, JACK *Combined Forces: Being the latter-day adventures of Major-General Sir Richard Hannay* (Buchan & Enright, 1983)

SNOW, E.E., *E. Phillips Oppenheim: Storyteller* (Evington, 1985)

SOMMER, DUDLEY, *Haldane of Cloan* (Allen & Unwin, 1960)

SPEAIGHT, ROBERT, *Life of Hilaire Belloc* (Hollis & Carter, 1957)

SPIES, S.B., *Methods of Barbarism* (Human & Rousseau, 1977)

SPOTO, DONALD, *The Life of Alfred Hitchcock* (Collins, 1983)

SPRING, HOWARD, *In The Meantime* (Constable, 1942)

STAFFORD, DAVID, *The Silent Game* (Viking, 1989)

STANDISH, ROBERT, *A Prince of Storytellers* (Peter Davies, 1957)

STREET, BRIAN, *The Savage in Literature: Representations of primitive society in English fiction 1858–1920* (Routledge, 1975)

SULLIVAN, JACK, *The Penguin Encyclopedia of Horror and the Supernatural* (Viking, 1986)

SWIGGETT, HOWARD, 'Introduction' in John Buchan *Mountain Meadow* (Literary Guild, 1941)

TAYLOR, JOHN RUSSELL, Hitch: The Life and Works of Alfred Hitchcock (Faber, 1978)

THORNTON, A.P., *For the File on Empire* (Macmillan, 1968)

TIDRICK, KATHRYN, *Empire and the English Character*, (I.B. Tavris, 1990)

TRUFFAUT, FRANCOIS, *Hitchcock by Truffaut* (Grafton, 1986)

TREDREY, F.D., *The House of Blackwood* 1804–1954 (Blackwood, 1954)

TURNER, ARTHUR, *John Buchan writer* (SCM Press, 1949)

USBORNE, RICHARD, *Clubland Heroes* (Macmillan, 1953). Revised edition (Barrie & Jenkins, 1974)

VINCENT, JOHN, (ed.), *The Crawford Papers* (Manchester University Press, 1984)

WALKER, DAVID, *Lean, Wind Lean* (Collins, 1984)

WARK, WESLEY, (ed.), *Spy Fiction, Spy Films & Real Intelligence* (Frank Cass, 1991)

WARNER, GERALD, *The Scottish Tory Party* (Weidenfeld, 1988)

WARNER, PELHAM, *Long Innings* (Harrap, 1951)

WARNER, PHILIP, *Field Marshal Earl Haig* (The Bodley Head, 1991)

WARWICK, PETER, (ed.), *The South African War* (Longman, 1980)

WEBB, PAUL, *A Buchan Companion* (Alan Sutton, 1994)

WEST, FRANCIS, *Gilbert Murray* (Croom Helm, 1984)

WHEATCROFT, GEOFFREY, *The Randlords* (Weidenfeld & Nicolson, 1985)

WHEATLEY, DENIS (ed), *A Century of Spy Stories*, (Hutchinson, 1938)

WILKINSON, BRUCE, *The Zeal of the Convert* (Smythe, 1978)

WILLIS-O'CONNOR, H. & MADGE MACBETH *Inside Government House* (Ryerson Press, 1954)

WILSON, A.N., *Hilaire Belloc*, (Hamish Hamilton, 1984)

WILSON, DUNCAN, *Gilbert Murray* (Clarendon, 1987)

WINKS, ROBIN, Introduction in John Buchan *The Four Adventures of Richard Hannay* (Godine, 1988)

WINKS, ROBIN, 'John Buchan: Stalking the Wider Game' in *The Four Adventures of Richard Hannay* (Boston, 1988)

WRENCH, EVELYN, *Alfred Lord Milner* (Eyre & Spottiswoode, 1958)

WRENCH, EVELYN, *Geoffrey Dawson and our Times* (Hutchinson, 1955)

WRIGLEY, CHRIS, 'In the Excess of their Patriotism: The National Party and Threats of Subversion' in *Warfare, Diplomacy and Politics* (Hamish Hamilton, 1986)

YACOWAR, MAURICE, *Hitchcock's British Films* (Archon Books, 1977)

YOUNG, KENNETH (ed.), *The Diaries of Sir Robert Bruce Lockhart, vols. 1 and 2* (Macmillan, 1973, 1980)

5. ARTICLES

ANNAN, NOEL, 'The Sweet Smell of Success', *New York Review of Books*, (17 February 1966)

BARNES, T.R., 'Prester John', *Use of English* (Spring 1964) 205–8

BARZUN, JACQUES, 'Meditations on the Literature of Spying' *American Scholar, (Spring 1965)*, 167–78

BAXTER, BEVERLEY, 'Lord Tweedsmuir's Vision of a New World', *Maclean's Magazine*, (11, 1940), ii

BECKINGHAM, C.F., *'The Quest for Prester John', Bulletin of the John Rylands University Library*, (1979–80) 290–310.

BEDELL, JEANNE, 'Romance & Moral Certainty: The Espionage Fiction of John Buchan', *Midwest Quarterly*, (Spring, 1981) 230–41.

BERGIER, JACQUES, 'Les Romans Prophetiques de l'Etonnant John Buchan', *Candide*, (July 1963), 24–31

BERGONZI, BERNARD, 'The Case of Mr Fleming', *Twentieth Century*, (March 1958), 220–8

BETTS, RAYMOND, 'The Allusion to Rome in British Imperialist Thought of the Late Nineteenth and Early Twentieth Centuries', *Victorian Studies* vol. XV, no. 2

BLAKENEY, T.R., 'Sherlock Holmes and Some Contemporaries', *Sherlock Holmes Journal*, (Winter 1964), 5–6

BOAS, F.S., 'John Buchan', *English* (Spring 1940), 5–6

BONNYCASTLE, R.H., 'Lord Tweedsmuir as a Mountaineer', *Canadian Alpine Journal*, (1943), 200–209.

BROWN, BARBARA, 'John Buchan and Twentieth Century Biography', *Biography* Vol. 2, No. 4

BUCHAN, JAMES, 'Romancers Entwined: How T.E. Lawrence and John Buchan Invented One Another,' *The Times Literary Supplement* (29 May 1992) 13–14

BUCHAN, JOHN, 'Adventure Stories', *John O'London's Weekly* (4 December 1926)

BUCHAN, JOHN, 'The Most Difficult Form of Fiction', *Listener* (16th January 1929)

BUCHAN, TOBY, 'A Line on the Aline', *Country Times* (August 1988), 44–47

BUTTS, MARY, 'Ghosties and Ghoulies: Uses of the Supernatural in English Fiction', *Bookman* (London), (February 1933), 433–5

CALENDRILLO, LINDA, 'Role Played and Atmosphere in Four Modern British Spy Novels', *Clues*, (1982), 111–19

CAMP, JOCELYN, 'John Buchan and Alfred Hitchcock', *Literature/Film Quarterly*, (1978), 230–40

CANBY, HENRY 'John Buchan' *Saturday Review of Literature* (17 February 1940)

CAVENDISH, RICHARD, 'Articles of Association: John Buchan Society,' *History Today* (October 1992), 62–3

CHAMBERLAIN, M.E., 'Lord Cromer's Ancient and Modern Imperialism', *Journal of British Studies*, (November 1972)

CHOWDHARAY-BEST, GEORGE, 'John Buchan', *The Salisbury Review*, (September 1995), 14–16

CHURCH, LESLIE, 'John Buchan: Happy Warrior', *London Quarterly Review*, (October 1947), 294–296

CODY, RICHARD, 'Secret Service Fiction', *The Graduate Student of English*, (Summer 1960), 6–12

COREN, MICHAEL, 'A Salute to the Governor', *Sunday Times* (11 Feb. 1990)

COREN, MICHAEL, 'Founder of Book Awards Unjustly Tarred', The Globe and Mail (21 November 1994)

COLDSTREAM, JOHN, 'When Cars were a new adventure', *Daily Telegraph*, (20 March 1978)

COLLINS, JOHN PHILIP, 'The Idealism of John Buchan', *Bookman* (London) (September 1922), 239–40

COMPTON, N.M., 'An Extraordinary Man', *Montreal Gazette*, (CLXIX, 1947), 25

COSGRAVE, PATRICK, 'John Buchan's Thrillers: The Ideology of Character', *Round Table*, (July 1972), 375–86

COUZENS, T.J., 'The Old Africa of a Boy's Dream: Towards Interpreting Buchan's "Prester John"', *English Studies in Africa*, vol. 24, no. 1 (1981), 1–24

COVENTRY, RICHARD, 'A Self-Made Patrician' *The New Statesman and Nation* (31 August 1940)

COX, J. RANDOLPH, 'The Genie and his Pen: The Fiction of John Buchan', *English Literature in Transition*, vol. 9, (1966), 236–40

COX, J. RANDOLPH, 'John Buchan, Lord Tweedsmuir: An Annotated Bibliography of Writings About Him', *English Literature in Transition*, vol. 9, No. 5 (1966) 241–91 and vol. 9, No. 6 (1966) 292–325

DAWSON, JOHN, *'The Poacher of Peebles' Country Life* (2 June 1988) 134–5

DANIELL, DAVID, 'John Buchan and Blackwood's', *Blackwood's Magazine*, (1975), 97–109

DANIELL, DAVID, 'John Buchan' *Words International*, (5 March 1988), 34–9

DANIELL, DAVID, 'The Scottishness of *The Thirty-Nine Steps*', *Gairfish* (1991), 4–14

DANIELL, DAVID, 'The non-fiction works of John Buchan', *Book and Magazine Collector* (June 1992), 4–11

ETHERINGTON, NORMAN, 'Buchan, Imperialism and Psychoanalysis', *John Buchan Journal* (Nos 6 and 7)

FRENCH, DAVID, 'Spy Fever in Britain 1900–15', *Historical Journal* vol. 21 no. 2 (1976) 355–70

GORDON, W., 'Tribute to a Great Man', *I.O.D.E. Magazine*, (March 1940), 1

GREEN, BENNY, 'Buchan: a Hundred Years on', *Spectator* (30 August 1975)

GREENSLET, FERRIS, 'John Buchan' *Atlantic Monthly* (September 1943)

GRIEVE, C.M., 'Contemporary Scottish Studies', *Scottish Educational Journal*, (19 June 1925), 648–9

GRIEVES, KEITH, 'John Buchan as a Contemporary Military Historian 1915–22', *Journal of Contemporary History* (July 1993)

HAGEMANN, SUSANNE, 'More News of Bonnie Prince Charlie after the '45: A Myth Debunked and Reaffirmed', *Forum for Modern Language Studies*', (April 1989), 147–153

HANKINS, KATHRYN, 'John Buchan: Classicist', *Classical Journal*, (December 1941), 164–7

HANNA, ARCHIBALD, 'A John Buchan Collection', *Yale University Library Gazette*, (July 1962), 25–9

HARVIE, CHRISTOPHER, 'For Gods are Kittle Cattle: J.G. Frazer and John Buchan', *The John Buchan Journal*, (Winter 1989), 14–26

HARVIE, CHRISTOPHER, 'Second Thoughts of a Scotsman on the Make: Politics, Nationalism and Myth in John Buchan', *The Scottish Historical Review*, (April 1991), 34

HARVIE, CHRISTOPHER, 'Six Steps to Buchan', *Scotsman* (15 April 1989), 2–3

HASTINGS, B.S., 'Story-teller', *Saturday Night* (LV, 1940), 7

HILL, SUSAN, 'On a Buchan Adventure', *Daily Telegraph*, (31 October 1981)

HILEY, NICHOLAS, 'Decoding German Spies: British Spy Fiction 1908–18', *Intelligence and National Security*, (October 1990)

HILEY, NICHOLAS, 'The Failure of British Counter-Espionage Against Germany 1907–1914', *Historical Journal*, vol. 28 no. 4, (1985) p. 835–62

HILLIER, KENNETH, 'Coy for the Top', *London Magazine*, (August/September 1982)

HIMMELFARB, GERTRUDE, 'John Buchan: An Untimely Appreciation' *Encounter* XV (September 1960)

HODGE, DAVID, 'John Buchan' *Bookman* (September 1922).

JEFFREYS-JONES, RHODRI, 'Lord Lothian and American Democracy', *The Canadian Review* (Winter 1986)

KERNOHAN, R.D., 'Age does not wither', *The Herald*, (25 April 1992), 8–9

KERNOHAN, R.D., 'John Buchan, the Presbyterian Cavalier', *Contemporary Review*, (February 1993) 96–100

KIRK-GREENE, ANTHONY, 'The Governors-General of Canada 1867–1952: A collective Profile', *Journal of Canadian Studies* (Summer 1977), 35–57

KIRK-GREENE, ANTHONY, 'John Buchan and His Appointment As Governor-General of Canada', *Brazen Nose*, (1976) 42–46

LOWNIE, ANDREW, 'The Friendship of Lawrence and Buchan', *The Journal of the T.E. Lawrence Society*, (Autumn 1995) 56–67

LOWNIE, ANDREW, 'T.E. Lawrence and John Buchan: The Story of a Friendship' *TE Notes*, (September 1995)

LOWNIE, ANDREW, 'The Life and Works of John Buchan', *Book and Magazine Collector*, (October 1995) 3–15

LOWNIE, ANDREW, 'John Buchan and Scotland', *Books in Scotland*, (Autumn 1995) 1–2

LOWNIE, ANDREW, 'John Buchan and Scotland', *Cencrastus*, (Winter 1995) 36–38

LOWNIE, ANDREW, 'John Buchan as a Short Story Writer', *Cencrastus*, (Spring 1997)

MARSH, R., 'Lesser-Known Writings of John Buchan, *Montreal Gazette* (28 February 1947)

MACDONALD, KATE, 'John Buchan', *The Countryman* (1990)

MACDONALD, KATE, 'Thirty-nine Steps on Road to Fame', *Scotland on Sunday*, (11th February 1990)

MACDONALD, KATE, 'Wells Correspondence with John Buchan', *Wellsian* (Summer 1990), 43–48

MACGLONE, JAMES, 'The Printed Texts of John Buchan's 'The Thirty-Nine Steps' 1915–40, *Bibliotheck* (1984), 9–24

MCCLEERY, ALASTAIR, 'John Buchan and the Path of the Keen', *English Literature in Transition*, vol. 29, no. 3, (1986), 277–86

MALLORY, J.R., 'Canada's Role in the Appointment of a Governor General' *Canadian Journal of Economics and Political Science* (February 1960)

MASSIE, ALAN, 'Buchan's Testament', *New Edinburgh Review*, (May 1979)

MITCHELL, GINA, 'John Buchan's Popular Fiction: a hierarchy of race', *Patterns of Prejudice*, (November/December 1973), 24–30

MOSKOWITZ, SAM, 'John Buchan: A Possible Influence on Lovecraft', *Fantasy Commentator*, (Spring 1948), 187–90, 205

NICHOLAISEN, W.F.H. 'Name that Past: Place Names In Autobiographical Writings', *Names* (September 1991), 239–248

NICOL, CHARLES, 'Early Buchan, Late Nabokov,' *The Nabokovian*, (Fall 1991) 42–44

NICOLSON, HAROLD, 'Ironside', *Foreign Affairs* (July 1940), 671–79

NIVEN, F.J., 'John Buchan – In Memoriam', *Saturday Night*, (LV, 1940), 6

PASKE, HELEN 'John Buchan's Pilgrimage', *NZ list*, (1982)

PETRIE, CHARLES, 'Author's Progress', *Illustrated London News*, (18 September 1965)

POWELL, GEOFFREY, 'John Buchan's Richard Hannay', *History Today*, (August 1987) 32–7

PRITCHETT, V.S., 'The Man From the Manse', *New Statesman*, (17 September 1965)

QUIGLEY, CARROLL, 'The Round Table Groups in Canada 1908–38', *Canadian Historical Journal*, (September 1962), 204–225

RAY, PHILIP, 'The Villain in the Spy Novels of John Buchan', *English Literature in Transition* vol. 24 (1981), 81–90

REEVES, NICHOLAS, 'The Power of Film Propaganda – Myth or Reality?' *Historical Journal of Film, Radio and Television*, (1993) 181–201

RICHARDS, BERNARD, 'John Buchan's aesthetic consciousness', *Brazen Nose*, (1976), 40–42

RICHLER, MORDECAI, 'Is he a Trendy?', *Nation*, (14 February 1966), 191–3

ROBINSON, TIM 'Poor Prolific John: John Buchan 50 Years After', *London Magazine*, (June/July 1993), 62–74

ROYLE, TREVOR, 'Buchan the Scot and Buchan the Briton', *Books in Scotland*, (Autumn 1979), 12–13

ROYLE, TREVOR, 'The Trial of John Buchan' *Scotland on Sunday* (11 February 1990)

SANDWELL, B.K., 'He Loved Canada and He Made Friends of Canadians', *Saturday Night*, (LV, 1940), 3

SANDWELL, B.K., 'We Have Lost a Friend', *Canadian Home Journal* (XXXVI, 1940), 6

SANDWELL, B.K., 'New Light on John Buchan By His Wife and Friends', *Saturday Night*, (LXIII, 1947), 26

SCHUBERT, LELAND, 'Almost Real Reality: John Buchan's Visible World', *Serif*, (September 1965), 5–14

SCOTT, J.D., 'Buchan and the British Guermantes', *New Republic*, (30 April 1966), 23–24

SISSONS, C.K., 'Lord Tweedsmuir Greets an Old Soldier', *Saturday Night*, (LV, 1940), 3

SMITH, CRAIG, 'Every Man Must Kill the Thing He Loves: Empire, Homoerotics and Nationalism in John Buchan's *Prester John*', *Novel: A Forum on Fiction*, (Winter 1995) 173–200

STAFFORD, DAVID, 'John Buchan's Tales of Espionage: A Popular Archive of British History' *Canadian Journal of History*, (April 1983)

STAFFORD, DAVID, 'Spies and Gentlemen: The Birth of the British Spy Novel, 1893–1914', *Victorian Studies* (1980–81), passim

STEVENSON, J., 'John Buchan', *Maclean's Magazine*, (XLVI, 1935) 11, 59, 60

SUTHERLAND, J.D., 'John Buchan's Sick Heart: Some Psychoanalytic Reflections', *Edinburgh Review* (1988) 83–101

TANGRI, DANIEL, 'Popular Fiction and the Zimbabwe Controversy', *History in Africa* (1990), 293–304

THOMSON, J.S., 'Lord Tweedsmuir', *Dalhousie Record* (XX, 1940), 102–4

TOYNBEE, PHILIP, 'Good Bad Books: Greenmantle' *Punch* (21 March 1962)

TROTTER, DAVID, 'The Politics of Adventure', *Intelligence and National Security* (October 1990)

TURNBAUGH, ROY, 'Images of Empire: George Henty and John Buchan', *Journal of Popular Culture*, (Winter 1975), 734–40

USBORNE, RICHARD, 'Whatever Happened to the Likely Lads?', *Spectator* (16 March 1974)

VOORHEES, RICHARD, 'John Buchan Today: The Richard Hannay Novels', *University of Windsor Review*, (1974), 30–39

VOORHEES, RICHARD, 'Flashman and Richard Hannay', *Dalhousie Review* (1973), 113–20

WEAVER, ROBERT, 'Visible Devils', *Reporter* (10 March 1966), 55–7

WEST, RICHARD, 'A Walk in the Galloway Hills', *Daily Telegraph*, (27 December 1983)

WRIGHT, DAVID, 'The Great War, Government Propaganda and English "Men of Letters" 1914–1916' *Literature and History*, (Spring 1978)

WYCHERLEY, H.A., 'Dubious Dialogue', *CEA Crit*, (May 1969)

YOUNG, MICHAEL, 'The Rules of the Game: Buchan's John Macnab', *Studies in Scottish Literature*, (1989), 194–211

6. THESES

EMERSON, SUSAN, 'Alfred Hitchcock and Isolationism in the Thirty-Nine Steps', MA, University of Kentucky, 1989

FURLONG, MICHAEL, 'John Buchan's Contribution to Literature', Ph.D., University of Montreal, 1948

GRACE, MAXINE, 'Sport and the English Gentleman as Viewed in Selected Novels of John Buchan', MA, University of Maryland, 1970.

HARRINGTON, ANDREW, 'Who Was Then the Gentleman?' Male Identity and Social Change in the Early Twentieth Century English Novel', Ph.D. Boston University, 1993

IVISON, DOUGLAS, 'Imagining the Empire: The Frontier and Masculinity in Fiction of Empire 1885–1910', MA, McMaster University, 1994

KADRAGIC, ALMA, 'John Buchan: The Social Concept', MA, City College of New York, 1966

LOEB, KURT, 'The Imperial Theme: A Study of Colonial Attitudes in English Novels Set in Africa', Ph.D., University of Toronto, 1984

MACDONALD, KATE, 'The Fiction of John Buchan with particular reference to the Richard Hannay novels' PhD University College, London, 1991

MACK, JAMES, 'John Buchan in Print: A Bibliography of the Published Writings and Addresses of John Buchan, First Baron Tweedsmuir of Elsfield', MA, Lehigh University, 1952

MCCAFFERY, SUSANNE, 'They Will Not Be the Same: Themes of Modernity in Britain During World War 1', MA, Virginia Polytechnic and State University, 1994

MURRAY, LEMUEL, 'The Techniques of John Buchan in His Novels', MA, Oklahoma State University, 1959

NEWPORT, VIVIAN, 'The Biographical Writings of John Buchan', MA, University of Arizona, 1961/Doctoral Dissertation George Peabody College for Teachers, 1961.

PEPERMANS, JEF, 'Image of Man and Philosophy of Life in the Novels of John Buchan', Lic Phil & Lit, Catholic University of Louvain, 1965

STEWART, EILEEN, 'John Buchan Borderer', Ph.D., University of Edinburgh 1980

TURNER, ARTHUR, 'John Buchan'. Ph.D. University of California, 1951

VANDERHAEGHE, GUY, 'John Buchan: Conservatism, Imperialism and Social Reconstruction', MA, University of Saskatchewan, 1975

WEISS, ALAN, 'Free Trade, Paratism, Protection: Studies in the Fiction of English Imperialism 1886–1910', Ph.D., State University of New York, 1972

WILCOX, VICTORIA, 'Prime Minister and Governor-General: Mackenzie King and Lord Tweedsmuir 1935–40', MA, Queens University, Kingston, 1976

YOUNG, MICHAEL, 'The Structure and Ideology of Romance Fiction', Ph.D, University of Minnesota, 1988

7. UNPUBLISHED LECTURES

DANIELL, DAVID, 'John Buchan and Anti-Semitism: The Creation of a Myth'.
ETHERINGTON, NORMAN, 'Imperialism in Literature: The Case of John Buchan'

8. REPORTS IN BUCHAN PAPERS

National Library of Scotland
January 1936, recapping on 1st two months
'Tour of Eastern Townships', March 1936
'Notes on Washington Visit'
'Notes on the Agricultural Conditions of the Prairies'
'Down North', August 1937
'The Land', August 1937
'The People', August 1937
'The Economics of the North', August 1937

Queen's University, Kingston
'Across Canada with King George VI and Queen Elizabeth'

INDEX